# College and University Business Administration

## FIFTH EDITION

Edited by
Deirdre McDonald Greene

NACUBO

# VOLUME 2
# Fiscal Functions

CHAPTER 5

# Overview of Financial Accounting and Reporting

by
Abbott Wainwright

# Sponsors

## ARTHUR ANDERSEN & CO.
1666 K Street, NW
Washington, DC 20006
202-862-3100

*Services that Arthur Andersen & Co. offers include accounting, auditing, financial consulting, and systems design and installation.*

## DELOITTE & TOUCHE
1700 Market Street
24th Floor
Philadelphia, PA 19103
215-246-2404

*Deloitte & Touche is a public accounting firm that provides accounting, auditing, tax, and management consulting services.*

## KPMG PEAT MARWICK
345 Park Avenue
New York, NY 10154
212-758-9700

*KPMG Peat Marwick is a leader in the development of accounting and reporting practices.*

## VIRCHOW, KRAUSE, HELGESON, & COMPANY
1100 TCF Tower
121 South Eighth Street
Minneapolis, MN 55402
612-341-3030

*Virchow, Krause, Helgeson, & Company provides accounting, auditing, tax, and consulting services to over 20 educational institutions.*

# Contents

## 5: Overview of Financial Accounting and Reporting

Complete, accurate, and timely financial accounting and reporting are essential to the management of colleges and universities. Financial reports are used by the governing board, president, and institutional managers for decision making; by creditors, grantors, state legislatures, and other agencies that have a financial interest in the institution; and by various constituencies, such as donors and alumni, to give them confidence in the management of the institution. The chief financial or business officer's responsibility in financial accounting and reporting is considerable, because the information he or she provides is the basis for many decisions that affect the institution and its programs. The way the information is presented to the governing board, the legislature, and others affects their decisions.

Until recently, the entity concept determined what accounting principles an institution followed--whether an institution was public or independent, it followed the accounting principles developed specifically for colleges and universities (they were the "entity"). This long-held practice has changed: the ownership concept now determines these principles. This means that the accounting principles that an institution follows are determined by whether it is public or independent; the fact that it is a college or university is secondary. This accounting dichotomy among institutions is a new dynamic that financial and business officers must be aware of, especially at public institutions. Whatever the size of an institution, whether it is public or independent, someone in the business office must monitor developments in standard setting so that the institution is informed of potential changes as well as the issuance of standards and their effective dates. Information on proposed standards, as well as the standards themselves, is available from the Financial Accounting Standards Board (FASB) and the Governmental Accounting Standards Board (GASB).

Much of the material in this chapter is excerpted from *Financial Accounting and Reporting Manual for Higher Education* (National Association of College and University Business Officers, 1990). A full discussion of financial accounting and reporting can be found there.

## Objectives of Financial Reporting

Among the objectives of accounting, for either a commercial enterprise or a college or university, is the provision of information to assist management in the effective allocation and use of resources and to assist others in understanding the financial operations of the organization. The nature of the organization, its resources, and its objectives influence the form and process by which accounting is accomplished and information is reported.

In a commercial enterprise, the emphasis on accounting and reporting is placed on matching expenses with revenues to determine net income. Because service, in which resources are consumed, is the objective of a college or university, the accounting and reporting process must focus on accounting for resources received and used rather than on the determination of net income. Because many funding sources stipulate the purposes for which resources provided to management can be used, there is also the need for adequate disclosure of the stewardship of resources, in accordance with the wishes of the funding sources.

The purpose of a commercial enterprise is to increase its owner's equity and provide a return on the owner's investment. The primary purposes of a higher education institution are instruction, research, and public service; an institution must obtain sufficient resources to provide these. Commercial entities typically receive revenues in exchange for goods or services. A higher education institution receives some of its revenues in exchange for goods or services and frequently receives contributions from outside parties that have no expectation of an economic benefit proportionate to the resources provided. These external parties may attach "conditions" concerning how these moneys can be used.

Commercial enterprises measure success through profit, return on equity, and earnings per share, which are easily measured in units of currency. Measures of success in not-for-profit organizations are efficient and effective use of resources and use of moneys for stated purposes in meeting donors' objectives and advancing the organization's mission ("service efforts and accomplishments").

The accounting records and financial statements of a college or university, as with any type of enterprise, must be adapted to the functions, purposes, and objectives of the organization and the needs of the users of the reported financial information. The institution's accounting system must observe any and all types of external restrictions and internal designations. The necessity of accounting separately for specific resources has resulted in the special form of accounting known as "fund accounting." In fund accounting, financial resources are classified for accounting and reporting purposes in accordance with their intended use or purpose and in accordance with laws, regulations, restrictions, or limitations imposed by sources outside the institution.

## A Historical View

An important goal of higher education administrators since early in this century has been the standardization of reporting: what is reported and how it is reported. The methods of reporting have been surveyed and studied more than the principles behind the reported information. For the greater part of this century, whatever improvements were made in higher education's accounting and reporting were made largely by the institutions themselves, acting through their national and regional associations.

World War II was the turning point for higher education. The involvement of university laboratories in research and development during the war and the G.I. Bill following the war changed the higher education environment forever. Both sponsored research and student aid programs have grown since then, as has their accountability. Accounting and reporting for these programs are a significant, costly, and specialized administrative responsibility; national associations now exist that monitor legislation and rule making in these areas. However, in spite of the changes in the higher education environment after the war, accounting principles were not affected. There were, of course, more reporting requirements by federal agencies, but these did not generally affect principles.

Several organizations, including the American Institute of Certified Public Accountants (AICPA), the National Association of College and University Business Officers (NACUBO), the National Center for Higher Education Management Systems, and the National Center for Education Statistics, have attempted to provide generally acceptable, rather than alternative, methods of recording and reporting financial data and to agree on revenue and expense categories that would be uniformly acceptable and applicable. These objectives have been achieved. The four organizations reached agreement in the mid-1970s concerning what should be reported, and this uniformity extends to financial data collection by the federal government through its annual Integrated Postsecondary Education Data Survey.

Until that time, and for several years later, it was assumed that, at the level of basic financial statements, little or no distinction would be made between public and independent institutions. However, the fabric holding public and independent institutions together is coming apart. This change has been subtle and indirect.

## Financial Accounting Foundation

The Financial Accounting Foundation (FAF), incorporated in 1972 as a Section 501(c)(3) tax-exempt organization, operates exclusively for the purpose of establishing accounting standards. The FAF created the Financial Accounting Standards Board (FASB) in 1973 and the Governmental Accounting Standards Board (GASB) in 1984. These two boards are designated as the authoritative accounting standard-setting bodies by the AICPA, the Securities and Exchange Commission, the General Accounting Office, and many state governments. The FAF's trustees are responsible for appointing the members, providing funds, and exercising general oversight (except with regard to technical decisions) of both FASB and GASB and their respective advisory councils.

## FASB

As a standard-setting body, FASB serves as successor to the Committee on Accounting Procedure of the AICPA (1936-59) and the Accounting Principles Board (1959-73), both of whose pronouncements remain in force unless amended or superseded by FASB. Since its inception, FASB has avoided promulgating accounting principles that specifically address governmental accounting principles and reporting standards. However, in 1980 FASB did issue Statement of Financial Accounting Concepts No. 4, "Objectives of Financial Reporting by Nonbusiness Organizations," which discusses financial reporting by not-for-profit organizations. Significant disagreement arose regarding FASB's authority to promulgate accounting principles for state and local governments. The problem was resolved by the creation of the Governmental Accounting Standards Board (GASB) in April 1984. The scope of FASB's jurisdiction comprises all private-sector entities, including businesses and not-for-profit organizations that are not units of state and local governments.

The primary responsibility of FASB is the issuance of "Statements of Financial Accounting Standards" (SFASs). These standards represent the views of the majority of the board and may amend existing standards or establish new ones. SFASs, along with FASB "Interpretations," are primary sources of authoritative, generally accepted accounting principles (GAAP). In addition to the authoritative sources of GAAP, FASB produces a number of nonauthoritative publications. The most significant of these are "Statements of Financial Accounting Concepts" (SFACs), which provide a basis for setting future accounting standards.[1]

One of FASB's early projects was an attempt to resolve the differences between the several audit guides and statements of position that AICPA had issued for "nonbusiness" organizations, including colleges and universities. In 1986, FASB formally added to its agenda several projects that are specific to not-for-profit organizations. These projects included evaluation of depreciation accounting, accounting for contributions and pledges, financial statement display, valuation of investments, and the definition of a reporting entity.

In December 1980, FASB issued SFAC No. 4, *Objectives of Financial Reporting by Nonbusiness Organizations,* as part of its conceptual framework project, which serves as the basis for the development of financial accounting and reporting standards.

***FASB conceptual framework.*** FASB undertook a conceptual framework project in 1978 and has since issued six interrelated SFACs, three of which are applicable to colleges and universities:

- SFAC No. 2, *Qualitative Characteristics of Accounting Information* (1980)

- SFAC No. 4, *Objectives of Financial Reporting by Nonbusiness Organizations* (1980)

- SFAC No. 6, *Elements of Financial Statements* (1985)

SFAC No. 4 and SFAC No. 6 are the most significant.

FASB itself is a major user and thus the most direct beneficiary of the guidance provided by its conceptual framework. However, knowledge of the objectives and concepts the board uses should enable all who are affected by or interested in financial accounting standards to better understand the content and limitations of information provided by financial accounting and reporting. That knowledge, if used with care, may also provide guidance in resolving new or emerging problems of financial accounting and reporting in the absence of applicable authoritative pronouncements.[2]

SFAC No. 4. SFAC No. 4 declares that the distinguishing characteristics of nonbusiness organizations include:

- Receipt of significant amounts of resources from providers who do not expect repayment or economic benefits proportionate to the resources

- Operating purposes other than to provide goods or services at a profit or profit equivalent

- Absence of defined ownership interests that can be sold, transferred, or redeemed or that convey entitlement to a share of residual distribution of resources in the event of liquidation of the organization

These characteristics result in certain types of transactions that are infrequent in business enterprises, such as contributions and grants, and in the absence of transactions with owners.

SFAC No. 4 states that the line between nonbusiness and business enterprises is not always sharp, since the incidence and relative importance of those characteristics in any organization are different. This suggests that, for purposes of developing financial reporting objectives, a spectrum of organizations exists ranging from those with clearly dominant nonbusiness characteristics to those with wholly business characteristics.

There are several common characteristics of financial reporting for nonbusiness organizations. Nonbusiness organizations generally have no single indicator of performance comparable to a business enterprise's profit. Thus, other indicators of performance usually are needed.

Financial reporting by nonbusiness organizations should provide information:

- that is useful to resource providers and other users in making rational decisions about the allocation of resources to those organizations;

- that is useful to resource providers and other users in assessing the services that a nonbusiness organization provides and its ability to continue to provide those services;

- about the economic resources, obligations, and net resources of an organization and the effects of transactions, events, and circumstances that change resources and interests in those resources;

- that is useful to resource providers and other users in assessing how managers of a nonbusiness organization have discharged their stewardship responsibilities and about other aspects of their performance;

- about the performance of an organization during a certain period. Periodic measurement of the changes in the amount and nature of the net resources of a nonbusiness organization and information about the service efforts and accomplishments of an organization represent the most useful information for assessing performance; and

- about how an organization obtains and spends cash or other liquid resources, about its borrowing and repayment of borrowing, and about other factors that may affect the organization's liquidity.

In addition, financial reporting should include explanations and interpretations to help users understand financial information provided.[3]

SFAC No. 6. SFAC No. 6 states that the elements of financial statements are the building blocks with which the statements are constructed—the classes of items that financial statements comprise. The items in financial statements represent in words and numbers certain entity resources, claims to those resources, and the effects of transactions and other events and circumstances that result in changes in those resources and claims.[4]

SFAC No. 6 defines ten interrelated elements that are directly related to measuring the performance and status of an entity:

- "Assets" are probable future economic benefits obtained or controlled by a particular entity as a result of past transactions or events.

- "Liabilities" are probable future sacrifices of economic benefits arising from present obligations of a particular entity to transfer assets or provide services to other entities in the future as a result of past transactions or events.

- "Equity," or net assets, is the residual interest in the assets of an entity that remains after deducting its liabilities. In a business enterprise, the equity is the ownership interest. In a not-for-profit organization, which does not have ownership interest in the same sense as a business enterprise, net assets are divided into three classes based on the presence or absence of donor-imposed restrictions—permanently restricted, temporarily restricted, and unrestricted net assets.

- "Investments by owners" are increases in equity of a particular business enterprise resulting from transfers to the enterprise from other entities of something valuable to obtain or increase ownership interests (or equity) in it. Assets are most commonly received as investments by owners and may include services or satisfaction or conversion of liabilities of the enterprise.

- "Distributions to owners" are decreases in equity of a particular business enterprise resulting from transferring assets, rendering services, or incurring liabilities by the enterprise to owners. Distributions to owners decrease ownership interest (or equity) in an enterprise.

- "Comprehensive income" is the change in equity of a business enterprise during a period as a result of transactions and other events and circumstances from nonowner sources. Comprehensive income includes all changes in equity during a period except those resulting from investments by owners and distributions to owners.

- "Revenues" are inflows or other enhancements of assets of an entity or settlements of its liabilities (or a combination of both) from delivering or producing goods, rendering services, or other activities that constitute the entity's ongoing major or central operations.

- "Expenses" are outflows or other using up of assets or incurrence of liabilities (or a combination of both) from delivering or producing goods, rendering services, or other activities that constitute the entity's ongoing major or central operations.

- "Gains" are increases in equity (net assets in the case of not-for-profit organizations) from peripheral or incidental transactions of an entity and from all other transactions and other events and circumstances affecting the entity except those that result from revenues or investments by owners.

- "Losses" are decreases in equity (net assets in the case of a not-for-profit organization) from peripheral or incidental transactions of an entity and from all other transactions and other events and circumstances affecting the entity except those that result from expenses or distributions to owners.

SFAC No. 6 defines three classes of net assets of not-for-profit organizations and the changes in those classes during a period. Each class is composed of the revenues, expenses, gains, and losses that affect that class and reclassifications from or to other classes.

- Change in permanently restricted assets during a period is the total of: contributions and other inflows of assets whose use by the organization is limited by donor-imposed stipulations that do not expire with the passage of time or cannot be fulfilled or otherwise removed by actions of the organization; other asset enhancements and diminishments during the period that are subject to the same kinds of stipulations; and reclassifications from (or to) other classes of net assets during the period as a consequence of donor-imposed stipulations.

- Change in temporarily restricted net assets during a period is the total of: contributions and other inflows during the period of assets whose use by the organization is limited by donor-imposed stipulations that expire by passage of time or can be fulfilled and removed by actions of the organization pursuant to those stipulations; other asset enhancements and diminishments during the period subject to the same kinds of stipulations; and reclassifications to (or from) other classes of net assets during the period as a consequence of donor-imposed stipulations, their expiration by passage of time, or their fulfillment and removal by actions of the organization pursuant to those stipulations.

- Change in unrestricted net assets during a period is the total change in net assets during the period less change in permanently restricted net assets and change in temporarily restricted net assets for the period. It is the change during the period in the part of net assets of a not-for-profit organization that is not limited by donor-imposed stipulations. Changes in unrestricted net assets include revenues and gains that change unrestricted net assets; expenses and losses that change unrestricted net assets; and reclassifications from (or to) other classes of net assets as a consequence of donor-imposed stipulations, their expiration by passage of time, or their fulfillment and removal by actions of the organization pursuant to those stipulations.

SFAC No. 6 eliminates the concept of expenditures—all outflows of resources are expenses. It defines all expenses as unrestricted—it eliminates the historical convention of restricted expenses.

SFAC No. 6 describes reclassifications between classes of net assets resulting from donor-imposed stipulations, their expiration by passage of time, or their fulfillment and removal by actions of the organization pursuant to those stipulations. Reclassifications simultaneously increase one class and decrease another class of net assets; they do not involve inflows, outflows, or other changes in assets or liabilities.

SFAC No. 6 indicates that net assets, including all enhancements to those net assets, should be classified as unrestricted unless restricted by donor stipulation or law. It also indicates that fund groups are not necessary for reporting and calls for more aggregated financial statements from not-for-profit organizations.[4]

# GASB

The FAF created GASB in 1984 to establish generally accepted accounting principles for state and local governments and their component units, including government-controlled not-for-profit organizations such as colleges and universities, hospitals, and many types of public utilities. GASB is the successor to the National Council on

Governmental Accounting (NCGA), which for many years promulgated accounting standards for the state and local sectors. The 1968 NCGA publication *Governmental Accounting, Auditing, and Financial Reporting* (1968 GAAFR) established GAAP for state and local governmental units. The AICPA endorsed these principles. In 1979, the NCGA issued NCGA Statement No. 1, "Governmental Accounting and Financial Reporting Principles," which was a restatement of earlier established accounting principles.

GASB's first standard-setting action was the adoption of all NCGA statements. The *Codification of Governmental Accounting and Financial Reporting Standards* contains each of these statements, which are in effect until GASB amends or supersedes them.

**GASB conceptual framework.** GASB issued Concepts Statement No. 1, "Objectives of Financial Reporting," in May 1987. This concept statement establishes the objectives of general-purpose external financial statements by state and local governmental entities and applies to both governmental-type and business-type activities. It supersedes NCGA Concepts Statement No. 1, *Objectives of Accounting and Financial Reporting for Governmental Units.*

SFAC No. 1 states that significant characteristics of the government environment that affect financial reporting of governmental-type activities need to be considered when establishing financing objectives.

The primary characteristics of government's structure and the services it provides are the representative form of government and the separation of powers; the federal system of government and the prevalence of intergovernmental revenues; and the relationship of taxpayers to services received.

The control characteristics resulting from government's structure are the budget as an expression of public policy and financial intent and as a method of providing control and the use of fund accounting for control purposes.

Significant characteristics also include the dissimilarities between similarly designated governments; the significant investment in capital assets that do not produce revenue; and the nature of the political process.

Primary users of external state and local governmental financial reports include the citizenry, legislative and oversight bodies, and investors and creditors.

Financial reports are used to compare actual financial results with the legally adopted budget; to assess financial condition and results of operations; to assist in determining compliance with finance-related laws, rules, and regulations; and to assist in evaluating efficiency and effectiveness.

Financial reporting objectives established for governmental-type activities are generally applicable to business-type activities. Public accountability should be a primary tenet in establishing government accounting standards. Financial reporting should provide information to assist users in assessing interperiod equity by showing whether current-year revenues are sufficient to pay for current-year services or how much of a burden future taxpayers will be required to assume for services previously provided.

State and local governmental financial reports should possess these basic characteristics: understandability, reliability, relevance, timeliness, consistency, and comparability.

Financial reporting should assist in fulfilling government's duty to be publicly accountable and should enable users to assess that accountability by

- providing information to determine whether current-year revenues are sufficient to pay for current-year services;

- demonstrating whether resources are obtained and used in accordance with the entity's legally adopted budget and demonstrating compliance with other finance-related legal or contractual requirements; and

- providing information to assist users in assessing the service efforts, costs, and accomplishments of the governmental entity.

Financial reporting should assist users in evaluating the operating results of the governmental entity for the year by

- providing information about sources and uses of financial resources;

- providing information about how it finances its activities and meets its cash requirements; and

- providing information necessary to determine whether its financial position improves or deteriorates as a result of the year's operations.

Financial reporting should assist users in assessing the level of services that can be provided by the governmental entity and its ability to meet its obligations as they become due by

- providing information about its financial position and condition;

- providing information about its physical and other nonfinancial resources having useful lives that extend beyond the current year, including information that can be used to assess the service potential of those resources; and

- disclosing legal or contractual restrictions on resources and the risk of potential loss of resources.[5]

***GASB standards.*** GASB issued its first standards statement, GASB Statement No. 1, *Authoritative Status of NCGA Pronouncements and AICPA Industry Audit Guide,* in July 1984. This gives authority to all NCGA pronouncements and to AICPA's *Audits of State and Local Government Units* until they are superseded by new GASB statements. The 12 principles of accounting and reporting applicable to state and local governments and their component reporting units listed in NCGA Statement No. 1 and the principles contained in GASB Concepts Statement No. 1 form the basis on which GASB will develop future standards. The list of these principles follows.

- Principle 1—Accounting and reporting capabilities

- Principle 2—Fund accounting systems

- Principle 3—Types of funds

  Governmental funds

  Proprietary funds

  Fiduciary funds

- Principle 4—Numbers of funds

- Principle 5—Accounting for fixed assets and long-term liabilities

- Principle 6—Valuation of fixed assets

- Principle 7—Depreciation of fixed assets

- Principle 8—Accrual basis in governmental accounting

- Principle 9—Budgeting, budgetary control, and budgetary reporting

- Principle 10—Transfer, revenue, expenditure, and expense account classification

- Principle 11—Common terminology and classification

- Principle 12—Interim and annual financial reports[6]

## The FASB-GASB Jurisdiction Issue

The 1984 GASB structural agreement provides that GASB will establish accounting and financial reporting standards for activities and transactions of state and local governmental entities and that FASB will establish standards for all other entities. GASB pronouncements rank above FASB pronouncements in the GAAP hierarchy for state and local governmental entities. A problem arises, however, for so-called special entities—more specifically, for the separately issued general-purpose financial statements of special entities, such as utilities, hospitals, and colleges and universities, that may be owned by either governmental or nongovernmental bodies. Although there have been questions about the wisdom of assigning jurisdiction solely on the basis of ownership, the 1984 structural agreement stands.

Because of the jurisdiction issue, colleges and universities are now separated for accounting purposes into "FASB institutions" and "GASB institutions": those that follow FASB principles and those that follow GASB principles. Actual jurisdiction, regardless of ownership, may not be obvious; for example, a state may have little control over a university, even if it is "governmental," and another state might have significant control over both its public and independent institutions. There is currently no accounting definition of "government" and "nongovernment," which would seem to be required for determining whether a special entity is an FASB or GASB institution.

Although the FASB-GASB jurisdiction issue is formally settled, it continues to be a problem because of the complexity of the ownership and control in colleges and universities.

# A Framework for College and University Accounting

Even though both FASB and GASB have conceptual frameworks, the historical framework is used because both FASB and GASB have ruled that accounting and reporting standards currently applicable to colleges and universities are established by the following pronouncements until modified by either board:

- *Audits of Colleges and Universities* (the AICPA audit guide)

- AICPA Statement of Position 74-8, "Financial Accounting and Reporting by Colleges and Universities"

- Part 5 of *College and University Business Administration,* 4th ed., now superseded by *Financial Accounting and Reporting Manual for Higher Education*

FASB's SFAS No. 32, *Specialized Accounting and Reporting Principles and Practices in AICPA Statements of Position and Guides on Accounting and Auditing Matters* (1979), specifies that the specialized accounting and reporting principles and practices contained in *Audits of Colleges and Universities* and in SOP 74-8 are preferable accounting principles for colleges and universities to use in justifying a change in accounting principles. This action recognizes *Audits of Colleges and Universities* as authoritative literature until FASB issues statements that modify such accounting treatments.

Although GASB has not explicitly sanctioned principles and practices contained in *Audits of Colleges and Universities* as authoritative literature for public institutions, it has implicitly recognized them through the adoption of NCGA Statement No. 7, *Financial Reporting for Component Units Within the Governmental Reporting Entity* (1984). This statement notes that a component unit such as a university may use accounting principles and reporting standards that are generally acceptable but are not in accordance with governmental GAAP. In 1991, GASB issued an exposure draft that would explicitly sanction *Audits of Colleges and Universities* for GASB institutions.

## CLASSIFICATION OF RESOURCES

The fundamental purpose of fund accounting is to properly account for all resources received and used. Fund accounting classifies all resources into funds according to specific limitations placed on their use by the resource providers. Classification recognizes the stewardship responsibility inherent in accepting restricted resources from external parties.

Each fund is a self-balancing set of accounts. Each fund has its own revenues, expenditures, transfers, assets, liabilities, and a fund balance. A change in fund balance represents the difference between fund additions (revenues and transfers in) and deductions (expenditures and transfers out). A fund balance is identified as the net difference between a fund's assets and liabilities.

Because of the variety of restrictions upon a higher education institution's resources, it is not unusual for even a small institution to have one hundred or more individual accounts. Large, complex research institutions can have thousands. Although each account needs to be internally monitored by the institution, for external accounting and reporting purposes similar funds are combined into fund groups. Higher education institutions typically combine their funds into the following fund groups:

- Current funds

- Loan funds

- Endowment and similar funds

- Annuity and life income funds

- Agency funds

- Plant funds

FASB's SFAC No. 6 indicates that fund groups are not necessary for reporting and calls for more aggregated financial statements. Because governmental financial statements typically contain many funds, GASB has not made a similar statement.

Brief descriptions of the above funds follow.

***Current funds.*** Current funds are those economic resources expendable for carrying out the primary missions of colleges and universities: instruction, research, and public service. Because current funds represent the resources available for general operations, a statement of current funds revenues, expenditures, and other changes is often viewed as the operating statement of an institution. Such a statement is not required, however, and is not included in the financial statements of many institutions.

CURRENT UNRESTRICTED FUNDS. Current unrestricted funds are resources received that have no limitations or stipulations placed on them by external agencies or donors. These funds are often deemed the most desirable resources for a college or university because they offer the widest range of flexibility concerning how moneys can be expended. Tuition and fees revenue and legislative appropriations are typical examples of revenue sources received as unrestricted current funds.

CURRENT RESTRICTED FUNDS. Current restricted funds are resources provided to an institution that have externally established limitations or stipulations placed on their use. At the direction of the external funding source, restrictions can be broad (for example, for scholarships) or quite specific (for example, analysis of the chemical composition of DNA).

Sponsored research is a type of current restricted fund received by many institutions. Expected to be consumed in the near term, sponsored research funding includes explicit external instructions as to its use. This funding may lack flexibility, but it is essential to institutions actively engaged in research.

Internal designations placed on resources by the governing board or institutional management (assuming delegation from the governing board) constitute an allocation of current unrestricted funds. These designations can change at any time. Any unrestricted resources designated to specific fund groups (plant, loan, or endowment) are included in such fund groups by a transfer, which can be either mandatory or nonmandatory, depending on the circumstances. Mandatory transfers from one fund to another are those transfers arising from

- binding legal agreements related to the financing of educational plant and

- grant agreements with agencies of the federal government, donors, and other organizations to match gifts and grants.

Nonmandatory transfers from one fund to another are made at the discretion of the governing board.

CURRENT FUNDS REVENUES. Current funds revenues include all unrestricted gifts, grants, and other resources earned during the reporting period, as well as restricted resources to the extent that they are expended. Current funds revenues do not include restricted current funds received but not expended, because these revenues have not yet been earned; instead, such receipts are classified as additions. Current funds revenues also do not include resources that are restricted by external persons or agencies to other than current funds, such as plant and endowment.

For example, University XYZ receives a $100,000 check on July 31 as a restricted gift. During the course of the next year, $60,000 of the gift is expended for the specified restricted purpose. This $60,000 would appear as current restricted funds revenue in the statement of current funds revenues, expenditures, and other changes and would also appear in the appropriate expenditure categories. In the statement of changes in fund balances, the $100,000 would appear as private gifts (an addition) and the $60,000 would appear in the appropriate functional category. The unspent $40,000 would be an increase in funds balance and would be reported as the excess of restricted receipts over transfers to revenues in the statement of current funds revenues, expenditures, and other changes.

Interdepartmental transactions between service departments and storerooms and other institutional departments or offices should not be reported as revenues of the service departments but rather as reductions of expenditures of the departments, because these intrainstitutional transactions, like intracompany sales in for-profit enterprises, are to be canceled out. The billed price of services and materials obtained from service departments and central stores by offices and departments of the institution should be accounted for as regular expenditures, just as if the services or materials had been obtained from sources outside the institution. Any difference between costs and billed prices as recorded in the service department account, whether a credit or debit, should be reported under the institutional support expenditures classification.

(See also Chapter 18, Materials Management.)

Certain intrainstitutional transactions, however, should be reflected in the operating statements as revenues and expenditures. Materials or services produced by an instructional department as a by-product of an instructional program and sold to auxiliary enterprises or hospitals—for example, milk sold by the dairy department to the dining halls—should be treated as sales and services revenues of the selling department and as expenditures of the receiving department. Sales and services of auxiliary enterprises to other departments—for example, catering by the food services department in the entertainment of guests of the college or university or sales by the college store to instructional departments—should be treated as sales and services revenues of the respective auxiliary enterprises and as expenditures of the unit receiving the services or materials.

Unrestricted and restricted current funds revenues should be grouped into the following major classifications by source of funds:

- Tuition and fees

- Federal appropriations

- State appropriations

- Local appropriations

- Federal grants and contracts

- State grants and contracts

- Local grants and contracts

- Private gifts, grants, and contracts

- Endowment income

- Sales and services of educational activities

- Sales and services of auxiliary enterprises

- Sales and services of hospitals

- Other sources

- Independent operations

CURRENT FUNDS EXPENDITURES AND TRANSFERS. Current funds expenditures represent the costs incurred for goods and services used in the conduct of an institution's operations. These include the acquisition cost of capital assets, such as equipment and library books, to the extent current funds are budgeted for and used by operating departments. If the amount of ending inventories or the cost of services benefiting subsequent fiscal periods is material (in terms of effect on financial statements), both inventories and deferred charges should be recorded as assets and previously recorded expenditures should be appropriately decreased. In a subsequent fiscal period, these inventories and deferred charges as consumed should be included as expenditures of that period. Significant inventories of materials are usually present in central stores.

Most institutional accounting systems provide for recording at least a portion of capital expenditures in the current funds expenditure accounts of the various operating units. Whether an expenditure is to be considered a capital expenditure is generally a matter for institutional determination; in the case of some public institutions, state regulations govern.

The general criteria for defining a capital asset are the relative significance of the amount expended and the useful life of the asset acquired or, in the case of repairs and alterations, the extent to which useful life is extended. Capital expenditures therefore include funds expended for land; improvements to land; buildings; improvements and additions to buildings; equipment; and library books.

A capital asset is defined as any physical resource that benefits a program for more than one year. However, some government agencies have different requirements for costing purposes. For example, OMB Circular A-21, "Cost Principles for Educational Institutions," stipulates an acquisition cost of $500 per unit and a useful life of more than two years as the threshold at which tangible personal property is considered a capital asset.

Interdepartmental transactions ordinarily should be accounted for as an increase in current funds expenditures of the department receiving the materials, services, or capital assets and as a decrease in current funds expenditures of the transferring department. (Auxiliary enterprises are not considered departments.) Thus, total institutional expenditures will not be inflated by such transactions. Examples are sales and services of service departments and central stores and transfers of material and equipment from one department to another. Any differences between charges to users for sales and services and the operating costs of service departments or central stores, whether debit or credit, are treated as institutional support expenditures. On the other hand, sales and services of an auxiliary enterprise to a department or to another auxiliary enterprise, or sales of materials produced by an instructional department or auxiliary enterprise, should be reported as an expenditure of the department or auxiliary enterprise receiving the materials or services and as revenue of the department or auxiliary enterprise selling the materials or services.

Expenditures differ from transfers. Expenditures are the recognition of the expending of resources of the current funds group in pursuit of the objectives of the respective funds of that group. Transfers are amounts moved between fund groups to be used for the objectives of the recipient fund group. The two types of transfers, mandatory and nonmandatory, are described under "Current Restricted Funds," above.

Expenditures and transfers may be classified in a variety of ways—by program, function, organizational unit, project, or object class. Factors bearing on the classification are

- the context in which appropriations, gifts, grants, and other sources of revenue are made to the institution;

- the mode best suited for preparing and executing the budget;

- the form that best serves the needs for financial reporting; and

- the presentation that will improve the quality of comparative studies among institutions.

Classifications by program often cut across organizational, functional, and even fund-group lines and are useful in the planning processes. The functional classification pattern—educational and general, auxiliary enterprises, hospitals, independent operations, and their subcategories—provides the greatest comparability of data among institutions. Classification by organizational units provides data corresponding to channels of intrainstitutional administrative responsibilities. Classification by projects provides data corresponding to the pattern in which gifts, grants, and contracts are used by the institution.

Classification by object class—according to materials or capital assets purchased or services received, such as personal services, employee benefits, printing and stationery, travel, communications, food, fuel, utilities, repairs, equipment, and library books—primarily serves internal management needs.

Published financial reports usually classify expenditures and transfers by function. The following functional classifications are used by educational institutions:

Educational and General

- Expenditures

    Instruction

    Research

    Public service

    Academic support

    Student services

    Institutional support

    Operation and maintenance of plant

    Scholarships and fellowships

- Mandatory transfers

- Nonmandatory transfers

Auxiliary enterprises

- Expenditures

- Mandatory transfers

- Nonmandatory transfers

Hospitals

- Expenditures

- Mandatory transfers

- Nonmandatory transfers

Independent operations

- Expenditures
- Mandatory transfers
- Nonmandatory transfers

*Loan funds.* Loan funds are used to account for resources that may be lent to students, faculty, or staff; they are provided by various sources. Some money may come from federal, state, or local appropriations or from private donors, while some money may be unrestricted current funds set aside for this purpose by the governing board. Loan funds arising from gifts, bequests, governmental grants, and student fees are generally operated on a revolving fund basis, with loan and interest repayments remaining in the loan fund group for future lending. Some loan moneys may be refundable to donors under specific conditions. In all cases, the identity of each loan fund must be specifically recorded in the accounting records, with details of all transactions into and out of the account.

*Endowment and similar funds.* This fund group consists of endowment funds, term endowment funds, and funds functioning as endowment (also known as quasi-endowment funds).

ENDOWMENT FUNDS. A true endowment fund may be established only by a donor and can never be expended. The traditional definition of an endowment fund is a fund of which only the earned income can be spent. The original principal of endowment funds must remain intact (nonexpendable) in perpetuity. However, the Uniform Management of Institutional Funds Act permits the prudent use of appreciation as well as income. If the income is restricted, it is classified as an addition to that particular fund and can be used only for the specified purpose. If unrestricted, the income should be reported in the current unrestricted fund group and can be used for any institutional purpose.

TERM ENDOWMENT FUNDS. Term endowment funds initially function exactly like "true" endowment funds. However, after a specific period or event, as defined by the donor, the nature of the principal of the term endowment changes.

For example, University XYZ receives a term endowment gift from Pat Smith. Pat Smith specifies that the principal of this gift is to be invested for the next 20 years, with the income earned on the gift restricted to undergraduate scholarships for the School of Fine Arts. At the conclusion of the twentieth year, Pat Smith says that the principal of the original gift is to be used to establish the Pat Smith Loan Fund, which is to be used for loans to students of the School of Fine Arts. When originally received, this gift would be recognized as a direct addition to the endowment and similar funds group (as a term endowment). During the next 20 years the income earned would be credited to the current restricted funds group and expended as scholarships. When the term of the endowment expired, the principal would be an addition to loan funds and a deduction from endowment and similar funds.

FUNDS FUNCTIONING AS ENDOWMENT. Funds functioning as endowment are also referred to as quasi-endowment funds. The decision to invest otherwise spendable resources is made by the institution's governing board or, through delegation from the board, by management. Since these are internal designations, they may be reversed. Unrestricted money received from outside the institution is first recorded in the current unrestricted fund. An addition to funds functioning as endowment is made by a nonmandatory transfer from current funds. Showing this transaction as a direct addition to funds functioning as endowment would misrepresent the sequence of the economic event, that is, a flow of funds that was initially received as spendable but was subsequently set aside by institutional action for long-term investment.

Income from investments of endowment and similar funds may be either unrestricted income that may be used for any purpose or restricted income that must be used according to the donor's stipulations. Unrestricted income is recorded as current unrestricted funds revenues. Restricted income is recorded as restricted funds in the current or other appropriate fund group. For example, a donor might specify that income earned is to be used for loans to students, in which case it would be recorded as an addition to loan funds.

Each endowment and similar fund must be accounted for separately. Each fund has its own cash and investments, but to facilitate the investment of endowment principal the amounts may be pooled. However, separate accountability of each fund's participating interest in the pool is still required. On some occasions, a donor may restrict how moneys may be invested. Such restriction could specify the actual assets permitted for investment or could prohibit investment in the pool. These restrictions must be honored in satisfying donor intent. (For a more detailed discussion of endowments, see Chapter 10, Endowment Management.)

*Annuity and life income funds.* Annuity and life income funds are funds received by an institution under deferred-giving agreements. These contracts provide that an income be paid to the donor, the donor's designee, or a combination thereof for the lifetime of the recipients(s) or for a fixed period of time. If the income payments are a fixed amount, the contracts are referred to as annuity contracts; if the income payments are based on earnings of the donated assets, they are referred to as life income contracts. At the termination of the contracts, the funds become available for general institutional purposes or for any restricted purpose designated by the donor in the contract.

For external reporting purposes, some institutions include annuity and life income funds in the endowment and similar funds group. This should be done only if the institution has but a few, small-dollar-amount agreements. While these contracts are in force, the income they earn is not available for institutional purposes; to report them with endowment funds, whose income is available for institutional purposes, could be misleading.

When these contracts terminate, the remaining principal of the contracts is reclassified in accordance with the terms of the contract. If the donor has not restricted its use and has allowed it to be used for general institutional purposes or some current restricted purpose, the principal is transferred to the current fund and recorded as revenue. If the funds are restricted by the donor for endowment, plant, or loan fund purposes, they are transferred to these funds and added to the appropriate fund balance.

Four types of deferred-giving contracts are most often used by colleges and universities. These are:

- Charitable gift annuity contracts (often referred to as annuity contracts)

- Pooled income contracts (sometimes referred to as life income contracts)

- Charitable remainder annuity trust contracts

- Charitable remainder unitrust contracts

If a donor is to receive current gift benefits for federal income tax purposes, the deferred-giving agreement must take one of these forms. Accordingly, the contract terms must follow IRS regulations.

***Agency funds.*** Agency funds are funds held by an institution acting as custodian or fiscal agent. The money is deposited with the institution for safekeeping, to be used or withdrawn by the depositor at will. These funds may be held on behalf of students, faculty, staff, organizations, or some other third party. Because they do not belong to the institution, these funds should be displayed as liabilities, not as fund balances. When agency assets are immaterial in amount, the assets and liabilities may be reported as assets and liabilities of the current funds group. Typical examples of agency funds are deposits by students and student organizations, publishing advances to faculty members who edit journals, college work-study funds for outside employers, and various breakage deposits.

***Plant funds.*** The plant funds group is used to account for unexpended plant funds to acquire long-lived assets for institutional purposes; funds set aside for the renewal and replacement of institutional properties; funds set aside for debt service charges and retirement of indebtedness on institutional plant; and the cost (or fair value at time of donation) of long-lived assets (other than those of endowment and similar funds) and the sources from which the cost is funded, including associated liabilities.

Four self-balancing subgroups are provided for the plant funds group: unexpended plant funds, funds for renewals and replacements, funds for retirement of indebtedness, and investment in plant.

The general sources of assets of the unexpended plant funds, the funds for renewals and replacements, and the funds for retirement of indebtedness are:

- Funds from external agencies

- Student fees and assessments for debt service or other plant purposes, which create an obligation equivalent to an externally imposed restriction and are not subject to the discretionary right of the governing board to use for other purposes

- Mandatory and nonmandatory transfers from other fund groups

- Borrowings from external sources for plant purposes

- Borrowings by advances from other fund groups

- Income and net gains from investments in the unrestricted and restricted elements of each subgroup

The distinction between unrestricted and restricted sources and uses should be maintained in the accounting records in order to disclose the limitations on the use of funds and the appropriate disposition of any excess funds. For example, funds transferred from unrestricted current funds at the discretion of the governing board may be retransferred in whole or in part from plant funds prior to commitment.

When funds are restricted by donors and other outside individuals and agencies for plant purposes, such funds should be credited directly to the respective fund subgroup and not passed through the current funds group.

Transfers from other fund groups to plant funds for the acquisition of properties, renewals and replacements, and debt service should be represented by appropriate amounts of cash and other liquid assets. Transfers from plant funds to other fund groups also should be represented by the appropriate transfer of liquid assets.

## New Dimensions

Various initiatives by FASB, GASB, the AICPA, and OMB may result in changes in accounting and reporting by colleges and universities in the 1990s.

*Accounting for contributions.* The FASB exposure draft "Accounting for Contributions Received and Contributions Made and Capitalization of Works of Art, Historical Treasures, and Similar Assets," issued in 1991, proposes that pledges be recognized by a donee at the time of pledge. In addition, it proposes that institutions record the monetary value of contributed services in a donee's financial statements and capitalize works of art and similar assets.

*Display of financial information.* There are several general areas in which the differences among the sources of authoritative literature for not-for-profit organizations are important enough to warrant resolution. These are:

- The display of financial information
- Accounting for investments
- Reporting entities

Although FASB has not given much attention to the second and third subjects, the display of financial information has received much attention. If advisory recommendations of AICPA become GAAP, they would significantly change the way college and university financial statements are presented. A complete set of statements for a not-for-profit organization would include a balance sheet; a statement of changes in net asset classes (for each of the three net asset classes: unrestricted, temporarily restricted, and permanently restricted); and a statement of cash flows.

***Service efforts and accomplishments.*** FASB and GASB continue to be interested in the subject of "service efforts and accomplishments." The basic indicators of input, output, outcomes, and efficiency are being refined, but mandatory reporting is some years away.

***Jurisdiction issue.*** The hierarchy of GAAP is expected to change, so that public colleges and universities would not be required to follow FASB standards unless the standards are adopted by GASB. A proposed AICPA auditing standard establishes two separate but parallel hierarchies of GAAP, one for governmental entities and one for private entities.

The FASB-GASB jurisdiction issue, although formally settled, will continue to pose problems for public institutions, whose financial or business officers will be required to devote more time to an understanding of accounting and reporting issues.

***OMB Circular A-21.*** OMB Circular A-21, "Cost Principles for Educational Institutions," may face changes. Certain expenses may become "unallowable for reimbursement," and there may be a limit on the rate of reimbursement of administrative costs to a specified percentage maximum of modified total direct costs. In addition, organizational changes at OMB may occur that will affect the administration of this and other circulars, including those concerning audits.

## Notes

1. National Association of College and University Business Officers, *Financial Accounting and Reporting Manual for Higher Education* (Washington, D.C.: NACUBO, 1990), p. 106.

2. *Financial Accounting and Reporting Manual for Higher Education*, p. 231.

3. *Financial Accounting and Reporting Manual for Higher Education*, p. 232.

4. *Financial Accounting and Reporting Manual for Higher Education*, p. 233.

5. *Financial Accounting and Reporting Manual for Higher Education*, p. 241.

6. *Financial Accounting and Reporting Manual for Higher Education*, p. 242.

# References and Resources

PUBLICATIONS AND ARTICLES

American Institute of Certified Public Accountants. *Audits of Colleges and Universities.* 2nd ed. New York: AICPA, 1975.

American Institute of Certified Public Accountants. *Audits of State and Local Governmental Units.* New York: AICPA, 1981.

American Institute of Certified Public Accountants. *Statement of Position 74-8: Financial Accounting and Reporting by Colleges and Universities.* New York: AICPA, 1974.

American Institute of Certified Public Accountants. *Statement of Position 78-10: Accounting Principles and Reporting Practices for Certain Nonprofit Organizations.* New York: AICPA, 1978.

Anthony, Robert N. *Financial Accounting in Nonbusiness Organizations.* Stamford, Conn.: Financial Accounting Standards Board, 1978.

Bailey, Larry P. *Miller Comprehensive Governmental GAAP Guide.* New York: Harcourt Brace Jovanovich, 1989.

Financial Accounting Standards Board. Statement of Financial Accounting Concepts No. 4: *Objectives of Financial Reporting by Nonbusiness Organizations.* Stamford, Conn.: FASB, 1980.

Financial Accounting Standards Board. Statement of Financial Accounting Concepts No. 6: *Elements of Financial Statements.* Stamford, Conn.: FASB, 1985.

Governmental Accounting Standards Board. *Codification of Governmental Accounting and Financial Reporting Standards as of June 15, 1987.* Stamford, Conn.: GASB, 1987.

Governmental Accounting Standards Board. Concepts Statement No. 1: *Objectives of Financial Reporting.* Stamford, Conn.: GASB, 1987.

Holder, William N. *The Not-for-Profit Organization Reporting Entity.* Stamford, Conn.: FASB, 1986.

National Association of College and University Business Officers. *Financial Accounting and Reporting Manual for Higher Education.* Washington, D.C.: NACUBO, 1990.

Scheps, Clarence, and E. E. Davidson. *Accounting for Colleges and Universities.* 3rd ed. Baton Rouge: Louisiana State University Press, 1978.

ORGANIZATIONS
American Institute of Certified Public Accountants (AICPA)
    1211 Avenue of the Americas
    New York, NY 10036
    212-575-6200

Financial Accounting Foundation (FAF)
    401 Merritt 7, P. O. Box 5116
    Norwalk, CT 06856-5116
    203-847-0700

Financial Accounting Standards Board (FASB)
    401 Merritt 7, P. O. Box 5116
    Norwalk, CT 06856-5116
    203-847-0700

Governmental Accounting Standards Board (GASB)
    401 Merritt 7, P. O. Box 5116
    Norwalk, CT 06856-5116
    203-847-0700

# CHAPTER 6

# Budgeting

by
Nathan Dickmeyer
Teachers College, Columbia University

# Contents

## 6: Budgeting

For any manager who has had an introduction to college and university budgets, the budgeting process seems perfectly natural: look toward the future and develop spending plans consistent with institutional goals. In fact, budgeting has a short history. In the not-so-distant past, higher education institutions spent only what they made or could borrow, as they made or borrowed it. They set aside only what donors required them to set aside. They constructed buildings only when they had raised funds to pay for the construction. If they ran out of funds, salaries were reduced or staff cut. When gifts for buildings were scarce, dormitories were built by stock companies, for-profit corporations formed by benefactors hoping for a return on their investments.

Budgets represent a move away from the hand-to-mouth, cash existence that colleges and universities once operated in. Budgets require both a forecast of the future and disciplined management as that future is realized. This chapter explores both year-to-year, or operational, budgeting and budgeting for projects that must be planned well in advance, or capital budgeting.

## Operational Budgeting

Budgeting for day-to-day operations, or operational budgeting, is one of many integrated management efforts that college and university administrative officers apply to move an institution toward its goals. Operational budgeting focuses on the control of financial resources, the evaluation of financial performance, and the facilitation of the institution's mission. Operational budgets are developed by calculating and ratifying expectations for revenues and expenditures. Because college and university personnel make daily decisions and set policies that bring in revenues and cause expenditures, the budget is used as a mechanism to manage expectations and behaviors. When the operational budgeting process is effective, individuals with revenue or expenditure authority know in advance what the institution expects by way of revenues and what they may spend.

Planning should be used to link institutional operations strategically to the institution's mission and to make the institution more responsive to internal and external changes. The planning process identifies priorities. Planning comprises many subprocesses, including academic program planning, marketing planning, and strategic planning. Each of these is closely linked. The focus of operational budgeting is on the next year, but at most institutions where the budgeting process runs smoothly, it incorporates objectives for three to five years into the future. Such a long-term view provides the link between planning and budgeting and the link to the capital budget.

Academic planning starts by relating the strengths of the institution to the needs of its market. As viewed and analyzed through the marketing function, strategic planning engages the institution's vision and mission, leading to a budget that is essentially a funded action plan for the institution. Good academic program planning thus provides much of the rationale for operational budgeting. Increases, decreases, creations, and eliminations of specific program budgets should be based on designs developed from an ongoing planning process—a process that can be more thoughtful and forward looking than the frenetic, once-a-year budget process. A good academic program planning process feeds the budget process with priorities, concepts, and campus designs. The constraints of the budget, moreover, should be allowed to feed back to planners to keep both planning and budgeting effective.

Institutions evaluate, improve, or eliminate services by reallocating resources in the framework of a formal strategic planning system or as part of day-to-day operations. Human resources planning (hiring, firing, evaluating, upgrading, training, and informing personnel) is linked to budgeting. Facilities planning and financial planning are also part of an institution's management structure. Operational budgeting is thus a critical management system in a constellation of linked systems.

## BUDGETING OVERVIEW

A key characteristic of an operational budget as a management system is its strong tie to accounting systems and periods of time. One year is typical for an operational budget to be applied, although budgets may be applicable for any period of time. Some states prepare biennial operational budgets, but these are in fact two one-year budgets prepared every other year.

This yearly cycle of activity has no real beginning or end: the final stage of one year is the first stage of the next. Nevertheless, the stages can be described as follows.

**Look ahead, assign responsibility.** In the first stage of budgeting, administrators and analysts examine the institution's fiscal situation, the institution's success in its markets, and future trends. The institution's strengths and weaknesses are examined, and trends from within the institution are projected. Important decisions about budget responsibility are made and goals for the budget are set or assumed (e.g., that the budget should be balanced).

**Submit the request.** If the institution is public, the budget request must be submitted to the institutional system or to the state. Each state has different guidelines for requesting the next year's budget.

**Exchange information.** The administration supplies information in the form of budget guidance, salary guidelines, and spending and revenue guidelines to those responsible for developing budgets. The revenue guidelines are based on revenue estimates, estimates of state funding, or actual appropriations, depending on the control of the institution and the state requirements (when the institution is publicly controlled). The people responsible for developing budgets produce estimates, develop proposals, list wishes, enumerate concerns, and try to develop budgets that will allow them to meet their goals, stated or unstated. For the purposes of this chapter, "budget officer" refers to those administrators who must prepare and follow budgets and "budget administrator" refers to those who are higher in the budget hierarchy than budget officers and who are involved in developing budget policy.

External reporting requirements affect the budgeting process. Budget procedures for public colleges and universities differ from those of independent colleges and universities because of requirements of external funding agencies. Timing and flexibility of budget procedures, for example, can be affected by the need to supply workload and enrollment data in support of budget requests. These data may also be requested on a regular basis throughout the budget cycle. As a result, the timing involved in the budget process for public institutions can become critical, with the budget officer involved not only with budgets for the current fiscal period but also with budgets for the most recent and upcoming fiscal periods.

*Negotiate.* In the negotiation stage, the need to make all the pieces fit in a manner consistent with the budget process requires upward as well as downward communication. While much negotiating can be eliminated by carefully phrasing the information passed down (e.g., "the institution will not accept requests for new positions this year"), the budget process should allow for budget requests to be negotiated. Instead of passing down a firm "bottom line," many institutions allow some flexibility at the request stage and then use a negotiation period to compress low-priority budgets with weak rationales and expand others.

*Ratify.* Resulting revenue goals and expenditure limits must be given legitimacy. The institution's president recommends the budget, the faculty often review the budget, and the governing board adopts the budget. Without legitimacy, the budget cannot function as a management guide.

*Implement.* The implementation stage occurs during the period of time covered by the budget. Over that period, revenues are received and expenditures are made and compared with the goals of the budget. The timeliness of the comparisons and the accuracy of the information available are of great concern. Deviations cannot be corrected if necessary information is late.

*Evaluate.* In the final stage, a number of evaluations are made. Was the budget process reasonable? Was it a burden? Did it foster discussion, understanding, and development of the institution's goals? Was it well-timed to take into consideration the needs of the community and the actual availability of information? If the goal of the budget process was to keep revenues and expenditures equal during the period, did it do so? If there were other financial goals, were they achieved? Finally, a more difficult evaluation needs to be undertaken. Did the institution move closer to achieving its planning goals during the budget period because of the budget process?

## MAKING CHOICES

Colleges and universities often have organizational structures shaped like a pyramid, in which those at the top are expected to lead and make decisions. This conceptual shape varies with the role that the faculty play in the management of the institution. Because there is in any case some sort of top and bottom, however, budget system designers must assign responsibilities and information flows. Good systems rely on clearly stated responsibilities for defining assumptions and priorities at the top and clear lines of upward communication by which those below can bring forward their ideas and values.

A few important choices determine the basic nature of a budgeting process as it is uniquely adapted to an institution. How decentralized will the process be? How much authority will people be given at each level of a decentralized process? How integrated will the budget process be with other management systems? How can the budgeting process be explained succinctly to those who must sometimes reluctantly engage with it? These choices depend heavily on whether the institution is public or independent and the management style of the institution's president. If the president does not face constraints by the state, he or she may choose to delegate authority and responsibility for various aspects of the budgeting process. Ultimately, however, the president is wholly responsible to the governing board of the institution.

***Centralized or decentralized budgeting.*** Most institutions manage the choice of a decentralized or centralized system with a compromise. For example, departments may be able to set their own budgets but only within strict overall guidelines. Divisions may control revenues and expenditures, but departments may not. Departments at all levels may request a budget, but administrators shape the request to fit a final budget. Some institutions have decentralized participation but not fully decentralized budgeting responsibility.

The more centralized the budget process, the less elaborate the procedures needed and the less time spent on the process. A negotiation stage is always necessary, however, so that requesters can come face-to-face with decisionmakers and express their concerns.

A more centralized process allows a smaller group of decisionmakers to shape the budget and make it match institutional goals or the goals of the legislature or state. Many decentralized processes are market driven and may force the institution to deviate from its mission or plan (e.g., an institution could become predominantly a business school because of tremendous demand in that area, while the plan calls for a liberal arts college). Thus, adherence to mission and goals, including recognition of size and location constraints, can steer institutions toward a more centralized budget process. Decentralized decisions can cause the institution to change in ways contrary to its mission.

However, decentralized systems allow the institution to react more quickly to the needs of the market. Decentralized processes are also believed to engender more effective budgets and more efficient performance, if only because people who have some control over their working lives perform better. The department, school, or division that sets all or some portion of its budget may be better motivated to solve its own problems. Departments whose budgets are set centrally may look only to the center for solutions.

*Setting authority at each level.* The decision to involve people in the budgeting process is one decision; determining their tasks and responsibilities is quite another. This decision thus has considerable impact on budgeting descriptions and procedures.

*Open-ended requests.* Budget officers (those with the responsibility for developing a budget at any level: college, school, division, department, office) may ask various people for their open-ended, or "blue sky," requests. The theory is that people's involvement in making a request motivates them to think about their needs. This in turn fosters creativity and may be useful during a period of budget growth or intense legislative interest in higher education. Too often, however, periods of growth are not sustained, and this style of budgeting can lead to bitterness and disillusionment.

Open-ended budgets, when they can be fulfilled, can cause unnecessary growth in expenditures, out of line with the institution's goals and needs. During subsequent downturns, the institution must find ways of cutting back.

*Recommended requests.* Some budget requests are developed under guidelines and can be regarded as little more than recommendations. Budget officers may be given request guidelines. Requests based on guidelines may or may not be honored, depending on overall pressures on the institution. Often the central administration has less information when it issues guidelines than when it begins to finalize a budget. Budget requests must then be changed before or during the negotiation stage.

Request guidelines may stipulate an overall dollar limit on expenditures; a percentage increase; differing percentage increases for the various lines in the budget (supplies might be held down, but a consideration for postal rate increases given); or number, dollar, and percentage guidelines. Some institutions allow budget officers to request only non-personnel-related items. These institutions may separate the personnel request system from the nonpersonnel request system.

*Mandatory requests.* After open-ended and recommended budget requests, the next conceptual step is mandatory budget requests. The institution guarantees that the requestor will (probably) receive the budget requested. Possible guidelines for mandatory budget requests:

- The budget officer is allowed to show that sufficient revenues are generated by the unit to cover expenditures plus an agreed-upon payment to the central administration for services.

- The budget request is made sufficiently lower than previous requests to make all the pieces fit (e.g., a system whereby each unit submits a budget 10 percent less than the previous year, plus a special request of 15 percent of the previous year's budget, which may be funded).

- The units have sufficient control over restricted reserves, especially from gifts directed to units, so they can fund the budget even if general revenues cannot.

Thus, delegated authority can range from simple consultation to having the budget officer make determinations. Because colleges and universities are made of many layers of organization units, there are many permutations for implementing these participation strategies.

Regardless of the style of budgeting selected, the process must be managed. The operational budget of the institution always requires assumptions, priorities, and the context of a long-range view. These assumptions, priorities, and views may purposely begin with a lack of definition so that the community can contribute its ideas, analyses, and beliefs. At some point, however, the assumptions, priorities, and views must be set and presented from above. Few institutions can proceed into budgeting without prescribed assumptions about inflation and energy costs, priority decisions about salary and tuition increases, priority decisions about program additions, and the working context of a three- to five-year financial projection model.

Good budgeting systems accommodate ideas from any level. The institution's assumptions and priorities can be developed with the advice of faculty and staff. Ideas about how to accomplish goals and put priorities into effect most often come from those faced with implementing policies day by day. Thus, a good system relies on firm decision-making responsibilities carefully apportioned to upper-level administrators, while keeping the system responsive to the ideas of all those affected by budgets.

***Integrating budgeting with other management processes.*** The administration of a college or university may choose to integrate other processes directly into budgeting. There are advantages and concerns with each type of integration. Many pieces of the budget puzzle are necessary for planning. The budget process can produce long-range financial forecasts, departmental reviews, and market analyses. Planning can be used to develop primary objectives for the budget. Many parts of the human resources management system can become part of the budgeting system.

***Operating budget process descriptions.*** Having chosen the appropriate levels of decentralization, responsibility, control, and management-system integration, budget managers can then select a particular budgeting technique. Descriptions of budgeting techniques are often vague as to whether they can or should be applied at all levels (departmental, division, school, or state), and each implementing institution has to work out its own design details. There are several choices.

OPEN-ENDED BUDGETING. Open-ended budgeting, or "blue sky" budgeting, forces budget management into the negotiation stage, because open-ended requests almost always exceed the resources available.

INCREMENTAL BUDGETING. The dollar increments allowed for individual budgets must be specified. The increments are usually specified so well that little creativity is allowed. Because increments are often imposed across the board, this technique cannot be used easily to tie to the budget those planning results that call for particular program reductions or expansions. Responsibility for setting assumptions and priorities may be shirked with incremental budgeting, while the flow of ideas from the lower levels is cut off. Nevertheless, when paired with a controlled process whereby lower-level budget officers make special requests that are then reviewed by higher administrators, a hybrid process can be an efficient budgeting mechanism.

ALTERNATIVE-LEVEL BUDGETING. Alternative-level budgeting is similar to incremental budgeting, except that several increments are specified by upper-level administrators. For example, three different budget requests may be required: one at last year's level, one at 5 percent above last year, and one at 5 percent below last year. Institutional planning priorities may be more easily fostered with this approach, because administrators select different support levels for different programs in line with planning priorities. There is a greater burden on budget officers, however, in that they must determine how to effect each level, especially if the limit is broadly placed. Many budget administrators have noted the tendency of budget officers to select a critical function to submit to a budget cut, rather than creatively trying to find ways of becoming more efficient. To implement alternative-level budgeting, budget administrators must apply firmness and reject requests that lack creativity.

QUOTA BUDGETING. Quota budgeting allows greater latitude for budget officers than incremental and alternative-level budgeting. Budget officers are given a single figure around which they may build a budget. Other critical decisions must be made by the chief budget officer. How is the quota determined? Does it result from planning and reflect priorities, or is it incremental? How stable is the quota? Do further negotiations have to occur when initial predictions prove to be wrong? This method implies more priority setting at the top of the organization and demands more creativity on the part of lower-level budget officers in working within the quota.

FORMULA BUDGETING. Formula budgeting is commonly found at the state level to allocate appropriations among institutions and to allow the state to respond to enrollment shifts. The formulas can be simple enrollment-driven measures or complex schemes to recognize differing missions and needs.

Formula budgeting favors or values measurable equity. Like most formulas, budgets can respond only to what can be measured, but they can do so in a way that is impartial to other effects. They can respond to enrollments, part-time students, number of majors or class points, number of Nobel prize winners, or number of students at risk, or to no designated area in particular. Few situations, however, are simple enough to ensure that participants will agree on a formula.

PROGRAM BUDGETING. Program budgeting requires a careful integration of budgeting and planning. Programs become planning units, and their managers must develop projections that can be supported with budgets. Program budgeting emphasizes the idea that budgets flow from plans.

ZERO-BASED BUDGETING. In zero-based budgeting, each function of a budgeting unit (or, for example, each major task of an office) is described in a collection of data called a "decision package." Each decision package includes a description of the goals, services, and purposes of the function at various levels of funding, including zero funding. Hence the name, zero-based funding. Each unit's budget officer is asked to rank his or her decision packages in priority order, and each administrator in the organizational hierarchy then ranks the decision packages of the various units. A budget is built by funding the decision packages with the highest priority at the top of the administrative pyramid, with input from each level below. The final budget is built by the top administrator from a collection of the highest priority activities (as represented by decision packages) at levels of activity appropriate to the priority.

Zero-based budgeting requires that administrators at each level of the organization take a hard look at all functions below them and select some that may be cut and some that may be improved. The system makes each budget officer responsible for achieving the goals of the functions funded.

Although zero-based budgeting is a remarkable learning experience, few institutions have managed to implement the system for more than three or four years. The system requires a great deal of paperwork to justify the alternatives. Institutions have found that cutting some areas is not as easily accomplished as giving a service a low ranking. Most institutions have found the technique better suited for administrative areas than for academic areas. Ranking functions in an orderly way within an academic department is difficult. A major improvement to the system may be to impose priorities early in the process to eliminate the need to explore certain alternatives.

INVESTMENT BUDGETING. Investment budgeting is an option when extra resources are made available because of enrollment growth, state appropriations increases, or revenue increases. Institutions with growing enrollments and relatively stable costs and nontuition revenues may have extra resources. Other institutions free up resources for investment budgeting by requiring reduced budgets each year. Investment budgeting is a strategy for budgeting these marginal revenues used in addition to a regular strategy (such as incremental or alternative-level budgeting) for the budget base.

To put extra money to work, the central administration, offices, or departments may put together investment proposals that outline the costs and benefits of a new function or an addition to an existing function. A minimum financial rate of return may be set, along with required intangible benefits supporting the priorities of the institution. The hurdle rate, or the minimum rate of return required on any such investment, should be set high enough to reflect the uncertainty of most of these forecasts. The budget is made by selecting a set of investments to ensure the viability of the new or added function.

INCENTIVE BUDGETING OR INTRAMURAL FUNDING. In incentive budgeting or intramural funding, a school or division is given authority over its revenues, except for a payment from the school to support central administration. This is a variation on formula budgeting, but the formula is directly tied to controllable revenues. However, incentive budgeting can rarely be used at the departmental level, because departments usually do not have the authority to carry it out. Schools within an institution may have good control over tuition income, but many students take courses outside their schools. Departments may strongly encourage students to take courses in their home departments. The result is internal conflict, rather than external competition, because departments are too interdependent.

Variations exist that give schools a range of budget control. At the loosest extreme, a school may be responsible for setting tuition, garnering enrollments, hiring faculty, and controlling expenditures. If the school needs more faculty than it can secure with current tuition, the school may increase the tuition rate, increase enrollment, or seek new endowments. The institution, however, may prevent the school from expanding unless it receives sufficient gifts to pay for a new building and its maintenance.

With the revenues collected, each revenue center must pay central administration for all central institutional operations and all functions not allocated to or the responsibility of the school or division. The payment to the central administration is negotiated on the basis of history, growth, potential, and equity with other schools. It is difficult to develop an easy formula. These payments may be fixed amounts negotiated each year or percentages of various kinds of revenue. They may also be based on expenses, like faculty salaries.

Fixed-rate payment protects the central administration better than variable-rate payment, but variable-rate payments can more adequately fund an administration faced with a growing school. Schools that fail to make the payment in any year may be forced to reduce expense levels or to raise tuition and fees. The system starts to break down when schools fail to make the payment several years in a row. The institution must decide if the system has failed and schools cannot survive on their own, or if a few schools need help from other richer ones, or if the failing schools need to make radical changes—new leadership, new markets, or closure. Within a school, however, a budgeting system must still be developed. For example, an institution may develop budgets for its schools using an incentive system, while the schools allocate funds using a quota system.

***Governmental control.*** In developing their budgets, public institutions must be aware of state and local restrictions on the expenditure of funds, such as purchasing regulations, travel restrictions, limitations on out-of-state enrollment, and restrictions on budgetary transfers imposed by state and local appropriating bodies. Public and independent institutions must also be aware of governmental restrictions on student aid and sponsored programs.

## OTHER ASPECTS OF THE BUDGETING PROCESS

When deciding on an operational budgeting technique, an institution must examine itself and make certain projections. Such examination has become formalized as part of or closely related to the operational budgeting process.

***Useful outcomes from financial analysis.*** Often called ratio analysis, financial analysis gives the institution a picture of its financial health in comparison with its peers and in comparison with itself over the last few years. Financial analysis causes institutions to spot problem areas and spurs further analyses to improve financial management and make strategic decisions. It also legitimizes the enforced discipline of the budget process. Institutions may use annual studies conducted by various organizations to justify changes in budgeting priorities.

Low and declining financial and nonfinancial resources, increasing financial risk exposure, and poor positioning to respond to risk justify greater discipline in the budget process. Worsening financial ratios mean that the increments in incremental budgeting and the quotas in quota budgeting must be lower and the priority of devices to channel resources into financial buffers and to gain flexibility must be raised.

A BALANCED BUDGET. Achieving a balanced budget sounds like a reasonable goal, but institutions define "balance" differently. An institution with ample financial reserves may set a goal of having operating expenses equal to revenues in three out of four years. Such a budget is constructed so that the estimates and control system can differ once every four years.

The issue of depreciation comes into play when discussing balanced budgets. Should the budget be balanced by including the funding of depreciation? If depreciation is not used, should the institution fund a reserve for repair and replacement in excess of depreciation? Are the institution's financial resources so depleted that revenues must exceed expenditures? Has the institution borrowed to continue operations? Should the repayment of these funds be budgeted? Responding to these situations requires a more stringent definition of balance. When the answers are difficult, financial analysis sets the stage for the appropriate degree of concern about the budget and helps determine the specific financial goal of the budget.

*Planning.* The results of planning can be so diffuse as to have no impact on budgeting. If planning fails to affect an institution, its usefulness must be challenged. Plans can result in inspirational goals, but often these goals should not be allowed to influence the budget excessively. For example, if planning calls for $10 million to be raised in gifts but the previous high is $8 million, budget administrators should not build $10 million into the budget.

Planning can result in institutional calls for budget changes. The institution may decide that, if the institution provided better services, the majority of its programs could compete against institutions with a better reputation. A strategy for effecting this plan might include higher tuition, more merit-based student aid, greater availability of computers, new lab equipment, more faculty, and a higher level of plant maintenance. All these items can be included in the budget.

Planning can result in the targeting of certain academic and nonacademic programs for reduction, elimination, addition, or emphasis, with or without a coherent strategic rationale. Budgets can be made to reflect such plans. The success of these maneuvers, however, depends heavily on the consensus of the community as the final version develops and on the right of the president to enact the changes.

**Long-range financial forecast.** A long-range financial forecast takes the previous budgets of the institution and projects future budgets, using assumptions about the environment, major policy variables, and models of the process that interrelate financial outcomes. Assumptions about inflation and postal costs, for example, can be used for projections. Policies about tuition and salary increases can be added. Models that tie federal grant assumptions to indirect cost recovery can also be constructed. Institutions have been able to use these factors to develop predictions of future balance sheets and financial ratios. A long-range financial forecast allows the institution to predict the impact of future strategic choices.

These forecasts can also allow the institution to evaluate risk better. By viewing a range of scenarios, the institution can better prepare for results that are less than predictions, including the development of contingency budgets and the creation of reserves to buffer the institution against these possible outcomes.

Long-range financial forecasts must reflect current reality and believable projections. Budgets based on unrealistic forecasts only cause administrations to lose their credibility as they scramble to balance budgets during the year, often doing long-lasting harm to themselves and their institution.

Long-range financial forecasts allow capital budgets to be better integrated into operating budgets. With a long-range forecast, an institution can try various new programs, capital construction, and financing scenarios to find which one best integrates with operating results. The impact of debt service and maintenance, including infrastructure costs such as utility corridors and roads, for a new building, for example, is a direct concern addressed by a long-range forecast. The impact on bond ratings of changes on the balance sheet is another important concern.

BUDGET GUIDELINES

As long as the operational budget technique falls somewhere between "autocratic" and "completely decentralized," some information must flow from those who put the final budget together to those who have some delegated responsibility for the budget. A set of guidelines should describe the budget technique, the outcomes of the financial analysis, the outcomes of planning, and the outcomes of the long-range financial forecast. These outcomes set the stage for budgeting by describing the strategies, assumptions, and methods of developing the budget.

Of particular interest to budget officers are the assumptions and policies that lead to the estimate of uncontrollable items in the budget. Most items termed uncontrollable are in fact semicontrollable. A primary example is the institution's endowment. Although investment returns may be largely out of the hands of the institution's administration, the spending formula is usually set by the board. Likewise, gift giving is almost always some function of the amount spent on fund raising. Rates for utilities are difficult to predict, but the institution can attempt to control usage. Assurances that estimates were reasonably and fairly developed are also useful when the budget is presented to the governing board.

State appropriations are difficult to predict and may be revised mid-year. Yet, budgeting requires some assumptions, however conservative. The more volatile an appropriation has been in the past, the greater the need for a contingency budget. New information or new strategies for influencing semicontrollable budget items may result in changes in estimates in the negotiation phase.

The stated guidelines must specify how information is to be collected and justified. Forms or computer software used for gathering information should be explained. Usually forms provide the expenses, by line, of at least one previous year and the budget for the current year. One of the great challenges of budgeting is that actual expense and revenue figures for the most recent budget year cannot be made available while the next year's budget is being prepared, because the year is in process.

Quotas, increments, and formulas must be specified, if applicable. The breadth of applicability of the quota needs to be specified (e.g., all expenditures or just nonpersonnel). Extra columns may be necessary for alternative budgets. Some institutions require separate columns for one-time-only requests like expensive equipment. These requests may go through a parallel evaluation process, but ongoing programs might take precedence for funding.

With broad quota budgets and incentive budgeting, only one

number needs to be provided by administrators for each department or office. This figure should represent how much may be budgeted for quota budgets or expense centers under incentive budgeting or how much contribution or subvention is expected from a school under incentive budgeting. The departments or offices must then spread the bottom line among all line items.

## NEGOTIATION

Under most budgeting techniques, budget officers are responsible for bringing the budget to the balance set in the goals. Budget officers must also ensure that all estimates are reasonable and that the probability of not meeting certain goals is not so great as to damage the institution.

Even within the most stringent guidelines, balancing a budget is difficult. The guidelines never seem to apply to everything. If the Occupational Safety and Health Administration suddenly demands that lab safety must meet new standards, then current guidelines may have little relevance. Planning may result in new programs to be developed outside of the guidelines. Contingencies may have been requested by top administrative officers. Increasing reserves may have been given a higher priority by the governing board.

Not only may the final set of budget requests be larger than resources, but the combined requests may show insufficient movement toward the planned new strategies and priorities of the institution. Actions at this point may take several forms.

New policies may be framed to improve the possibility of balance. For example, new fees for the use of labs and computers may be instituted or caps may be placed on financial aid levels.

Strategic adjustments can be imposed to better reflect plans. Reduction of staff or denial of requests for staff may be necessary if the budget does not balance or does not reflect new strategic elements.

Cuts might be allocated across the board or for each division to allocate as it sees fit. This step works only if central administrators are tough negotiators, are capable of analyzing budgets for appropriate cuts, and can deflect the attempts of administrators who strongly defend their budget requests. This step seldom succeeds without face-to-face negotiations.

***Contingency budgets.*** One method of making cuts more palatable at this stage is to develop a two-way contingency budget. Items that are cut might be put on a contingency budget and get a higher priority for funding if certain revenue goals, such as fall enrollments or actual appropriations, are exceeded. At the same time, budget officers should be required to specify primary cuts to go into a second contingency budget if these goals fall short by a certain level.

In some institutions, budgets for vacant positions are withdrawn from the budget unit allocation and pooled centrally in the contingency fund, or they are reallocated on an institutionwide basis. At other institutions, the department involved is able to retain these savings and use them for other purposes. At state-supported institutions, however, these savings may revert to the state.

Contingency budgets are especially useful for funding one-time-only expenses, even if the funding lags by one year. If the institution meets its goals, some portion of the reserve created might be apportioned to items on the contingency budget list, after the institution has the funds in hand. However, institutions should be hesitant to use transitory revenues to fund ongoing expenses.

## RATIFICATION AND IMPLEMENTATION

The last step in the determination of the operational budget in independent institutions is approval of the budget by the institutional governing board; public colleges or universities, however, often must gain approval for their requests from state education agencies. Before final approval is given, other constituencies, such as faculty and students, are frequently asked to be heard by the administration. Many institutions use budget hearings, newspaper briefings, and the planning process to widen the number of constituents who can participate in budget decisions.

In institutions where faculty, staff, and/or students have input into the budget process, the institution should try to apply that influence early rather than late in the process. Negotiations between the central administration and schools or departments are difficult enough without other parties pressing for influence. Educating faculty committees about the particularities of each line of the budget as it is coming together leaves top administrators exhausted and faculty feeling as though they have no influence—they are shown only the results; they do not play a part in what led to the results.

The most effective place for faculty influence is in the planning process, where strategic objectives are set, long before budget requests are compiled. As the budget is formed, faculty, staff, and student committees should ask, "Does this budget move the institution toward the strategic priorities developed in planning?" This should be easy for budget officers to demonstrate. Final ratification is difficult when some constituencies feel disenfranchised.

After the budget is adopted and made official, changes may occur before the budget is actually implemented. In many cases, contingencies for salary increases are set aside as a lump sum and allocated only after the governing board adopts final salary guidelines. It may not be possible to budget individual salary increases until negotiations between employee representatives and the institution's representatives are complete. When negotiations are complete, the salary contingency pool is drawn down and allocated to individual budgets.

Budget changes that may occur throughout a budget year include:

- Transfers among nonpersonnel items

- Transfers from personnel to nonpersonnel

- Transfers from nonpersonnel to personnel

- Transfers to or from contingency funds

- Transfers without sources (appropriations)

Many public institutions have only limited authority to make these transfers. The rules of the institutional system govern. Independent institutions need to set up stringent procedures for each of these transfers.

***Transfers among nonpersonnel items.*** Unless the institution must prevent transfers among nonpersonnel items because of line-item control by the state, institutions can allow transfers among nonpersonnel items if the transfers are made within a simple notification system with departmental budget officer approval.

***Transfers from personnel to nonpersonnel.*** An institution may wish to limit transfers from personnel to nonpersonnel funds, anticipating some savings from turnover (new people are hired at lower salaries or with a delay) and believing that the original nonpersonnel budgets were adequate. An institution might appropriate turnover savings to a central or decentralized contingency fund that is either budgeted or not. Some institutions do not allow such transfers. Instead, they budget a certain amount in expectation of turnover savings and transfer the savings as they occur. Transfers of turnover savings would not occur at the institutional level under most forms of incentive budgeting or similar philosophies, because the amount owed by the school would normally be determined in advance or by formula.

*Transfers from nonpersonnel to personnel.* Most institutions with even minimal levels of control in their budgeting procedures do not allow transfers from nonpersonnel to personnel. Personnel commitments are much stronger than nonpersonnel commitments. A blanket prohibition on such transfers averts the temptation to use $5,000 saved in nonpersonnel costs to hire a $20,000-per-year employee in the last quarter of the year with the result that, in the following year, either the employee must be let go or $20,000 (not $5,000) must be found to keep the position filled.

*Transfers to or from contingency funds.* There is no real difficulty with transfers from contingency funds as long as the contingency fund is not overspent and only one senior administrator has responsibility for each contingency.

*Transfers without sources (appropriations).* Many institutions make "transfers without sources" without notifying the governing board. They may, for example, authorize a student aid program to be paid for from new tuition. If the institution's tuition budget is not raised and if the higher revenue goal is not met, the institution is spending money without a source. Administrators should not authorize appropriations without telling the institution's governing board. Institutions that follow this rule find that they have few unbudgeted items.

In general, where the policies of the institution do not require that budget changes be disclosed to the board, the governing board needs only general information about transfers. However, if the relative proportions of income and expenditure shift between the time of the budget request and the time of the transfers, the governing board should be informed. Changes of one to two percentage points in relative share are significant and should be of interest to the board.

Once the fiscal period begins, the objectives of implementation are easy enough: to provide through managerial financial reporting timely information on how budget officers are proceeding against their budget goals and to make evident sanctions for violating those goals. (For a full discussion of this subject, see Chapter 8, Managerial Financial Reporting.)

***Automation.*** The automation of budgeting by using interactive database management systems presents new opportunities and new challenges. In the past, reports were available monthly at best; with an interactive budget system, a budget officer can instantly see all changes to the budgets and charges to the account. With some systems, budget officers can learn to design their own reports. There may be, however, large financial and computer transaction-time costs to these installations. Automated systems make it easier to apportion annual budgets into monthly budgets. They also make it easier for administrators to spot spending rates that are too aggressive or income rates that fall below what is necessary to meet the budget.

A comparison by account number of what has been budgeted, what is spent, what is committed, and the resulting balance is minimally necessary output from an automated system. The information on what is committed may be new information for some institutions. This information includes personnel contracts, purchase requisitions, purchase orders, and standing orders. The transactions that stand behind these numbers need to be easily available to budget officers: original budgets, budget adjustments (whether permanent or temporary), journal vouchers, invoices, payrolls, purchase orders, and purchase requisitions. Detailed listings should include enough information to allow a budget officer to trace any transaction and investigate discrepancies.

***Reporting.*** Top administrators need several kinds of reports: exception reports, payroll reports, and program reports. Exception reports show those budget areas that significantly deviate from budget expectations. Easy to develop when monthly budgeting is used, they are more complicated when a broad formula must be used to pick out the exceptions.

Several types of payroll reports are necessary to show that there have been no deviations from authorized staffing levels. These reports need to pinpoint exceptions to budget expectations caused by salary adjustments and excessive overtime use.

Program reports can be employed by institutions using program budgeting or program-oriented planning to track expenditures by major function in the institution, regardless of its organizational placement. Similarly, responsibility reports can show total budget deviation by an aggregate of units reporting to one person, regardless of their organizational placement.

## EVALUATION

*Process evaluation*. Colleges and universities often fail to review systematically the process of developing the budget. How many staff hours were required? Was information provided and received in a timely fashion? Were deadlines reasonable? Evaluations emphasize the more subtle purposes of budgeting. Did people come to understand the institution better because of the process? Did people understand the institution's financial constraints better? Did they understand better that those constraints are largely imposed by the institutional environment? Administrators need to decide whether the budgeting system continues to match their management style and the needs for motivation and autonomy of the other participants.

*Budget goal evaluation.* Did the institution achieve its budget goals? If not, why not? How much money was lost to a lack of expenditure control? How much money was lost because of inaccurate or late information? How much money was lost by decisions made centrally? By decisions made at lower levels of management? How much budget loss was caused by external shifts like utilities increases? Should the institution have reacted or prepared better?

*Planning goal evaluation.* The more explicit the planning goals are, the easier it is to evaluate success. If the institution wishes to hold down administrative costs, was some figure or proportion chosen? Did the budget achieve that? Did the actual figures achieve that? If the institution wished to enter new markets, was it successful? How much of the incremental items in the budget are dedicated to that initiative?

One of the challenges of operational budgeting is that the cycle may be 18 months long but must recur every 12 months. Planning must be going on for the next budget cycle while negotiations are being concluded on the current cycle. When the planning effort is well-integrated, the cycle might be as long as two or three years. Thus, an institution could be evaluating a budget one year after the next budget has been implemented.

Operational budgets are effective management tools because people respect the need for visible constraints and are willing to join an effort to ensure the financial integrity of the institution. For that reason, operational budgeting systems must have integrity built into them at every level; they cannot abuse people's willingness to have their expectations managed. In short, operational budgets symbolize the financial integrity of the institution.

# Capital Budgeting

Capital budgeting is a discipline for examining plans and alternatives for projects that could bring major changes to an institution's asset or expense structure. This planning framework is usually imposed on projects that require several years of advance planning, projects that are expected to have a long life, and projects that require major infusions of capital.

Like operational budgeting, capital budgeting is a planning and control process. Capital budgeting, however, is concerned with planning for expenditures too large and too irregular to be easily made part of the operational budgeting process. Often the size and unusual nature of the activities being budgeted require greater involvement of the governing board than does operational budgeting. The activities involved are complex, last longer than a single fiscal year, and commonly require specialized assistance.

Capital budgeting is most often required as part of the planning for building projects. The construction of a new building demands focused attention to planning, construction, and phase-in over a period much longer than a year. In almost all cases, the funding for such a project cannot be accommodated within an operational budget. As a capital asset, the project presents opportunities to develop funding sources often unavailable to the operational budget.

Similarly, renovations of existing buildings or other fixed assets are candidates for the capital budgeting process. Major equipment purchases such as boilers, mainframe computers, major pieces of scientific equipment, water chillers, and new heating, ventilation, and air-conditioning installations can be planned within a capital budgeting framework. Land purchases and sales may also be best budgeted within this framework. Capital budgeting is necessary not only for new buildings but also for the infrastructural changes that they make necessary.

New academic programs are less often considered as subjects of capital budgeting because the financing options are more limited. Nevertheless, adding a new program is an institutional investment that should be examined with the same discipline and depth of planning as the construction of a new building. The planning should cover many years, and start-up funding is critical.

Capital budgeting must reflect the directions in which the institution plans to grow. As such, the capital budget must be integrated into the campus master plan and academic program plans of the institution. Academic program plans can show where capital investments will produce the greatest benefit to the institution in terms of increased enrollment, more efficient operations, increased services, and greater research productivity and revenues.

The campus master plan reflects the institution's mission, the academic plan, and, sometimes, the state's plan for higher education. Like academic program plans, the campus master plan must set the context for the institution well into the future and reflect local economic growth, demand for graduates, housing availability, demographic shifts, traffic patterns, and land usage. It essentially represents a set of physical constraints. Besides dictating building design and location, campus master plans show campus traffic patterns and power, water, and sewage provisions. Campus master plans are based on assumptions about basic campus characteristics drawn from projections of academic plans: the future number of students by department; number of residential students; proportion of graduate students by department; number of commuters; number of faculty; and number of staff. A well-articulated campus master plan is critical to capital budgeting.

## PURPOSES

Capital budgeting has four major purposes: to facilitate institutional growth, to permit systematic exploration of alternatives, to manage balance sheets, and to communicate the institution's options to the board.

Capital budgeting is necessary to permit institutional growth without undue strain on continuing operations. Capital projects undertaken without the discipline and framework of capital budgeting can jeopardize normal operations. A new building or academic program demands cash for planning, debt service, and operations. Without planning, cash demands can take an institution by surprise and result in a weakened financial position, loss of programs, and demoralization.

Capital budgeting permits systematic exploration of alternatives so that the college or university may maximize its opportunities. The capital budgeting stages require a systematic exploration of debt vehicles, project timing, project scope and size, and project design. Taking shortcuts on any of these steps can result in unnecessary financial burdens for the institution.

Balance-sheet strength requires that the financial or business officer actively manage the balance sheet, that is, the asset-and-liability position of the institution. This management orientation goes beyond year-to-year operational budgeting because cash, debt, and other liability positions must also be managed. Capital budgeting, along with operational budgeting and cash management, is a critical and necessary ingredient in balance-sheet management. Balance-sheet strength can be achieved only by predicting and understanding the impact of capital decisions, especially those that require substantial borrowing.

Capital budgeting also produces information that enables board members to understand the long-term needs and options facing the institution as it grows and preserves its capital assets. Keeping the governing board informed of needs and showing them the process used to manage and meet those needs is a major reason for capital budgeting.

## OBJECTIVE

With these purposes in mind, the objective of any capital budgeting system should be to integrate uneven capital needs with smooth year-to-year needs. A college or university will know that it has a working, worthwhile capital budgeting system when capital needs are well-planned and do not result in surprises to the operating budget. Capital planning does not make an institution rich, but it should enable the institution, through choice, discipline, and strategy, to avoid a number of crises.

## PHILOSOPHY

Capital projects that are not adequately planned can put enormous strain on the institution and can lead to severe financial problems for the institution, both during and after the project. On the other hand, an overly constrained capital budgeting process can limit the flexibility necessary to take advantage of new opportunities.

There is no easy answer to the question, "What do you do when a donor wants to give $3 million toward a $7 million building that is low on the priority list?" A function of capital budgeting, however, is to have available the cost of the project and the data needed to forecast financing costs and future financial impact. Indeed, part of capital budgeting is to have a priority list, even if it is one that is easily altered.

There is as much art, but less politics, in capital budgeting as in operational budgeting. Nonetheless, a mistake in capital budgeting can be much more devastating than a mistake in operational budgeting. More colleges have been challenged by choosing to build a building than by choosing the wrong tuition price. The mistake itself is much more obvious.

After personnel costs, plant expenditures are the largest investments made by most colleges and universities. Superior capital management can make the difference between affordable and unreachable long-term capital expenditures. A college or university with an inadequate capital budgeting system may not be able to make future capital purchases.

## PRELIMINARY REQUIREMENTS

The most important conceptual prerequisite for a chief financial or business officer when successfully engaging in capital budgeting is an understanding of capital management. Managing the capital position of the institution means watching the ratios that bond-rating firms and foundations use to assess institutional financial health. Ratio analysis of the balance sheet and operating statement is used to answer lenders' questions. Is there too much debt? Can the institution be relied upon to service new debt? Is the debt reasonably proportioned to the value of the assets of the institution? Has the institution adequately planned its capital position well into the future? Besides this conceptual preparation, the institution needs to have a number of systems and networks in place.

***An integrated approach.*** The institution should have an integrated approach to planning and financial policies (see Chapter 2, Decision Processes). Important financial policies include the amount of risk the institution is willing to sustain, its projected growth, and timetables and strategies for reaching financial and capital equilibrium (if it has not already done so). Academic and capital planning must be done within the constraints and risk-tolerance levels of financial policies and plans.

*Long-range financial forecasts.* Capital planners must have access to long-range financial forecasts in order to project revenues, expenditures, assets, liabilities, and fund balances. These projections are necessary to produce the ratios that allow lenders to assess the institution's financial condition. Approximate bond ratings, necessary when showing lenders how debt will be serviced, can be constructed from these projections. Many institutions project revenues and expenditures, but few translate those projections into balance-sheet results. Many of the critical ratios from a lender's perspective, however, come from the balance sheet. The approximate bond ratings can help the institution estimate costs of debt service for future projects.

College and university balance-sheet ratios for bond-rating estimates must be used with caution. For example, the ratio of total long-term debt to operating revenues is often used to identify institutions with "too much debt," when in fact the ratio is not directly proportional to financial health. In general, optimistic, healthy institutions borrow more, borrow less expensively, and plan better. The ratio of long-term debt to plant assets is suspect for two reasons: because of the cost basis of plant accounting and because of the lack of accounting for depreciation. Perhaps the introduction of depreciation accounting will make this ratio more useful. Understanding financial assessment by the bond-rating industry is quite helpful. The industry has grown more sophisticated in recent years, using indicators of faculty and student quality, enrollment trends, student application pool size, financial resources, and general management to determine bond ratings.

*Integration of capital plans into operational budgets.* The ability to integrate capital plans into operating budget projections of the long-range financial forecast is necessary. The institution must be able to quantify the financial impact over time of each variation of each project and then integrate those results into the operating projection. This is a fairly sophisticated capability. While many institutions can project operating budgets ahead and many can calculate the result of various capital budgets, few have been able to merge the two. The more automatic the merge, the less impediment there is to exploring options.

The capital budgeting process described in more detail below enables administration to achieve an integrated budget.

**Debt financing resources.** Before beginning to plan a project, an institution needs to make sure that it can obtain funding. Most institutions need access to a variety of debt-financing resources. There was a time when no structure was built until all the financing was in hand. Unfortunately, if colleges and universities were forced to follow that rule now, there would be few new buildings and the old ones would deteriorate to uselessness. Banks, state lending authorities, federal programs, and national lenders like Sallie Mae have helped institutions with capital projects. (For a full discussion of this subject, see Chapter 12, Debt Financing and Management.)

**External help**. For most projects, an institution needs outside assistance. Architects and bond counsel are two professional groups that are often called upon. The list of participants in the capital financing process is growing rapidly and includes guaranteeing (letter of credit) banks, title companies, bank counsel, funding agencies, secondary market providers, and counsel for the funding agency. Preparation for any project means keeping up with the strengths and weaknesses of any firm that is engaged in the project.

## THE CAPITAL BUDGETING PROCESS

The framework for capital budgeting assumes that, at any given time, any project could be at any stage: planning, development, construction, or completion. As each project moves ahead, more information is obtained. That information affects the capital budgeting process. Thus, not only must the institution go through these stages on a regular basis, it must go through these steps whenever significant new pieces of information become available.

Planning for a shopping center on campus is tremendously different from planning for a new academic program. Projects vary according to size and institutional mission. Although it is most applicable to new construction and renovation of buildings, the framework outlined below is sufficiently simple and generic to apply to other kinds of projects. In using this framework, planners need to go through it as many times as it takes to clearly define the project before spending money on design. With each iteration of the process, new information brings the project more clearly into focus and places it more clearly in relation to other projects on the institution's priority list.

***Analyze needs and create a campus master plan*** (see Chapter 2, Decision Processes). Existing buildings may require maintenance to keep them suitable for habitation. They may need to be renovated or enlarged to accommodate current or projected academic or administrative programs. New buildings may be necessary because plans call for greater capacity, plans call for new functions, or existing buildings cannot be converted to new, necessary uses.

In the eye of the capital budgeter, then, a campus master plan consists of a list of projects, prepared project timings, and project priorities. The list contains building projects, renovation projects, building renewals, infrastructure investments, and academic program developments.

Developing a campus master plan requires a planning process whereby the views of all decisionmakers are reconciled. Not every idea is within the mission, scope, or means of the institution. The purpose of a planning process is to identify viable ideas without inhibiting creative thinking.

The campus master plan should be pared down to those items that cannot be done within the operating budget. Administrators should then be able to create a manageable list of projects with priorities and visible ties to the academic plans and financial strategies of the institution.

A campus master plan can be prepared that gives a vision of the physical campus in the future. The plan may also reveal the need to eliminate projects because of land use or space constraints. The plan should enable management to visualize the completed project list and thus relate the future campus directly to the academic plan and financial strategies.

***Develop costs for the capital outlay.*** Putting together a list of projects within a suitable campus master plan can be done only tentatively until cost estimates are complete. Administrators probably will have to repeat the campus master planning stage if costs exceed expectations. New information can always change preferences. The campus master planning stage is highly political. Unsigned agreements are likely to break down when constraints tighten and people begin to see that everyone's wishes may not be fulfilled.

The need for precision on cost estimates varies. During early iterations of the capital budget plan, when firm decisions have not been made about priorities and sequences on the project list, cost estimates can be approximate. Architects' estimates (with the required markup for total project costs, including design fees, contingencies, site acquisition and/or preparation, related infrastructure costs, project management and legal fees, and environmental compliance) or estimates derived from similar projects can be useful during the early phase. Firm bids may become necessary for the final iteration, when the projects may be placed on a timeline. In that case, only projects scheduled to begin within the next two or three years may require firm cost estimates.

*Create a timeline for projects.* A timeline should include a range of start and completion dates based on the campus master plan. The use of project planning tools is very helpful at this stage. The administrator needs to be able to move projects around to lessen demands for capital and administrative oversight. Delays in projects are possible. There may be times when smaller projects must be substituted for larger projects.

The original timeline, usually based on priorities, may be altered by the estimated availability of funding and the ability of the institution to absorb debt service and on-line costs brought about by the project.

*Calculate follow-up operating costs.* A new building requires upkeep, noncapitalizable equipment, utilities, telecommunications, cleaning, and maintenance. A new building may require major infrastructure additions, such as roads or campus electric power. A new mainframe computer usually has a hefty service agreement, and it may need new systems programmers and new software packages. A new academic program can require more follow-up costs than start-up costs.

A project to reduce deferred maintenance, where the institution has also established a preventive maintenance program funded within the operating budget, may not have follow-up costs. If adequate funding for ongoing maintenance is included in the operating budget plan, then provision need not be made for ongoing maintenance costs in the capital budget. However, delays in reducing deferred maintenance can exponentially increase the amount needed for the project. A delay in repairing a roof may result in rusting of structural steel and much greater future expense, for example.

Many projects have follow-up revenues or cost reductions. These should be calculated at this stage. Many projects change the institution's cost-recovery structure. For example, construction of a new dormitory or dining hall may be based on future revenue streams, or new heating plants may save future fuel and personnel costs.

*Evaluate and match financing.* Financing comes in many forms. Donors may give money toward specified projects. State debt authorities may offer tax-exempt, lower-interest funding. Banks and other commercial establishments can be sources of taxable and occasionally tax-exempt funding. Leaseback arrangements are possible, although rather restricted. State or federal appropriations are another form of financing.

An institution may buy finished buildings or lease them for long periods with a buyout option. The same is true of equipment. State authorities often have arrangements for shorter-term financing for equipment, renovations, or "bridge" capital (for financing during the construction phase of a project).

Interest may be fixed or variable, insured or hedged, straight or "swapped." The number of possibilities is immense. There are three important elements to consider when developing a financing package: cost, timing, and risk. The lower the debt-service burden, the lower the impact on the operating fund. Timing may be important when, for example, the project has a future impact on enrollments or when replacement of a mainframe can reduce high maintenance costs. Risk is increased when variable rates are accepted, especially when the rates are pegged to something as volatile as the prime rate.

Most institutions approach this problem by finding the cheapest available options (usually tax-exempt or subsidized funding) and then making these options fit their timing needs while trying to keep them within their risk profiles. When these relatively inexpensive options are not available, as when an institution has reached the $150 million cap on independent institution tax-exempt borrowing, then new sources must be found and timing must again be examined.

The same is true of risk. When a package appears to be unnecessarily risky, the institution may work with financial partners to arrange insurance or interest rate swaps to lower the risk to the institution, while keeping costs to a minimum.

*Test feasibility.* At this stage, the institution should have a set of projects, their costs, the proposed timing of the projects, and the timing of project costs. Some costs may be financed, in which case debt service has the most direct impact on the operating budget. Other costs may have a direct impact on the operating budget, especially the follow-up costs and many preliminary costs.

These costs must be integrated into the long-range financial forecast to determine financial feasibility. If the institution is thrown out of financial equilibrium, two alternatives must be pursued. First, the institution should examine the financial strategies of its operating fund to see if changes in projected tuition rates, enrollments, or program and expense containment can bring financial feasibility back to the plan. Second, the institution may wish to return to the campus master plan and add or delete projects, depending on the results of this integration.

***Evaluate risks.*** Even if the integrated budget appears to allow the institution to maintain or approach financial equilibrium, the risks inherent in the capital plan need to be evaluated. Interest rates may change. If the institution has used a variable rate plan, what is its exposure? What would be the impact of a shift in rates? What happens if the return from the project is below estimates? If dormitories do not fill or if indirect cost recovery increases are negated by a reduction in rates and/or a reduction in successful proposals, then what are the revenue projections? Similarly, what happens if regulations change?

A change that may have a major impact is a change in collateral value. A stock market decline may hurt the value of investments intended as collateral. Changes in donor eagerness to fund a project, often for similar reasons, can greatly affect timing and cost equations. An enrollment decline has the same kind of impact.

While few institutions have the resources to build full models of these risks, best- and worst-case analyses can prepare the institution for any possibility. The institution may find the risk too great and act to reduce risk with special insurance, interest rate swaps, or changes in investment policy. The institution may also develop contingency plans against some of the possible difficulties.

One method of preparing a contingency plan is to base capital plans on an expectation that 10 to 20 percent of the expected funding will not occur. In this way, a reduction in gift expectations or a short-term budget deficit will not disrupt the project or the financial base of the institution.

Contingencies are also typically built into construction cost estimates and financing cost estimates. Bond-financing agreements almost always require debt-service reserves as well.

*Revise scenario.* After completing each step above, administrators may wish to repeat certain steps—or even all of them from the beginning. Even if the administrator makes it through the full process to this stage, the results may be unsatisfactory for a combination of reasons: projects with higher priority have surfaced, risk levels are marginal, or equilibrium is threatened.

Administrators may wish to change strategies and start over. Projects may have to be delayed. The scope of projects may have to be reduced. The quality of a program may have to be altered. Modules in a project may have to be staggered, or new sources of financing may have to be sought.

Two elements improve the chances of success in implementing a plan. The first is establishing the roles and coordinating the members of the capital budgeting team. Rarely will one administrator perform every task. Responsibilities may be divided among those who understand the costs of the projects, those who understand debt, those who develop the projections and integrate the models, and the person who manages the budget, the institution's capital position, and the team. The chances of success are also improved by an effective information system. Data and ideas should be readily integrated into the quantitative information for projecting and planning and easily input and retrieved. The data and the assumptions behind projections should be easy to check and validate.

KEY ISSUES

Certain key issues that affect the outcome of the capital budgeting process demand attention.

*Use of depreciation accounting.* Based on Statement of Financial Accounting Standards No. 93, *Recognition of Depreciation by Not-for-Profit Organizations,* colleges and universities following the accounting rules of the Financial Accounting Standards Board (FASB) are required to depreciate fixed assets. Some institutions may use this discipline to change the nature of their capital budgeting. One institution has successfully imposed some of the costs of depreciation on its operating budget while maintaining budget balance in a way that builds up sizable reserves for the maintenance and replacement of plant and equipment. Institutions have always had the choice of setting aside funds for capital projects. Enforced accounting for depreciation may now give greater credibility to this method for FASB institutions, although the amounts may still be insufficient for new buildings or other growth-based projects.

Institutions that are governed by the Governmental Accounting Standards Board (GASB) may wish to use the disciplines of depreciation to set aside funds (without including depreciation in their financial statements), but many may be constrained from setting aside reserves by their state governments.

Depreciation is not the only possible discipline used to fund long-term maintenance. There are several methodologies for determining the portion of the budget that should be set aside as a reserve for renewal and replacements. These calculations are often based on the age and expected life of various building systems, such as roofs, heating, air conditioning and ventilation, and windows. Often these calculations, which do not include provisions for deferred maintenance or infrastructure improvements, require 3 percent of the budget to be set aside in a reserve each year.

**Use of reserves, endowment, gifts, or debt.** In general, reserves are best used for supplementing operating funds when revenues drop or expenses increase. Reserves are also appropriate funding for major repair work that occurs regularly. The institution should have a reserve plan that allows it to save for many years to repair one aspect of a building, while saving for and taking care of other predictable building system needs.

Endowment is an absolute last resort. The cost of tax-exempt debt seldom exceeds the return on a well-managed endowment over the long run. Of course, gifts are always desirable and gifts restricted to plant projects are usually unrelated to and seldom supplant giving for other purposes. Of the four funding options, debt has become the most common primary means of financing new projects or projects required by growth. Careful analysis is necessary to develop a preferred financing plan. Several references listed at the end of this section are very helpful in this regard.

**Debt funding options.** Tax-exempt funding is not always the least expensive solution to every problem. The institution should also explore taxable options. There have been times when the gap between taxable and tax-exempt interest rates has been very narrow. Costs of bond counsel and other up-front closing costs can be considerably lower in taxable financing. Moreover, tax-exempt financing can require more institutional time to prepare analyses and longer waiting periods than does taxable financing.

***Matched or "lumped" financing.*** One way to simplify the financing process is to group a number of projects together for a single financing. However, more options may be possible when separate projects are matched to separate financing packages. Matching allows easier trade-offs between project and financing risks, and it can improve cash-flow timing.

***Modularization of projects.*** Some projects can be broken down into modules to allow a more flexible analysis of options. Modularization makes it possible to delay certain portions of the project.

***Contingent start dates.*** An institution may add special decision rules to the capital budgeting process. For example, an institution could stipulate that a project will not start until 50 percent of the financing through donors is in hand. While this complicates the cost analysis and the impact on the operating budget analysis, in many cases it simplifies the risk analysis.

***Crisis funding.*** The primary purpose of capital budgeting is to obviate crisis funding. Nonetheless, crisis funding remains an option. However, administration should never lose sight of the cost to the institution if it stops capital budgeting and must meet a crisis with funds on hand.

The lessons and discipline of capital budgeting are powerful and worth pursuing. Administration and governing boards should have a solid understanding of the ways in which capital budgeting and operational budgeting can be integrated for the institution's benefit. For many institutions burdened with many years of deficits, an exploration of capital budgeting may reveal previously unavailable avenues of debt management. While a balanced budget may not result from such an exploration, it is a learning process that cannot fail to strengthen the institution's financial outlook.

When capital budgeting is incorporated into the management of the institution's economy, its administration has ready access to a feasible, minimum-risk campus master plan, complete with well-understood contingencies and empowered with flexibility. Together, operational budgeting and capital budgeting permit participation at all management levels, averting unwelcome surprises while meeting the reasonable expectations of the campus community for stability, growth, and a balanced budget.

# References and Resources

Association of Governing Boards and National Association of College and University Business Officers. *Financial Responsibilities of Governing Boards of Colleges and Universities.* 2d ed. Washington, D.C.: NACUBO, 1985.

Bennett, Karen H., Larry S. Owen, and Timothy R. Warner. "Implementing Zero-Base Budgeting at Stanford University." *NACUBO Writers on Financial Management.* Washington, D.C.: NACUBO, 1983.

Dickmeyer, Nathan, and K. Scott Hughes. *Financial Self-Assessment: A Workbook for Colleges and Universities.* Washington, D.C.: NACUBO, 1987.

Forrester, Robert T. *A Handbook on Debt Management for Colleges and Universities.* Washington, D.C.: NACUBO, 1988.

Gordon, Lawrence A., and George E. Pinches. *Improving Capital Budgeting: A Decision Support System Approach.* Reading, Mass.: Addison-Wesley, 1984.

Hyatt, James. *A Cost Accounting Handbook for Colleges and Universities.* Washington, D.C.: NACUBO, 1983.

Kaiser, Harvey H. "Funding of Facility Repairs and Renovation." *NACUBO Writers on Financial Management.* Washington, D.C.: NACUBO, 1983.

Landry, Lawrence L., and Rodney Mebane. "Capital Crisis in Higher Education." *NACUBO Writers on Financial Management.* Washington, D.C.: NACUBO, 1983.

Meisinger, Richard J., Jr., and Leroy W. Dubeck. *College and University Budgeting: An Introduction for Faculty and Academic Administrators.* Washington, D.C.: NACUBO, 1984.

Meyerson, Joel W., and Peter M. Mitchell. *Financing Capital Maintenance.* Washington, D.C.: NACUBO, 1990.

Sherman, Douglas R., and William A. Dergis. "Funding Model for Building Renewal." *NACUBO Writers on Financial Management.* Washington, D.C.: NACUBO, 1983.

Standard and Poor's. "Private Universities." *CreditReview,* 24 (September 1990): 10-12.

Strauss, Jon C., and Linda B. Salamon. "Using Financial Incentives in Academic Planning and Management." *NACUBO Writers on Financial Management.* Washington, D.C.: NACUBO, 1983.

Turk, Frederick J. "Intramural Funding Applied by Universities." *Management Issues* (October 1990): 1-4.

# CHAPTER 7

# Costing and Pricing

by
Hans H. Jenny
VISTA, Limited

# Contents

## 7: Costing and Pricing

C osting and pricing decisions are pivotal to the efficient allocation of college and university resources. When the costing and pricing processes that precede and define operating and capital budgets are technically flawed or capricious, budgets have little, if any, significance. For budgets to reflect rational and efficient allocations of resources, appropriate costing and pricing decisions must be made.

As sellers, colleges and universities must determine the appropriate prices for their numerous services; in turn, the prices they pay as buyers of the human and material resources they deploy determine the cost of what they offer. Costs and the related levels of current expenditures and capital outlays thus determine the prices charged. This chapter considers college and university costing first, followed by a discussion of pricing.

## The Nature, Scope, and Purposes of Costing

Costing, a complex and evolutionary undertaking, is not unique to higher education. Although costing has always been a requirement in the management of colleges and universities, state-of-the-art approaches to costing and a widespread consensus on when and how to use cost information are recent developments. In 1975, the National Association of College and University Business Officers (NACUBO) found that conventional cost definitions and cost determination methods and approaches were not uniform or expressed in language that was readily applicable to higher education. Despite considerable progress since then, there is still no general consensus on costing methodology in higher education.

An important reason for this lack of consensus is inherent in the notion of costing: cost information can serve many purposes and there are numerous cost concepts. It is important to know which concepts are best suited for specific costing objectives. Because higher education costs are increasingly scrutinized by the public, institutional administrators must be prepared to defend them. It may be advantageous to reduce the multiplicity of approaches to costing and urge adherence to uniform costing formats. However, the variety of costing objectives, coupled with the diversity of colleges and universities, may point away from the use of a single system. Especially where cost information serves internal purposes, managers should be free to explore and use approaches that they perceive to be best suited for their circumstances. Nevertheless, because higher education cost information often becomes useful only when it is compared with information from other institutions, the need for uniform costing practices is evident.

The choice of costing approaches is often influenced by strategic and tactical considerations, which may include political concerns. The application of costing techniques also depends upon the expertise of those charged with budgetary and resource allocation responsibilities. Because resource allocation is ongoing in many offices of the institution, business or financial officers should assist in developing costing skills among key management personnel.

## TYPES OF ACCOUNTING AND COSTS

The meanings of the term "cost" derive from the contexts in which costing takes place. The most commonly used cost definitions are derived from financial accounting, cost accounting, economics, and law.

***Financial accounting.*** Financial accounting defines cost in historical terms as amounts paid or charged for something with a dollar value in the "current" period. Neither future expenses associated with the acquisition of assets nor deferred expenses are included in financial accounting costs. Financial accounting supplies much of the raw material for all other costing endeavors (along with the underlying ledgers).

***Cost accounting.*** Cost accounting is concerned with accumulating, classifying, summarizing, interpreting, and reporting the costs of personnel, goods, and services used in institutional operations, as well as the costs resulting from the use and financing of assets (materials) and capital investments (foremost, plant and equipment), including the cost of debt. A major purpose of cost accounting is to determine different types of program, project, activity, and unit or service unit costs.[1] Unit costs often are a prerequisite for setting prices. Cost accounting uses financial accounting information, supplemented by nonfinancial data such as enrollment figures or the number of personnel in key job classifications. Whereas financial accounting stresses institutional costs by organizational function and for line item object categories, cost accounting normally involves the synthesis of financial accounting and other relevant information and the creation of appropriate costing models. The budget line item detail and the underlying financial accounting ledgers serve as the initial cost accounting sources.

**Economic cost accounting.** Economic cost accounting focuses chiefly on the concept of "opportunity costs." Every investment (or expenditure) decision is based on a choice. Choosing A means giving up B. The economic or opportunity cost is the value of what is given up when a specific investment or expenditure is made.[2] Closely related to the concept of opportunity costs is the concept of "cost-benefit" analysis, where the costs and the value of benefits are studied in relation to a specific level of investment or spending.

**Costs and the law.** The law adds a different dimension to the meaning of costs. Laws and government regulations stipulate cost definitions that may or may not correspond with normal business practice, logic, or current industry convention. Government agencies frequently provide specific cost definitions or guidelines for calculating costs. Most important for colleges and universities with large research components are the limitations imposed by government agencies and others on allowable costs for indirect-cost reimbursement. Sometimes both the law and regulations are vague or overly complex, allowing program officers and auditors to interpret them individually, thus creating uncertainty about the meaning of particular costing requirements. When the law and regulations impose definitions of and limits on costs that differ significantly from those suggested by technology or market forces, the financial viability of the involved institution can be affected, sometimes dramatically.

From time to time, the Financial Accounting Standards Board (FASB) and the Governmental Accounting Standards Board impose new accounting standards and cost definitions. The effect of new standards has often been to increase reported current expenditures, to lower reported current revenues, and to decrease reported fund balances. The immediate result of the implementation of new standards and definitions may be that an institution's or the industry's financial condition appears to have worsened or improved. In truth, only the account of the condition is different; the actual condition did not change at all.

The types of costs most frequently used in costing terminology follow.

*Aggregate costs.* Aggregate costs, or total costs, are the sum of variable costs plus fixed costs. They encompass a range of otherwise distinct cost elements. For instance, aggregate operating costs for an entire institution might include the total expenditure budget or the budget for a self-supporting professional school, a hospital, and departments.

*Variable costs.* Variable costs vary with the size of enrollment, output, or sales.

*Fixed costs.* Fixed costs remain the same regardless of changeable elements, such as the size of a class or the amount of a product sold.

*Average costs.* Average costs, or mean costs, are the total cost divided by a number of input or output (e.g., total full-time equivalent [FTE] enrollment, FTE teaching staff, or any other appropriate "unit" measure).

*Marginal costs.* Marginal costs, also called marginal variable or marginal fixed costs, are the change in total costs resulting from a (unit) change in input or output. Marginal costs are of special interest as institutions consider long-range plans or retrenchment. When an institution plans to introduce a new program, hire additional staff, or build a new classroom, new costs will be added to the existing ones. When an institution decides to eliminate an activity, costs will be reduced. These marginal costs should be determined as precisely as possible and preferably before implementing an action. Institutions may overstate marginal cost savings and underestimate marginal cost increments when costing procedures do not encompass every cost element affected by the proposed change or when certain necessary assumptions are based on questionable estimates.

*Direct costs.* Direct costs are costs that are directly related to an activity being conducted (e.g., the salary and benefits for a professor are direct costs of the courses he or she teaches).

*Indirect costs.* Indirect costs, sometimes referred to as "overhead," "prorated," or "marked" costs in the budget, can be charged legitimately to a specific activity but are not necessarily caused by it. In higher education, "indirect-cost recovery" for research and educational projects is a topic of intense interest. The indirect-cost concept is an aspect of full costing (see below). If a research project is housed in an existing building and occupies a significant portion of a laboratory, maintenance and plant costs do not need to increase to generate indirect costs. However, the same research project may cause laboratory maintenance costs to rise, resulting in "marginal" costs. Colleges and universities must therefore distinguish between marginal or incremental costs and those that are in fact nonincremental.

*Historical costs.* Historical costs are the monetary value of economic resources acquired by cash disbursements or liabilities incurred; they can be incurred on a cash or accrual basis. The accrual basis is recommended for colleges and universities.

*Standard costs.* Standard costs are benchmark or predetermined costs that serve as a target or basis of comparison with the actual costs of services rendered. Standard costs are based on historical and/or comparative analysis or cost studies. They can be used in internal pricing and performance evaluation.

*Imputed costs.* Imputed costs encompass forgone resources (e.g., income) as a cost. For instance, an imputed cost is the interest income forgone when a specific amount of money is spent rather than invested.

*Replacement costs.* Replacement costs are the financial resources required to replace equipment and/or plant at current or specific future prices. They are different from depreciation.

*Projected costs.* Projected costs are estimates or forecasts of costs to be incurred in future periods under specific economic and program assumptions.

*Committed costs.* Committed costs normally derive from contractual commitments to specific expenses or investments without which some funding or other event might not occur.

*Discretionary costs.* Discretionary costs derive from management decisions or changes in fiscal policy and need not be directly related to any particular service or activity.

*Full costing.* Full costing is, in a sense, the equivalent of total long-run costs, where an activity's costs include not only variable and fixed operating costs but also equipment and facility costs, debt service, and depreciation.

*Common or joint costs.* Common or joint costs are associated with "joint-product" costs, as when an expenditure (e.g., a professor's salary) results in two or more outcomes (e.g., a research effort combined with a teaching, a public relations, and/or an administrative outcome).

***Short-run versus long-run costs.*** Economists distinguish between "short-run" and "long-run" costs. Short-run costs are costs involved in operating a business without considering fixed costs. Long-run costs encompass the entire range of variable and fixed costs, including the cost of equipment and plant assets (including capital consumption and replacement) and the cost of tenured faculty, which can be viewed as a fixed "asset." The distinction between short-run and long-run costs is crucial for evaluating the relative adequacy of prices and the demand for collegiate services. If prices and resources cover variable costs only, the institution will not be financially viable in the long run. For a college or university to be viable over the long run, its prices and/or revenues must be high enough to cover all variable and fixed costs.[3]

Each type of costing has its uses and limitations. For instance, full costing is an attempt to identify the total cost elements surrounding a given activity—all variable and fixed costs, including all associated capital costs, plus the cost of capital consumption and replacement. In contrast, direct costing covers only the total costs that arise from an activity, without regard to those general administrative and institutional costs that arise independent of it. Marginal costing can be used when looking at changes in aggregate or total costs or in average costs. Institutions also need to know which costs are variable and thus change with the volume of output and which are fixed and do not vary as output changes. The relationship (or ratio) between changes in output and changes in variable costs and the points where changes in output necessitate the addition of fixed costs are of special interest. An understanding of "indivisibilities," typically those fixed-cost entities that must be acquired or exist as indivisible units (e.g., a piece of equipment, a building, even a full-time employee), is also necessary.

Ideally, costing is a comprehensive and integrated process encompassing the entire institution. Figure 7-1 depicts this process.

## COSTING STANDARDS

Foremost among the factors affecting the costing process are costing standards. "Costing standards" are principles and rules that

FIGURE 7-1
Dimensions of Costing

**Purposes of
Cost Information**

| Definitions of Cost | Cost Objectives and Costing Units | Types and Classifications of Cost | Relationship of Financial Accounting and Statistical Data to Costing |
|---|---|---|---|

**Cost Determination
Methods and Approaches**

| | Specific Service Method | | | Continuous Service Method | |
|---|---|---|---|---|---|
| Full Costing | Variable or Direct Costing | Standard Costing | Full Costing | Variable or Direct Costing | Standard Costing |

**Implementation-
Cost Analysis**

| Full-Cost Analysis | Cost-Volume-Revenue Analysis | Controllable Cost Analysis |
|---|---|---|

Source: *Indirect Costs of Sponsored Programs* (Washington, D.C.: National Association of College and University Business Officers, 1981).

must be adhered to in any costing endeavor. There are 12 costing standards.

• The purposes for which cost information is to be used should determine the framework within which cost information is developed. Clear definitions of costing purposes are needed in order to specify the cost-determination approach to be used.

• Cost information should be based on the accrual method of accounting. The cash basis method of determining costs recognizes expenditures when cash is paid, whereas accrual accounting recognizes expenditures when materials are used and services are performed.

The accrual method provides valid and consistent costs when used by colleges and universities.

- Cost data should be reconcilable to official financial accounting data. Reconciliation is the process of identifying and considering differences in sets of data.

- Nonfinancial data should be reconcilable to official institutional records.

- Definitions used in cost determinations should be applied uniformly.

- Cost information and related costing units should cover the same period.

- Cost information should be consistently determined. Cost data cannot be comparable unless they are consistently collected and recorded. Consistency depends on uniform definitions, methods, and interpretations, as well as judgments exercised in the cost-determination process.

- Cost should be attributed to a cost objective based on a causal or beneficial relationship; all costing endeavors must relate to a specific activity, project, program, or department.

- Indirect cost should be allocated on the basis of quantitative measures that can be applied in a practical manner. The quantitative measures used should represent the relationship of costs to the cost objective, so that indirect costs are equitably distributed. There are instances when the most equitable distribution may not be the most practical, in terms either of time or of expense involved in collecting and tabulating quantitative measures. In such cases, the most practical measure should be selected, provided the results are not materially different.

- Common costs incurred to provide two or more services should be allocated in an equitable manner. Separate costing of jointly produced services can be subjective.

- Capital costs should reflect the applicable capital costs (i.e., depreciation) for the period, determined on the basis of the estimated useful life of each asset being depreciated.

◆

- Cost information should be accompanied by a disclosure statement. Disclosures should describe the costing method and approach used, the cost definition used, the types of cost included, identification of cost objectives and costing units, and other information pertinent to the cost-determination effort.

These costing standards have evolved over time, and new ones may be added if experience dictates. Each standard is stated in relatively broad terms. These standards will not ensure uniform cost determinations, because individual judgment and other factors come into play. Institutions differ in their methods of carrying out activities that may have common labels in higher education. Identically labeled activities will not necessarily produce identical cost information across institutions even if basic cost factors, such as salary levels and support costs, are similar.

In practice, except for financial accounting, the costing process is circumscribed and defined by the specific activity (or activities) whose cost must be ascertained. Specific financial and managerial objectives can sometimes be expressed in terms of more than one cost concept. Although cost standards may serve different purposes at the same time, and some of them may appear to have a life of their own, all cost standards are interrelated. The appropriateness of specific standards is determined in part by the costing objective and in part by the suitability of the standard within the framework of a particular costing methodology.

## PURPOSES OF COSTING

Cost information is used both externally and internally. Externally, federal, state, and local government agencies require cost information in relation to appropriation, grant, loan, and legal compliance matters. These agencies usually specify the manner in which cost information is to be provided. Private foundations, businesses, and others who make grants to institutions may request cost information. Banks and other lending agencies are also interested in cost data. When colleges and universities bid for research and other contracts or sell their services, cost information is needed not only to set the prices for these contracts and services but also to document relevant costing details.

Costing within a college or university is used most frequently for the following purposes.

- Annual operations and capital budgeting: Costing helps determine prices (to generate revenues) and expenditure budget allocations (to minimize or optimize costs).

- Controlling operations: Cost analysis verifies and corrects allocations and prices for improved current and future budget construction and management results.

- Evaluating performance and operational analysis: Costing in this context focuses on educational, financial, and operational objectives and assists in their implementation.

- Internal pricing: Internal pricing is both a rationing and a cost allocation device.

- Indirect-cost recovery: Indirect-cost recovery is a revenue-generating device defined as reimbursement of overhead costs associated with externally funded research projects.

- Long-range planning: A full understanding of the costs of an institution's activities, the long-range behavior of these costs, and knowledge of the cost interactions within an institution is necessary to design an effective long-range plan.

- Interinstitutional comparisons: Comparative costing is practiced both within the confines of the current budget and in long-range planning; unless certain precautions are taken, interinstitutional cost comparisons may be based on incompatible or inconsistent methodologies and cost content.

In each instance, one or several cost concepts and costing methodologies may be appropriate and several costing techniques may be applied simultaneously.

## COSTING METHODOLOGIES

Costs can be viewed from a number of management perspectives, and costing methodologies may differ with the nature and purpose of specific costing applications.

***Costing of broad management systems*** (the institution overall, separate campuses, individual professional schools, and major academic divisions). Broad aggregate costing presents few technical difficulties and is based on an institution's financial accounting information supplemented by data on deferred expenditures and the cost implications in the use and obsolescence of capital.

***Costing of discrete organizational subsystems*** (a single academic department or discipline, a single administrative unit, specific academic and administrative programs, and specific academic and administrative activities). As costing focuses on administrative subsystems, a need for precise costing, prorating, and allocating procedures arises. In addition to relying on financial accounting data reflected in functional and line-item budget reports, administrators should distinguish between direct and indirect and variable and fixed costs. They also must decide whether the final objective is full costing within the context of the operating budget alone or in the economist's "long-run" sense. The indirect-cost recovery issue and the perennial controversies surrounding it are a primary example of the difficulties and complexities that arise in costing.

***Costing project-by-project.*** There is a major difference between costing of discrete organizational subsystems and costing project-by-project. The logical approach of project-by-project costing calls first for a "from-the-bottom-up" identification of the cost elements. The initial and primary focus should be on the direct costs of the project, including direct overhead costs, followed by consideration of indirect and long-run capital costs. Most higher education costing that relates to efficient resource allocation (cost-effective budgeting, long-range planning, cost studies focusing on alternative uses of available resources) is of the project-by-project type. Projects and, in the broader sense, programs often cut across administrative jurisdictions; therefore, costing frequently requires the assembling of relevant cost elements across jurisdictions. Project-by-project costing is also a form of marginal costing, whereby the incremental costs of specific activities are considered.

In the above instances, the cost elements must be clearly articulated. At the same time, specific individuals responsible for carrying out costing tasks should be identified and made accountable for implementing appropriate and sound costing practices. Because each costing application and costing requirement may be carried out in different ways, it is crucial that institutions start the costing process with a clear definition of objectives, an understanding of available methodologies, and appropriate internal communications and decision processes.

Although truly dynamic long-range cost models may be difficult to construct, they are preferable to linear models because of the complexity of collegiate interactions. Thus, certain costing objectives (e.g., forecasting, projections, and long-range planning) may require statistical manipulations. These should be appropriate to the quality and scope of the cost information and other relevant data. Managers have numerous choices of statistical methodology; where data are sound and have adequate historical depth, sophisticated statistical tools can and should be used.[4] Managers may develop unique interpretations of complex financial matters and apply them to the costing methodologies that they feel are most suitable for an occasion, specific activities, or the institution's special mission and character. There is ample room for creativity.

Many costing endeavors occur in social and political contexts. For instance, when institutions determine the cost of academic instruction or of specific administrative activities, they may run into sensitivities involving human relations and potential political tensions (i.e., the faculty-versus-administration issue). To those whose costs are being studied or publicized, the elements of the costing formula may matter very much. They may want to have a say in the formulation of the costing procedure. Because the determination of program and activity costs depends to some extent on judgments rather than firm rules, the determination can be affected by what, if any, consensus building has taken place during costing and how well and widely a costing approach is accepted by those affected by the results. Managers responsible for costing need to be alert lest such endeavors become discredited because they are controversial. The political content of cost information should not be ignored, especially in the academic setting, where the faculty play important decision-making roles.

## APPLICATIONS OF COSTING

***Allocating resources.*** The most important uses of costing in higher education relate to the efficient allocation of resources. In this context, the objective is not merely to determine the cost of services or products but also to allocate limited resources in economically sound ways.

Minimum-cost models and optimum resource allocation models are useful in the construction of cost-effective current and long-range operating and capital budgets and assist in the external pricing of institutional services and indirect-cost recovery. (Internal pricing is a special and essential aspect of costing related to budgeting and budget control.) Minimum-cost models alone, however, will not necessarily guarantee the efficient allocation of limited resources; costs can be reduced to a point where the quality of service may suffer.

Financial accounting normally precedes the development of cost accounting; as cost accounting needs change, financial accounting can gradually be adapted to accommodate many cost accounting requirements. In an institution with a well-developed cost accounting tradition, it is easy to produce many different types of cost accounting information with computer software by assembling data available in accounting ledgers and elsewhere in the institution's management information system.

Starting with the financial accounting system, an institution can break out direct and indirect costs by individual cost centers. Although this technique will not meet every cost accounting need, it does help to align the two systems and can be carried out in great detail. For instance, plant maintenance costs may be distributed not only to the various plant units but also to the "purchasers" of maintenance services; institutions routinely prorate a percentage of general administrative costs to auxiliary enterprises and sometimes to operating departments.

Prorating results in lump-sum cost allocations (usually percentages of aggregate relevant costs.) For instance, prorating "general administrative costs" to auxiliary enterprises in a lump sum may be appropriate for broad cost accounting purposes. However, such prorating may not be suitable for determining unit costs of specific activities within the auxiliary enterprise category. General administrative costs represent, among other things, a variety of personnel costs in different administrative departments. Prorating compresses this diverse and complex cost into one crude number of limited usefulness.

***Determining costs.*** Because cost accounting normally requires the merging of financial and nonfinancial data, it must be viewed as a separate and distinct accounting activity. A large percentage of cost information, from academic and administrative departments especially, involves joint services (or joint products), which require specialized accounting ledgers that bring together the cost elements from two or more sources. Determining the direct or indirect and variable or fixed cost of instruction per student, per credit hour, or per faculty member or some other unit of measure requires software and management information specifically designed to assemble all the pieces of the puzzle.[5] Similarly, many student services cut across administrative and educational departments, making precise costing a complex undertaking.

**Budgeting and analyzing.** The operating budget represents a composite of discrete resource allocation and optimization opportunities, for which cost accounting is fundamentally important.[6] Two aspects are worth noting.

The cost-effective use of utilities, the optimal management of materials and supplies, and the cost-effective management of personnel represent one aspect of the use of cost accounting in budgeting; other examples are cost-effective travel, computer use, data processing, telecommunications, custodial services, security, and all the other routine services normally supervised by the chief financial or business officer. A second aspect is the nature of the specific activity whose costs are being determined. For instance, how is the cost of an academic department, a new course to be offered, or a specific student advisement function determined? In terms of costs, what is the real meaning of student services, housing, institutional advancement, instructional support, and academic or institutional research?

Costing requires an understanding of the institution's underlying financial policies, in particular the institution's rules governing capital financing, maintenance, and renewal. The costs of capital can vary enormously depending upon the financial policy ground rules. If full costing is used to formulate a competitive price for a specific service, the financial policies governing capital costs must also be based on competitive considerations.

Costing in general and cost accounting in particular assist administrators in understanding the behavior of costs over time. Once initial cost studies have been completed, administrators should develop procedures for determining the costs in question at appropriate intervals. Before settling on one number, the complexity of many collegiate undertakings may call for the use of more than one type of analysis or policy.

Financial accounting and costing involve the use of unrestricted and restricted funds. While administrators should not ignore such differences in the sources of funds, their primary consideration must be the nature and cost composition of the activity in question. A fixed budget does not make an activity "cost free"; it merely indicates what funds can assist in financing it.

## COSTING AND INTERNAL PRICING

Internal pricing provides a direct link to costing by charging departments fees for using the institution's supplies and other resources. When fees are established for the use of central computer services, the consumption of electricity, or the maintenance of facilities, using departments can allocate their budget resources appropriately. At the same time, the institution works with budget information that reflects cost charges where resources are actually used, rather than having to rely on a miscellaneous budget category or simple prorating.

Internal pricing informs users of the cost to the institution of departmental activities. In the economy at large, prices serve the purpose of clearing the shelves; in an institution, internal pricing helps "clear" and often "reallocate" the budget. For instance, departments such as maintenance or computer services may charge fees to user departments, resulting in corresponding debits and credits vis-a-vis the respective line item budget allocations. A budget allocation divided by a prevailing price for service will encumber (use up) the allocation at a certain rate. Depending on whether users are held to strict line-item budgets or to broader budget allocations, internal pricing may enhance a manager's freedom to control how budgeted amounts are used. In highly decentralized management systems, internal pricing replaces the more authoritarian type of budget discipline normally associated with specific spending rules. For instance, institutions often stipulate exact specifications of supplies, modes of travel, or types of vendors that users must adhere to. Internal prices often can be substituted for rigid guidelines, leaving the choice of what, how much, and from whom to buy to the user and letting the price determine both the quality and amount purchased within broad budget authorizations.

In setting internal prices, the costs that they cover must be decided on. The costing standards that underlie internal prices then should be clearly communicated to users. Such communication is especially important when full or indirect-costing standards are adopted. When institutions do not take economies of scale sufficiently into account, even direct-cost internal prices may exceed those charged by the local commercial competition. When internal prices are not competitive, or when they are expected to recover significant internal overhead costs, the manager needs to ensure that users understand what is intended and that the internal pricing system is accepted as fair. Internal pricing should enable both departments and budgets to succeed; it should not create incentives for bypassing the system. A properly conceived internal pricing system is one that is generally accepted within the management hierarchy, does not merely shuffle costs from one department to another, and, most important, contributes to cost-effective management throughout the institution.[7]

## Costs of Sponsored Programs

It is relatively easy to determine the direct costs of the activities of a professor who engages in research under a grant or contract. Salaries, health and other benefits, supplies, travel, and the cost of assistants represent straightforward cost elements. The determination of other less obvious costs may be somewhat more difficult. How much of the heating and cooling bill, of janitorial services and plant maintenance, should be allocated to the grant? What percentage of general administrative expenditures should be written off against it? How should the depreciation and replacement of capital be accounted for? In other words, exactly what should be included in indirect costs and who should pay for them?

The first formal attempt at establishing guidelines for indirect-cost recovery came with the publication of *Explanation of Principles for Determination of Costs under Government Research and Development Contracts with Educational Institutions,* referred to as the "Blue Book." This publication relied heavily on the principle of averaging. A single indirect-cost rate was applied to all allowable cost categories within the institution. Calculations were based on the audited annual financial report.

In 1957, Bureau of the Budget Circular A-21, "Principles for Costing Research and Development under Grants and Contracts with Educational Institutions," replaced the "Blue Book." Circular A-21 abandoned the single indirect-cost notion, increasing considerably the workload associated with calculating indirect-cost recovery. The audited financial report was no longer the sole source for indirect costing, and henceforth supplemental cost data needed to be collected.

Several subsequent revisions to Circular A-21 have been published. In 1976, the Office of Management and Budget (OMB) assumed jurisdiction over it. Now titled "Cost Principles for Educational Institutions," Circular A-21 was last revised in 1986. There is still no uniformity in different government agencies' definitions of indirect costs.

## INDIRECT AND DIRECT COSTS

Section F of Circular A-21 describes each cost category and the allocation base preferred by the federal government. It addresses the following major concepts and concerns.

***Indirect-cost categories.*** Indirect-cost categories include:

- Depreciation and use allowances

- Operations and maintenance expenses

- General administration and general institutional expenses

- Departmental administration expenses

- Sponsored-programs administration

- Library expenses

- Student administration and services

***Allocable costs.*** Allocable costs are costs assignable to a cost objective or sponsored activity, if the assignment can be based on a cause-and-effect relationship, benefit derived, or logic and reason. Allocable costs include direct and indirect costs. A potential allocable cost can be determined by answering the following questions:

- Does the cost serve to advance the work of the final cost objective?

- Does the cost benefit both the project and other objectives of the institution?

- Is the cost necessary and reasonable for the overall operation of the institution?

**Reasonable costs.** Reasonable costs are incurred within the bounds of prudence, determined by such issues as conflicts of interest, fair value received, the necessity of the costs in question, and adherence to institutional policies.

**Allowable costs.** Not all allocable or reasonable costs are "allowed" under Circular A-21. Section J describes the costs that are not allowed. The major ones are interest expense; fund-raising and investment management costs; intramural student activities costs; cost overruns, general public and alumni relations activities; and entertainment, commencement, and convocation expenses.

**Allocation base.** The allocation base is the common measurable base used when allocating indirect costs to a major function (e.g., operation and maintenance cost charged to major functions on the basis of net assignable square footage).

**Distribution base.** The distribution base refers to the base or denominator from which the indirect-cost rate is computed and to which it is applied. The most common base includes salaries and wages, employee benefits, materials and supplies, and services, travel, and certain subgrant and subcontract expenditures.

## INDIRECT-COST RATE

In calculating indirect costs, institutions whose total volume of federally sponsored activities does not exceed $3 million per year may use the simplified method described in Section H of Circular A-21; all others are required to use the "regular" or long-form method. In the simplified method, the indirect-cost rate is a percentage of the salary and wage base, not of the modified total direct cost base. Under both methods, indirect-cost rates are developed in total and not for individual projects. The result of the approval process is an institutional indirect-cost rate. Sections G3, G4, and G5 provide information on the types of rates institutions may negotiate.

Once an indirect-cost rate has been calculated, the resulting cost proposal is officially assigned to a "cognizant" federal agency for negotiation and audit. OMB Circular A-88, "Indirect Cost Rates, Audit, and Audit Follow-Up at Educational Institutions," provides that indirect-cost rates must be audited by and negotiated with a cognizant federal agency in order for an institution's indirect-cost rate to be applied to federal grants, cooperative agreements, and contracts. For most higher education institutions, the cognizant agency is the Department of Health and Human Services. Less often, cognizant agencies are the Department of Defense, the National Science Foundation, the Department of the Interior, and the Department of Education. These agencies may differ in their interpretations and implementation of Circular A-21.

An ongoing dispute between higher education and OMB concerns the adequacy of cost recovery. Colleges and universities argue that Circular A-21 principles fail to provide for full indirect-cost recovery. Government agencies suspect that higher education institutions submit requests for excessive and unjustified cost reimbursements. From time to time, the U.S. Congress and the national media focus on alleged abuses. To avoid charges that colleges and universities are squandering taxpayers' money by charging the federal government for inappropriate (even fraudulent) costs, higher education may need to implement more uniform and reasonable indirect-cost recovery as well as general costing procedures. There are large differences in the indirect-cost recovery rates among institutions, and indirect costing may be as much art as it is science.[8] Negotiating skills may also play a role. But the foremost need is for a greater consensus among higher education officials and the government on proper and uniform costing standards for colleges and universities.

Federal indirect-cost recovery may cause a dilemma for public institutions, depending on how the state views such "revenues." In the eyes of some state authorities, recovery is seen as reimbursement for prior state appropriations in support of federally funded research and educational activities. Thus, the state and not the college or university is entitled to the reimbursement. Indeed, states sometimes recapture all indirect-cost reimbursements. In other instances, anticipated cost recovery is incorporated into the institutional budget and state appropriations are adjusted fully or in part. Some states may provide incentives for leaving a portion of reimbursements at the disposal of the institution. Indirect-cost recovery rates, on average, tend to be significantly smaller for public than for independent institutions.

For independent colleges and universities, indirect-cost recovery is supposed to ensure an adequate academic infrastructure by supporting the basic services expected of the institution. However, because such costing relies on judgment, a question of what charges are reasonable and what may be excessive always exists. If business- or government-sponsored research requires an infrastructure, and if without such an infrastructure institutions could not qualify for grants, how much of the infrastructure costs should institutions charge to others? Given the full range of indirect costs, specifically depreciation and use allowances, how do institutions distribute the reimbursed money among their various funds? Specifically, is any money transferred to equipment replacement and plant funds? In most independent institutions, reimbursements are treated as unrestricted revenues and often revert back to the cost-originating departments. Indirect-cost rates for the top 20 independent universities ranged from 63 to 79 percent in fiscal year 1991. Institutions should be wary of their dependence on operating revenues from this source.

## Policy Implications of Costing

### INTERNAL POLICY IMPLICATIONS

Reporting of cost data provides essential information for evaluating the financial performance of management and the institution. The critical analysis of cost information is essential in determining how efficiently financial, human, and material resources are being deployed. Cost information is central to sound budget planning, to formulating effective financial controls and policies, and to carrying out the trusteeship function of the governing board. It is also essential to long-range financial and program planning.

Costing is directly linked to financial policy in two noteworthy aspects. The first concerns the appropriateness of full costing: what it means and when to use it. To the extent that college and university operating and capital budgets incorporate full-costing principles in the long-run sense, they also raise the revenue horizon under which they need to function. Conversely, to the extent that institutions relax their full-costing stance, long-run revenue requirements will appear to become less demanding. If long-run full costing is applied to project, activity, and program costing but not to budgeting and long-range planning, a fundamental policy discrepancy exists. Such inconsistency could damage an institution's long-run financial condition.

The second linkage of costing with financial policy concerns the question of how much current and future revenue should depend on indirect-cost recovery—particularly, how much of it should depend on federal sources. Colleges and universities should answer this question in terms of both academic and financial policy implications.

Internally, costing highlights the comparative costs of academic and operating departments, the latter especially. Many policy concerns may arise from these differences. For instance, where cost differences are the result of more or less efficient uses of resources, management can focus on improving the performance of less-efficient managers. When differences are based on salary and wage discrepancies, questions of equity may arise. Although cost differences alone should not determine which departments or activities survive, very costly operations that cause operating deficits should be scrutinized carefully. Even the smallest college is a complex institution, and many costs cannot be linked directly to offsetting revenues. Careful cost analysis therefore is essential if management is to ensure the cost-effective allocation of resources.

Interinstitutional cost comparisons are useful, provided the cost information is based on common costing principles and is consistent over time. To assist in efficient resource allocation, college and university cost information can and should be applicable and comparable with similar cost data from the for-profit sector and noneducational non-profit organizations. Examples are plant custodial and maintenance costs and the cost of managing a college store. Standard costs and target cost ratios used in the for-profit sector can be applied to higher education.

## EXTERNAL POLICY IMPLICATIONS

The most obvious external policy implication of costing stems from the public's interest in the cost of higher education. The cost of doing business influences the prices that institutions charge and the taxes that citizens pay in support of higher education directly (through appropriations, grants, and contracts) and indirectly (through tax exemptions for philanthropic support).

For public institutions, external policy issues arise from the need to justify annual government appropriations. In this regard, cost information has always been a major factor, with unit and marginal cost data playing special roles in many states' funding practices. Higher education institutions usually derive funding from a variety of governmental and private sources. Private entities that provide funding for colleges and universities, including individual donors, increasingly are requesting certain types of cost information or asking for assurances that resources are used efficiently. Given the public's interest in higher education, rising costs in the nation's colleges and universities will continue to be a major and legitimate public concern in the 1990s and beyond.

## Pricing

When a business offers a product or service, it tries to set a price at which it expects sales to cover its costs and help it realize a profit. Although revenues from investments may supplement revenues from sales, product and service prices are the principal sources of income that shape the eventual profit-or-loss outcome.

In higher education, pricing must be seen in a broader context. Colleges and universities depend on one or more non-price-based revenues. In addition, these institutions normally are engaged in a variety of pricing situations that are related to the multiple services they render. In this sense, colleges and universities resemble multiproduct or multiservice firms in the for-profit environment.

Because multiple revenue sources are the norm in higher education, pricing often focuses on the share of total revenues that the sale of a specific service is expected to produce or the budget target that it is to achieve. Although prices in higher education—as in for-profit businesses—must cover the cost of rendering institutional services, the relationship between price setting and costing in higher education is not as direct as in the for-profit world. How closely prices and costs are related to one another in higher education depends upon the type of service for which a price is established and how "price-dependent"— the relationship or ratio between price-based and non-price-based revenues—the institution is.

There are two types of tuition pricing situations in higher education: those in which costs are an important but not the sole criterion of price (typically, the price of tuition and fees in multirevenue institutions) and those in which non-price-based revenues are negligible and the institution derives substantial revenue from its tuition and fees and self-supporting activities.

## Tuition and Fees

The best-known college and university price—the charge for tuition and fees—is not always or necessarily a direct function of total educational costs, and it is seldom directly related to total institutional costs. A key issue in tuition pricing is the amount of current revenue that tuition and fees are expected to produce. The answer will depend upon a number of factors, chiefly the institution's competitive standing, its budget plan, the anticipated revenues from nontuition sources, and the administration's perception of the potential public relations impact of any increase in price.

TYPES OF TUITION CHARGES

Tuition revenues fall under an institution's educational and general revenues. In independent colleges and universities, tuition revenues usually represent the largest single source in this category; when enrollment-based government appropriations are added, the same can be said for public institutions. Some institutions, most of them in the public sector, may supplement low tuition with a variety of fees.

Higher education institutions distinguish among the following types of tuition and fee charges:

- Undergraduate tuition

- Tuition for professional schools and for general and specialized graduate schools

- Tuition per single course, for a specific degree, or for a specific time frame

These categories do not exhaust all possibilities; tuition types proliferate and each institution may have its own type of tuition. Nevertheless, these categories accommodate most, if not all, types of tuition.

***Undergraduate tuition.*** The expression "tuition" usually refers to undergraduate tuition, meaning the price charged or listed for rendering educational services leading to a two- or four-year degree. As a published price, it is legally binding unless a college or university expressly reserves the right to make changes without prior notice. Public and media attention tend to focus on the officially announced and published price and rarely on the real (frequently discounted and highly differentiated) prices paid by many students who qualify for student aid grants and scholarships.

Unless otherwise noted, the announced undergraduate tuition is valid for one academic year and payable in installments, depending on whether the institution's academic year is divided into semesters, trimesters, or quarters. Because many institutions, especially in the public sector, enroll large numbers of part-time students taking less than a normal course load, undergraduate tuition is also quoted per course or per credit hour.

Many institutions offer payment plans managed by the college or university or administered by banks or other independent agencies. An institution may "guarantee" (usually with an appropriate and legally sound escape clause) the tuition for two or more years for a matriculating class of students; this is sometimes accompanied by a not-to-be-exceeded maximum percentage of annual increments (e.g., increments equal to or less than the prevailing rate of consumer price inflation).

From time to time, especially when tuition at independent colleges and universities has increased rapidly, colleges and universities have experimented with "tuition stabilization" plans. Such plans may distinguish between tuition for returning and new students. Annual tuition increases for returning students may be set at zero or at less than the percentage rate by which the tuition for new students rises. For colleges where retention is a problem, differentiated tuition may have appeal.

Some independent colleges and universities charge a comprehensive fee, rather than separating tuition from room and board charges. This practice occurs chiefly among residential colleges, where the percentage of part-time students is relatively small. One objective of the practice is to create a price incentive for students to use institution-owned student housing and food services. Colleges and universities that use this structure publish comprehensive fees that encompass tuition, room and board, and miscellaneous fees, or partial combinations of these. These institutions also must offer an alternative tuition-only choice for off-campus residents and part-time students. Comprehensive fee plans usually result in tuition-plus-housing and tuition-plus-food-service fee alternatives. Where such plans exist, the financial or business officer is responsible for prorating revenues to auxiliary enterprises.

The average cost to students of the first two years of college tuition is considerably less than that of the last two years, in the usual four-year undergraduate degree program. Some have perceived this phenomenon as justification for formalizing it as policy—setting higher tuition rates for junior and senior class years. However, the notion has few adherents because of its predictable impact on upper-class enrollment and student aid policies.

Complex tuition plans may complicate accounting and always give rise to certain management risks. However, today's computer-based accounting systems are up to the task. Institutions should use all computer capabilities to investigate the potential advantages and pitfalls of tuition refinements. Properly managed, innovative tuition plans can be rewarding both in their financial and their public relations impact, and they may enhance student retention.

***Tuition for professional degrees and graduate studies.*** Multiple levels of tuition that reflect cost differences for academic programs are more prevalent among professional schools and for graduate studies. While a general graduate tuition may exist, such disciplines as business, law, engineering, and medicine may charge their own "prices," influenced by the underlying cost differentials, the institution's competitive position, and the fact that these degree programs are often offered by independent entities within a college or university.

***Tuition per course, per degree, and for special periods.*** Rather than establishing a tuition for a semester or a quarter, many institutions provide an alternative whereby the tuition is expressed in terms of dollars per credit hour or per course. This approach is especially useful for colleges and universities with large numbers of part-time students and adult learning programs such as continuing education.

Special degree programs or course offerings culminating in a certificate of completion may have price tags that focus on the total work to be performed, rather than on a series of smaller prices for each step in the process. The prices of such degrees encompass the cost of all the services rendered, and tuition may be high enough to produce a sizable "profit" for the institution. Some institutions do not offer these more specialized degree programs unless there is a high probability of realizing an operating surplus. Whether or not the price in question is based on the principle of full costing determines the adequacy of the realized surplus.

Many institutions set a separate tuition for summer terms or such special periods as a "January quarter" (or any academic term during which a limited number of credits can be earned). Sometimes the cost to students of a special term is part of the normal tuition; if this is the case, there may be an ancillary requirement that a student be enrolled in the subsequent academic term. A special price for such academic terms may add a degree of flexibility for financial managers.

Summer terms help students catch up or accelerate their progress toward degree completion, and they engage the use of institutional facilities throughout the calendar year. However, some institutions have discovered that there may not be an adequate market for a summer term among their preferred type of student body. Summer terms may result in entirely different, often specialized, enrollments—often high school teachers and others enrolling in search of college credits for professional advancement. Although such shifts in enrollment may be both legitimate and desirable, they may not serve the institution's mission. A particularly careful financial analysis is required when summer programs are undertaken at reduced tuition rates. Reduced tuition for summer terms among independent institutions often is a response to public-sector pricing when the institution competes for the same clientele. At the very least, the "reduced" price should cover the total marginal costs of summer school operations, so that marginal revenues equal marginal costs without adding a deficit to the institution's current funds account.

## MISCELLANEOUS FEES

Colleges and universities customarily charge educational and general fees for a variety of services and purposes. The most common fees and the ones of longest historical standing are laboratory and athletic fees. In recent years, some institutions, especially government-supported institutions, have charged multiple fees for various educational and ancillary purposes. These fees are popular in low-tuition institutions and may include fees for the use of libraries or computers. Special fees of limited or indefinite duration may be charged to help defray building loans or to support parking facilities or plant renovations. Critics argue that some fees charged by colleges and universities represent a form of disguised tuition.

Fees may represent a problem for colleges and universities, and there may be an ethical consideration: Where does the legitimate tuition charged for all students stop and the fees for selected students or purposes begin? However, every college and university has experienced the need to find new revenues, and fees offer a convenient way to do this. Institutions must determine the purposes for which special fees are charged. Once this determination is made, institutions should establish clear policy guidelines about who makes decisions about fees, who collects and accounts for them, and who has discretion to spend them. When an academic department or an individual professor can set and charge fees, special oversight is indicated; the area of fees is fraught with the potential for abuse. A low tuition, in combination with multiple fees, often translates into a high price, higher than the "list price" that supposedly is determined on the basis of students' ability to pay and competitive considerations. A low-tuition policy that includes many fees can be financially counterproductive, especially if it creates ill will or restricts enrollment. At worst, such a policy may promote dishonesty.

## FACTORS INFLUENCING TUITION POLICY

Tuition pricing decisions are driven by several considerations: competition, the budget for educational and general expenditures, and total institutional cost trends. There are almost as many different tuition prices as there are colleges and universities.

***Peer comparison.*** When administrators plan a budget and study tuition alternatives, they look at a list of the college or university's principal competitors and its perceived peer institutions. Administrators may or may not have access to the tuition decisions of others, but they should have a sense of where within the array of prices the institution's tuition should be positioned. The relative price ranking among peers or competitors is an important factor affecting tuition policy.

***Public relations.*** The anticipated reaction of returning students, as well as that of potential new students, is another major factor affecting tuition policy. In the public sector, the legislature may influence a tuition decision directly or indirectly, depending upon who has jurisdiction over pricing.

Tuition policy is an important aspect of the managerial art of positioning the institution vis-a-vis specific potential clienteles by strategies that focus on mission and academic orientation. In theory, demand is a function of an institution's academic reputation and available academic programs. In reality, product differentiation among colleges and universities is often in the eye of the beholder. Some people believe that a reputation for high quality comes with a high market price: high prices speak for themselves. Consumer behavior often supports the notion that quality finds expression in prices. Others view a high price as the result of an expensive operation and inefficient management; they suggest that lower costs followed by lower prices do not endanger academic quality. Because there is no formal consensus in higher education about the relationship between a quality education and pricing, institutions must rely on individual tuition-setting methodologies and competitive perceptions.

***The budget.*** Tuition policy evolves from year to year and is geared to the budget cycle. The tuition decision is an integral part of the budgeting process. In spite of the competitive and public relations considerations that enter into the tuition decision, a crucial aspect of the decision centers on the need to provide adequate revenues for balancing the next operating budget. (For institutions that operate with a budget deficit, the tuition or price decision establishes a key revenue target.) Once the tuition decision has been made, whether or not the underlying assumptions will eventually occur, a specific revenue constraint will have been imposed on the budget.

Demand analysis addresses the determination of student demand for higher education. There is no single demand for higher education; it offers numerous services (undergraduate and graduate instruction, adult instruction, certificate instruction, public and extension services, sporting and other entertainment events, and applied and pure research). Demand analysis must focus on each service separately and collectively. Colleges and universities must analyze all of their "demands": each type of enrollment and each type of service rendered confronts the college or university with unique demand functions and thus with a unique pricing task. The tuition or price-setting function concentrates on enrollment demands.

Of all the types of enrollment or student demand, only undergraduate enrollment has received the consistent attention of researchers. Given the high percentage of revenues derived from undergraduate enrollment, this preoccupation is not surprising. Depending on the type of college or university, however, the changing structure of total enrollment over time suggests that traditional nomenclatures may not always be the most suitable. Undergraduate enrollment today is a composite of full-time and part-time students, traditional teenagers and a growing cohort of adults. There are differences in what is generically called "graduate" enrollment, divided between master's degree candidates and a smaller group in doctoral programs. Programmatic interests among these types of students differ widely, as does their ability to pay and to allocate time for study. Sound tuition policy recognizes these differences.

Tuition has generated great public concern—especially when tuition is announced for the coming academic year—because tuition increases continue to exceed the rate of inflation as measured by the consumer price index (CPI). Studies have indicated that tuition in independent colleges and universities has risen by 2 to 3.5 percent more than the annual CPI rate of inflation since the late 1950s. During the 1980s, the differential was at times even greater, a fact that received wide publicity. Among public and smaller institutions, tuition increases—starting from a lower base—often exceeded these differentials. Facing growing criticism, higher education finds itself on the defensive, although there may be sound reasons for the persistence of the CPI-related price-increase differential. Because tuition represents such a significant revenue source, the only way tuition increases can be held in check is by limiting increases of the numerous expenditures that constitute a college or university budget. Before institutions embark upon a major containment of price increases, they are well-advised to investigate how a reduction of their current and capital expenditures will affect the quality of the services they offer.[9]

The public controversy about tuition increases aside, for many institutions, budget escalation and tuition increases over time may constitute a "catching-up" syndrome, whereby budget plans incorporate substantial salary and wage increases, employee benefit improvements, and academic program enhancements in response to competitive needs (or perceptions), internally developed benchmarks, and specific external challenges supported at least initially by government or private grants. This catching-up can be pronounced among "developing" tuition-dependent institutions with relatively low tuition. As new catch-up budgets are implemented, tuition increases may accelerate.[10]

***Changing structure of enrollments.*** Whether the final tuition decision is influenced primarily by competitive or cost considerations, a fundamental element in the decision is the changing structure of the types of student enrollment. In terms of tuition revenues, there are at least two ways in which to look at enrollment structure. One stresses enrollment by academic level. In this sense, long-range enrollment trends reflect matriculation and attrition rates and permit a weighing of tuition revenue contributions (and their trends) by each class. The second emphasizes enrollment by classification of net tuition revenues (after student aid grants). In practice it is useful to combine the two methods to obtain a basis for projecting the financial effect of existing policies and trends. Where there are significant and rapid changes in enrollments and net price structures, the tuition decision requires an understanding of these changes. Total tuition revenues are the sum of the revenue contributions made by each cohort in the aggregate enrollment structure.

***Tuition discounting.*** The "net tuition" or the "net price" actually paid by each student is of great importance in tuition decisions. Total enrollments and the institution's bottom line are in part a function of the net prices charged rather than of the published list price. Demand analysis requires net price information. Every college and university faces both elastic and inelastic demand; some students will matriculate regardless of price, while others are extremely price sensitive. Of course, the many different listed tuitions available in the market have their own weeding-out effect, assisting students and parents to decide where to apply for admission. Once such a decision has been made, multiple admissions being the norm, price-sensitive students will begin to pay close attention to net tuition.

For the purposes of this chapter, "net tuition" is defined as listed tuition plus fees minus fellowships and/or student aid grants. The "net price," especially for full-time resident students, is defined as listed tuition plus fees, plus charges for room and board, plus any other required charges minus fellowships and/or student aid grants. Institutions that have carefully analyzed their net prices have discovered that they charge multiple net prices, with discounts that range from 90 percent or more to 10 percent or less. Administrators can array the discounts from high to low, student by student, to develop a statistical distribution pattern. A useful method is to construct a decile distribution in which the number of students in each decile, multiplied by the respective average net price, produces the corresponding net tuition (or, as the case may be, net tuition plus room and board revenues). By adding this net revenue flow to that produced by students paying the full price, the net student revenues available in the budget can be estimated.

The extensive tuition discounting practiced by colleges and universities is not only a pragmatic response to enrollment competition but also provides an interesting opportunity for student cash flow management. The discount structure can be influenced by management to produce a better or a worse financial outcome. It is therefore the responsibility of the chief financial or business officer to provide relevant information and leadership to bring about the desired results.

***Other factors.*** Finally, two other factors that may affect the tuition decision marginally are worth mentioning: estimates of tuition receivables and student loans that may go into default. Normally college and university budgets contain allowances for uncollectible receivables and loans in default. In an institution where tuition is the sole revenue source, such allowances would clearly affect tuition directly. For colleges or universities with multiple unrestricted revenues, the cause-and-effect relationship may be less clear but nevertheless present. Tuition increases may reflect any significant rise in uncollectibles.

Aggregate tuition revenue analysis alone is not adequate when one looks at "tuition pricing" in all of its complexity in higher education. Institutions need to ask themselves periodically how well financial aid policies and their implementation support financial objectives and the extent to which student aid practices weaken or strengthen the long-range financial posture of the institution.

# Break-Even or Full-Cost Pricing in Higher Education

A range of services are rendered by colleges and universities where break-even or full-cost pricing are taken for granted. The methods require an understanding of appropriate policies concerning applicable costs.

## AUXILIARY ENTERPRISES OR SELF-SUPPORTING ACTIVITIES

The most conspicuous auxiliaries are student housing, food services and catering, and college stores. Auxiliary enterprises are generally understood to be self-supporting activities. There are vast differences in definitions of "self-supporting." On a full-costing basis, the phrase means that current and long-run revenues, collected through the prices charged for auxiliary activities, equal long-run costs. However, institutions differ in their treatment of certain costs, such as allocations for space, utilities, and housekeeping services.

The prices charged for these services depend upon historical precedent, competitive conditions, and the costing philosophy in force. In some instances, specific segments of auxiliary enterprises may be subsidized by revenues generated elsewhere within the institution. A percentage of current general administrative expenditures is legitimately (and routinely) charged to auxiliary enterprises, but the specific percentage varies greatly. Despite a general expectation that auxiliary enterprises are to be self-supporting, research has shown that operating deficits tend to occur regularly in some sectors.

Student housing costs include activities and budgets that are not part of maintaining the facilities but that may stem from decisions made by student life officers and academic administrators. Student housing officers, for instance, determine the density of dormitory capacity, frequently favoring lower numbers of residents. This can have severe adverse dormitory revenue effects that in turn may lead to increases in housing fees. Many institutions provide educational services (classes, seminars, lecture series, computer networks) in student housing units. Institutions need to be conscious of where the totality of housing costs originates and be systematic in allocating or prorating cost categories to the appropriate cost centers. College stores and other auxiliary enterprises carry substantial inventories of supplies and merchandise for sale; some institutions charge interest for money tied up in inventories, either because it was borrowed short term or because they consider it to be forgone revenue. Unless a manager is familiar with prevailing accounting and costing practice, he or she cannot know the true significance of a specific auxiliary enterprise's net revenue balance, be it positive or negative. Therefore, before the adequacy of existing auxiliary enterprise prices can be judged, the specific short- and long-run costs that these prices enable the institution to cover must be determined. Ideally, in the absence of consistent non-price-based revenues (i.e., gifts, grants, and endowment income), the prices are "correct" only if they cover long-run economic costs.

## SALES AND SERVICES OF EDUCATIONAL ACTIVITIES, HOSPITALS, AND AMBULATORY CARE CENTERS

Nursery schools, reading and speech laboratories, theaters, hotels and restaurants operated for student instruction, demonstration schools, farm services and product stores run by agricultural extensions, psychological and other clinics, and hospital services rendered to the public by medical schools are considered "sales and services" activities by a college or university's educational departments that draw income from the community. Because the basic financial support for the various departments and schools comes from the institution, these services are often priced on the basis of direct average or marginal costs. The funds derived from selling goods and services help to support departmental budgets. Financial administrators should be involved in setting specific prices, and policies on how departments should spend and account for funds should be explicit. If full-cost pricing is used, the business office should ensure that it is implemented properly. Close cooperation and mutual understanding between the business office and the educational departments are necessary for successful management of such operations.

Some institutions encourage individual professors and department chairs to engage in the sale of such services. The resulting revenue enhancement can serve as a supplementary resource, or it can help the institution limit its contribution to the activity. Although the primary objectives of these activities have traditionally been viewed as academic because they support education and research, in some institutions they have led to moonlighting and the production of supplementary incomes. Institutions should prevent "off-the-books" sales and services; specific prices and fees charged should have official sanction.

## INTERCOLLEGIATE ATHLETICS

For many colleges and universities, intercollegiate athletics are big business. History suggests that managers who are responsible for athletic programs should be especially vigilant. They should watch carefully how the specific sports are managed and in particular how the "business" and financial aspects are controlled. Setting prices is but one of the managerial details. Revenues of intercollegiate athletic activities may include season ticket sales, gate receipts, student activity fees, receipts from merchandise, food and beverage sales, guarantees, radio and television royalties, program sales, parking income, and gifts and grants for current operations. In some instances, endowment income may play a role. Except for endowment income, these types of revenues involve pricing decisions that must be made by an executive or manager. The role of the business office is to help coordinate policy and decision making to ensure that the financial outcomes are in the institution's long-range interest. Managers of intercollegiate athletics and other lucrative activities may be tempted to hold the institution's business office at arm's length; the college and university president should prevent this from happening.

## PRICING DECISIONS: TWO PRINCIPLES

In conjunction with other factors, pricing decisions determine major college and university revenue streams. These decisions are fundamental to sound budget construction and play a major role in defining the institution's financial condition.

Pricing encompasses a variety of institutional activities, and pricing decisions are made by many different individuals throughout an institution. Because colleges and universities differ significantly in the percentage of total net revenues derived from their major sources, certain pricing decisions may assume greater importance than others in individual circumstances. For instance, a residential four-year liberal arts college may make relatively few major external pricing decisions, focusing primarily on tuition and fees and room and board charges if there are few large-scale sponsored activities, no expensive intercollegiate athletic programs, and no extensive adult education and extension programs. In contrast, a major state university usually faces a far more complex set of pricing opportunities that involve many academic and administrative departments. Because of such differences, there is no single best way to administer pricing decisions in higher education.

However, two principles should be kept in mind. First, the president, through the chief financial or business officer, is responsible for ensuring that pricing decisions, wherever they are made, adhere to legal requirements and agree with the financial policies established by the governing board and the institution's administration. Second, the chief financial or business officer should be an informed and integral participant in the price-setting process. Even when decision making is decentralized, participation and supervision by the financial or business officers are not only legitimate but essential.

Proper pricing requires knowledge about markets, an understanding of the cost composition of institutional services, proper internal control and accountability procedures, and the ability to steer numerous micromanagement decisions toward the institution's financial and educational objectives. In higher education, individual managers and members of the faculty cherish decision-making autonomy. They can enjoy that autonomy within the bounds of the law and within a generally understood financial policy framework, but the chief financial or business officer must ensure that these and related requirements are met.

## The Relationship among Costing, Pricing, and Institutional Quality

Costing and pricing decisions give meaning to operating and capital budgets. In the short run and in the long run, these budgets define the quality of the institution. The relationship between costs and prices may be clear at some times and ambiguous at others. Costs clearly influence prices and prices clearly tend to limit costs. The ambiguity rests in the uncertainty of the causal relationship between price and cost. Even more difficult to determine is the issue of how costs and prices affect institutional quality.

Some higher education administrators have suggested that cost information and cost analyses are essential in evaluating the comparative quality of college and university programs. Conversely, some believe that price comparisons can indicate differences in institutional quality. In a simplified fashion, both contentions are accurate. The highest-priced institutions do seem to have the largest expenditure budgets per student. In addition, high tuition seems to embody a certain prestige element: institutions that charge high tuition, it is inferred, must be good, because they get away with charging so much.

While high costs per unit of output may signify that the service in question has superior quality and uses expensive resources, high unit costs can also mean inefficient resource use. Do higher costs mean more educational "bang" or just higher costs? When high prices and high unit costs are combined, is the educational outcome better or is it simply produced in a more expensive fashion?

A more fundamental reason for skepticism in evaluating the quality of higher education in terms of costs and prices is that cost information refers to human input and not merely material input. Both kinds of input create value in the students' minds and in their intellectual and professional capabilities. Moreover, student academic achievements, public service, and the institution's cultural and intellectual contribution to its community and society at large are the true measures of higher education quality. These are not the primary province of financial and business officers. Rather, as guardians of the institution's financial resources, financial and business officers can only facilitate or hinder these outcomes.

Administrators must compare production functions in terms of specific input mixes and their corresponding outputs. A production function is a mathematical concept whereby the output is expressed as a function of specific combinations of input. In higher education, production functions incorporate assumptions about enrollment size; however, other things being equal, institutions of identical size but with different costs may set different prices, especially in the absence of non-price-based revenue enhancements. Again, numbers alone cannot tell the whole story.

When costs incurred and prices charged by colleges and universities are expressed in constant (deflated) dollars, any net change is called "real" change. In other words, something other than inflation has been operating. But does a rise in expenditures per student, adjusted for inflation, prove an increase in value to each student, and has it brought about an improvement in the institution's perceived quality among financiers, prospective faculty, funding agencies, and desired student populations? Comparisons of "real" cost differences are fraught with hazards; to begin with, the cost information compared across institutions may not be consistent. As a guide to institutional and program quality, neither real costs nor real prices are sound indicators, although differences in them between institutions may provide rough approximations of quality differences.

Costing and pricing are interconnected activities in higher education, without a clear cause-and-effect relationship. Some costing activities, essential to budget construction and long-range planning, are not directly linked to the eventual pricing of institutional services. In other instances, particularly in the case of tuition, competition and other factors may influence the pricing decision and lead to the imposition of a revenue constraint within which expenditures and costs must be accommodated. Even where self-supporting activities are involved, competitive and public relations considerations may constrain future expenditures.

The ultimate objective of costing should be the rational, cost-effective allocation of scarce resources. The purpose of pricing is to produce adequate revenues for institutions to defray their long-run costs and to impose a constraint on expenditures and thus on costs in the aggregate.

Because expenditures and costs are not necessarily the same thing—although expenditures are a part of costs—financial managers should try to gain an accurate perception of costs. They should distinguish between cost descriptions and analysis, which are after the fact, and costing exercises, which are before the fact and designed to produce cost-effective managerial decisions.

Institutions should periodically determine their long-run or full costs of operations, that is, calculate costs in terms of both current expenditures and the long-run impact of variable and fixed costs. The concept of long-run costs imposes the obligation to define the financial policy parameters within which capital (and/or fixed) costs are determined. College and university financial managers have traditionally understated capital costs by assigning unrealistically high life spans to plant and equipment and by understating the rate of true capital consumption. The extent to which deferred maintenance exists—in the billions of dollars—is a clear indication of this defect in collegiate finance. But there are also long-run effects in current variable program costs, most notably employee benefits, which are a function of both the number of employees and salary levels and are driven by external forces such as the escalation in medical costs. Even if an institution's actual budget does not reflect a realistic long-run or full-costing policy, institutions should attempt to construct hypothetical full-cost, long-range budget plans based on realistic assumptions about obsolescence, the costs of entitlements, and the costs of future obligations. While this may appear to be principally a long-range planning budget issue, it is really an exercise in costing.

The gap between financial accounting and cost accounting is normally widest at the point of full costing within realistic (in competitive and technological terms) long-run costing parameters. Few college or university accounting systems reflect the full costs of an institution. As suggested above, an institution's full costs exist whether the accounting system captures them or not.

In one sense, colleges and universities are properly concerned about the nature and scope of their efforts to recover indirect costs, but the revenue-enhancing aspects of indirect costs can take on far too much importance. Moreover, in order to maximize cost recovery, the temptation arises to bring in cost elements that have nothing to do with the research or contract activity that raised the issue of indirect costs in the first place. More fundamental than indirect costs are a program's marginal or incremental costs. Institutions should understand the marginal costs of all their activities. Changes in prices need to occur when marginal costs increase. There is no direct- or indirect-cost concept in economics. All incremental costs are either variable or fixed direct costs. It is to be hoped that colleges and universities will pay as much attention to marginal costs in the future as they have to indirect costs in the past.

Costing and pricing occur within a firm managerial process and the existing managerial system. Costs develop whenever a manager allocates specific resources and/or initiates a new activity or program. Conversely, when an activity is eliminated, its associated costs should disappear. Moreover, what today may appear to be a cost-effective allocation may become cost-ineffective next month; what may look cheap today may prove to be costly next year. There is always more than one way to allocate resources or means. What are the procedures used by managers (and by top management) to ensure that resource allocation is and remains cost-effective? What are the procedures ensuring rational pricing decisions by the many individuals in the institution who make such decisions? These questions must be addressed continuously, as a function of the technical skills of financial or business officers and of the specific control procedures established to ensure that costing and pricing decisions produce value for the institution and its mission.

# Notes

1. "Project" refers to something limited and distinct, for instance, a specific research project or a narrow plant maintenance task reflected in a "job order." "Activity" refers to the management of janitorial and campus security services or other tasks of a relatively homogeneous nature. "Program" (as in program budgeting) is broader and may involve several jurisdictions, for instance, "academic program," "student life program," or "capital development program." "Unit costs" refers to a broad group of "average costs" frequently used by business officers and financial managers in almost every aspect of the budget.

2. Don R. Hansen, *Management Accounting* (Boston, Mass.: PWS-Kent Publishing Co., 1990), 31; William A. Koivisto, *Principles and Problems of Modern Economics* (New York: John Wiley & Sons, 1957), 595-604.

3. Current revenue deficiencies are prevalent in higher education, as are large amounts of deferred maintenance. Both conditions point to a precarious long-run financial condition, particularly in the chronic underfunding of existing plant and equipment.

4. Variance and multiple regression analyses are favored by some costing experts; similarly, linear and dynamic programming techniques are sometimes advocated. These are sound methodologies but require appropriate depth and quality of data.

5. See National Center for Higher Education Management Systems (NCHEMS) Resource Requirement Prediction Model; see also George Wheathersby et al., Induced Course Load Matrix, which assists in allocating costs to individual courses and instructors for calculating or estimating aggregate and unit instructional costs.

6. Efficient resource allocation involves the solution of quantitative optimizations; these are often couched in cost-minimization terms such as "to achieve a specific outcome with as few resources as possible" or "to produce a maximum result with few resources."

7. Occasionally, a college or university may allow academic departments to set internal prices as part of its budget and expenditure control procedures; the chief financial or business officer should participate in the pricing.

8. In 1990-91, indirect-cost ratios as a percentage of direct cost ranged from 40 to 79 percent in independent institutions and from 35 to 43 percent in public institutions. Bill Workman, "Stanford Wants 76% Rate for Overhead...," in *San Francisco Chronicle* (July 4, 1991): A 15.

9. See Hans H. Jenny and Richard G. Wynn, *The Golden Years: A Study of*

*Income and Expenditure Growth and Distribution of 48 Private Four-Year Liberal Arts Colleges, 1960-1968* (Wooster, Ohio: College of Wooster, 1970); and Hans H. Jenny and Richard G. Wynn, *The Turning Point: A Study of Income and Expenditure Growth and Distribution of 48 Private Four-Year Liberal Arts Colleges, 1960-1970* (Wooster, Ohio: College of Wooster, 1972).

10. Tuition increases during the 1960s and 1970s show a clear wedgelike effect, whereby the relative spread between high- and low-priced institutions narrowed over time. See Richard G. Wynn, "Inflation Indices in Liberal Arts Colleges." Ph.D. diss., University of Michigan, 1974.

# References and Resources

Abowd, John M. *An Econometric Model of Higher Education.* Chicago, Ill.: University of Chicago Press, 1981.

Abowd, John M. *An Econometric Model of the U.S. Market for Higher Education.* New York: Garland Publishing Co., 1984.

Adams, Carl R., Russell L. Hankins, and Roger G. Schroeder. *The Literature of Cost and Cost Analysis in Higher Education.* A Study of Cost Analysis in Higher Education, Vol 1. Washington, D.C.: American Council on Education, 1978.

Ahlburg, Vinod B., et al. "The Outlook for Higher Education: A Cohort Size Model of Enrollment of the College Age Population, 1948-2000." *Review of Public Data Use* 9: 211-227.

Alexander, E. R., III, et al. "An Econometric Estimate of the Demand for MBA Enrollment." *Economics of Education Review* 3 (1984): 97-103.

Allen, R. H., and P. T. Brinkman. *Marginal Costing Techniques for Higher Education.* Boulder, Colo.: National Center for Higher Education Management Systems, 1983.

Andersen, Charles A. *Conditions Affecting College and University Financial Strength.* Higher Education Panel Report, no. 63. Washington, D.C.: American Council on Education, 1985.

Anderson, Richard E., and Joel W. Meyerson. *Financing Higher Education in a Global Economy.* American Council on Education Series. New York: Macmillan, 1990.

Berg, D. J., and S. A. Hoenack. "The Concept of Cost-Related Tuition and Its Implementation at the University of Minnesota." *Journal of Higher Education* 58 (1987): 276-305.

Bowen, Howard R. *Investment in Learning: The Individual and Social Value of Higher Education.* San Francisco, Calif.: Jossey-Bass, 1977.

Bowen, Howard R. *The Costs of Higher Education.* San Francisco, Calif.: Jossey-Bass, 1980.

Bowen, William G. *The Economics of the Major Private Universities.* Berkeley, Calif.: Carnegie Commission on the Future of Higher Education, 1968.

Brinkman, P. T. "Factors Affecting Instructional Costs at Major Research Universities." *Journal of Higher Education,* vol. 52, no. 3 (1981): 265-279.

Brinkman, P. T. *Instructional Costs Per Student Credit Hour: Differences by Level of Instruction.* Boulder, Colo.: National Center for Higher Education Management Systems, 1985.

Brinkman, P. T. "Marginal Costs of Instruction in Public Higher Education." Ph.D. diss., University of Arizona, 1981.

Broomall, L. W., et al. "Economies of Scale in Higher Education," ERIC No. ED 162604. Paper presented to the Southern Association for Institutional Research, Nashville, Tenn., October 26-27, 1978.

Buckles, S. "Identification of Causes of Increasing Costs in Higher Education." *Southern Economic Journal* 45 (1978).

Calkins, R. N. "The Unit Costs of Programs in Higher Education." Ph.D. diss., Columbia University, 1963.

Chaffee, Ellen E. *Rational Decision Making in Higher Education.* Boulder, Colo.: National Center for Higher Education Management Systems, 1983.

Cohn, E., and J. M. Morgan. "The Demand for Higher Education: A Survey of Recent Studies." *Higher Education Review* 1 (Winter 1978): 18-30.

Gardner, C., et al. "Stanford and the Railroad: Case Studies of Cost Cutting." *Change* (November/December 1990).

Gulko, Warren W., and K. B. Hussein. *A Resource Requirements Prediction Model.* Boulder, Colo.: Western Interstate Commission of Higher Education, 1971.

Hoenack, Stephen A., and Eileen A. Collins, eds. *The Economics of American Universities: Management, Operations, and Fiscal Environment.* New York: State University of New York Press, 1990.

Hyatt, James A. *A Cost Accounting Handbook for Colleges and Universities.* Washington, D.C.: NACUBO, 1980.

Hyatt, James A., and A. A. Santiago. *Financial Management of Colleges and Universities.* Washington, D.C.: NACUBO, 1986.

James, Estelle, and Stephen A. Hoenack. "Student Financial Aid and Public Policy." *Economics of Education Review,* no. 1 (1988): 127-34.

Jenny, Hans H., and Richard G. Wynn. *The Golden Years: A Study of Income and Expenditure Growth and Distribution of 48 Private Four-Year Liberal Arts Colleges, 1960-1968.* Wooster, Ohio: College of Wooster, 1970.

Jenny, Hans H., and Richard G. Wynn. *The Turning Point: A Study of Income and Expenditure Growth and Distribution of 48 Private Four-Year Liberal Arts Colleges, 1960-1970.* Wooster, Ohio: College of Wooster, 1972.

Jenny, Hans H., G. C. Hughes, and Richard E. Devine. *Hang-Gliding or Looking for an Updraft: A Study of College and University Finance in the 1980s—The Capital Margin.* Wooster, Ohio: College of Wooster, 1981.

Kaiser, Harvey H. "Capital Needs in Higher Education." *Financing Higher Education: Strategies after Tax Reform.* Edited by Richard E. Anderson and Joel W. Meyerson. San Francisco, Calif.: Jossey-Bass, 1987.

King, George A. "Rethinking Higher Education Capital Finance." Parts 1, 2. *Capital Ideas* 3, nos. 2-3 (1988).

Langfitt, Thomas W. "The Cost of Higher Education: Lessons to Learn from the Health Care Industry." *Change* (November/December 1990): 8-38.

Leslie, Larry L., and Paul T. Brinkman. "Student Price Response in Higher Education: The Student Demand Studies." *Journal of Higher Education,* vol. 58, no. 2 (1987): 181-204.

Massy, William F. "A Strategy for Productivity Improvement in College and University Academic Departments." Paper presented at

Forum for Postsecondary Governance, Santa Fe, N.M., October 31, 1989.

Massy, William F. "Productivity Improvement Strategies for College and University Administration and Academic Support." Paper presented at Forum for College Financing, Annapolis, Md., October 26, 1989.

National Association of College and University Business Officers. *Indirect Costs of Sponsored Programs.* Washington, D.C.: NACUBO, 1981.

National Association of College and University Business Officers. *Policy Statement and Guidelines on Educational Business Activities of Colleges and Universities.* Special Action Report 87-6. Washington, D.C.: NACUBO, 1987.

National Center for Higher Education Management Systems. *Costing for Policy Analysis.* Boulder, Colo.: NCHEMS, 1980.

Nerlove, Marc. "On Tuition and the Costs of Higher Education: Prolegomena to a Conceptual Framework." *Journal of Political Economy* 80 (1972): 178-218.

O'Neill, June. *Resource Use in Higher Education.* Berkeley, Calif.: Carnegie Commission on Higher Education, 1971.

Porter, Michael E. *Competitive Strategy: Techniques for Analyzing Industry and Competitors.* New York: Macmillan, The Free Press, 1980.

Radner, Roy, and Leonard S. Miller. *Demand and Supply in U.S. Higher Education.* New York: McGraw-Hill Book Company, 1975.

Robinson, Daniel D. *Capital Maintenance for Colleges and Universities.* Washington, D.C.: NACUBO, 1986.

Russel, John Dale. *The Finance of Higher Education.* Chicago, Ill.: University of Chicago Press, 1954.

U.S. Department of Education. *Higher Education Prices and Price Indexes: 1990 Supplement.* Washington, D.C.: Government Printing Office, 1991.

U.S. OMB Circular A-21, "Cost Principles for Educational Institutions." Washington, D.C.: Government Printing Office, 1986.

Weathersby, G. B. *The Development and Application of a University Cost Simulation Model.* Berkeley, Calif.: University of California, 1967.

Werther, W. B., Jr., et al. *Productivity Through People.* New York: West Publishing Co., 1986.

Witmer, David R. "Cost Studies in Higher Education." *Review of Educational Research* 42 (1971): 99-127.

Wynn, R. G. "Inflation Indices in Liberal Arts Colleges." Ph.D. diss., University of Michigan, 1974.

# CHAPTER 8

# Managerial Financial Reporting

by
Hans H. Jenny
VISTA, Limited

# Sponsor

**KPMG PEAT MARWICK**
345 Park Avenue
New York, NY 10154
212-758-9700

*KPMG Peat Marwick assists managers in developing financial reports
that focus on critical success factors to support decision making.*

# Contents

## 8: Managerial Financial Reporting

The principal objective of managerial financial reporting is to provide useful information for evaluating the financial effects of administrative or managerial decisions. Such reporting is built around the information needs of managers who must achieve specific financial and nonfinancial objectives. It focuses on the financial dimensions of whether, how, and why specific institutional objectives are achieved. Managerial financial reporting should be viewed as a distinct area of professional interest, different from the more formal "business reporting" that normally emanates from the business office. Managerial financial reporting is an ongoing rather than a periodic process.

In the narrow sense, the management of a college or university's financial resources is normally entrusted to and supervised by the chief financial or business officer, who is directly responsible for overseeing the management of the institution's financial resources, for recording all financial transactions, and for identifying and articulating the financial aspects of resource allocation.

In a broader sense, the chief financial or business officer shares with other key administrators decision-making responsibilities that have significant financial consequences. Within the context of the annual operating budget, decisions about resource allocation tend to be decentralized. Institutions differ in how key allocation decisions are made and in how much revenue-producing responsibility or spending authority is delegated throughout the managerial structure. The governing board and the president (and in some instances, the legislature) are ultimately responsible for defining the specific institutional objectives and the persons responsible for achieving them, as well as the nature and the scope of managerial reporting in general and managerial financial reporting in particular. The president and others turn to the chief financial or business officer when they look for the articulation of financial objectives, the coordination of decisions that have a financial effect, and the refinement of operational and analytical managerial financial reporting.

Managerial financial reporting is institutionwide in scope and transcends the operational responsibilities of the business office. Its data requirements go beyond financial and accounting information. In its most simplified form, managerial financial reporting conveys a picture of an institution's financial condition. In a more complete sense, it relates this condition to an institution's specific short- and long-range objectives. College and university missions are nonfinancial in nature, and managerial financial reporting must try to reflect the interplay between the financial means (limited) and nonfinancial objectives (open ended). A major challenge for the business officer lies in linking reports of financial outcomes to the institution's primary mission.

This chapter discusses the concept of managerial interaction, the concepts and considerations inherent in managerial financial reporting, the types of managerial financial reports, and the constraints of managerial financial reporting.[1]

## Managerial Interaction

At its best, financial management is an "enabling" activity that provides an institution with financial discipline, top management with financial accountability, and key administrators with an understanding of the financial consequences of their decisions. Three steps can be used to develop a comprehensive managerial financial reporting system:

- The accountability structure should be described by identifying the sources of management reports, focusing on reports with financial content.

- The financial and nonfinancial data elements that, together with management decisions, produce financial outcomes should be identified and the "theoretical" financial model of the institution should be described.

- A matrix identifying the specific management reports, their audiences, who is responsible for issuing them, and their frequency should be created.

While managerial financial reporting focuses on the college or university's financial performance, its principal value as a management tool lies in highlighting the complex managerial interactions and decisions that lead to a particular financial outcome. By formalizing the reporting requirements of key managers, the managerial financial reporting matrix underscores the ultimate financial accountability of key administrators whose managerial responsibilities are not primarily financial in nature.

A managerial financial reporting matrix has a number of levels that correspond to the types of reports produced. The first level should provide an institutionwide perspective, emphasizing reports that describe the financial performance of the college or university. The second level should identify operational reports that deal with the financial condition of major units of the college or university, such as separate campuses in a multicampus system, professional schools and institutes, major academic divisions, and departments. A third level should identify specific administrative departments and individuals within the college or university with predetermined financial management reporting responsibilities. Figure 8-1 identifies some of these elements.

College and university management is a team effort, regardless of whether or not this is always made explicit in an institution's organization chart. Team management is also needed at numerous operational levels. It often cuts across normal official organizational structures—a team's composition depends on the specific management tasks to be accomplished. Figure 8-2 delineates key players whose daily decisions, professional competence, and analytical skills contribute to a major financial outcome: reaching a net tuition and fees revenue (budget) target.

Not every financial management decision requires a team effort. Many financial micromanagement tasks are performed by individuals with duties that have precise and limited objectives. The managerial financial reporting matrix should define each manager's reporting responsibilities in detail. Where a team effort is required, the matrix specifies the roles to be played by each participant.

# A Managerial Financial Reporting Model

The reporting matrix can be adapted to become an institution's managerial financial reporting model, which should focus on the following:

FIGURE 8-1

Sample Managerial Financial Reporting Matrix

| Type of Report | Manager Issuing Report | Contributors or Preparers | Audience or Recipients | Frequency or Due Date | Commentary |
|---|---|---|---|---|---|
| **State of the Institution** | | | | | |
| Expanded annual financial reports | Chief executive | Chief financial officer Chief academic officer | Governing board | Annually | Highlights financial and pertinent academic issues |
| Budget | Chief executive | Chief financial officer with assistance from others | Governing board | Annually with monthly updates | Monthly updates go beyond variance analysis, focusing on reasons for any deviations |
| **Operational Managerial Financial Reporting** | | | | | |
| Tuition revenue estimates | Chief financial officer | Admissions director Student aid director Registrar Others | Budget committee Chief executive Enrollment manager | When needed: Monthly or every two weeks | New and returning student estimates translated into net revenue estimates |
| **Utility Consumption Reporting** | | | | | |
| Electricity Coal, gas Telecommunication | Maintenance manager Chief financial officer | Maintenance manager or appropriate office manager | Chief financial officer Appropriate committees | Monthly and on request | In addition to status, must include comparisons with prior years and periodic cost minimization or analysis |

- Identification of the necessary reports, with precise specifications as to their purposes and contents, taking into account:

    Identification of the report's issuer, its recipient or user, and those who must contribute information for it

    Definition of the recipient's information requirements

    The most appropriate means of presentation

- Specification of the message and the data elements to be included

- Postpresentation critique and evaluation of the report preparation and communications process

FIGURE 8-2
Institutional Managers and Their Functions within a Managerial Financial
Reporting System

- Admissions officer: Sets new student enrollment objectives and provides periodic reports tracking prospective matriculants.

- Registrar: Estimates number of returning students by various groupings such as academic level, discipline, and/or department.

- Student financial aid officer: Classifies new and returning students in terms of their net tuition and fee contribution, their long-term student loan exposure, and estimates of future loan and/or tuition and fees delinquency.

- Chief academic officer: Determines potential short- and long-range effects of changes in academic programs and course and graduation requirements on enrollment and student retention.

- Financial or business officer: Measures the effect of pricing alternatives and the adopted pricing policy on enrollment objectives; synthesizes information provided by the other participants; coordinates data analysis.

- Accounting/data processing personnel: Assist participants in generating report formats; obtain appropriate software; and cooperate in producing timely and understandable models and reports.

- Institutional research office (if there is one) personnel: Assist team in data analysis, creation and testing of models, and experimenting with reporting formats.

## THE ART OF REPORTING

Once a report's message and data requirements have been identified, administrators must decide whose point of view the report should convey. Financial management information may have different meanings to different administrators. The particular point of view of a report should be identified clearly.

The level of detail in a report may not be the same as that in an oral presentation. Reports are often the culmination of extensive research, analysis, and synthesis. Analysis may lead to more than one possible conclusion or may give rise to additional questions rather than providing clear answers. Thus, a system should be developed that allows written reports to be criticized by others prior to dissemination and presentations to be rehearsed before an audience that provides constructive advice.

Because managerial financial reports involve more than traditional year-end statements and reach diverse internal and external audiences, they must address diverse communication needs. Administrators should consult experts in effective communications in order to ensure that their messages are being understood.

Users should be included in the design of report formats, and oral presentations should be rehearsed before a group of one's peers. In the complex managerial environments in which most managerial financial reports originate and are disseminated, the process of reporting can be more important than the reports themselves. The proper interaction among users and report originators is of paramount importance. Other administrators can become useful support groups, offering suggestions, experimenting with alternative formats, and constructively criticizing proposed reporting schemes. Even the choice of the presenter may be important.

Computers enable others to participate in modeling activities, on-line data retrieval, and experimenting with graphics or report creations. Executives with direct computer access have wide latitude in experimenting with report formats, the creation and testing of models, and the formulation of theories, ratios, and key indicators.[2]

## Concepts and Considerations of Managerial Financial Reporting

AUDIENCE

Managerial financial reporting is aimed at internal as well as external audiences. The internal audience is defined by an organization chart, ad hoc management teams, and the decision-making hierarchy, as articulated in the matrix discussed above. The external audience is defined by the "publics" and agencies to whom the college or university reports regularly on a mandatory or voluntary basis. These include the state that granted the institutional charter, specific government agencies (federal, state, or local), private entities (foundations, corporations), accrediting agencies (regional and professional), and the institution's alumni.

## PURPOSES

The ultimate purposes of managerial financial reporting are to measure or evaluate institutional, financial, and managerial performance and to enhance decision-making effectiveness. Other purposes are

- to maintain control over management policies and procedures;

- to document short- and long-range plans, budget and program requests, and major managerial and policy decisions; and

- to enhance—through communication—managerial cooperation and coordination, as well as a sense of inclusion or participation among managers and information recipients.

More specifically, managerial financial reporting should accomplish the following objectives, which should be seen as complementary:

***Managerial financial reporting should provide information on the financial position of the institution and on financial performance.*** This is most easily achieved through the traditional year-end balance sheet and the statements of changes in fund balances and current funds revenues, expenditures, and transfers. In addition, a variety of financial performance indicators can be developed on the basis of these statements and other specialized analyses. These statements and reports should be accompanied by appropriate commentary that compares objectives with results. Normally comparisons over time (trends) and with peer institutions are included.

***Managerial financial reporting should provide information on nonfinancial performance.*** Special performance considerations include conclusions concerning the effectiveness of institutional programs and changes in institutional productivity. Whether or not institutional productivity and service quality are improving is an important question answered in part by financial analysis.

***Managerial financial reporting should define the locus of accountability.*** Because numerous managers, as well as the governing board, are charged with certain specific financial and fiduciary responsibilities, clear definitions of who is accountable for what and to whom are a basic requirement.

***Managerial financial reporting should identify audiences and users of reports and adapt content and format to special audience needs.*** Because users' information needs differ, format and content (sometimes even style of presentation) should be sensitive to such differences.

***Managerial financial reporting should help managers and institutions achieve their stated objectives and help them improve performance.*** Managerial financial reporting is normally "after-the-fact" reporting that discloses results. Financial results can be reported on a daily, weekly, monthly, quarterly, term (semester, quarter, trimester), or annual basis. For best performance results, managerial financial reporting should be as timely as possible to enable managers to take corrective action as quickly as possible.

When the objective of managerial financial reporting is improving performance, information covering shorter periods (days, weeks, months) and smaller units (departments, specific events, subcategories in budgets) is normally more useful than annual or institutionwide reports. There is an inevitable time lag between the receipt of a monthly budget report, for instance, and the financial data it describes; there is a further time lag between the receipt of such a report and the analysis of why specific events occurred. Thus, corrective actions tend to be delayed under the best of circumstances. Waiting a long time before taking corrective or reinforcing steps nullifies the objective of reporting.

***Managerial financial reporting must support financial forecasting and financial long-range planning.*** Few colleges and universities are not engaged in long-range planning, and every institution is expected to make short- and long-range forecasts about the availability of or need for resources. A financial model describing the myriad dynamic interactions among key financial and nonfinancial variables enables managers to simulate financial outcomes under alternative assumptions. Because the internal financial structures of colleges and universities normally do not change dramatically from year to year, the financial model should be relatively stable, even over long periods. This makes it easier to understand how key financial and other variables interact and how they produce change.

***Managerial financial reporting should facilitate method-***

*ological, analytical, and expository innovation.* Higher education is given certain specific, but relatively few, managerial financial reporting guidelines. There is little consensus on some of the most important areas of financial reporting, particularly with respect to institutional outcomes, institutional quality, and the meaning of higher education productivity. Institutional managers are essentially free to develop reporting systems and performance measures that are suited to their insights, to their available talent, and to their particular financial circumstances.

**Quality managerial financial reporting should achieve the following principles.**

CONSISTENCY. Managerial financial reporting should adhere to generally accepted accounting principles as set forth in *Audits of Colleges and Universities,* published by the American Institute of Certified Public Accountants. In addition, managerial financial reporting should maintain consistency over time and, for interinstitutional comparisons, with the reporting practices of other institutions and with the data collection surveys of public agencies (e.g., the Department of Education's Integrated Postsecondary Education Data System [IPEDS]) and private organizations (e.g., the Higher Education Price Index [HEPI]).

COMPARABILITY. When information is compared among institutions, the subject matter must compare with that of other institutions. Comparability is not the same thing as "consistency"; one can compare consistent data that is not comparable. Activities that bear a common label may differ in form or organization. An example is a cost comparison for a biology "lab" course, where one institution uses traditional laboratory instruction while another uses videotapes of laboratory demonstrations and students never set foot in a lab. Comparability issues also arise when accounting practices differ among institutions.

SUMMARIZATION. Brevity for its own sake may not be appropriate, but "a picture is worth a thousand words" is a useful criterion in managerial financial reporting; the key to summarization is to provide what is necessary to convey the meaning. The detail should be appropriate to the user's level of responsibility. Thus, a member of a governing board investment committee often would be given more detailed information on investment performance than the board as a whole. Furthermore, because management styles differ even at the board level, some executives may be provided with more detail than others. Reports should be detailed enough to enable managers to understand what is going on and how to carry out their duties.

Reports that provide analysis may require supporting information; reports that highlight certain information may be adequate when they rely on only the most summary data. In practice, all reports generate questions on the part of recipients. If similar questions are asked repeatedly over time by the same report recipients, the report format may be too brief or may need to be changed.

***Managerial financial reporting should reflect changed demands.*** Reporting systems evolve over time; managerial financial reporting is no exception. New reporting requirements sometimes arise from external agencies, particularly government entities. Innovation may result from external research efforts or analytical advances made by professionals within and outside the institution. Members of the governing board and its committees also contribute to reporting innovations. The task of keeping up with state-of-the-art analysis and reporting belongs to the chief financial or business officer and his or her staff.

***Managerial financial reporting should be performed by knowledgeable administrators.*** The business offices of small colleges are usually staffed with "jack-of-all-trades" types who may lack in-depth expertise for managerial financial reporting. Larger institutions are often able to hire more specialists for such key financial management functions. When internal reporting know-how is lacking, external sources of expertise may have to be called upon. However, colleges and universities have pools of unused or hidden talent at their disposal in the form of the governing board, faculty, alumni, and students. Where this potential low-cost talent is used effectively, financial reporting, as well as managerial practice, may be improved.

## CONFLICTING AND MULTIPLE OBJECTIVES

It is almost impossible to operate consistently, on the basis of singular and noncompeting objectives, in complex management systems. The more complex an institution, the greater the likelihood that certain segments will succeed in implementing objectives that, upon closer analysis, may not be fully consonant with the objectives that central management is trying to achieve. Even when there is an apparently unified institutional objective, some divisional and departmental objectives may be in conflict. In addition, multiple and simultaneous objectives frequently must be achieved within constraints of money and time.

**Short- and long-range financial objectives.** Short-range financial objectives are embodied in the operating budget. If the operating budget does not adhere to or strive toward the program and finance principles of the long-range plan, a major conflict exists. One frequent conflict concerns the imperative—at any cost—to balance the operating budget. Another possible conflict concerns the desire to maximize short-term endowment investment income payout at the expense of sound long-range investment and payout policies. Managerial financial reporting must address these conflicts between short- and long-range financial objectives and indicate how they are being resolved.

Long-range planning objectives, articulated in the institution's long-range financial plan, should be based on a balanced overview of the institution's competing demands for resources.

**Cost-effective financial objectives.** Sound financial policy stipulates that all resources must be allocated in a cost-effective manner. Some practitioners may interpret this responsibility to mean that in all instances least-cost solutions must be found and financial targets set accordingly. But least-cost and cost-effective allocations may not be the same thing. Because higher education outcomes cannot be quantified easily, the definition of cost-effectiveness is often difficult, if not impossible, to determine. It is therefore not unusual that financial objectives that are linked to specific cost minimization, cost-effectiveness, or cost-revenue optimization targets may be perceived as adverse to the quality of institutional outcomes.

**Staffing objectives.** In financial terms, human resources costs represent the largest single cost component of a college or university operating budget, especially when capital elements are excluded. A perennial conflict seems to exist between staffing academic functions and the personnel requirements of institutional administration. A budget may merely indicate how the conflict has been resolved; it may not focus on either the redundancies or shortages that can be part of the picture. Managerial financial reporting should go beyond the straightforward facts about human resources expenditures and costs and deal with the broader questions of personnel productivity and adequacy. Reports about staffing needs, performance objectives, and productivity are useful adjuncts in this case.

*Quality objectives.* Specific strategic quality objectives for academic and administrative departments, professional schools, academic divisions, and administrators should be formulated. Long-range quality objectives may differ from short-range quality objectives. Managerial financial reporting should focus on the intended progressions that lead to the implementation of the long-range quality objectives.

*Capital and operating requirements.* The conflict between an institution's financial requirements for capital resources on the one hand and those for current operations on the other is a long-standing one and must be addressed by the articulation of a sound capital finance policy.

In these areas of actual or potential conflict, it is important that the institution's nonfinancial objectives be linked with its financial goals. Managerial financial reporting should articulate this interaction clearly by identifying all relevant objectives for the audiences.

Conflicting objectives are normal in human endeavors; in managerial financial reporting they should not be viewed as an obstacle but as an opportunity for greater precision in articulating institutional mission, objectives, financial policy guidelines, and the difference, if any, between stated goals and actual achievements.

## THE FOCUS OF MANAGERIAL FINANCIAL REPORTING

There are a variety of perspectives for managerial financial reporting.

*State-of-the-institution reporting.* Managerial reports on the financial (and programmatic) performance of the institution as a whole usually originate at the presidential level and involve the governing board as their primary audience. Such broad, institutionwide reporting normally includes reports by administrators at divisional and departmental levels.

Institutionwide managerial financial reporting should reflect the inherent and relatively simple logic of collegiate finance. For example, a college or university has a well-integrated long-range programmatic and financial plan. From this plan, it develops an annual operating budget and a capital budget that are updated whenever necessary. At the end of the fiscal year, on the basis of year-end financial statements, the long-range financial plan is updated. Any programmatic changes not in the plan that have been made or are being contemplated are also factored into the revision, as are any changes in the institution's financial policies. These revisions establish the base for the next annual operating and capital budgets.

Institutionwide managerial financial reporting can be limited to a one-line statement about aggregate changes in institutional net worth, or it may encompass analyses using the operational budget and audited year-end financial reports. Because year-end statements seldom address program issues or even refer to the size of enrollments, the number of degrees granted, or the number of personnel employed, the chief financial or business officer must decide which environmental nonfinancial factors to include. The following list provides guidance on the types of information that might be included:

- Enrollment and student profile information and key aspects of financial aid

- Human resources: faculty and staff information, salary and wage levels, nonsalary benefits, and professional quality of personnel

- Instructional and public service program information: instructional programs (student-to-faculty ratio, course offerings, special issues), academic support (libraries, laboratories, academic computing), and public service outreach programs

- Administrative support issues

- Institutional advancement (alumni, donors, bequests)

- Physical plant and equipment (inventory, condition of facilities, deferred maintenance issues, equipment replacement issues)

- Research

- Grants and contracts

- Auxiliary activities (condition of plant and equipment, bottom-line issues)

Each area can be used as a topic for data collection and analysis as it relates to the overall financial environment of the institution.

***Program, service unit, and activities reporting.*** This type of microreporting addresses specific subsystems and discrete activities. Examples are the financial analysis of a specific program of instruction (a foreign language major, a required course, a library acquisition program for an academic department), the bottom-line analysis of an institution's food service program, and the study of how the costs of electricity consumption can be reduced without impairing service.

***Performance reporting.*** Performance reports identify original managerial objectives and describe how well they have been achieved. If performance is less than satisfactory, these reports should give reasons why and indicate the steps to be taken for remedial action. Performance reporting normally involves the transformation of accounting and other data into information that serves a specific purpose, requiring data analysis and interpretation. Where complex analyses are required, they need not be part of a financial management report proper but can be attached as supplements or produced separately.

***Operational reporting.*** Operational reports focus on the day-to-day operations of the institution. Managers must keep each other informed. Upward and sideward reporting are used to carry out management and operational assignments. In this way managers remain informed about the institution's progress toward stated goals. This type of reporting is especially important where nonfinancial management decisions produce significant financial results. Upward and sideward reports should

- identify the specific managerial levels (and individuals) where managerial financial reporting must occur, and

- formalize reporting links and management teams.

Because some managers may not immediately understand the financial consequences of their decisions, an appropriate and constructive learning environment should be part of setting up an operational reporting system.

***Baseline reporting.*** "Baseline reporting" refers to descriptive historical and indicator reporting, a task often assigned to an institutional research office. In this sense, the basic purpose of reporting is to establish norms and to define departure points, trends, and key relationships. Because colleges and universities are composites of complex interactions among numerous activities, managerial financial reporting must describe relationships between the financial variables and the nonfinancial variables, which are also indicators of financial activity. A description of these relationships can be expressed in the institution's financial model. Because such a model is not static, reports need to focus on the following:

- Identification of general and unique internal environmental variables that affect institutional behavior and financial outcomes.

- Historical information that may identify trends or cycles for key financial indicators. Because institutions differ in this information, data are subject to the special characteristics of each institution.

- Definition of the key cause-and-effect relationships. These relationships are the heart and soul of the financial model. Comparative ratio analysis can help establish benchmarks against which future action and progress can be measured. Baseline reports are more than a stringing together of unrelated data; they should reflect the institution's financial model and behavior.

- Forecasting (or predicting) future financial outcomes, which gives rise to variance analysis and may, in turn, lead to changes in the original targets or plans.

TYPES OF ANALYSIS

Several types of analysis must be applied to a college or university's financial data and reports:

- Comparative analysis

- Constant-dollar analysis

- Indicator and ratio analysis

- Trend analysis

- Productivity analysis

- Return-on-investment analysis

- Variance analysis

*Comparative analysis.* Comparative analysis provides an effective performance perspective. Specific internally stipulated objectives (e.g., compensation levels, student achievement scores, and revenue and expenditure per student) are measured against achievements at similar institutions using generally accepted or widely used indicators of comparative performance.

Most institutions have peer-group cohort preferences; others have aspiration-group cohorts as well. For specific statistical comparisons, special groupings must be created. Research universities, community colleges, and law and medical schools have their own preferred universes. Objectivity is critical when assembling a comparative sample.

***Constant-dollar analysis.*** An important step in managerial financial reporting is to distinguish between current- and constant-dollar trends. Several states and colleges and universities have developed cost indexes to assist them in sorting out the effect of inflation on institutional budgets. The point of departure is the line-item budget.

From the standpoint of managerial financial reporting, constant-dollar budget information is most easily derived by deflating current-dollar budgets by higher education industry price indexes such as the HEPI or specific state-developed indexes. A well-established professional consensus on how to construct a price or cost index exists. Constant-dollar analysis should not be restricted to revenues and expenditures. The institution's capital (plant, endowment, and investment capital) also is affected by inflation. Managerial financial reporting should include appropriate trend analyses in both current and constant dollars.

***Indicator and ratio analysis.*** Indicator analysis determines financial and nonfinancial variables that best describe the behavior of the institution. From the viewpoint of managerial financial reporting, indicator analysis is perhaps the most important type of analysis: it evaluates how the system works and how one institution differs from others in interactions among key quantitative and qualitative variables. Indicator analysis provides the foundation for long-range planning.

Ratio analysis can and should be a major feature of trend analysis, because ratios depicted over time display the inherent stability or instability of key relationships among important institutional components.

Financial ratios communicate information drawn from financial statements in an accessible manner that can aid in assessing the financial health of an institution. In addition, ratios can identify trends. Ratio analysis also permits comparison of an institution with an aspiration or peer group. There are several types of ratios:

- Balance-sheet ratios
- Creditworthiness ratios
- Net operating ratios
- Contribution and demand ratios

CURRENT FUNDS (BALANCE-SHEET) RATIOS. The balance sheet is an important feature of the annual financial report. Because a balance sheet represents the financial picture at a given moment, balance-sheet trends are a central requirement in any analysis. Some balance-sheet components help explain the institution's capacity to support specific types of expenditures. How liquid are its assets? Is the annual cash flow from other than debt sources adequate to finance the current budget? In other words, is the institution financially viable? If not, what are the problems and likely solutions? Balance-sheet analysis sheds light on the financial structure and relative fiscal health of the various funds. Even positive fund balances may hide poor financial conditions, lack of liquidity, and other potential between-the-lines problems.

Balance-sheet ratios include:

- Quick (or liquidity) ratio
- Current ratio (current assets:current liabilities)
- Long-term assets:long-term liabilities
- Fund balance:debt
- Fund balances:types of expenditures and mandatory transfers

CREDITWORTHINESS RATIOS. Creditworthiness ratios are significant to lenders, suppliers, and credit-rating agencies, who are interested in whether or not an institution is capable of paying its bills, servicing debt punctually, and incurring additional indebtedness. They answer the question, What is the degree of risk that lenders and suppliers face? Students and their parents are also interested in these issues, because the bankruptcy of an institution could prevent students from completing their degrees or diminish the value of degrees earned. Employees, too, have an interest in institutional creditworthiness, because their employment might be affected.

NET OPERATING RATIOS. The term "operating ratio" is slightly different from "operating result," in that capital items and debt service are assumed to be part of the operation. Three net operating ratios are:

- Net total revenues:total revenues

- Net educational and general revenues:total educational and total revenues

- Net auxiliary enterprise revenues:total auxiliary enterprise revenues

In each instance, net revenue is the net gain or loss as a percentage of the three revenue sources.

Positive ratios or percentages signify surpluses; negative results signify deficits. The ratios are similar to expressing the profit or loss of a for-profit business as a percentage of sales or revenues.

CONTRIBUTION AND DEMAND RATIOS. Contribution and demand ratios can help determine the weight of one item in relation to another element or an appropriate composite. In contribution ratios, each revenue source is taken as a percentage of educational and general expenditures (e.g., tuition as a percentage of education and general expenditures), showing the adequacy of coverage. Demand ratios compare major expenditure categories to educational and general revenues.

DISAGGREGATION BY DEPARTMENT, DIVISION, OR SCHOOL. Because institutionwide ratio analysis can mask strengths and weaknesses in individual departments, divisions, or schools, managers may wish to use ratio analysis to assess the financial health or impact of subunits. Unless balance sheets are routinely prepared for subdivisions, ratio analysis for them tends to be limited to operational concerns, that is, to revenue and expenditure components. Ratio and trend analysis may need to include many nonfinancial components as well.

An effective way to proceed from revenue and expenditure ratios is to disaggregate the previously mentioned ratios, as well as to create new ones that are suitable for the type of subdivision studied. Law and medical schools have developed standard measures, and hospitals use specific indicators of financial health.

It is useful to compare some ratios and percentages among the several subdivisions, but managers must remember that the divisions may be inherently different. It may be more constructive to find suitable comparisons among competing or peer subdivisions at other institutions.

***Trend analysis.*** Trend, or historical, analysis is widely practiced in higher education finance; it is used to describe the long-range behavior of institutional variables, as well as to compare interinstitutional data over time. Management reports comparing year-to-date results for the current year and prior years are the most commonly used historical comparisons, particularly in interim and financial reports. This type of analysis has two dimensions. Data in a trend analysis should span a sufficiently long period to describe turning points, discontinuities, or cycles in the elements that influence financial performance. Institutional rhythms frequently run in multiyear cycles; the specific rhythms should define the trends' length. A three- to five-year trend is appropriate in most instances but will not always be adequate.

***Productivity analysis.*** A college or university has three essential functions: instruction, research, and public service. Productivity analysis should address each of these functions. However, there is little agreement on how colleges and universities should measure changes in institutional productivity.

Facing the multitude of institutional objectives and activities, some institutions prefer to address productivity by focusing on the activities of instructional departments, specific research projects, or key micromanagement areas. For some activities, the physical or quantitative changes are more easily defined. Less attention has been paid to productivity changes in research and public service endeavors than to productivity changes in instruction.

Physical changes in productivity can be defined as changes in physical output per physical or monetary (constant-dollar) unit of input. Higher education has long worked with physical input and output measures such as student-faculty ratios; teaching or workload parameters; unit costs per course or per instructor; cost per kwh or miles traveled; unit mailing costs; cost per person hour in research; and operating costs per student housed or fed.

Qualitative changes in productivity can be defined as any change in quality associated with a unit change in resources input. Parameters for changes in service quality are elusive, but measuring devices exist, among them institutional inventories; questionnaires addressed to students, alumni, and professional peers on their perceptions of changing quality; and models set forth by accrediting agencies for their visiting teams. In general, the college and university accreditation process—though overly diverse, decentralized, and relatively imprecise—serves the purposes of guarding quality.

Higher education is a service industry. Colleges and universities operate at a disadvantage when it comes to a need for long-range (if not continuous) improvement in productivity similar to what is expected from the for-profit world. Higher education managers at times fall into the trap of assuming that any constant-dollar change in output represents a quality change. Such a change may signify activity or program expansion. Whether or not such a change is an improvement in quality must be carefully determined.

***Return-on-investment analysis.*** Return-on-investment (ROI) analysis is fundamental to financial analysis. It is sometimes used in a limited fashion in terms of the returns achieved by a short-term cash or long-term endowment investment or, more narrowly, in terms of investment yield.

Economists use ROI in a number of ways. Trade-off analysis is a form of ROI in which the return on a new investment (or expenditure) must be equal to or greater than that of the expenses that it replaces. Plant maintenance, replacement, investment, and improvement expenditures should be subjected to trade-off analysis.

Another type of ROI analysis involves the use of optimization techniques. Optimization formulas attempt to maximize benefits (revenues, cash flow, profits) with a certain amount of resources or to minimize outlays or investments (personnel, physical inputs, costs) for a certain outcome.

Cost-benefit ROI is also widely used. For instance, in the realm of student and faculty morale, the provision of adequate equipment in laboratories or improved facilities in student housing or recreation can be related to the amount of money to be invested. Differences in the amount of capital required can produce significant differentials in perceived quality, which can affect morale and institutional marketability. Thus, cost-benefit analysis is an important tool.

Risk management is also a type of ROI analysis. The problem of liability and the minimization of short- and long-term liability costs and the broader problem of exposure are matters of risk management. Because current and capital budget resources related to risk represent significant percentages in institutional budgets, risk management is a major managerial financial reporting concern. (For a full discussion of risk management, see Chapter 14, Risk Management and Insurance.)

***Variance analysis.*** Variance analysis, or exception reporting, is well-established in managerial financial reporting. Its most widespread use occurs with the budget, but it can be applied to many operational phases of financial management. Variance analysis works best within a historical (i.e., compared to the same quarter in the previous year) or a planning (i.e., compared to parameters set forth in a plan) context. Data consistency is crucial for sound variance analysis. An important issue in variance analysis is the degree of deviation considered normal or acceptable. Variance analysis and specific financial policies are closely connected.

Variance analysis also concerns forecasts and projections that extend beyond the current period. Do current results indicate that proposed actions can be implemented? Variance analysis is an essential step in bringing long-range plans into focus with current events.

***Analysis supported by graphics.*** Colleges and universities often combine verbal and graphic presentations for enhanced communication. The arsenal of statistical methodology now available is extensive and becomes more sophisticated and more challenging each year. Computer software easily translates complex data into meaningful "pictures." For certain trend reports, it is advisable to consider the use of semilogarithmic graphs rather than decimal presentations. Because some managers are more comfortable with "pictorial" explanations of complex data, semilogarithmic graphs can be an important communications tool. These presentations can save time once the audience understands them.

# The Tasks of Financial Management

College and university financial management encompasses three fundamentally different yet integrated tasks. These tasks can be divided by various levels of management responsibility:

- Management of current funds revenues

- Management of current funds expenditures

- Management of capital resources

These three tasks are a comprehensive, all-inclusive description of financial management. Revenue management focuses on the numerous types of revenue, including tuition, government appropriations, gifts and grants, endowment and investment income, and income from auxiliary activities. Expenditure management encompasses the entire line-item structure of the operating budget for each managerial function, including instruction, physical plant maintenance, student services, and auxiliary enterprises. Revenues and expenditures include both unrestricted and restricted funds, although managers may face differences in the degree of freedom that an institution has in the "management" of restricted and unrestricted funds. In many instances, restricted funds may have to be spent not merely for specific purposes but in prescribed ways. Sometimes institutions have discretion in how they allocate restricted revenues. The management of capital resources includes new construction and the management of existing facilities and equipment, student and other loan funds, endowment and other capital resources, and the means of financing them.

These financial management tasks should be the focus of managerial financial reporting. Managerial financial reports should address bottom-line results, including an evaluation of the adequacy of resources in terms of long-run costs and prices, and the following issues.

- What noteworthy changes in available or expendable financial resources have occurred during the latest period (month or year) and over longer periods (five years or ten years)?

- What are the institution's current and future cash-flow requirements, and what changes are occurring (or necessary) to the institution's indebtedness? Can the institution afford current and/or contemplated debt?

- What are the scope and "quality" of the institution's debt, and what ratings are given by rating agencies to institutional debt instruments and to its financial condition?

- Does the institution have adequate long-range expendable reserves in the event of adverse revenue trends? Assuming a specific level of deficit, how many years will the reserves last before they are completely exhausted?

- What, if any, academic and administrative program deficiencies are there and what, if any, is the gap between available and needed resources? Are there substantial unused resources?

- What is the institution's specific revenue dependency? Is it overly dependent on tuition revenue? If yes, what, if anything, can be done about it? Is the structure (percentage distribution) of all current revenues changing? If so, how is it changing and what steps are being taken to correct adverse trends? If the institution is public, what favorable or adverse changes are there in the amount and composition of state appropriations?

- What, if any, changes have been occurring in the institution's functional and line-item expenditure structure or distribution? If the trends are adverse, what actions are being taken or recommended to remedy the situation?

- Does the institution have an adequate physical capital budget? How is this determined? Is there a significant amount of deferred maintenance? What are the institution's new equipment needs and budgets? What are its facilities maintenance and improvement budgets? What is the inventory of planned new construction? What will be the inventory's impact on future operating budgets?

- Does the institution have a reliable method for determining the marginal costs of new programs? What is it?

- What are current investment results (endowment funds, funds functioning as endowment, and others)? How do they compare with results achieved by other colleges and universities, mutual funds, and other types of investment managers? What has been the net effect of inflation on the purchasing power of permanent investments?

- What is the institution's competitive (and comparative) standing in tuition and fees, room and board charges, student financial aid, the quality of enrollments, the quality of educational and research programs, faculty and staff compensation, and the nature and scope of the nonsalary benefits package? Specifically, what are the cost trends of social security, pension plan, and medical plan coverage?

- Are enrollments rising or falling? Is the mix of net revenues (after student aid grants) improving or deteriorating? What are the causes for specific changes, and what corrective steps, if any, are being taken or recommended?

- For research universities and others with significant research programs, what is the institution's dependency on indirect-cost recovery, and how would sharp reductions in grants, contracts, and/or cost recovery affect future budgets and programs?

- Is the institution financially viable? How is "viability" defined by the institution? If the institution is not financially viable, what steps are recommended to make it so?

- Is the institution academically viable? What is its standing in the accreditation and reaffirmation process? Did recent accreditation visits disclose specific financial or other weaknesses, and what, if any, corrective action has been instituted or is being recommended?

## TYPES OF REPORTS

*Annual financial management reports.* Annual financial management reports can answer either all or some of the questions listed above. Because the issues are of interest to a variety of audiences, the reports may have to be tailored to both the public relations needs of the institution and the recipients' particular information requirements. Internally, it is important that such reports clarify the relationship between results and institutional goals in an objective manner.

*The annual operating budget.* The annual operating budget is the financial expression or plan of an institution's activities for a certain year. It represents the summation as well as the details of divisional and departmental plans. Although it may differ in its expository details, the budget is one document or instrument used by every college and university.

*The short- and long-range capital plan.* The capital plan

encompasses all of the institution's funds: current funds, student loan funds, endowment and similar funds, plant funds, and miscellaneous funds. It should address past, present, and future changes in fund balances. In addition, there should be a separate plan for physical capital (equipment and facilities).

*The long-range financial plan.* The long-range financial plan should address the future or long-range adequacy of revenues and capital.

*Ad hoc financial reports addressing specific financial and programmatic topics.* Ad hoc reports can be performance-oriented financial reports or special analyses focusing on financial trends, ratios, interinstitutional comparisons, program costs, or any special financial issue facing the institution.

Specialized managerial financial reports include:

- Cash-flow analysis identifying the various sources of current cash flow, highlighting cash-flow deficiencies, if any

- Net current cash-flow analysis pertaining to revenues from and on behalf of students that distinguishes among student types, levels of enrollments, and other characteristics unique to the institution and takes into account the effect of student aid grants, loans, and payment delinquencies on cash flow

- Consolidated net worth in current and constant dollars, both aggregate and expendable portion only

- Analysis of total return on investments

- Constant-dollar purchasing power of endowment (including new gifts to endowment)

- Endowment payout policies and formulas and their effect on the budget

- Current and long-range preventive maintenance and physical capital plans

- Revenue and expenditure distributions—the former by source, the latter by function and major line-item groupings

- Structure of student aid grants (or discounts)

- Miscellaneous micromanagement operations reports, emphasizing unit costs, marginal costs, productivity measures, resource-allocation optimization, and rate of investment

- Institutionwide cost-of-living index

***Internal control and managerial effectiveness.*** Internal control and managerial effectiveness reports should disclose how well specific financial policies and procedures are being carried out. Topics covered by these reports include:

- Cash control

- Payroll and benefit control

- Budget variance

- Costing targets by cost center and cost minimization or the optimal allocation of resources in specific areas such as utilities, postage, telecommunications, travel, and supplies

- Restricted funds additions, deductions, and balances, by fund and fund groups

- Analyses of recruitment expenditures in relation to matriculation results (number and quality of new enrollments, student aid dependency)

- Analyses of fund-raising expenditures in relation to current and capital funds objectives

- The least-cost issue, i.e., the documentation of why management believes specific budget allocations reflect the most economical use of resources

- Cost-effective inventory control and purchasing procedures and outcomes

# Managerial Financial Reporting

POLICY CONSTRAINTS

Because financial reporting takes place in an environment of specific financial policy assumptions, the financial results produced by a given set of accounting records can change, often significantly, when these policy assumptions are altered.

Financial policy is both explicit and implicit: policy must be formally stated but it may be deduced from the nature of the accounting methodology embodied in the formal financial statements.

Where key financial issues are involved, institutions should have written documentation of the financial policies in effect. The audit usually points out whether or not major changes in accounting procedures have occurred. Financial policy constraints must be clearly articulated in managerial financial reports so that the reader can interpret the data correctly.

For example, a number of financial policy constraints can affect a college or university's bottom line, referred to as a change in the current (usually unrestricted) fund balance. The most conspicuous of these concern the rules governing capital expenditures.

Assuming no borrowing for acquisition or replacement of equipment or for plant improvements and a requirement to balance the budget, capital expenditures would be limited—regardless of programmatic needs—to available current revenues (including capital gifts). If borrowing is allowed, the duration of the indebtedness is an important question. Institutions usually establish rules concerning this, but a prolonged debt obligation's superficial effect may be to make the immediate bottom line look better than it really is. An even more serious matter arises when colleges and universities do not allow for modest capital consumption by not debiting modest depreciation charges against the current budget. The presence of any significant amount of accumulated deferred maintenance is a sign that current revenues are not up to the task of maintaining the institution (including its plant equipment) as a going concern in the long run.

Managers should realize that rules of financial policy concerning capital will affect the bottom line, which must be judged within the relative severity of prevailing policy constraints. Balanced budgets can also be achieved at the expense of institutional quality or by falling behind schedule in implementing the long-range financial plan. Institutions may wish to accompany their normal managerial financial reports with an internal document highlighting program and facilities "deficits."

Financial policy in the form of rules established by the governing board or the legislature on how endowment funds are to be invested and what expendable investment returns are also directly affects the bottom line and the revenue side of the budget. This is a complex issue, and depending upon how key questions are resolved, the effect on the bottom line can be significant. The long-range questions that arise include: Is the payout limited to interest and dividends? Does the institution operate with a total return payout formula? Does this formula maximize payout in the short run or allow the return to be reinvested for payout stabilization or meet the inflation-induced reduction of endowment capital purchasing power? Depending on the answers, the payout may provide more or less current revenue for the budget and simultaneously influence the size of the endowment fund balance.

## BUDGETARY CONSTRAINTS

Beyond the budget's bottom-line constraints, two broad elements must be considered:

- Assumptions (or forecasts) about current revenues and expendable (or budgetable) resources
- Expenditure targets that may be line-item specific down to the smallest accounting unit

In many public institutions, the budget format and detail are prescribed; independent colleges and universities have greater freedom and thus greater variety in budget format. The separate line-item budgets are grouped according to the functional expenditure categories of the accounting system, such as instruction, academic support, general administration, and auxiliary enterprises. In complex institutions, budgets may also be aggregated in terms of the institution's major subdivisions, such as freestanding institutes, professional schools, hospitals, or separate academic divisions. In multicampus institutions, a budget usually exists for each campus. In any situation, however, there is usually one document that summarizes the institution's overall budget.

Although functional subdivisions are routinely displayed in the traditional audited statements, the line-item structure of the budget reveals how the institution allocates resources within each function.

Yet, this aspect of higher education finance is not well-documented, in spite of the fact that institutional staff work with this line-item structure on a daily basis.[3]

*Current revenues from and on behalf of students.* "Current fund revenues from and on behalf of students" means all expendable funds—unrestricted and restricted—that are paid directly by students (including those based on student loans), plus those expendable gifts and grants (private and public) and investment returns that the institution allocates to student accounts and that appear as current restricted revenues in the current funds statement. Most institutions receive the bulk of current revenues "from and on behalf of students." Because of peculiarities in higher education accounting, however, it is almost impossible to measure this important revenue stream. Student-related cash-flow data are even more difficult, if not impossible, to measure.

Revenues from and on behalf of students are made up of the following components:

- Tuition and fees

- Enrollment-based government appropriations

- Housing and food-service fees

- Sales of other services and goods (books, supplies, etc.) to students

- Private and/or government grants for scholarships and student aid

- Private gifts for scholarships (restricted)

- Endowment income or payout for scholarships and student aid grants

- Public and private student loans

The student-by-student effect on institutional net revenues (after student aid grants) differs vastly among institutions and over time. A managerial financial report that focuses on these issues must answer the following questions:

- What percentage of students receive tuition discounts via grants and scholarships? Is the percentage increasing or decreasing?

- What is the range of discounts expressed as a percentage of the student's gross invoice? Is the discount distribution shifting upward (higher average discounts) or is it shifting downward (lower average discounts)?

- What percentage of the grants are being financed through restricted private and public grant revenues? What percentage represents institutional revenues forgone? Is this percentage rising or falling?

An increasing number of institutions are reporting total revenues from and on behalf of students and are experimenting with financial reports that track all relevant financial and nonfinancial variables. Figure 8-3 illustrates one possible summary report format.

## THE SHORT- AND LONG-RANGE CAPITAL PLAN

The balance sheet is often referred to as a summary of the capital structure of a business. In fact, the balance sheet provides only a temporary picture of this structure, which can change dramatically in a very short time. To assess the nature and scope of a higher education institution's capital, documents summarizing history, current condition, and future plans are appropriate and informative supplements.

*Capital structure.* Reports on an institution's capital structure should address the following:

- Physical capital, which takes many forms, such as real estate, plant, equipment, and furnishings (some institutions also capitalize books, periodicals, software, and art collections)

- Unused capital (from gifts or reserves available for future use)

- Short-term cash-equivalent investments

- Unrestricted and restricted working capital

- Endowment (investment) capital and unrestricted funds functioning as endowment or designated investment capital

- Short- and long-term loan capital (the latter in the form of bond issues), long-term lines of credit

- Student loan capital

FIGURE 8-3
Components of Revenue from and on behalf of Students

    Tuition and fees revenue

+    Student-derived auxiliary enterprises revenue (principally housing, food services, and bookstore revenue)

=    Gross revenue *from* students

+    Government appropriations in lieu of tuition

=    Adjusted gross revenue *from* students

-    Scholarships, fellowships, student aid (unrestricted and restricted from all sources)

=    Net revenue *from* students

+    Restricted revenue from private gifts and grants for scholarships and student aid

+    Restricted endowment payout for scholarships and student aid

+    Restricted federal, state, and local students aid grants

=    Net revenue *from and on behalf of* students

-    Allowances for questionable current receivables and bad student loans

=    Adjusted net revenue *from and on behalf of* students

Note: To the extent that College-Work Study wages are included in a student's aid package, and when student loans are reduced or forgiven (not counting allowances for bad debt), appropriate adjustments to the formula can and should be made.

The capital management responsibility lies with the institution's governing board, president, and chief financial or business officer.

*Reporting on management of physical capital.* The management of physical capital entails financial, business, and engineering skills. Certain background information regarding physical capital is needed in a comprehensive managerial financial reporting scheme, including:

• Historical inventory of real estate, plant, furnishings, and equipment, including original cost, value of improvements since acquisition, and fair market or present replacement value

- Description of condition of facilities and equipment, including repair and replacement schedules and dollar estimates

- Estimates of "implied" depreciation cost, assuming appropriate useful life for plant and equipment, taking into account technological or educational obsolescence

- Plans for future physical capital requirements not related to past acquisitions

This information serves as a basis for formulating a long-term capital maintenance plan, a long-range capital plan, and the ensuing financing mechanisms to implement them. Not every aspect of these plans will be implemented; therefore old plans should be updated periodically and amended to reflect any "unfinished business." The management objective for existing physical capital is to minimize or eliminate any kind of deferred maintenance.

***Reporting on management of endowment capital.*** The management of endowment and similar funds is generally acknowledged to belong to the governing board. Endowment management is not merely a reporting issue but a major policy issue that focuses on payout policy. Is the endowment payout keeping pace with general inflation or the specific cost inflation to which the institution is exposed? Figure 8-4 sketches a historical table that may assist managers in tracking the answer.

Endowment investment reporting has tended to focus on the relatively few "endowed" institutions, which are only a small portion of the more than 3,000 higher education institutions in the U.S. As a result, many colleges and universities with relatively small endowments (less than $10 million) view endowment investment reporting as a minor matter. Modern investment management techniques and reporting practices should be applied regardless of an endowment's size. (For a full discussion of endowments, see Chapter 10, Endowment Management.)

## DEBT MANAGEMENT

In its broadest sense, managerial financial reporting on debt manage-

FIGURE 8-4

Measure of Endowment Purchasing Power over Time

    Base-year endowment capital at market

+    Current additions to endowment from gifts, bequests, etc.

+    Current earnings (dividends, interest, net appreciation)

-    Endowment payout

=    Year-end market value of endowment

-    Inflation effect (using HEPI, Consumer Price Index (CPI), or individual institution's inflation index)

=    Constant-dollar value of endowment

Note: There is widespread agreement that investment results alone may not be sufficient to shelter endowment capital from inflationary erosion; gifts and bequests can be used as anti-inflation protection.

ment should focus on all of the liabilities of the institution, regardless of the fund in which they are located. As far as the current fund is concerned, the evolution of receivables must be part of any analysis, because they lead to short-term borrowing. When receivables increase, debt rises. Worse, debt that appears as a short-term liability may turn into a quasi-permanent liability. Some institutions transfer such indebtedness into the plant fund. Managerial financial reporting can define these problems.

Long-term indebtedness usually arises from the financing of plant; it also arises from bond issues that support institutional student-loan funds, which are becoming more common. Basic financial statements detail debt burden, debt service, and debt maturities, but there is no consensus on an acceptable level of long-term debt in higher education. The issue is not solely an internal matter: the financial rating of colleges by external firms is a concern of managerial financial reporting. (For a full discussion of debt, see Chapter 12, Debt Financing and Management.)

## MANAGING, PLANNING, AND REPORTING FOR THE LONG RUN

Long-range managerial financial reporting enables a college or university to indicate in as much detail as necessary (or desired) its mission, strategies, and action plans for future years. The financial plan is a subset of the institution's program and facilities plan. Because the execution of the program plan is constrained by available resources, the two major issues of long-range financial planning are best defined under the headings of "adequacy of capital" and "adequacy of revenues."

***Adequacy of capital.*** If an enterprise decides to stay in business over the long run, it must generate sufficient income to pay for its fixed and variable costs. The expression "long run" has come to mean that fixed costs are covered by income.

Many colleges and universities are undercapitalized, that is, they do not possess the capital resources needed to function efficiently and effectively within their individually articulated missions and plans. One problem lies in the fact that the higher education industry does not work with norms that define adequacy of physical capital, meaning that

- current revenues are inadequate to cover routine maintenance and replacement costs, leading to a buildup of deferred maintenance;

- capital consumption (obsolescence, deterioration) is not included in the cost of capital, therefore current revenues are not expected to cover it; and

- existing capital is either unavailable or technologically obsolete.

Deferred maintenance, depreciation, and obsolescence are so widespread in higher education that the industry cannot be called a going concern in the long run, because revenues are not consistently large enough to support fixed (or capital) costs. Thus, an essential step in financial long-range planning is to attempt to define an institution's "capital deficit" — not necessarily to set it as a practical planning goal but to establish financial benchmarks.

This approach can be of strategic importance for an institution. For example, physical capital represents a significant aspect of an institution's program quality. The working condition of the physical capital has an effect on quality. Institutions must have the appropriate physical capital in good working order. This is not merely a long-range planning issue but a strategic concern: adequacy and condition of the physical plant are major factors in positioning an institution with regard to other institutions.

***Adequacy of revenues.*** The issue of financial adequacy over the long run with respect to an institution's academic program has two dimensions:

- Long-range support of the existing program

- Long-range support of a dynamic, changing program

Inherent in any situation is "unfinished business," which refers to the plans of an institution, already in progress, that may be left unfinished or undone at various stages of execution. Because institutional management is a continuing chain of incremental actions, "next-step planning" is a logical option, especially since most comprehensive institutional plans are implemented gradually.

Although spreadsheets and projections are useful communication tools, narratives and supporting documentation are an essential aspect of managerial financial reporting within the long-range planning context.

Institutions that engage in long-range planning know that planning for expenditures differs from planning for revenues. Assumptions about future revenues define and limit future expenditures. Furthermore, revenues tend to fluctuate from year to year. The success or failure of financial long-range planning depends more on revenue than on expenditure planning. Expenditure planning comes rather easily. Revenue planning is true performance planning: there is no plan without the revenues.

The focus in financial planning must be on the major revenue sources. Financial long-range planning stresses:

- Enrollment management

- Government relations with respect to appropriations and grants

- Student aid policies

- Endowment capital development

- Private gift and grant development

- Cost-effective management of auxiliary enterprises and hospitals, emphasizing the optimization of net revenues

By identifying their particular major revenue sources, colleges and universities can develop the most realistic revenue plans, to which they can subordinate expenditure aspirations. In the final analysis, the revenue capacity determines whether or not a college or university will remain a financially viable institution as well as one that achieves its highest educational aspirations.

## Summary

The traditional financial statements, particularly those relating to the yearly audit, represent a mere beginning to managerial financial reporting, which depends upon a careful and ongoing analysis of an institution's direct financial components and of all managerial decisions that lead to significant financial consequences.

Managerial financial reporting encompasses the transformation of accounting information and the identification of financial and nonfinancial data. Research and analysis of data are important elements, as are modeling and simulation.

Because the ultimate objective of managerial financial reporting is to monitor and improve managerial performance, and because management decisions with financial effects tend to be highly decentralized in higher education, managerial financial reporting is, for the most part, operational reporting. Thus, it is upward and sideward reporting. It also is result-centered reporting for the institution as a whole. In the final analysis, however, operational reporting should bear the most fruitful results.

The examples and lists of reports provided in this chapter should be viewed as illustrations. College and university financial and business officers are aware of a variety of reports that come across their desks or are found in the professional literature. Each one has invented, adopted, and adapted reports based on what he or she has seen and read. Peer example is always a good instructor, and individual initiative, where it is allowed, is the most promising road to innovation and diversity.

## Notes

1. This chapter is adapted from *Financial Accounting and Reporting Manual for Higher Education* (Washington, D.C.: NACUBO, 1990), Chapter 7, Managerial Financial Reporting; and James A. Hyatt, *Presentation and Analysis of Financial Management Information* (Washington, D.C.: NACUBO, 1989).

2. What should be reported, how to structure reports, or what media to use when reporting will depend on institutional needs and preferences. *Presentation and Analysis of Financial Management Information* provides more than 100 financial management report illustrations. The suggestions contained in this chapter should be viewed as illustrations.

3. Most financial surveys focus on functional expenditures rather than major line-item expenditures for key functions. The structures of line-item expenditures vary by function and among institutions.

# References and Resources

Chamberlain, Don, and Relmond VanDaniker. "Service Efforts and Accomplishments Reporting." *Business Officer* 24, no. 1 (July, 1990): 32-36.

Financial Accounting Standards Board. Statement of Financial Accounting Concepts No. 2, *Qualitative Characteristics of Accounting Information*. Stamford, Conn.: FASB, 1980.

Gordon, Teresa P., and Mary Fischer. "Reporting Performance: Using Financial and Nonfinancial Data." *Business Officer* 24, no. 1 (July, 1990): 28-31.

Hansen, D. R. *Management Accounting*. Boston, Mass.: PWS-Kent Publishing Co., 1990.

Hyatt, James A. *Presentation and Analysis of Financial Management Information*. Washington, D.C.: NACUBO, 1989.

National Association of College and University Business Officers and Association of Governing Boards of Universities and Colleges. *Financial Responsibilities of Governing Boards of Colleges and Universities*. 2nd ed. Washington, D.C.: NACUBO and AGB, 1985.

National Association of College and University Business Officers. *Financial Self-Assessment: A Workbook for Colleges and Universities*. 2nd ed. Washington, D.C.: NACUBO, 1987.

Peat, Marwick, Mitchell & Co. *Ratio Analysis in Higher Education: A Guide to Assessing the Institution's Financial Condition*. New York: Peat, Marwick, Mitchell & Co., 1988.

# CHAPTER 9

# Taxation

by
Kaye B. Ferriter
Coopers & Lybrand

Bruce R. Hopkins
Steptoe & Johnson

Elyse I. Summers
Steptoe & Johnson

# Sponsor

## KPMG PEAT MARWICK

345 Park Avenue
New York, NY 10154
212-758-9700

*KPMG Peat Marwick assists clients with matters pertaining to employee benefits, independent contractors, unrelated business income tax, and maximization of donor deductions in capital campaigns.*

# Contents

## 9: Taxation

C olleges and universities, though generally exempt from federal income tax, face a panoply of taxation issues that are of particular importance and relevance to institutional financial and business officers.[1] These issues include the maintenance, through proper and conscientious organization and operation, of a college or university's tax-exempt status; the treatment and reporting of charitable contributions; the treatment of income derived from activities unrelated to the pursuit of the exempt educational purpose of a college or university (i.e., unrelated business income); the tax treatment of faculty housing and tuition remission; and the compliance responsibilities with respect to employment and state and local taxes. In an era of growing federal and state budget deficits, colleges and universities face increased scrutiny from taxing authorities at all levels of government.

This chapter is intended to provide a broad overview of many of the tax-related issues that are of concern to higher education institutions. Many of the following topics are the subjects of entire books. The scope of this chapter does not permit a detailed discussion of any one.

## Obtaining and Retaining Tax-Exempt Status

For a college or university to receive recognition of its tax-exempt status from the Internal Revenue Service (IRS), the institution must be organized and operated primarily for exempt purposes as described in Internal Revenue Code (IRC) section 501(c)(3). Independent institutions must seek recognition under IRC section 501(c)(3); public institutions, already "passively" exempt as state institutions under section 115, may choose to apply for recognition under section 501(c)(3). Exempt purposes recognized by the IRC and the Treasury regulations promulgated thereunder include religious, educational, literary, and/or scientific objectives.[2] To be exempt as an organization described in IRC 501(c)(3), an institution must meet two tests: an organizational test and an operational test.

The organizational test requires that an institution's articles of incorporation limit its purposes to one or more exempt purposes and do not "expressly empower the organization to engage, otherwise than as an insubstantial part of its activities, in activities which in themselves are not in furtherance of one or more exempt purposes."[3] Organizational documents that mandate or allow a substantial involvement in lobbying or activities unrelated to an exempt purpose may preclude an organization from receiving tax-exempt status as a charitable organization or cause an organization to lose its charitable exempt status.

The operational test requires that an institution be "operated exclusively" for one or more of its stated exempt purposes, which is defined by the Treasury and consistently interpreted by the courts to mean "primarily."[4] Therefore, for example, lobbying and unrelated business activities (discussed below) will not cause an exempt organization to lose its status unless they become substantial in relationship to the overall activities of the organization.

An institution of higher education may be recognized as either a tax-exempt "charitable" organization (insofar as the definition of "charitable" includes the "advancement of education") or an educational organization (which "normally maintains a regular faculty and curriculum and normally has a regularly enrolled body of pupils or students in attendance at the place where its educational activities are regularly carried on").[5] An organization may be educational even though it advocates a particular position or viewpoint so long as it presents a sufficiently full and fair exposition of the pertinent facts as to permit an individual or the public to form an independent opinion or conclusion.[6] An organization is not educational if its principal function is the mere presentation of unsupported opinion.[7]

## INUREMENT

As stated above, to qualify for and maintain exemption as a charitable organization, an entity must be both organized and operated for exempt purposes. As part of this requirement, the IRC provides that no part of the net earnings of a charitable organization can inure to the benefit of any private shareholder or individual.[8] Moreover, the Treasury regulations state that an organization is not organized and operated exclusively for one or more exempt purposes unless it serves a public rather than a private interest.[9] Thus, to meet this requirement, an organization must prove that it is not organized or operated for the benefit of private interests such as designated individuals, the creator or his or her family, shareholders of the organization, or any other persons. The concept of private inurement, although it lacks precise definition, is broad. The IRS has stated that "[i]nurement is likely to arise where the financial benefit represents a transfer of the organization's financial resources to an individual solely by virtue of the individual's relationship with the organization, and without regard to accomplishing exempt purposes."[10] The IRS has also stated that the "inurement issue . . . focuses on benefits conferred on an organization's insiders through the use or distribution of the organization's financial resources."[11] The essence of the concept is to ensure that an exempt charitable organization is serving a public and not a private interest.[12]

The IRS has stated that, as a general rule, "[a]n organization's trustees, officers, members, founders, or contributors may not, by reason of their position, acquire any of its funds."[13] Stating the proposition another way, the IRS has observed that "[t]he prohibition of inurement, in its simplest terms, means that a private shareholder or individual cannot pocket the organization's funds except as reasonable payment for goods or services."[14] The existence of private inurement can lead to the revocation of an institution's tax exemption.

Obviously, employees of educational institutions are entitled to reasonable compensation for services rendered; such payments do not constitute inurement. However, excessive compensation can result in a finding of private inurement. The question of whether compensation is reasonable is a question to be decided in the context of each case, taking into account the experience, skills, and services provided by the individual, as well as the compensation paid to employees performing comparable services elsewhere. In making the determination of whether compensation is reasonable, all elements of the compensation package must be considered, including salary and fringe benefits, such as automobiles, employee benefit plans, below-market loans, and relocation allowances. Compensation arrangements must be carefully evaluated. If uniform performance standards are used to evaluate employees and to justify compensation, private inurement generally does not exist. Moreover, an educational institution making grants and providing scholarships may wish to review procedures for awarding them to ensure that certain individuals do not receive preferential treatment and, therefore, directly or indirectly receive a private benefit.

The possibility of private inurement also arises if an institution is involved in partnerships or other joint ventures with individuals and other nonexempt entities. Such activities may be impermissible inurement if the nonexempt participant in a joint arrangement with a tax-exempt entity receives an unreasonable and more-than-incidental benefit at the expense of the college or university.

POLITICAL CAMPAIGN ACTIVITIES

A college or university cannot qualify for or maintain tax-exempt status as a charitable organization if it participates or intervenes in any political campaign on behalf of, or in opposition to, any candidate for public office. This prohibition has been interpreted by the IRS to be absolute.

A political expenditure is any amount paid or incurred by a college or university in connection with any participation or intervention in any political campaign on behalf of or in opposition to any candidate for public office. Intervention includes the publication or distribution of statements opposing or supporting a candidate. (Intervention does not include the participation by students in a political campaign of their choosing in satisfaction of the requirements of a political science course, nor does it include positions taken by a student newspaper that is run by students as an educational endeavor.[15]) An institution that participates in a political campaign on behalf of or in opposition to a candidate for public office may, in addition to losing its tax-exempt status, expose itself to tax liability in the amount of an initial tax equal to 10 percent of the amount of the political expenditure.

An expenditure may be "corrected" by recovery of the expenditure to the extent possible, establishment of safeguards to prevent future political expenditures, and other additional action provided for under Treasury regulations. If the political expenditure is not corrected within a prescribed period, the institution may face an additional tax equal to 100 percent of the amount involved in the political campaign expenditure.

In addition to the revocation of an institution's exemption for participating in political campaign activities, severe penalties may be imposed on the individuals involved in approving or participating in political campaign activity on behalf of the institution. A college or university administrator who knowingly agrees to such expenditure may be subject to a tax equal to 2.5 percent of the political expenditure. This tax is paid by the administrator. There is a reasonable cause exception to this general rule.

A second tax in the amount of 50 percent of the political campaign expenditure may be assessed if the administrator refuses to agree to a correction of the initial expenditure. Again, this tax is paid by the administrator. The maximum taxes are $5,000 and $10,000, respectively, for the first and second levels of liability.

## LOBBYING

A college or university cannot qualify as, and may lose its status as, a tax-exempt charitable organization if it engages in more than an insubstantial amount of lobbying activities. The term "insubstantial" has never been defined precisely by either the courts or the IRS.

In reaction to this uncertainty, Congress enacted IRC section 501(h) in 1976 to help clarify the situation. Institutions may elect to be governed by the provisions of section 501(h). These guidelines define permissible ranges of legislative activities in terms of expenditures of funds and sliding scales of percentages. Entities that do not make the election provided for in IRC section 501(h) continue to be governed by the "insubstantial part" test. Because lobbying is usually insignificant in terms of the overall programmatic activities pursued by a college or university, it may be in the interest of most institutions to choose to be governed by the insubstantial part test, notwithstanding its inherent uncertainty.

"Safe harbor" guidelines under section 501(h) are set out in terms of declining percentages of total expenditures. (In this case, the safe harbor guidelines describe acceptable types and amounts of an activity or activities; if the guidelines are not adhered to, an organization will face a penalty—taxes.) The annual level of expenditures for legislative activities is fixed at 20 percent of the first $500,000 of an organization's exempt purpose expenditures, 15 percent of the next $500,000, 10 percent of the next $500,000, and 5 percent of any remaining expenditures. However, in no event may the expenditures in any one taxable year for legislative activities made by a public charity exceed $1,000,000. Grass-roots lobbying (i.e., lobbying of the general public as opposed to lobbying of a legislative body or regulatory agency) expenditures are limited to 25 percent of the amounts derived under the above formula.

A charitable organization that has made the election under section 501(h) and that exceeds the limitations is subject to an excise tax of 25 percent of the excess lobbying expenditures. If an electing organization's lobbying expenditures exceed 150 percent of either the lobbying limit or the grass-roots limit over a four-year period, it may lose its tax-exempt status.

The term "influencing legislation" is defined to mean any attempt to influence any legislation through an attempt to affect the opinions of the general public or segments thereof, and through communication with any member or employee of a legislative body or any other governmental official or employee who participates in formulation of the legislation. Exclusions from the definition of influencing legislation are provided for five types of activities:

- Making available the results of nonpartisan analysis, study, or research

- Providing technical advice to a governmental body in response to a written request

- Appearing before or communicating with any legislative body with respect to a possible decision of that body that may affect the existence of the organization, its powers, its duties, its tax-exempt status, or the deduction of contributions

- Communicating with the organization's bona fide members with respect to legislation or proposed legislation of direct interest to them, provided that the communication does not directly encourage the members to influence legislation or directly encourage the members to urge nonmembers to influence legislation

- Communicating with nonlegislative government officials or employees

## Charitable Contributions

Charitable contributions are a key source of revenue for many colleges and universities.[16] Therefore, it is important for institutions to be aware of the charitable contribution reporting and documentation requirements that affect their donors. Two areas of particular concern for universities are the treatment of noncash property donations and the implications of certain fund-raising efforts.

Certain reporting requirements exist with respect to the donation of noncash property. If an individual or partnership donates noncash property worth more than $500, the donor is obligated to complete and attach IRS Form 8283, *Non-cash Charitable Contributions*, to his or her tax return to claim a contribution deduction. Corporations making noncash contributions of $5,000 or more are also subject to this requirement. In addition, a noncash contribution by any taxpayer in excess of $5,000 requires acknowledgment of receipt by the institution on Form 8283 and, in many cases, requires certification by a qualified appraiser. The donee's signature on Form 8283 merely acknowledges receipt of the donation and does not constitute agreement with the donor's stated valuation.

Charitable organizations, including colleges and universities, that dispose of noncash contributions worth more than $500 within two years of receipt are required to file IRS Form 8282, *Donee Information Return*. The form is due within 125 days of disposition. The donor must receive a copy of the form. An exception to this filing requirement is property that is given away or used by the institution in furtherance of its tax-exempt purpose. A disposition of property that occurs within two years of receipt by the institution, for an amount substantially less than that claimed by the donor on the occurrence of the original donation, may cause the IRS to challenge the original valuation of the gift.

Colleges and universities are advised to exercise caution when accepting gifts of property that may have significant costs, either in the form of recurring costs such as insurance and real property taxes or in the form of huge one-time outlays, such as the cost of cleaning up a hazardous work site. They should also be aware of potential unrelated business income when accepting gifts of partnership interests.

With respect to fund-raising, the IRS is concerned about fund-raising practices that allow contributors the opportunity to obtain something of value while taking a charitable deduction for the full amount paid. Under federal tax law, a charitable contribution deduction must be reduced by the fair market value of any benefit received. For example, if a college or university holds a raffle, a raffle ticket purchaser may be tempted to claim a deduction for the amount paid for the ticket because the payment is made to a charitable organization. However, no deduction would be allowed in that instance because the purchaser is buying a chance to win something. Alternatively, where an amount paid exceeds the value of the thing received, the taxpayer may take a deduction for the difference. For example, if a taxpayer pays $75 for a ticket to a benefit dinner and the actual value of the dinner is $50, the taxpayer is entitled to a deduction for the amount that exceeds the $50 value of the meal, in this case $25. Tax-exempt organizations are encouraged to inform donors of the tax-deductible amount of a contribution.

The IRS has issued guidelines that govern the issue of providing a token item in return for a contribution. Generally, items costing $5 or less (indexed for inflation) are covered by a *de minimis* rule and need not be used to reduce the amount of a donation. Moreover, items bearing the college or university's logo, such as T-shirts, calendars, or key chains, do not generally reduce the amount of the deductible contribution if the donation is $25 (indexed for inflation) or more. In addition, the amount of the donation is not reduced if the fair market value of the benefit received in the form of a token gift does not exceed the lesser of 2 percent of the donation or $50.

To meet the IRS rules for token benefits, colleges and universities are required to communicate both the deductible and nondeductible portion of donations in all solicitations, including written, broadcast, and telephone materials. In situations where only insubstantial benefits are provided by the institution, the IRS suggests that the following disclosure statement be provided in any solicitation materials: "Under Internal Revenue Service guidelines, the estimated value of the benefits received is not substantial; therefore, the full amount of your payment is a deductible contribution."

## Unrelated Business Income Tax

Colleges and universities, though otherwise tax-exempt, are required to pay federal income tax on their unrelated business income.[17] For the unrelated business income tax (UBIT) to apply, the following three conditions must be met:

- The activity earning income must be a trade or business.

- The trade or business must be carried on regularly.

- The trade or business must not be substantially related to the college or university's exempt purposes.

For UBIT purposes, a trade or business includes any activity undertaken to produce income, regardless of whether it is profitable. Whether an activity is "regularly carried on" depends on the frequency and continuity with which the activity is conducted. Ordinarily, an activity is not substantially related to a college or university's exempt purpose if there is no causal relationship between the activity and the achievement of the institution's exempt purpose.

There are a number of circumstances, the "UBIT exceptions," in which certain income-producing activities are statutorily exempt from the imposition of UBIT, notwithstanding that the activities are, in fact, unrelated. These include:

- The volunteer exception: This may occur when substantially all of the work performed in pursuit of the unrelated activity is done by volunteers.

- The donated goods exception: This may occur when the unrelated income derived from a particular activity is from the sale of merchandise, substantially all of which was donated to the college or university.

- The convenience exception: This may occur when the trade or business is conducted by the college or university primarily for the convenience of its members, patrons, visitors, officers, or employees.

- The research exception: Income derived from the performance of basic research is generally excludable from UBIT.

Another exception to UBIT involves the exchange or rental of donor membership lists between tax-exempt charitable organizations. Though "unrelated" in the ordinary sense of the word, this activity has been held by the IRS and the courts not to generate UBIT. In addition, there are specific exclusions from UBIT for certain types of passive income, such as rents, royalties, dividends, interest, annuities, securities, loans, and capital gains.

In the situations that give rise to UBIT, taxable income generally is gross income from all of an organization's unrelated trade or businesses, less allowable deductions directly connected with the conduct of these activities. In addition, there are several other allowable deductions:

- A specific deduction of $1,000

- A deduction for net operating loss carryforwards

- A deduction for charitable contributions

If facilities and personnel are used for both exempt functions and unrelated business activities, expenses, depreciation, and similar items such as overhead must be allocated between the exempt and the taxable activities. This allocation is necessary to determine the net income from the unrelated business activity. For example, if an employee of a college or university spends 10 percent of his or her time on an unrelated business activity, 10 percent of his or her salary and benefits should be allocated as a deduction against the unrelated activity.

Where dual use of a facility occurs, the expenses associated with operating the facility must be allocated between both uses, according to the following formula:

$$\frac{\text{Number of hours facility used for unrelated purposes}}{\text{Total number of hours facility used for unrelated and related purposes}^{18}} \quad X \quad \begin{array}{l}\text{Expenses associated with operating the facility}\end{array}$$

## ADVERTISING

Income from advertising is generally taxable as unrelated business income. Colleges and universities typically solicit and feature advertising in their periodicals and sports programs. One court has held that advertising in collegiate sports programs for events that are conducted for only a few weeks each year, such as the National Collegiate Athletic Association basketball tournament, is not regularly carried on and, therefore, does not result in unrelated business income.[19] However, it should be noted that the IRS has publicly disavowed the court's holding.[20]

Income from a publication is categorized either as gross advertising income or circulation income. Circulation income is all income other than advertising income realized from the publication, its circulation, or its distribution. Expenses are divided into direct advertising costs and readership costs. If direct advertising costs exceed gross advertising income, the loss is recognized for tax purposes and may be used to offset other sources of unrelated business income. If gross advertising income exceeds direct advertising costs, the institution may compare circulation income to readership costs. If circulation income is greater than readership costs, the taxable income is the gross advertising income less direct advertising costs. If readership costs exceed circulation income, the excess readership costs may affect the previously computed income from advertising.

## RENTAL INCOME

Many colleges and universities rent housing, tennis facilities, skating rinks, stadiums, and chapels to alumni and others. Although rental income is specifically excluded from unrelated business income tax, it is taxable if:

- fifty percent or more of the rent is for personal property;
- the rent is tied in whole or part to the income or profits derived by the lessee;
- the property is "debt-financed property" and not used in an exempt activity; or
- significant services are provided.

In general, the lease or rental of property to the general public is excluded from UBIT as passive income. Rents based on a fixed percentage of net income or profits are not excluded from UBIT. (Otherwise, an institution could use a net profit rental agreement to operate an unrelated trade or business and disguise taxable profits as tax-free rents.) However, rents based on a fixed percentage of gross receipts or sales are excluded. If a substantial portion (more than 15 percent but less than 50 percent) of rental income is from the rental of personal property, the proceeds attributable to the use of personal property are unrelated business income.

For purposes of the rental exclusion, certain services may be provided without tax implications as long as they are customarily rendered in connection with the lease of the facility. Such services include:

- Furnishing of heat, light, and other utilities
- Provision of security
- The cleaning and maintenance of public areas
- The collection of trash

If additional services are provided that are primarily for the convenience of the user and not customarily rendered, the entire amount received from the party receiving the services is considered unrelated business income because the institution is viewed as conducting a service business. Some examples of services that may give rise to unrelated business taxable income are:

- Maid service
- Extensive grounds and playing field maintenance
- The provision of towels, linens, or laundry service
- The provision of food, beverage, or other catering services
- Video or audio production services
- Valet parking
- The resurfacing of an ice rink
- Lifeguard services at swimming pools

ROYALTIES

A royalty is a fee for the license of a property right such as a patent, copyright, or mineral interest. Royalties are generally excluded from UBIT. However, a distinction must be made between royalties and personal property rents. Many institutions allow others to use their donor lists for a fee. Is the income unrelated business income or is it excluded as a royalty for the use of the institution's name? The IRS tends to treat mailing list rental or sales proceeds as unrelated business income if a tax-exempt charity and a noncharity enter into such an agreement.

## CREDIT CARDS

Some colleges and universities offer specially designed bank credit cards, called "affinity cards," to alumni. The institution receives payments from the issuing bank, in the form of either a flat fee or a percentage of purchases charged by the user of the affinity credit card. The IRS has indicated that such arrangements are analogous to providing membership lists to a commercial organization and, thus, are taxable transactions. That is, the net income from these activities constitutes unrelated business income.

## BOOKSTORES

Net income from the operation of a college or university bookstore is generally not unrelated business income because it serves the educational purposes and programs of the institution. However, employing the "fragmentation rule," the IRS will analyze the overall operation of the bookstore as well as each activity and product line to determine whether or not it is related to the accomplishment of the institution's exempt purposes. For example, sales of computers by a college bookstore may generate unrelated business income if the sales are not limited to students and faculty members or if multiple purchases are allowed. Moreover, the convenience exception has been held by the IRS to be limited to nondurable goods (for example, soap and toothpaste) with a useful life of one year or less, rendering sales of certain items, such as stereos and nonlogo clothing, tax-generating events.

## ATHLETIC FACILITIES

Many colleges and universities lease their athletic facilities to outside promoters for athletic and other entertainment events. In a situation where a college or university rents its sports facilities to an outsider and the use of the facility includes operation by employees of the institution's athletic department, the college or university is engaged in an unrelated trade or business. As alluded to above, the provision of substantial services by institutional employees would render this situation a taxable event, not covered by the general UBIT exclusion for income received from the rental of real property. Alternatively, if an institution leases facilities for a fixed fee to an unrelated individual or entity that operates a club for the public, but the institution provides no services (such as food, security, maintenance, or laundry), the rental income is excluded from UBIT under the general exception for rent from real property.

Another common activity of colleges and universities that may be subject to UBIT is the provision of health club facilities to those beyond the student, faculty, and employee population, such as alumni and the general community. Alumni are considered by the IRS to be the "general public" for purposes of determining whether users are members of the college or university community covered by the convenience exception.

## DAY CARE

Income from the operation of a day-care center may qualify for exclusion from UBIT if the center is operated primarily for the convenience of employees of the college or university, faculty members, and students or if it is operated as an integral part of the institution's educational program. On the other hand, if a college or university runs a day-care center for unrelated third parties (and none of the other exceptions apply), the income generated is probably subject to UBIT, unless it can be proved under IRC section 501(k) that substantially all of the care provided is for the purposes of enabling individuals to be gainfully employed and the services are available to the general public.

## RADIO AND TELEVISION

A college or university may operate a radio or television station as an activity in furtherance of its exempt, educational purpose, if the raison d'etre of such a station is to offer students education and training in the broadcasting industry and it is not run in a commercial way. The revenue generated by a radio or television station operated in such a manner does not constitute unrelated business taxable income. However, the operation of a radio or television station by a college or university may be an unrelated trade or business if the station is operated purely as a commercial enterprise with little teaching or training involved.

## INVESTMENTS IN PARTNERSHIPS

The investment in a partnership by a college or university may give rise to unrelated business income, regardless of the tax status of the other partners. The test here, as in all other unrelated business income determinations, goes to the nature of the activity pursued by the partnership. If the partnership is involved in an activity that would be an unrelated trade or business activity if it were directly carried on by the college or university, the participation by the college or university in such a partnership does nothing to change the character of the activity carried on by the partnership. Therefore, an institution's allocable share of gross income from a partnership pursuing an unrelated activity constitutes unrelated business taxable income. Even if the income earned by a partnership would otherwise be exempt from UBIT, it will not be exempt if the income is earned by a "publicly traded partnership" and if the partnership has interests that are traded on an established securities market or on a secondary market. Partnerships must report unrelated business income information to all tax-exempt partners.

## LENDING SECURITIES

In an effort to enhance their financial cushion in hard economic times, many colleges and universities undertake sophisticated financial transactions, including those involving securities. An issue that frequently arises is whether securities lending creates debt-financed income that is taxable as unrelated business income. Where an institution uses its own assets as collateral to borrow stock that it has sold short, and the value of the collateral equals the fair market value of the borrowed stock, the transaction does not result in unrelated business income. However, if the borrowing is not fully collateralized, the income derived from the short sale is taxable.

## LIFE INSURANCE POLICIES

An institution may receive deductible contributions by being the named beneficiary on a donor's life insurance policy. In this case, the contributor pays the annual premiums on the donated policies. As a means to significantly increase its revenue, the donee institution can withdraw the accumulated cash value, paying approximately 5 percent in interest per year to the insurance company while earning over 10 percent on the reinvestment of this cash in marketable securities.

Ordinarily, passive investment income such as interest and dividends is excluded from unrelated business income and, therefore, is not taxable. However, it has been held by the IRS that, because insurance policy loans have generally been regarded as a valid form of indebtedness, the income earned through the reinvestment is unrelated business income to a college or university.

## AUXILIARY ENTERPRISES

Auxiliary enterprises do not generate unrelated business income if they serve the educational purposes of the institution. As alluded to above, if a college or university opens its auxiliary enterprises to the public, it should be aware of the existence of potential generation of unrelated business income.

## DEBT-FINANCED PROPERTY

Income received from debt-financed property is generally subject to UBIT. This includes dividends, interest, royalties, and rents derived from property that is subject to an indebtedness, as well as gains from the sale of a capital asset that is subject to an indebtedness at any time during the 12 months prior to the sale. The amount of debt-financed income recognized as UBIT is determined by the ratio of debt outstanding during the year and the tax basis for a property. The following are specifically excluded from treatment as "debt-financed property":

- Any property that is substantially related to the college or university's educational purpose

- Any property that is already treated as unrelated business income

- Any property that is used in a trade or business in a manner covered by one of the exceptions discussed above, including the volunteer exception, the research exception, the convenience exception, and the donated property exception[21]

## FOR-PROFIT SUBSIDIARIES

Many institutions have wholly owned, for-profit subsidiaries that operate unrelated activities. If a college or university causes a wholly owned, for-profit subsidiary to incorporate and capitalize a network of taxable subsidiaries, the activities of the subsidiaries do not jeopardize the parent's exempt status. Institutions that have multiple for-profit subsidiaries should consider having them all owned by a single for-profit holding company, so that losses of one subsidiary might offset the income of another. In addition, the existence of any number of financial relationships may give rise to unrelated business income in the parent. For example, the fact that a subsidiary may be allowed to use the parent's name and logo in return for royalty payments, and may pay interest on loans made by the parent, will generate unrelated business taxable income in the parent charitable organization to the extent that the subsidiary is able to benefit from the deduction of these amounts.

# Employee Benefits

To attract and retain faculty and staff, higher education institutions may offer benefits such as tuition reduction and faculty housing.

TUITION REDUCTION

Employees of educational institutions are allowed a "qualified tuition reduction."[22] A qualified tuition reduction is any amount of reduction in tuition provided to an employee of a college or university for the education of the employee, spouse, dependent children, and certain retired and disabled employees and surviving spouses. Amounts excluded from the gross income of an employee as a qualified tuition reduction are not subject to monetary limitations.

The tuition reduction benefit may also be provided to graduate students who attend a higher education institution and are engaged in teaching or research activities. However, if they do not receive fair compensation for their research or teaching, the tuition reduction may be deemed by the IRS to be disguised compensation.

To meet the qualified tuition reduction tests, the reduction must be provided to an employee or graduate student of a college or university that normally maintains a regular faculty and curriculum and normally has a regularly enrolled body of students in attendance at the place where its educational activities are regularly carried on. It is unclear whether or not institutions may have reciprocal tuition reduction agreements or provide cash payments to students to attend another institution.

The tuition reduction benefit must be available to employees on a nondiscriminatory basis in order to qualify for the exclusion from gross income of the employee. In the event that the tuition reduction program discriminates in favor of highly compensated employees or officers, such persons cannot exclude such benefits from their gross income.

FACULTY HOUSING

Another benefit for employees of educational institutions is the provision of faculty housing to the employee by the institution. Gross income of an employee does not include the value of "qualified campus lodging" furnished to that employee by the institution so long as the employee pays rent equal to at least the lesser of 5 percent of the appraised fair market value of the lodging or comparable market rate rents.[23] Qualified campus lodging is lodging that is located on or in the vicinity of the institution's campus and that is furnished to an employee, spouse, or any dependent by or on behalf of the institution for use as a residence.

The appraisal requirement does not need to be met annually; however, the appraisal must be reviewed annually. If the rental period involves one year or less, the value of the lodging may be determined at any time during the year in which the rental period begins.

# Reporting and Withholding Requirements

Most colleges and universities are required to file IRS Form 990, *Return of Organization Exempt from Tax*, each year. It must be made available for public inspection. Most public colleges and universities are not required to file Form 990.[24] In addition, every higher educational organization that earns more than $1,000 in gross unrelated business income in a year is required to file Form 990-T, *Exempt Organization's Business Income Tax Return*.

Form 990 requires detailed information on a vast variety of activities and functions, ranging from income-producing programmatic activities to the compensation of officers, directors, and trustees. It requires that the revenue of a reporting organization be broken down into the following three categories:

- Related or exempt function income
- Unrelated business income

- Income that is not exempt from tax but that is specifically excluded from treatment as unrelated business income (e.g., dividends, interest, rent, income from activities performed by volunteers or for the convenience of students or that is derived from the use of donated merchandise)

The degree of detail required to comply with this requirement makes it necessary for institutions to conduct an in-depth review of all revenue accounts. In order to complete Form 990, an institution must segregate all accounts into the three classifications listed above. In addition, an explanation is required to describe how a particular item fits a particular category. An exclusion code (provided by the IRS) is required for each category of excluded income. Unrelated income reported on the Form 990 must agree with that reported on Form 990-T.

## EMPLOYMENT TAXES

Colleges and universities are generally required to withhold federal income taxes and funds on employee wages under the Federal Insurance Contributions Act (FICA) and to remit the funds to the federal government. Public colleges and universities may be required to make payments to the state retirement system in lieu of FICA payments. The IRS has stepped up its examination and collection activity in this area, including the use of payroll audits of colleges and universities, in an effort to stem a rising tide of employment tax deficiencies. In addition, certain state and/or local taxes will likely need to be withheld from the pay of an individual determined to be an employee.

## EMPLOYEE VERSUS INDEPENDENT CONTRACTOR

A college or university that utilizes the services of both employees and independent contractors must understand and be able to communicate clearly the difference between an employee and an independent contractor. The determination is based on facts and circumstances and is based on the degree of control that the employer exercises over an individual's performance.

Adjunct faculty, for example, may be more properly classified as employees rather than as independent contractors. The following factors indicate that a college or university has the right to control and direct individuals in regard to their performance of teaching services, thereby making them employees:

- The institution provides equipment and materials.

- The institution has the ability to select textbooks.

- The institution establishes the hours of instruction.

- Courses are taught at regular intervals.

- Substitute teachers must be approved by the institution.

- The institution or the employee can terminate the relationship without incurring additional liability for compensation or to perform services.

- The services of the faculty are an integral part of the institution's business.

- Adjunct faculty teach the same courses, with the same books and under the same guidelines, as regular faculty.

Section 530 of the 1978 Revenue Act provides that, although an individual may be a common-law employee, in certain circumstances the individual is not treated as an employee for federal tax purposes. Under section 530, an institution may treat a worker as an independent contractor rather than as an employee subject to payroll tax withholding if the institution has a reasonable basis for doing so. A reasonable basis exists if the institution relies on:

- Judicial precedent, a published IRS ruling, or technical advice or a private-letter ruling addressed to the institution

- A past IRS audit that resulted in no assessment as to the institution's employment tax treatment of individuals with positions substantially similar to the position of the individual whose employee status is at issue

- A longstanding recognized practice of a significant segment of the industry in which the individual is engaged

The above exceptions to employee status do not apply to a worker if the institution has treated another worker holding a substantially similar position as an employee for tax purposes.

The IRS has become more interested in identifying misclassifications of employees as independent contractors and in that regard has begun to levy significant fines for any misclassifications.

As discussed above, where the person performing services is deemed to be an employee, the college or university must withhold a certain portion of income for federal income tax purposes and under FICA. In addition, certain state and/or local taxes will likely need to be withheld from the pay of an individual determined to be an employee. Independent contractors are subject to the self-employment tax.

## STUDENT-EMPLOYEES

Where payments constitute wages, students performing services for a college or university are generally subject to federal income tax withholding. Some students may be in a position to eliminate this tax by certifying on an annual Form W-4 that they did not incur a federal income tax liability in the prior year and that they do not anticipate such a liability in the current year.

Students who are enrolled in a college or university and are regularly attending classes are not subject to FICA withholding for amounts received for services provided to the institution during the school year.[25] In addition, the exemption from FICA may apply to students employed by certain nonprofit corporations operating in support of public or independent colleges and universities. If a student works for a college or university during the summer months and is not regularly attending classes, the payments may be subject to the FICA tax. If they are, the FICA tax must be withheld even if the student has an exemption from federal income tax withholding.

## SCHOLARSHIPS AND FELLOWSHIPS

Scholarships and fellowships are excluded from degree candidates' gross income for amounts used for tuition and course-related fees, books, supplies, and equipment; as such, they are not subject to federal or FICA withholding.[26] Thus, institutions that make such payments are not required to report them to the IRS. This exclusion does not apply to any amount received that represents payment for teaching, research, or other services as a condition for receiving the scholarship.

The student-recipient is responsible for determining whether the scholarship, in whole or in part, is included in gross income (i.e., it was not used for qualified tuition and related expenses). However, to assist students in understanding their federal tax liabilities, it is recommended that colleges and universities formally advise the recipient in writing about the tax treatment of amounts received. For example, the student should be notified that amounts granted are taxable income if the aggregate received exceeds tuition and fees (not including room and board) required for enrollment or attendance at the institution and fees, books, supplies, and equipment required for courses of instruction.

## MISCELLANEOUS REQUIREMENTS

***Nonresident aliens.*** Generally, all payments for services performed by a nonresident alien within the U.S. are subject to federal income tax withholding. Wages paid to a nonresident alien generally are subject to 30 percent withholding unless an agreement is entered into with the IRS under which graduated rates can be used. Nonwage payments are also subject to withholding, generally at 30 percent. However, the withholding rate is reduced for scholarships and fellowships received by nonresident aliens temporarily in the U.S. under "F" visas (foreign students) or "J" visas (students, scholars, trainees, teachers, or research assistants).

Payments to nonresident aliens may also qualify for an exemption from withholding or reduced withholding under a treaty between the U.S. and the nonresident alien's country of residence. The nonresident should file IRS Form 1001, *Ownership, Exemption, or Reduced Rate Certificate*, to ensure the reduced rate or exemption. The exemption generally applies only for a limited number of years.

Payments made to nonresident aliens must be reported and filed with the IRS annually on IRS Form 1042S, *Foreign Person's U.S. Source Income Subject to Withholding.*

***Wages.*** All payments that are wages must be reported on Form W-2 along with federal income tax, FICA, and state tax withholding.

***Miscellaneous income.*** Colleges and universities are required to file IRS Form 1096, *Annual Summary and Transmittal of U.S. Information Returns*, with the IRS by the last day of February each year. Form 1096 reports the total number of IRS Forms 1099 issued by the institution. Two examples of Form 1099 are Form 1099-DIV for dividend distributions and Form 1099-MISC for miscellaneous items, such as distributions of $600 or more during the calendar year in payment of rents and payments for services to a nonemployee, prizes, and awards. Form 1099-MISC is also used to report gross royalty payments of $10 or more. A Form 1099-MISC must be filed for every noncorporate provider that received $600 or more during the tax year. Thus, colleges and universities are required to file these forms for legal and accounting partnerships that provide services to the institution.

*Magnetic media.* Magnetic media reporting may be required to file information returns such as Forms W-2, 1099, and 1042S with the IRS. Acceptable forms of magnetic media are magnetic tapes; tape cartridges; 3 1/2-, 5 1/4-, or 8-inch diskettes; and electronic submission. Financial or business officers may obtain a copy of IRS Publication 1220 from their local IRS office; this publication contains specific rules and procedures governing magnetic filing. Magnetic media filing is required if an institution is required to file 250 or more information returns. The 250-or-more requirement applies separately to each type of return.

An institution must request approval from the IRS for magnetic media filing by submitting IRS Form 4419, *Application for Filing Information Returns Magnetically/Electronically.* The application must be filed at least 30 days before the due date of a return. The IRS will reply with additional instructions within 30 days and will send a package including labels and transmittals.

An institution may request a waiver from the magnetic media filing requirements by submitting IRS Form 8508, *Request for Waiver from Filing Information Returns on Magnetic Media.* A waiver request must be filed 45 days before the due date of a return.

Failure to file information returns through magnetic media without an approved waiver may result in a penalty of $50 per information return.

# Notes

1. Higher education institutions are exempt from federal income tax under the Internal Revenue Code of 1986, as amended, section 501(a), as charitable organiza-

tions described in IRC section 501(c)(3) or as political subdivisions described in IRC section 115. This latter exception is available only for public institutions.

2. IRC section 501(c)(3) and Treasury regulation 1.501(c)(3)-1(d)(1)(i).

3. Treasury regulation 1.501(c)(3)-1(b)(1)(i)(a) and 1.501(c)(3)-1(b)(1)(b)

4. Treasury regulation 1.501(c)(3)-1(c)(1) and *Better Business Bureau v. United States* (326 U.S. 279 (1945)).

5. Treasury regulations 1.501(c)(3)-1(d)(2) and 1.501(c)(3)-1(d)(3)(ii)(1).

6. Treasury regulation 1.501(c)(3)-1(d)(3)(b).

7. Treasury regulation 1.501(c)(3)-1(d)(3)(b).

8. IRC section 501(c)(3).

9. Treasury regulation 1.501(c)(3)-1(d)(1)(ii).

10. GCM 38459.

11. GCM 38459, citing *Kemper Military School v. Crutchley*, 273 F. Supp. 125 (W.D. Mo. 1921).

12. *Ginsburg v. Commissioner*, 46 T.C. 47 (1966); Rev. Rul. 76-206, 1976-1 C.B. 154.

13. IRS Exempt Organizations Handbook (IRM 7751), section 381.1(1).

14. IRS Exempt Organizations Handbook (IRM 7751), section 381.1(3).

15. Rev. Rul. 72-512, 1972-2 C.B. 246 and Rev. Rul. 72-513, 1972-2 C.B. 246.

16. IRC section 170 and the regulations promulgated thereunder provide the statutory and regulatory basis for the acceptance and treatment of charitable contributions.

17. IRC section 511-515 and the regulations promulgated thereunder cover the imposition of tax on, definition of exceptions from, and treatment of unrelated business income.

18. Although there is authority for this position in *Rensselaer Polytechnic Institute v. Commissioner*, 732 F.2d 1058 (2d Cir. 1984), *aff'g* 79 T.C. 967 (1982), the IRS believes the proper method to allocate fixed expenses is based on a 24-hour-a-day, 12-month-a-year period, using a ratio of hours used for unrelated activities to total hours in the year.

19. *NCAA v. Commission*, 914 F.2d 1417 (10th Cir. 1990).

20. AOD 1991-015.

21. IRC section 514

22. IRC section 117(d).

23. IRC section 119.

24. Treasury regulation 1.6033-2(g)(1)(v).

25. IRC section 3121(b)(10).

26. IRC section 117.

# References and Resources

PUBLICATIONS

Galloway, Joseph M. *The Unrelated Business Income Tax.* New York: John Wiley & Sons, 1982.

Hopkins, Bruce R. *The Law of Tax-Exempt Organizations.* New York: John Wiley & Sons, 1987.

National Association of College and University Business Officers. *Guidelines for Filing 1990 IRS Forms 990 and 990-T.* Washington, D.C.: NACUBO, 1991.

PERIODICAL

*The Exempt Organization Tax Review*

# CHAPTER 10

# Endowment Management

by
David A. Salem
Grantham, Mayo, Van Otterloo & Co.

# Sponsors

## THE COMMON FUND
363 Reef Road, P.O. Box 940
Fairfield, CT 06430
203-255-7000

*The Common Fund provides comprehensive investment management programs for endowment and operating funds for its member colleges, universities, and independent schools.*

## FIRST QUADRANT CORP.
800 East Colorado Boulevard, Suite 900
Pasadena, CA 91101
818-795-8220

*First Quadrant serves as an institutional asset manager for endowments and pensions.*

## KPMG PEAT MARWICK
345 Park Avenue
New York, NY 10154
212-758-9700

*KPMG Peat Marwick conducts studies of college and university treasury functions and endowment funds reporting.*

## TWENTIETH CENTURY INVESTORS
P.O. Box 419385
Kansas City, MO 64141
816-932-4732

*Twentieth Century offers investment management and no-load mutual fund services for college and university retirement plans, endowments, foundations, and operating funds.*

# Contents

## 10: Endowment Management

The principles that guide investment management for endowed educational institutions do not differ greatly from those followed by other institutional investors. Educational endowments do have characteristics that distinguish them from other pools of investable wealth: they are exempt from taxation, they have a very long-term investment horizon (in theory, a perpetual one), and they are supposed to generate a stream of earnings to support current operations that will remain stable (or grow) in real or inflation-adjusted terms. Because other pools of investable wealth share some of these attributes and aims, the similarities between the way educational endowments are managed and the way other institutional funds are managed outweigh the differences. The investors pursue essentially the same investment policies; they allocate their assets in a similar fashion; and they delegate day-to-day responsibility for investment decision making to many of the same professional investment managers.

It is not surprising that educational institutions pursue investment policies similar to those pursued by other institutional investors, because endowment trustees quite naturally adopt policies and practices that have served them well in other contexts, especially in the management of other institutional funds for which they serve as fiduciaries. Some policies and practices are conducive to investment success regardless of the character of the assets being deployed. Approaches that work well when applied to taxable assets, for example, can also work well when applied to endowment assets. Nevertheless, governing boards and officers must understand fully how endowments differ from other pools of capital, for without such understanding it is unlikely that they will exploit to the maximum extent possible their funds' tax-exempt and perpetual life status.

This chapter provides an overview of endowments, discusses the legal aspects of endowment investing, analyzes alternate endowment investment policies, and explains types of deferred-giving assets.

# Types of Endowment and Similar Funds

The three principal categories of endowment and similar funds are endowment funds (sometimes referred to as true endowment), term endowment funds, and funds functioning as endowment (sometimes referred to as quasi-endowment funds). "Endowment funds" are funds received from a donor with the restriction that the principal is not expendable. "Term endowment funds" are funds for which the donor stipulates that the principal may be expended after a stated period or upon the occurrence of a certain event. A "fund functioning as endowment" is a fund that is established by the governing board to function like an endowment fund but may be expended at any time at the discretion of the board. All three types of funds—endowment funds, term endowment funds, and funds functioning as endowment—should be reported in the "endowment and similar funds" section of the institution's balance sheet, and the identity of each type of fund should be clearly differentiated in the section on fund balances.

Institutions may receive gifts or bequests subject to payment of income or specified amounts to one or more beneficiaries for life. In this instance, the institution functions as a trustee for federal tax purposes (except for gifts received for a charitable annuity contract). Such funds—often referred to as "annuity and life income funds"—are not "institutional funds" within the scope of the Uniform Management of Institutional Funds Act (discussed below) but become such on the death of the last beneficiary if they are restricted for endowment purposes. The funds nevertheless possess many characteristics of institutional endowment funds for administrative and investment purposes. Regardless of the reporting method used, the funds must be labeled clearly as "subject to life income reservation."

## USE OF ENDOWMENT PRINCIPAL AND EARNINGS

For the purposes of this chapter, the term "spendable return" is used to describe the amount of endowment income or income and appreciation allotted on a regular, periodic basis by the institution for current expenditures. The term "income" is not used, because many institutions have adopted "total return" spending formulas (discussed below) under which they may expend not only the current yield but also a prudent portion of appreciation. Such formulas can at times produce

◆

a spendable amount that is less than the fund's current yield, especially when the current yield is abnormally high.

In accounting records and financial reports, endowment and similar funds should be classified according to any limitations placed on the expenditure of their principal and spendable return. For example, if a donor specifies that the principal must be retained but makes no stipulations concerning use of the spendable return, the fund is an "unrestricted endowment fund." If the donor specifies that the spendable return from the fund is to be used for a certain instructional department or other specific purpose, the fund is a "restricted endowment fund." Similar situations may exist with respect to use of spendable return from term endowment funds.

If a donor makes a gift to an institution, specifying only that it be used for a specific institutional purpose and not stipulating that the principal of the fund be maintained in perpetuity or for a period of time, and if the governing board elects to invest the fund and expend only the spendable return for the purpose stipulated by the donor, the fund becomes a "restricted fund functioning as endowment." Similarly, the governing board may create an "unrestricted fund functioning as endowment" by authorizing the transfer of unrestricted funds to the "endowment and similar funds" group with the intention of retaining the funds on a long-term basis and using only the investment earnings for current expenditures.

Assets of endowment funds must not be hypothecated or pledged for any purpose and normally should not be loaned to or invested in the institution's physical plant. Such conveyances of true endowment assets, whether actual or potential, violate the institution's legal obligation to maintain endowment principal inviolate. Funds functioning as endowment, however, can be used for these purposes, because their functional status stems not from donor stipulations but rather from board action.

## Accounting and Reporting of Gifts

The appropriate accounting and reporting of gifts for endowment and similar funds depend on the conditions under which funds are accepted and received by an institution. It is therefore essential that these conditions be communicated to the chief financial or business officer, or his or her designee in the accounting office, to ensure proper recording of funds in the institution's accounting records. If conditions of the gift stipulate that the principal of the fund is to be retained in perpetuity or for some stated period, the funds received should be accounted for as direct additions to the endowment and similar funds group. On the other hand, if funds received are determined to be spendable, they should be accounted for as current fund revenue. The importance of this determination is highlighted by cases in which incorrect classification of funds received by an institution has resulted in understatement of the institution's current funds.

## ENSURING COMPLIANCE WITH FUND RESTRICTIONS

The chief financial or business officer or other designated officer is responsible for ensuring that applicable restrictions are honored fully until they either lapse or are removed. Compliance with such restrictions is both necessary and expedient. It is necessary because the restrictions carry the force of law, and their violation could trigger private litigation or intervention by state authorities. It is expedient because there is a close and demonstrable link between good stewardship of gifts and bequests and long-term fund-raising success. The officer responsible should therefore have a thorough understanding of the legal environment in which these funds are administered and used.

Every institution should establish policies to ensure compliance with restrictions imposed by donors and designations imposed by the governing board on the use of funds and their spendable return. The chief financial or business officer or designee and independent auditors should periodically examine administrative policies and practices. Such examination should be supplemented from time to time with a review by legal counsel.

A detailed accounting of all endowment and similar funds should be maintained. The register should include such information as:

- Name of the donor and members of his or her family, with brief biographical comments

- Amount and date of donation

- Identification of the type of fund

- Restrictions by the donor or designations by the governing board on use of the fund or its spendable return

- Identification of the source of such limitations (donor, grantor, or governing board)

- Limitations on investments

- Reference to formal acceptance and other actions by the governing board

DONOR RELATIONS

Although a register of endowment and similar funds is a useful administrative tool, its limitations should be recognized. It may present terms and limitations in summary form, when in fact they may have been developed through correspondence with a donor over many years. It is therefore essential that an institution maintain complete files of all original gift instruments and related correspondence, as such documents provide an authoritative basis for interpreting donor intent. Fund-raising personnel must ensure that information essential to the administration of an endowment fund is memorialized in a written instrument at the time a gift is made.

Conferences with donors can be especially useful, not only in clarifying and ultimately codifying donor intent but also in demonstrating the need for unrestricted resources. Such resources are essential to ensure the continued quality of the institution's academic programs and supporting services and to sustain and enhance the institution's financial strength and flexibility. If a donor seeks to restrict the use of a gift or bequest, the institution should, insofar as possible, ensure that such restriction will not prevent effective use of the funds in the future. When a donor is informed that such restrictions are not consistent with the institution's mission, he or she is often willing to grant broad latitude, not only in the use of the fund and its spendable return but also in the manner in which it is invested and administered. Most donors recognize that a gift that unduly hampers an institution's freedom of action is ultimately a poor memorial to their generosity.

A representative of the institution should review gift instruments in draft form to suggest changes in terms or wording that will help the institution comply with the donor's wishes. As defined by the Uniform

Management of Institutional Funds Act, "gift instrument" is a will, deed, grant, conveyance, agreement, memorandum, writing, or other governing document (including the terms of any institutional solicitations from which an institutional fund resulted) under which property is transferred to or held by a college or university as an institutional fund. One change in gift instruments commonly suggested by representatives of a college or university is the inclusion of a "changed conditions" clause permitting the use of funds for purposes other than those initially stipulated by the donor, should future conditions dictate such a change.

Although most gifts to institutions are motivated by charitable impulses, estate planning and tax factors can also be quite important. It is essential, however, that representatives of the institution avoid rendering formal legal or tax opinions or appraising the value of noncash gifts. The value that donors assign to noncash gifts for purposes of computing income tax deductions is in no way binding upon the receiving institution when it assigns its own book value to such gifts. Because tax regulations normally require that receipts for noncash gifts be based on independent appraisals, institutional representatives should avoid rendering their own appraisals of noncash gifts and should refrain from any acts or statements that might be construed as tax or legal advice. The donor should be advised to seek counsel on such matters.

***Standard donor agreement.*** Whether or not the administration elects to conduct an internal full-scale review of existing awards and endowments, a standard donor agreement should be created. Figure 10-1 presents a sample donor agreement that is meant to provide a basis for discussion. The draft is basic, brief, and in need of refinement. It is included to illustrate the type of structured questionnaire that should be administered to memorialize fully each donor's wishes. Figure 10-1 is provided for illustrative purposes only.

The objective of a standard donor agreement is to ensure the donor's understanding and acceptance of legal and administrative realities. An agreement should be drafted jointly by the development office, the financial aid office, graduate departments, and other interested departments. The final agreement should be distributed campuswide to the entire community of interest.

FIGURE 10-1
Standard Donor Agreement

1.  **Nature of the award contemplated:**

    _____

    _____

    _____

    _____

2.  **Type of award:**

    |  |  |  |
    |---|---|---|
    | Student scholarship | _____ __ |
    | Student bursary | _____ __ |
    | Prize | _____ __ |
    | Research award | _____ __ |
    | Graduate student award | _____ __ |
    | Fellowship | _____ __ |
    | Other (_____) | _____ __ |

3.  **Amount of donation/award disbursement**
    Amount of donation to create capital pool: $_____
    Envisioned annual disbursement: _____ award(s) x $_____

    PLEASE NOTE: The university will normally distribute awards
    on the following basis:

    | | |
    |---|---|
    | < $500 | Pooled in faculty or departmental general endowments |
    | $500 - $5,000 | Normally pooled; individual awards of less than five years' duration considered |

$5,001 - $25,000     Individual awards with five-year duration

\> $25,000     Individual awards in perpetuity (normally 25-year maximum)

Is this acceptable?                Yes/No
If not, please explain:

_____

_____

_____

_____

## 4. Eligible recipient restrictions

PLEASE NOTE: Awards should be free of criteria based on personal characteristics such as race, ancestry, place of origin, color, ethnic origin, sex, creed, age, marital status, family status, sexual orientation, or handicap. Notwithstanding the above, the university may from time to time establish awards specifically intended to improve the participation of certain groups.

Is this acceptable?                Yes/No
If not, please explain:

_____

_____

_____

_____

## 5. Capital investment restrictions

PLEASE NOTE: The university is normally obliged to invest only those funds authorized for investment under the Trustee Act. These authorized investments are of a fairly standard, conservative nature.

Would you consider exempting your donation from the
restrictions of the Act for investment purposes?          Yes/No

If not, please explain:

_____

_____

_____

_____

### 6.  Capital preservation policy

PLEASE NOTE: The university's capital preservation policy typically
envisions annual spending at a maximum of the average of the past three
years' CPI (in %) times the then current market value of the endowment.

Is this acceptable?                                      Yes/No
If not, please explain:

_____

_____

_____

_____

### 7.  Administrative fees

PLEASE NOTE: The university normally charges an administrative cost
recovery equal to 1/10 of 1 percent of market value monthly, to recognize the
costs associated with fund-raising and award management. Further, investment manager fees are normally a direct charge to endowment income.

Is this acceptable?                                      Yes/No
If not, please explain:

_____

_____

_____

_____

**8. Discretion to university**

PLEASE NOTE: Given changing circumstances and priorities, the right to utilize both the capital and income from a donation would normally revert to the complete discretion of the university 25 years from the date of the donation.

Is this acceptable?                                      Yes/No
If not, please explain:

_____

_____

_____

_____

**9. Calendar description/award name**

PLEASE NOTE: Only individually categorized awards normally receive separate calendar descriptions. The nature of the description envisioned:

_____

_____

_____

In acknowledgment of the terms and conditions and amendments thereto listed above, please sign below:

_____

Donor Signature                          Date

## TREATMENT OF NONCASH GIFTS

Educational institutions typically receive many noncash gifts, including gifts of securities in kind, and the number of issues held by a fund can easily grow beyond reasonable bounds if steps are not taken to routinely liquidate securities not held strictly on investment grounds. The greater the number of issues held by a fund, the higher administrative expenses tend to be. Appropriate diversification of endowment assets can be obtained with a reasonably small number of carefully selected holdings, and maintenance of a large number of small positions in individual issues generally entails costs that are disproportionate to any diversification benefits that their retention provides. To guard against unproductive diversification of fund holdings, many institutions maintain a policy requiring the prompt sale of all securities received by a gift or bequest unless prohibited by the terms of the gift or bequest or unless a particular security is already held in the institution's portfolio or is under consideration as an addition to the portfolio in the near future.

# Cy Pres

In some instances, a donor may, by the terms of his or her gift, have so limited either the purposes for which an endowment fund may be used or the manner in which it may be invested that the value of the fund to the institution is severely limited. In such cases it is often undesirable, impractical, and sometimes impossible for the institution to continue to comply with the donor's wishes. To gain relief from impractical restrictions, the institution may bring a so-called cy pres action in an appropriate court.

Cy pres ("as near as may be") is a procedure for releasing a limitation on a restricted gift if the donor is no longer living. An institution may seek to depart from the original terms of the gift to make the fund useful while adhering, as nearly as possible, to the donor's original intent. Cy pres is a last resort and often a futile one. It has been attempted in some jurisdictions against living donors, but the courts have refused to approve it in such cases.

The cy pres doctrine has not been a satisfactory solution and is applied reluctantly in some states. Therefore, the Uniform Management of Institutional Funds Act provides a statutory procedure for the release of restrictions with the consent of the donor. If the donor is deceased, unable to consent, or cannot be identified, the appropriate court may, on application of the institution's governing board, release a limitation shown to be obsolete, inappropriate, or impractical. Many institutions include a "sunset clause" in donative instruments that gives the institution complete discretion to dispose of principal and income after a stated period, typically 25 years. (See Figure 10-1, item 8.)

## Legal Status of Endowment Funds

Endowment funds have been the subject of considerable legal discussion. The most serious question is whether fund appreciation, realized or unrealized, must be treated as principal and therefore considered unexpendable. The answer depends upon the extent to which trust law is deemed applicable to educational institutions, which are considered charitable corporations under the laws of most states and hence subject to a regulatory framework that combines elements of corporation and contract law with traditional trust principles. Because corporation, contract, and trust law are derived not only from statutes but from centuries of common-law jurisprudence, the regulatory framework in which endowments are managed is at times ambiguous and uncertain. Nonetheless, there are touchstone principles that governing boards and officers can rely upon, and there is such widespread acceptance of the legitimacy of certain policies and practices that the institutions following them can be relatively certain that these procedures will withstand legal scrutiny.

There are two generic views of the legal status of endowment funds. The traditional, and by now somewhat discredited, view of an endowment is that it is a trust fund per se, regardless of whether the written instrument establishing it contains the appropriate "terms of art"— specific words or phrases that unambiguously justify the invocation of trust principles. It is inconsequential, to those who insist on viewing endowments only through the prism of trust law, that endowed institutions may hold property in trust for themselves, or that the three-way separation of trustee, life beneficiary, and remainderman—the cornerstone of private trust law—does not exist in an endowment setting. The more modern view, embodied in the Uniform Management of Institutional Funds Act, is that educational institutions hold endowment funds for their own benefit as their absolute property, that the laws applicable to charitable corporations apply, and that principles of private trust law are largely inapposite.

## THE TRADITIONAL VIEW: ENDOWMENTS ARE TRUSTS

Under the trust fund theory, the principal of an endowment fund must be maintained inviolate in perpetuity. Principal includes:

- The market value of the fund at the moment it was established

- The market value of any additions to the fund at the moment they were added

- Realized appreciation in the value of the fund's assets

For example, assume that an endowment fund of $100,000 was established in Year 1 with the stipulation that all current income be used for faculty salaries. If an additional $60,000 were donated to the fund in Year 5, and if the fund realized investment gains (exclusive of dividends, interest, or rents) of $40,000 in Years 1-10, at the end of Year 10 the entire $200,000 would be deemed inviolate.

Perhaps the most glaring anomaly in treating endowments as trust funds is the nearly universal practice of commingling assets for investment purposes. In private trust law, the rule forbidding trustees from commingling investments of two or more separate trust funds is still strictly applied, at least in theory. In practice, however, this rule is honored more in the breach than the observance, with the assets of many private trusts being invested in commingled investment vehicles such as mutual funds. Also, the anticommingling provisions of trust law have a slightly hollow ring in an era of "certificateless" trading, where the indicia of ownership of most publicly traded securities take the form not of stacks of certificates bearing individual investors' names but rather of a record etched on a silicon wafer in the computer of a custodial bank. (Most custodial banks are members of centralized depository networks that permit them to buy and sell securities without physically exchanging stock or bond certificates. Indeed, most U.S. Treasury obligations do not exist in certificate form.) Banking regulations explicitly permit banks to commingle the assets of trusts for which they serve as trustees, but this is the only exception to the general rule that trust assets cannot legally be commingled.

If endowments are viewed as trust funds, commingling endowment assets for investment purposes is thus not permissible. However, most educational institutions have for many years pooled the assets of the many individual funds (thousands, in the case of a major research university) that collectively constitute their endowments, and this practice has never been challenged. The nearly universal acceptance of the commingling of endowment assets materially weakens the argument that such funds are properly regarded as trusts.

Another problem that arises when endowments are viewed as trusts is that trust principles prohibit the governing board from delegating day-to-day responsibility for fund administration to an institution's officers, even if such delegation is the norm with respect to other aspects of the institution's affairs. The extent to which investment discretion can be delegated by an institution's governing board depends on the charter and bylaws under which it operates and the laws of the state in which it is situated; legal counsel should be consulted before the board delegates such authority to others. In some jurisdictions the governing board, or a committee composed of board members, must technically be involved in the selection of individual securities. This is undeniably sound from a legal point of view but perhaps not the most effective means of maximizing investment returns within acceptable volatility constraints, which is the end result that fund fiduciaries seek. Fortunately, many states have adopted the Uniform Management of Institutional Funds Act or variants thereof that permit trustees to delegate considerable discretion to investment and financial professionals who are not members of the board.

## THE MODERN VIEW: ENDOWMENTS ARE NOT TRUSTS

The many states that have rejected the trust theory have opted instead to view educational institutions as charitable corporations that hold endowment funds solely for their own benefit. Investment and administration of such funds is governed by the law of charitable corporations and not the law of private trusts. This does not result in unalloyed gains for educational institutions in these states, however, because the law of charitable corporations is loosely applied and often confusing, drawing on a mixture of corporate, trust, and contract principles. It is possible, for example, for a court in an "absolute ownership" state to reach the conclusion that appreciation must be considered part of principal as in private trust law, contrary to the general rule of corporation law that realized gains may be treated as income and therefore spent.

Depending on the law of the state of incorporation or provisions in an institution's charter, its governing board has some freedom to delegate authority in connection with investment functions to a committee of its members or to appropriate corporate officers. Investment discretion may also be delegated to professional investment managers who are not members of the governing board or officers of the institution, but responsibility for investment activities ultimately rests with the governing board and is thus, in a strictly legal sense, nondelegable. In other words, the governing board may fully delegate the authority to make investment decisions, but it cannot delegate the responsibility it ultimately bears to ensure that endowment assets are invested prudently.

## THE UNIFORM MANAGEMENT OF INSTITUTIONAL FUNDS ACT

The Uniform Management of Institutional Funds Act (the Uniform Act) is one of a series of nonbinding "model" statutes recommended to individual state legislatures by the National Conference of Commissioners on Uniform State Laws, a private advisory panel that is operated under the auspices of the American Bar Association and the bar associations of individual states and territories. Conceived in the late 1960s and adopted by the National Conference in 1972, the Uniform Act aims to clarify and codify what can and cannot be done by persons administering endowment and similar funds. The Uniform Act prescribes a standard of care and prudence to guide governing boards in exercising their duties. It countermands two important tenets of trust law by specifically permitting endowment trustees to spend a prudent portion of realized endowment gains and to delegate investment discretion to qualified professionals. As of January 1, 1991, the District of Columbia and the following states had adopted the Uniform Act or variants thereof: California, Colorado, Connecticut, Delaware, Illinois, Kansas, Kentucky, Louisiana, Maine, Maryland, Massachusetts, Michigan, Minnesota, Missouri, Montana, New Hampshire, New Jersey, New York, North Dakota, Ohio, Oregon, Rhode Island, Tennessee,

Vermont, Virginia, Washington, West Virginia, and Wisconsin. In addition, Pennsylvania passed a similar act before the Uniform Act was promulgated in 1972.

The Uniform Act provides the following definitions.

"Institutional fund" is a fund held by an institution for its exclusive use, benefit, or purposes; it does not include a fund held for an institution by a trustee who is a natural person (as distinct from an institution) or a fund in which a beneficiary who is a natural person has an interest other than the rights that could arise on violation or failure of the fund's stated purposes.

"Endowment fund" is an institutional fund, or any part thereof, not wholly expendable by the institution on a current basis under the terms of the applicable gift instrument. (Implicit in this definition is the continued maintenance of all or a specified part of the original gift.)

"Historic dollar value" is the aggregate value in dollars of an endowment fund at the time it became an endowment fund; each subsequent donation to the fund at the time it is made; and each accumulation made pursuant to a direction in the applicable gift instrument at the time the accumulation is added to the fund.

"Appreciation" is the appreciation over historic dollar value. Therefore, if the market value is below the historic dollar value of the fund, the institution may spend only the current yield ("income" in the traditional trust law sense) that the fund generates in the form of dividends, interest, or rent. If the market value exceeds the historic dollar value of the fund, the institution is free to expend the appreciation in excess of the historic value.

## Pooling Endowment Assets

To the extent legally possible, colleges and universities may find it advantageous to commingle investments of endowment and similar funds in an investment pool or pools. An investment pool permits broad diversification of investments with attendant protection of principal and relative stability of revenue. In addition, it permits economies in administration and accounting.

Even though assets are invested as a pool, the identity of separate funds must be maintained. Individual accounts must be kept, usually in subsidiary records, for the principal of each fund in the investment pool.

This is particularly important if the pool is administered on a total return basis in conformity with the Uniform Act or other applicable state law. Although the market value of assets of the entire pool may exceed aggregate historic dollar value of the individual funds invested, the value of the proportionate share of the pool's assets related to a particular fund may be greater or less than the historic dollar value of that fund. If the value of the fund's share of the assets is less than its historic dollar value, only the yield may be used.

A consolidated pool may be desirable for investment of endowment funds, term endowment funds, and funds functioning as endowment. However, it is preferable to have separate investment pools for funds such as life income and annuity funds, which have objectives and characteristics different from endowment and similar funds (see "Pooled Life Income Funds").

The terms of some gift instruments may prohibit pooling or commingling of assets. Legal interpretation of complex language in gift instruments is often necessary, but generally the requirement that a fund be "held separate" is construed as meaning only that the fund balance be separately identified at all times and not that assets of the fund be separately invested. Language to the effect that the fund be "invested separately" or that "its assets shall not be commingled" requires that the fund be separately invested. When it is possible to guide a donor in drafting a gift document, benefits to the fund and to the institution of pooling investments should be explained and the donor's consent sought for participation in the pool.

Separate investment sometimes may be necessary because of special provisions in the gift instrument or because of the nature of gift property. For example, a donor may require retention of a particular investment, limit investments of the fund to certain types of securities or other property, or contribute assets that are unmarketable (restricted stock), not income producing, hard to value, or uncommonly risky. These characteristics might disqualify the gift property as a proper investment for an endowment pool. The only solution is to establish a separately invested fund in the donor's name. That fund alone will suffer the consequences of any change or loss of value occurring because of the nature of the gift property. If the character of the asset changes, as when restrictions on the sale of securities are removed, the fund may then be invested in a pool.

## OPERATING INVESTMENT POOLS

Operation of an investment pool necessitates procedures permitting equitable distribution of spendable return and assignment of market values to the individual funds invested in the pool.

Investment earnings are distributed to various participating funds on the basis of the assignment to each fund of a number of units calculated on the market value of assets of the pool at the time of entry of each fund into the pool. This procedure is known as the "market value" or "unit" method of accounting for investment pools. Under this method, when an investment pool is inaugurated, or when a change is made from a historic dollar value to a market value method, an arbitrary value is assigned to each share or unit. Each institutional fund then is considered to have the number of units directly proportional to its historic dollar value at the time the market value method is inaugurated. For example, if $100 is assigned for each unit, a fund of $10,000 would have 100 shares.

Thereafter, the pooled assets are valued at specific intervals, usually monthly or quarterly, and a new unit value is determined by dividing the new total market value by total number of units. This new unit value is used to determine the number of units assigned to, or "purchased" by, a new fund as it enters the pool. The new unit value also is used in calculating the value of a fund that may be withdrawn from the pool. For example, the market value of assets of an investment pool having a total of 100,000 units may be $15 million at a given monthly or quarterly valuation date; the value of each unit, therefore, would be $150 ($15 million divided by 100,000 units). A new fund of $30,000 entering the pool on that date would be assigned 200 units ($30,000 divided by $150). A fund holding 300 units that is withdrawn from the pool would have a value of $45,000 (or 300 units multiplied by $150).

Either of two procedures may be followed in admitting funds to or withdrawing funds from the pool. One is to admit funds to or remove them from the pool only on valuation dates. The other is to admit or remove them at any time, with valuation of units being that of the latest valuation date. (Under the provisions of the Tax Reform Act of 1969, the latter method cannot be used for pooled life income funds.) If the latter method is employed, unit values should be determined with sufficient frequency to avoid inequities resulting from variations in unit market value.

A separate account is maintained to which realized gains and losses are charged. No units are assigned and no income is distributed to this account. Regular income (interest and dividends) is prorated to the various funds that compose the total endowment on the basis of the number of units in each fund. The institution may distribute gains and losses to each fund in this pool on a pro rata basis, but some institutions may not consider the work involved as justified. Realized gains and losses on separately invested funds should be distributed directly to the funds; thus, the fund balance will change each time a gain or loss is realized.

In the past, many colleges and universities followed the historic dollar value method of distributing earnings. When there was little or no change in the valuation of assets held, this method equitably distributed investment revenue. However, because equity securities and other assets that fluctuate in value are of increasing importance to investment pools, the market value method provides a more equitable distribution of income and realized and unrealized gains and losses to each fund. The historic dollar value method is no longer considered acceptable. As a collateral advantage, fluctuations in unit value of the pool provide a useful measure of performance of the investment pool, undistorted by additions or withdrawals of funds.

## Setting Endowment Spending Rates

Endowment management has been significantly affected by the trend toward "total return investing." Until the 1970s, most educational institutions spent only income (yield) of endowment funds, treating appreciation as an addition to principal. In the early 1970s, several published studies suggested that institutions could enhance the return on their endowment funds by investing more heavily in equities, especially low-yield "growth" stocks. To avoid the immediate reduction in distributable endowment earnings that a redeployment of fund assets from relatively high-yield bonds to lower-yield stocks would have entailed, many institutions moving more heavily into stocks adopted spending policies that permitted the expenditure of both current income and a portion of appreciation. Unfortunately, these policy changes occurred at what proved in hindsight to be the end of a long-term secular rise in stock prices in general and "growth" stock prices in particular; the subsequent decline in endowment capital values caused serious reconsideration of the total return approach in the late 1970s. This approach remains the most widely used method of determining annual spending rates, but its risks are better understood than they were when it was first introduced, and the importance of diversifying endowment assets is better appreciated.

## ALTERNATE SPENDING RULES

The most common variant of the total return approach in use today links available endowment spending to endowment market values. An example is a percentage (such as 5 percent) of a moving average of market values (a three-year average is common). The use of a moving average asset base dampens the impact of market fluctuations on available spending, thereby making it easier for an institution to formulate and adhere to annual budgets. In pursuit of even greater certainty in the budgeting process, some institutions have adopted a variant of the total return approach under which distributed endowment earnings are set at a prudent initial dollar level (such as the dollar equivalent of 5 percent of the endowment's market value on the date the formula is adopted) and then permitted to grow at a fixed annual rate equal to the fund's expected long-term real or inflation-adjusted rate of return.

## RATIONALE FOR SPENDING RULES

Most spending policies aim to balance the need for current income with the need to preserve the purchasing power of both endowment principal and endowment earnings. Excessively high spending rates undermine achievement of the latter objective, while reinvesting too large a portion of total return can cause significant program disruptions. The pre-1970s approach of spending all current yield proved acceptable in an era when bonds were the asset of choice for most endowments and a policy of spending all income led to a reasonable and sustainable payout of 4 to 6 percent per year. High rates of inflation in the 1970s and early 1980s caused stock and bond yields (as distinct from total returns) to rise and put many institutions that had clung to a spend-all-yield rule in the untenable position of spending at unsustainably high rates of 8 percent or more.

Striking an appropriate balance between present and future institutional needs can be difficult: to determine what portion of its existing endowment assets an institution can prudently spend each year, its governing board must estimate the endowment's expected long-term real or inflation-adjusted rate of return. By definition, the institution can spend at a rate equal to (but not exceeding) its expected real or inflation-adjusted rate of return without jeopardizing the purchasing power of existing endowment assets. However, to estimate a fund's expected real rate of return, the governing board must make certain assumptions about the endowment's long-term asset mix, which is dependent on the fund's return objectives or desired spending rate. (The higher a fund's long-term return objective, the more aggressively its assets must be invested.)

To escape this vicious circle, most governing boards make defensible assumptions about sustainable spending rates based on capital market history and then review and if necessary revise spending policies later in the planning process, after appropriate long-term asset mixes have been identified. Over the long term, equities have produced an average annual real total return approximating 6 percent. The corresponding return for long-term high-quality bonds has been approximately 2 percent, while cash equivalents have produced a long-term real return of approximately 1 percent. An institution that committed 65 percent to stocks, 30 percent to bonds, and 5 percent to cash equivalents (a typical long-term asset mix) might therefore expect to earn a long-term real return of 4.5 percent—perhaps higher if it aggressively invests in "alternative assets" (discussed below) or if the strategies and tactics it employs within conventional asset classes produce incremental returns above a purely passive buy-and-hold approach.

Given the complexities of determining appropriate spending rates and the interrelationship of spending and investment policies, it is not surprising that educational institutions have adopted widely varying endowment spending rules. Selection of an appropriate endowment spending policy is one of the governing board's most important responsibilities, and the typical board spends considerable time ensuring that the policy that it has adopted truly reflects the institution's financial condition and risk tolerances. Particular attention is paid to estimating the expected additions to specific endowment accounts (e.g., an endowed chair) from fund-raising efforts: the larger such additions are expected to be, the higher the spending rate from an endowment account can be without eroding the purchasing power of its remaining assets.

## REVENUE STABILIZATION RESERVES

To minimize the effect of year-to-year fluctuations in the amount of current revenue available from an investment pool, some institutions have established revenue stabilization reserves by allocating to a special reserve account a portion of the current yield that endowment assets generate.

Under this procedure all earnings from an investment pool are distributed to participating funds. The amount applicable to unrestricted endowment funds is reported in full as unrestricted current funds revenue under a title such as "endowment earnings," and the amount set aside for the stabilization reserve is shown in the same statement as a transfer to "unrestricted current funds balance—allocated." Under this method, the reserve relates only to earnings from the unrestricted endowment funds and is reflected in the balance sheet as a separately listed equity of unrestricted current funds balance—allocated. Amounts not spent in restricted fund accounts remain as balances to be carried forward to the next period.

This method is acceptable to the American Institute of Certified Public Accountants. The need for and size of the reserve are determined by each institution according to its needs.

# Investment Planning

Investing an institution's endowment assets effectively is difficult in the absence of a comprehensive investment plan, for several reasons. Endowment management entails the ongoing resolution of many interrelated issues. Modern financial markets are volatile; when asset prices are fluctuating widely, the natural human tendency is to act, and without the restraint imposed by a well-prepared and well-understood investment plan, action sometimes leads to the sale of volatile assets at temporarily depressed prices. Also, in recent years the number of available investment vehicles has proliferated, as have the number and variety of firms professing an ability to invest effectively. This has heightened the need for policies and guidelines that fund fiduciaries can consult as they perform their duties, especially as they evaluate and select investment vehicles and managers.

An effective means of preparing a comprehensive investment plan is to divide the planning process into a logically ordered series of discrete tasks.

## IDENTIFYING INVESTABLE FUNDS

The first step is to identify investable funds. Investment management for an institution of higher education primarily involves true endowment funds, term endowment funds, and funds functioning as endowment. (The investment of life income and annuity funds is discussed below.)

Most educational institutions have current funds not needed immediately for operating purposes, as well as other funds earmarked for plant construction or other capital improvements. These are often invested in high-quality fixed-income instruments that generate high levels of current income. The maturities of such instruments are either very short (to preclude principal losses should interest rates rise) or staggered so that the instruments mature on or about the dates that cash withdrawals must be made to fund expenditures. Although short-term investing is a very important function, long-term funds are the primary subject of this chapter. (For more detail on short-term investment, see Chapter 11, Cash Management.)

Some institutions are responsible for the stewardship of employee pension assets, typically in accordance with policies that differ (albeit not markedly) from those governing investment of endowment assets. As long-term pools of capital exempt from taxation, college and university pension funds have much in common with endowments and can often be invested in similar vehicles, using similar strategies and tactics. Where differences exist, they are often dictated by the distinct contractual and regulatory framework in which pension fund fiduciaries must operate, including the adherence to collective bargaining agreements, the Employee Retirement Income Security Act of 1974 (ERISA) and related regulations, state laws, and other external constraints.

## ORGANIZING TO INVEST

The second step in preparing a comprehensive investment plan is to assign responsibility for the ongoing formulation and implementation of investment policies, strategies, and tactics. For the purposes of this chapter, "policies" refers to the allocation of investable funds across asset classes, based on long-term objectives and risk tolerances. "Strategies" refers to the allocation of funds across asset classes (or across outside professional managers) based on short- or medium-term return assumptions. Strategic insights sometimes cause assets to be allocated in proportions that differ from policy norms. "Tactics" refers to the allocation of funds across individual securities based on short-term return assumptions.

For most governing boards, policy formulation is a task that cannot be delegated. Governing boards may choose to delegate policy decisions, but the decisions their designees make are merely de facto choices by the governing board. Strategic decisions may be delegated entirely, partly delegated, or retained by the institution's governing board. Tactical decisions also may be delegated or retained but are almost always delegated to full-time investment professionals. Whatever the amount of an institution's investable funds, these funds must have continuous, enlightened supervision. Each institution should select the form of management organization best suited to its return objectives and to the amount of investable funds that it controls.

***Establishing an investment committee.*** Most boards delegate ongoing authority for endowment management to an investment committee, which may be separate from the board's finance committee or subcommittee. Typically, the investment committee is a policy-making body that does not directly manage the institution's investments by attempting to select securities for the portfolio. To facilitate timely decision making and to focus authority, the investment committee should be small. It should be composed of members who understand how modern investment and capital markets function or who can lend other useful skills or perspectives to the committee's work. To ensure that investment committees have the requisite expertise, some institutions appoint as either voting or nonvoting members individuals who are not technically members of the governing board.

It is important to consult legal counsel concerning delegation of investment authority to ensure that such delegation conforms with state laws and institutional bylaws. If the governing board delegates investment authority to an investment committee, the committee may, in turn, delegate to an officer of the college or university or to a portfolio manager the discretionary authority to buy and sell securities and to perform other essential investment functions.

*Establishing an investment subsidiary.* Several institutions with large endowments have created wholly owned subsidiaries to manage their endowment assets under the supervision of an independent board of directors appointed by and responsible to the parent institution's governing board. This arrangement shifts investment decision-making authority (but not ultimate responsibility) to a group of individuals that monitors investment and capital markets on a continuous basis and that has well-defined personal incentives (including, in the case of the subsidiary's professional staff, pecuniary incentives) to deploy investment assets in a manner that comports fully with an institution's return objectives and time horizon.

*Obviating conflicts of interest.* Real or apparent conflicts of interest can and do arise as investment committees go about their work; it is essential that an institution have written policies that define what is and what is not a conflict of interest and that outline procedures to be followed when such conflicts arise. Governing boards and officers do not need to make immediate or certain financial gains for investments to be construed as conflicts of interest; an institution's written policies should compel prompt and complete disclosure of any means by which governing boards or officers could benefit personally from recommended investment decisions.

## FORMULATING AND CODIFYING INVESTMENT POLICIES

Once investable funds have been identified and agreement is reached as to who will make which decisions, the next step in preparing a comprehensive investment plan is to formulate and codify the institution's investment policies. The preparation of a written statement of investment policies is usually the responsibility of the investment committee, but the governing board should confirm these policies through review and ratification of the committee's work.

A comprehensive statement of investment policies and practices addresses the following issues.

*Return objective.* In most cases, the return objective is to invest funds in a manner that will preserve the purchasing power of income and principal. Alternate objectives are to achieve a prespecified level of income (expressed in either dollar or percentage terms), to maximize current income while ignoring total return, or to maximize capital values while ignoring current income. Regardless of the return objective chosen, the institution should explain the rationale underlying its choice so that all institutional constituents understand clearly what its investment program is designed to accomplish.

***Time horizon.*** Return objectives are not useful unless they incorporate a specified time horizon. Given the perpetual life status of most endowments, total fund objectives typically have a very long-term time horizon (e.g., 10 or more years). Stated time horizons for individual fund components vary widely: the more volatile and less liquid (i.e., less readily salable) an investment vehicle is, the longer the time horizon that should be used to evaluate its results.

***Long-term asset allocation guidelines.*** Asset allocation guidelines should outline what asset classes and subclasses constitute permissible areas for investment of fund assets and the minimum, maximum, and normal allocation of fund assets to each of these areas. The policy statement should also outline the criteria to be used in determining whether and to what extent funds should be committed to particular areas. These criteria should be as clear and specific as possible, so that all interested parties will understand why certain investments are held and how their performance should be measured and evaluated. Alternate criteria to be used in evaluating proposed investments include:

- To enhance current income

- To enhance principal

- To enhance liquidity

- To reduce market value fluctuations, either generally or in specific economic environments (e.g., deflation, high inflation)

Long-term asset allocation guidelines typically divide endowment assets into at least three parts: a fixed-income component to generate an adequate level of current income and to hedge against deflation; a component that is a multiasset agreement, typically including cash equivalents and other variable income assets, to hedge against high rates of unanticipated inflation; and an equity component to enhance inflation-adjusted returns within acceptable risk parameters. Over time, portions of these components might be allocated to alternate investments such as venture capital or oil and gas drilling partnerships, primarily to enhance returns but also to diversify the fund's holdings and hence keep total fund volatility within acceptable bounds. Some institutions further diversify their fixed-income and equity holdings by the addition of international securities. A number of recent studies have shown that these actions tend to reduce volatility.

EVOLUTION OF INVESTMENT VEHICLES HELD BY ENDOWMENTS. Until the early 1980s educational endowment funds were invested almost exclusively in established asset classes, primarily domestic common stocks and fixed-income instruments. These traditional investments were held either directly or, especially in the case of smaller endowments, through mutual funds. In recent years, however, educational endowments and other institutional investors have made extensive use of such nontraditional investments as equity real estate, foreign securities, small capitalization stocks, leveraged buyouts, and derivative instruments (options and futures). They have also turned increasingly to professional investment managers who employ highly specialized and aggressive investment approaches.

The results have been mixed. Where success has been achieved, it has been because trustees have recognized that the markets for virtually all investment vehicles, even seemingly long-term assets such as equity real estate, are inherently cyclical. They also recognize that the total return an asset produces is ultimately a function of two variables: entry prices at the time it is acquired and exit prices at the time it is sold. Paying careful attention to investment cycles and avoiding the natural human tendency to extrapolate recent return trends, especially large gains or losses, are crucially important principles for the achievement of investment success, especially with respect to new or unfamiliar asset classes or techniques.

An institution's asset mix should be reviewed continually. An unusually large appreciation in the value of particular types of holdings (whether held directly or through outside managers) should not necessarily dictate an increase in their size, nor should an unusually large depreciation dictate their sale. Rather, asset classes and subclasses in which endowment funds are invested should be reviewed on a case-by-case basis with an eye toward determining whether the original thesis underlying their use remains intact. If it does, the investment should either be retained or perhaps augmented (if its price has fallen) to the extent that fund guidelines permit. The rationale for increasing exposure to an investment that has fallen in price is that it now offers higher expected returns; whether it offers higher risk-adjusted expected returns is the critical question that must be addressed. Clearly, if the policy aims that motivated the institution to make the investment are no longer achievable or desirable, sale of the investment should be considered.

*Short-term asset allocation guidelines.* The segregation of assets into discrete segments in accordance with long-term asset allocation guidelines does not address the separate issue of how to exploit temporary opportunities to make asset allocation shifts for total return purposes. These shifts are extremely difficult to make with respect to illiquid investments such as venture capital and equity real estate and can often be counterproductive (because of timing errors) with respect to liquid investments such as stocks and bonds. In practice, most investment committees refrain from making material and frequent shifts themselves. Instead, they either maintain more or less static asset allocations, rebalancing segment weights as needed to offset cash flows or market movements, or they delegate responsibility for short-term asset allocation to full-time investment professionals. Given the difficulties of short-term asset allocation and the risks to an institution of ill-timed shifts, the written statement of guidelines should specify precisely how much flexibility those responsible for short-term allocation decisions enjoy and how their results will be evaluated.

*Manager selection and evaluation criteria.* Selecting an investment manager or managers is one of the most significant actions taken by the investment committee. Some institutions may have a board member willing to manage the portfolio and serve as chair of the investment committee. The risks of such an arrangement almost always outweigh the potential rewards. Competent talent is rarely available on a continuous and volunteer basis, conflicts of interest may exist, and if returns prove unacceptable, the arrangement may be difficult to dissolve.

Institutions with sufficiently large endowments can achieve continuous supervision by hiring a staff of full-time investment managers and support personnel, often through a wholly owned investment management subsidiary. Under this arrangement, the investment committee retains responsibility for making policy but delegates responsibility for investment strategy and tactics. The committee also retains responsibility for monitoring and evaluating the investment staff's performance.

Most institutions, especially those with small endowments, achieve continuous supervision by retaining external investment advisors. Outside management has many advantages. Modern financial markets are complex and highly volatile, and few investment committees have both the expertise and the time to make profitable strategic and tactical investment choices. Reliance upon outside managers also facilitates objective evaluation of performance. The immediate costs of relying upon outside managers exceed the costs of relying upon volunteers, but the long-term net returns (total net returns of manager fees and related expenses) are often higher than they would be in the absence of professional management.

The weights assigned to criteria used in selecting and evaluating investment managers differ, depending on the asset class (or classes) in which prospective managers invest. With respect to active equity managers, for example, the prerequisites for success arguably include a clearly defined investment philosophy, an asset base that is appropriate to this philosophy (neither too small nor too large), and strong incentives to act in the client's long-term interests. These criteria might be applied to managers specializing in other asset classes, but in applying them trustees must carefully consider the distinctive characteristics of the markets in which individual managers will be operating. A proprietary investment philosophy, for example, is not necessarily a prerequisite for success in managing a short-term fixed-income portfolio, nor is asset size as significant a concern for managers of diversified bond portfolios as it is for managers of focused equity portfolios.

While the weights assigned to individual criteria differ, depending on the investment vehicles and management approaches being considered, a checklist of aspects of an investment management organization that should be evaluated can be quite useful.

THE PHILOSOPHY UNDERLYING THE MANAGER'S APPROACH. The consideration includes the investment vehicles that will be used, the likely degree of concentration or diversification in a typical portfolio, the economic and industry sectors that will be favored, the criteria to be used in selecting individual holdings, the portfolio's expected performance during rising and falling markets, and the past and expected evolution of the philosophy.

An important question trustees must address in evaluating alternate investment philosophies is where, along the spectrum of risk or diversification, they believe a fund component should lie. This spectrum is quite broad: it ranges from extremely passive approaches, such as those employed to manage stock index funds, to extremely active approaches, such as those employed by commodity traders. When determining the position of a desired approach along the risk spectrum, trustees must consider many variables, including the "efficiency" of the markets in which a prospective manager operates. An efficient market is one in which the widespread availability and rapid dissemination of data affecting asset prices make it impossible for investors to earn superior returns through intensive research or skilled trading. Many studies suggest that the U.S. stock market is highly efficient, a hypothesis that is supported by evidence suggesting that active equity managers on average tend to underperform passive stock portfolios. Unfortunately, however, the statistical techniques used to measure the market's efficiency do not work very well, because the professional life spans of managers do not generate a sufficient number of data points to produce valid results. Also, while there is universal agreement that the returns a manager produces should be adjusted for risk, there is no agreement on how investment risk should be defined or measured.

The widespread use of approaches lying all along the risk spectrum underscores the diversity of opinions regarding the issue of market efficiency. However diverse these opinions might be, there is no question that most investment markets, including the U.S. stock market, are becoming increasingly efficient in a valuation sense. Approaches that have worked well in the past could continue to add value, but endowment trustees should be prepared to adjust their return expectations downward to reflect the sophistication and competitiveness of most present-day investment markets. If the search for potentially remunerative approaches causes trustees to doubt the efficacy of active techniques, the trustees should employ passive or semipassive managers. Retaining an active manager in whom endowment trustees have less than total confidence is extremely dangerous, because temporary setbacks caused by normal portfolio volatility can induce skittish trustees to terminate the relationship when the assets a manager has selected are trading at temporarily depressed prices.

THE MANAGER'S PERFORMANCE. Measuring a manager's performance includes comparisons of the manager's returns with the performance of (in order of significance):

- Other managers espousing a similar philosophy

- Other managers specializing in the same asset class or investment vehicles

- A benchmark index (passive portfolio) for the asset class or subclass in which the manager invests

Results should be measured over sufficiently long time periods—rolling three- to five-year intervals, in the case of most stock and bond managers.

OTHER VARIABLES. Other variables to consider in evaluating managers include the following.

- Organization, including the breadth and depth of a firm's overall product line; the depth, experience, and retention of key individuals; the allocation of responsibilities within the firm; and its compensation and ownership structure. The number and type of portfolios for which key investment decisionmakers are responsible should be carefully analyzed, as should the percentage of their time spent on noninvestment activities such as administration and marketing. If the institution has a separately managed account, as distinct from units in a commingled pool or mutual fund that the firm offers, the importance of the institution's account in relation to the firm's other portfolios should also be considered, as should the firm's method of supervising individual portfolio managers to ensure their adherence to stated account objectives and guidelines.

- Asset size, including recent trends and the reasons underlying them. Some institutions have experienced difficulties with firms that have grown too fast. Declining assets can indicate that clients have lost confidence in a firm.

- Research conducted by the organization, including the character and quantity of research, the degree of reliance on outside sources, the extent to which a firm has harnessed available technologies to the research function, and the degree to which successful implementation of its approach requires extensive and perhaps proprietary analytical tools.

- The organization's trading history, including the organization's ability to execute purchase and sale orders promptly and economically, taking into account both commissions and price impact.

- The organization's control, including the supervision of portfolio managers and their results, and adherence to stated objectives and institutional policy.

- The organization's lines of communication, including the frequency and manner of reporting and past success at retaining accounts.

When applying these criteria, the governing board should recognize that it is impossible to select the single best manager. It is possible to identify a manager who has performed well historically, but there is no assurance that superior performance will continue and considerable evidence that superior managers' returns tend to regress to the mean. Given these facts, many institutions have sought to limit manager-selection risk through the hiring of multiple managers or by delegating responsibility for manager selection and evaluation to a "manager of managers," such as the not-for-profit Common Fund.

## Manager Relations

The investment authority granted to managers should be as broad as legally possible to provide managers with the flexibility that they need in order to make timely and profitable decisions.

### CONTROLLING MANAGER ACTIONS

Few institutions require prior committee approval of individual purchase and sale decisions, because such a requirement inhibits effective portfolio management. Some institutions maintain "approved lists" of permissible investments, but in practice the lists are either extremely broad (to encompass all issues a manager is likely to consider) or revised periodically to include issues that may already have been purchased. As an alternative to prior committee approval of decisions or approved lists, most institutions formulate written guidelines for managers to follow in deploying portfolio assets. The topics covered in a set of guidelines differ depending on the asset class and manager approach in question.

Equity manager guidelines may include limits on the size and number of individual investments. Percentage limits may be set for total equity positions in any industry or group classification, over-the counter securities, securities in foreign issues, and outstanding shares of any one company. Fixed-income manager guidelines may include percentage limits on the total issues in any one industry or group, on securities of any one issuer, and on the amount of private placements. Such guidelines may also specify any maturity or quality limits to which managers must adhere. Regardless of their exact content, managerial guidelines should be flexible and should be reviewed periodically to ensure their continued appropriateness in light of available investment opportunities and the committee's ongoing assessment of the institution's return objectives and risk tolerances.

## REVIEWING MANAGER ACTIONS

Regular reports to the investment committee concerning investment strategies and tactics are extremely helpful, especially if the manager's approach is very active and entails a high degree of volatility. Periodic face-to-face meetings can be quite useful also, although trustees should recognize that time spent traveling to and attending client meetings is time a manager might otherwise spend on investment functions. The committee's principal concern should be to ensure that managers are faithfully implementing the philosophies that they espouse. Manager performance should be evaluated in accordance with a timetable that is specifically suited to the investment vehicles and approach being employed. As a general rule, managers of longer-term vehicles such as stocks and bonds should be evaluated on a three- to five-year basis, unless it becomes obvious at an earlier date that they are not implementing faithfully or successfully the philosophy of the board.

Investment managers should provide the institution with written reports, preferably monthly but at least quarterly, analyzing recent performance, performance since inception, and diversification and income characteristics. Detailed analyses of holdings showing cost and market values may also be provided by the investment manager but are typically supplied by custodial banks. The institution's expectations regarding the frequency and content of reports and the methods that will be used to evaluate manager results should be codified in writing, typically in the investment advisory contract executed in accordance with relevant state or federal securities laws. Investments in registered mutual funds are not typically covered by separate contracts between the funds' managers and fund shareholders. Rather, such relationships are governed by the Investment Company Act of 1940, which provides mutual fund shareholders with an extensive array of protective safeguards, including the requirement that the board of each investment company (mutual fund) be composed of a specified number of independent directors. Use of registered mutual funds does not insulate the institution from fiduciary liability, but it does afford an additional layer of regulatory protection not available outside the mutual fund setting.

## USING AN INVESTMENT CONSULTANT

A number of organizations offer consulting services designed to assist governing boards in the preparation and implementation of comprehensive investment plans. In selecting an investment consultant, the investment committee or governing board should probe carefully for any conflicts of interest that might prevent the consultant from acting solely in the institution's best interest.

# Enhancing Endowment Returns Through Securities Lending

To enhance earnings, some colleges and universities lend securities to broker-dealers. A security loan is a transaction in which the owner of securities gives up physical possession of certificates to the borrower and in return receives cash or other collateral equal to the full current market value of the securities. While continuing to receive the equivalent income from the securities, the lender also has the unrestricted use of collateral, representing the full value of the securities for the period they are on loan.

Several firms make a specialty of servicing large portfolio accounts by generating security loan arrangements. Although the practice of securities lending is well established, any institution contemplating participation should first learn all of the procedures, including protective controls. In contracting for security loans, care should be exercised to evaluate the financial stability of the broker-dealers involved. Lending institutions should continuously monitor the market values of securities loaned and require the borrower to maintain the cash or other collateral at levels specified in the agreement. Because competition among broker-dealer firms offering securities lending is very intense, the incremental returns that can be earned through securities lending are not as large as they were in the 1970s and early 1980s, prior to the entry of pension funds into this field.

## Measuring Total Fund Results

An important responsibility of the governing board is to ensure that endowments and other funds of the institution are invested to produce stated objectives. Productivity depends on many factors, such as the degree of volatility and risk the governing board is prepared to accept in the market value of investments, restrictions imposed on investments by donors, and the relative emphasis on current income versus long-term growth. Whatever criteria are used to judge the return on investments, it is essential that the rate of return be properly measured and that timely reports be made to the governing board.

The historic dollar value accounting method does not provide the information required to compute investment returns in a manner that permits accurate analysis of investment results. The most accurate method uses the market value unit method of accounting.

A fund's gross return has two components: yield and market value change. Yield is the income earned on investments from dividends, interest, and net rental income for the period, stated as a percentage of the fund's market value during the period. Market value change is the net increase or decrease in market value over a designated period, allowing for cash added to or taken away from the pool during the period, expressed as a percentage of the beginning market value. The combination of yield and market value change is the total gross return on the fund. It is important that both components of gross total return be computed and reported to the governing board at regular intervals and that a net total return also be reported that reflects the deduction of all expenses incurred in the safekeeping and investment of assets.

Costs of investment management include direct expenses, such as costs of supervision of securities, investments in real estate, and other types of investments, plus the cost of custodial arrangements. Indirect costs also may be included. Each fund may bear its proportionate share as a charge against income, or an institution may choose to accept such costs as part of general institutional expense. Proportion of market value is a method used for indirect cost allocation of this type; proportion of activity is another.

Significant cash flows into or out of invested funds can seriously affect the rate of return earned on the total fund. Use of a time-weighted rate of return makes it possible to compute measurements that eliminate the effect of cash flows. The time-weighted rate of return, as opposed to the dollar-weighted rate, is the appropriate measure of results achieved by the fund's investment manager. In averaging rates of return over successive periods, arithmetic averages (adding the rates of return and dividing by the number of periods) should be avoided. A geometric average return (the $n^{th}$ root of a compound return over n periods) is the best measure of how profitably the portfolio has been managed.

Many institutions are interested in comparing their investment results with the rate of return achieved on widely quoted indexes, such as Standard & Poor's 500 Stock Index. In making such comparisons, governing boards should employ indexes that are appropriate to the assets whose performance is being measured. Stock indexes are appropriate benchmarks for the measurement of equity managers' performance, but they are inappropriate for the measurement of total fund results, which by definition also reflect the performance of nonequity holdings. Evaluation of total fund results can be made by constructing a composite benchmark that weights the performance of individual asset class benchmarks, such as stock or bond indexes, in accordance with their representation in the overall endowment. The best measurements adjust both the portfolio and the selected indexes for dividends and/or interest. A more comprehensive review of performance may also include measurements of the variability of returns and comparisons of turnover rates on individual fund components.

Many organizations offer performance measurement services. These services measure total fund returns and returns produced by individual fund components; they also categorize managers by investment philosophy and compare managers' returns to returns produced by competing firms with similar investment philosophies.

The National Association of College and University Business Officers (NACUBO) publishes an annual comprehensive endowment study that contains performance, asset allocation, and other data on endowment management practices supplied by participating institutions. Participants typically include institutions representing more than 90 percent of the total endowment of American higher education, and the study has become an important resource for governing boards and administrators seeking to compare their policies and practices to those employed by peer institutions.

In computing rates of return for purposes of evaluating the quality of investment management, it is important to exclude unappraised or unmanaged investments, as well as investments not under control of the governing board or the firms to whom the board has delegated investment discretion. Unmanaged investments include such items as unregistered or "letter" stock, gifts of securities that donors require to be held in the portfolio as a condition of such gifts, or funds invested in institutional buildings. It may be useful to report earnings on all investments, including such items, but they should not be included for purposes of evaluating investment management prowess.

## Social Responsibility

The objective of managing endowment and other funds is to seek maximum long-term investment return without incurring excessive risk. However, the governing board should be aware that social responsibility might also be considered. Advocates of investment responsibility have called on educational institutions to be concerned with social, moral, and ethical considerations in their investments.

Traditionally, institutional investors have tended to follow the "Wall Street rule"—they may support positions taken by corporate management unless there is disagreement, in which case that particular stock is sold. However, in recent years, the trend has moved away from strict adherence to this rule. The more thoughtful investor now makes choices beforehand as to the desirability of involvement with individual portfolio companies.

Many institutions accept the premise that corporations have a moral obligation not to inflict injury on society. As investors and therefore owners of the corporation, institutions have an obligation to communicate their concern to corporations and to seek the prevention of social injury. In addition, some institutions may expect corporations to contribute time, talent, materials, or money to social activities. An investor can encourage or attempt to alter a corporation's practices in at least three ways:

- Through the purchase or sale of stock or other securities

- Through the use of a proxy, available to the owner of voting stock

- Through correspondence or other forms of communication

In exercising an institution's freedom to invest, the board or its agents should bear in mind that this freedom is subject to certain legal and fiduciary responsibilities. For example, state law may prohibit the use of institutional investments to support a particular political point of view.

When analyzing a corporation's level of social responsibility, it is wise to separate those issues that are mandated by law from those that truly represent the corporation's actions within society. Minimal societal involvement should not be construed as lack of interest. Rather, consideration should be given to the nature and size of the business and to the level of involvement that is justified. Conversely, magnanimous corporate activity may raise questions about objectives and values. What may appear to be a "sound social investment" may, on review, produce neither tangible nor intangible returns.

These are but a few of the concerns that the governing board should consider in assessing the complex issue of an institution's social responsibility. Serious consideration should be given to adopting a separate policy concerning issues of social responsibility in investment management. Institutions lacking such a policy may be open to the accusation that such issues are of little or no concern to them. If a policy statement on investor responsibility is adopted by a governing board, it should describe responsibilities of officers and committees and the decision-making process related to social and political issues in investment decisions.

Colleges and universities may find it helpful to use the services of organizations whose purpose is to provide impartial and timely analysis, without recommendations, of corporate social responsibility.

# Custodial, Safekeeping, and Execution Services

A custodial or safekeeping arrangement with a bank or trust company is essential to implement an institution's investment program safely and efficiently and to monitor results. Services performed by a custodian typically include preparation of up-to-date portfolio appraisals, timely exercise or sale of stock rights, presentation of called bonds for payment, conversion or sale of convertible securities, handling and deposit of dividends and interest income, and carrying out policies related to proxy voting. Service can be extended to include use of the custodian's nominee name. A nominee is an individual, partnership, or other legal entity established for the limited purpose of facilitating the transferability of record ownership of securities without regard to beneficial ownership or interest. This device facilitates compliance with the requirements of the organized securities markets: the custodial nominee typically is a member of automated clearinghouses for securities transfers and, as such, acts as an agent for its custodial clients in delivering and receiving securities.

Custodial services should be specified by written agreement and, in addition to the items mentioned above, may include classification of securities holdings, amount of interest and dividends received, accrued interest schedules, and amortization schedules. Under certain arrangements, verified custodial reports may serve as subsidiary records for the institution. If all security transactions flow through the custodian, computer-to-computer transmission may be possible and relatively inexpensive.

Under custodial arrangements, receipt and delivery of securities usually are from or to brokers against payments charged or credited to a designated bank account or received or remitted by check or wire transfer.

The arrangement for buying and selling investments varies with the nature of the portfolio and form of management organization. When an institution has its own internal investment organization, the full-time manager employed by the institution should be responsible for executions. When an independent advisor is employed—whether a bank, trust company, or investment management firm—it should have its own trading department, staffed with persons whose principal responsibilities are executing transactions, checking markets, and identifying prospective sellers or purchasers of particular securities. This arrangement provides for the most advantageous purchases and sales.

It is important to select investment banking and brokerage firms that execute orders promptly and efficiently and that invest idle cash quickly; that have research divisions capable of providing investment information; that are active in underwriting new issues or in managing private placements; and that make a market for, or deal in, certain securities. An investment performance measurement service is also necessary.

Even though the investment management firm executes transactions, the allocation of the institution's business should be determined by the manager in consultation with the institution. Care should be exercised to avoid conflicts of interest. It is not only appropriate but good practice to require allocation of commissions to those investment brokerage firms providing services. Because of the recent transition from standard commissions to negotiated commissions, available services have varied widely. Good execution and commission prices are important considerations in routing business. Other services provided by brokerage firms may be negotiated into the commission or purchased separately. It is also good practice to review quarterly the allocation of brokerage commissions paid by the fund, including identification of individuals in the brokerage firms and reasons for using them.

## Deferred-Giving Assets

The principal of funds received under deferred-giving agreements, more commonly referred to as life income and annuity funds, generally cannot be expended for the benefit of the institution until the death of the donor or donor-designated beneficiaries. Also, state laws may require that the assets of such funds be invested separately. However, in some cases endowment funds and certain annuity and life income funds may be commingled for investment purposes. The chief difference between annuity and life income funds and endowment funds is that annuity and life income funds are held for the benefit of named beneficiaries until their death, and during this time the income is not available to the institution for its use. These funds may ultimately become endowment funds or funds functioning as endowment—the former by donor restrictions and the latter by decisions of the governing board. However, life income and annuity funds should be reported as a separate fund group in the financial statements until they become legally available for other uses.

## LIFE INCOME AND ANNUITY FUNDS

A life income agreement is an agreement whereby money or other property is made available to an institution on condition that the institution bind itself to pay periodically to the donor and/or donor-designated individual(s) the income earned by assets donated to the institution for the lifetime of such beneficiaries. If the institution is obligated to pay stipulated amounts rather than only the income actually earned by the assets, the term "annuity agreement" should be used. An annuity agreement is an agreement whereby money or other property is made available to an institution on condition that the institution bind itself to pay periodically to the donor and/or donor-designated individual(s) stipulated amounts, which terminate at a time specified in the agreement.

Prior to passage of the Tax Reform Act of 1969, arrangements with donors were often informal. Many institutions sought to avoid a trust relationship, as defined by local law, by use of "life income agreements" and scrupulous avoidance of the word "trust." The Tax Reform Act of 1969 clearly established the existence of a trust relationship (for Internal Revenue Service purposes) when educational institutions issue qualified life income or annuity agreements. The act stipulates that gifts or bequests subject to life income must be made to qualified pooled life income funds or charitable remainder unitrusts or annuity trusts (as defined in the act) in order to qualify for the income, estate, or gift tax charitable deductions. Definitions of these methods of deferred giving prepared for the information of donors must include detailed provisions governing administration of various types of trusts. Donors may make additional gifts to existing pooled life income trusts or unitrusts. However, additions to annuity trusts are not permitted under the act.

Institutions that now administer or plan to administer deferred-giving agreements should seek advice from counsel to ensure compliance with relevant provisions of federal and state laws. The officer responsible for deferred-giving agreement administration and investments should be thoroughly familiar with the legal, tax, and accounting complexities of deferred-giving programs, and should analyze carefully the utility to the institution (and to potential donors) of various sizes and types of deferred gifts.

Guidelines should be established by the governing board with respect to methods of deferred giving accepted by the institution. These guidelines could include the following:

- Suitability of each type of agreement to the institution's needs and operating capabilities

- Minimum gift amount required to establish the type of trust in question

- Maximum number of life beneficiaries permitted

- Minimum age for beneficiaries

- Cost of investment management and whether to charge a fee to cover these costs

Many institutions refrain from charging beneficiaries for investment management. Because of this, many donors recognize that giving a life income fund may produce an income stream somewhat greater than might other alternatives; it is important that an institution consider carefully how management costs will be allocated. Management costs are associated with any investment fund, and such expenses should be recognized and accounted for. The institution should consider whether such costs will be charged to specific funds or offset by general funds.

Four types of deferred-giving agreements qualify the donor for federal income tax benefits: charitable gift annuity contracts, pooled life income funds, charitable remainder unitrusts, and charitable remainder annuity trusts.

*Charitable gift annuity contracts.* A gift of cash or other assets may be given to an institution by a donor in return for an agreement by the institution that it will pay the donor and/or named beneficiaries periodic annuity payments for the donor's and/or beneficiaries' lifetime. The full faith and credit of the institution stand behind these contracts. The cash or assets donated become the assets of the institution and can be used for any purpose the institution wishes or any restricted purpose the donor specifies. Even though the assets are technically available for immediate use and are not legally required to be set aside for income-producing purposes, most institutions do set these assets aside in a separate fund to produce income until the donor and/or beneficiaries have died. Some institutions have accepted non-income-producing real estate (private homes) in return for charitable gift annuity contracts. In these cases the cash used to cover the periodic payments is drawn from the current fund or some other fund until the asset is sold.

The rates of return paid to the donor and/or beneficiaries are generally based upon their respective ages. The Committee on Gift Annuities, an organization that comprises many of the charitable organizations that issue charitable gift annuity contracts, has established payout rates using actuarial methods that presumably leave the institution a residual of 50 percent of the original value of the assets given to the institution. Most colleges and universities that issue charitable gift annuity contracts follow the rates established by the Committee on Gift Annuities.

***Pooled life income funds.*** A pooled life income fund is a trust, defined in Section 642(c)(5) of the Internal Revenue Code, to which donors make irrevocable gifts of money or securities that are commingled with the property of other donors who have made similar transfers. Each donor retains a life income interest, as do named beneficiaries living at the time the gift is made. Each beneficiary is entitled to a pro rata share of the pooled fund's earnings each year for his or her lifetime. At the death of the last beneficiary, the charitable organization severs the donor's share of the pooled fund and uses it for charitable purposes.

Assets of pooled life income funds may be commingled with assets of other institutional funds—such as assets of an endowment pool. However, institutions must carefully consider using a consolidated pool, as certain legal restrictions, such as those concerned with self-dealing and investments in tax-exempt securities, apply to life income and annuity funds. If an institution adopts a total return spending policy for its pooled endowment and similar funds, life income funds must be invested in a separate pool, under the requirements of the Tax Reform Act of 1969. Institutions not using the total return method may continue to invest life income funds in a pool (or registered mutual fund) with other institutional funds as long as adequate accounting records are maintained that specifically identify the life income portion of the pool and the income earned by and attributable to that portion. Any institution with a significant number of life income funds should establish one or more separate life income pools to facilitate compliance with the stringent operating rules established by the act. Tax law requires that the market value, unit method of accounting be used for all pooled life income funds, whether or not the assets are commingled with assets of endowment funds.

The institution may delegate its trustee responsibility for the investment management of a pooled life income fund to a bank, as long as the institution retains the power to change trustees. Moreover, a bank may use a common trust fund as an investment vehicle; by using this device, it may be possible for smaller institutions to effect considerable cost savings and achieve greater diversification of their pooled life income funds. As noted, responsibility for investing life income assets may also be delegated to a registered investment advisor.

Management of a pooled life income fund presents no unique problems, but as with any investment pool, the institution should articulate clearly the fund's return objectives. Institutions operating only one pooled income fund often opt for a balanced fund aimed at moderate income and some growth. Larger institutions may wish to operate more than one life income pool in order to give donors a wider array of income and growth options; an individual donor's selection of an option will depend on his or her charitable objectives for the institution and the ages of beneficiaries and their financial circumstances.

***Charitable remainder unitrusts.*** There are three variations of the charitable remainder unitrust.

STRAIGHT UNITRUST. In a "straight" unitrust, a donor irrevocably transfers money, securities, or property to a separate trust that has a charitable remainderman, with payments to be distributed to named beneficiaries at least annually in an amount equal to a fixed percentage (not less than 5 percent under the act) of the net fair market value of trust assets determined annually. On the death of the last beneficiary, the trust terminates and assets are distributed to the charitable remainderman. The donor may designate him- or herself and/or other beneficiaries to receive these payments as long as designated beneficiaries are alive at the time the trust is created, and payments are made for their lifetimes or for a term not to exceed 20 years.

In a straight unitrust, a stated percentage of the market value of trust assets must be distributed annually regardless of whether this amount is earned by the trust. To meet the payout obligation, tax law specifies that the trustee must first pay all ordinary income from the current year or prior years, then pay realized capital gains from the current year or prior years, and finally return principal to the beneficiary, if necessary. Moreover, the payments retain their character in the hands of the beneficiaries and the beneficiaries are taxed accordingly. Hence the straight unitrust is primarily of interest to donors in high tax brackets who seek maximum appreciation and minimum ordinary income. This dictates an active, closely supervised, growth-oriented investment program.

NET INCOME UNITRUST. The "net income" unitrust is similar to a straight unitrust except that payments to beneficiaries are limited to the actual income earned by the trust up to but not exceeding the fixed percentage stated in the trust agreement. Once the initial investment is made, investment activity in such a trust must be executed with care to ensure that income payments are not reduced.

NET-PLUS-MAKEUP UNITRUST. In the "net-plus-makeup" unitrust, payments are limited to ordinary earned income as in the case of the net income unitrust, except that payments may exceed the stated percentage up to but not exceeding the amount required to make up any accumulated deficiencies from prior years (years in which the trust earned less than the stated percentage). This option usually is chosen by younger donors seeking capital appreciation until retirement and maximum income thereafter. The investment strategy therefore is similar to that for a straight unitrust initially and shifts to a net income strategy at a later date. The development office is responsible for informing the investment officer of the donor's objectives in such cases.

Net income and net-plus-makeup unitrusts differ from pre-1969 separately invested life income funds only in that the payout rate stated in the instrument imposes a ceiling on distributions, expressed as a percentage of the fair market value of trust assets.

Administratively, several options are available for managing unitrusts. The institution can, in effect, run a small "trust department," making individual decisions with respect to the investment of each straight unitrust. This is difficult and costly for a large number of trusts. It may be possible, however, for the institution's investment advisor to prepare a list of a limited number of low-yield, growth-oriented securities in which all straight unitrusts will be invested. These ordinarily will be issues held in the institution's regular portfolio. Such a list should be monitored closely and reviewed regularly.

An institution may elect to have a bank serve as trustee of its unitrusts, in which case the investment vehicle for all but the largest trusts ordinarily is the bank's growth-oriented common trust fund. Such an arrangement may permit an institution to accept smaller straight unitrusts than it could afford to accept if it retained direct investment responsibility. An institution also may elect to invest its straight unitrusts in a minimum number of growth-oriented mutual funds.

***Charitable remainder annuity trusts.*** A charitable remainder annuity trust is defined in Section 664(d)(1) of the Internal Revenue Code as one created by a donor irrevocably transferring money or securities for the benefit of a charitable organization in exchange for a fixed dollar amount (at least 5 percent of the initial fair market value of the transferred property) to be paid at least annually to a designated beneficiary or beneficiaries for their lifetimes or for a fixed term not to exceed 20 years. At the death of the donor or the last surviving beneficiary, the trust terminates and assets of the annuity trust are transferred to the charitable organization for which the trust was created.

Except that the dollar amount of annual payment is fixed at the outset, the annuity trust is essentially similar to a unitrust; the same "tiered" payout rule applies to annuity trusts and straight unitrusts. Because of the fixed annual payment, the donor has an interest in how trust assets are invested only to the extent that it affects the character of the payments and the trustee pursues a strategy that, at a minimum, preserves sufficient assets to make required payments for the life of the beneficiary.

Two variants of annuity trusts are the term-of-years trust and the tax-free trust. A term-of-years trust pays the donor income over a period of years rather than over a lifetime. Scheduling payments for the years when the donor's children will be in college is one popular use of this trust. Tax-free trusts are identical to other annuity trusts but are funded with cash or municipal bonds, the income from which is exempt from federal tax.

## CHARITABLE LEND TRUSTS

Charitable lend trusts also may be called front-end charitable trusts, charitable income trusts, or Clifford Trusts for Charity. These trusts essentially lend assets to the institution. When establishing such trusts, donors specify that income will be distributed to a nonprofit charitable organization for a specified time, after which the assets will revert to a noncharitable beneficiary (such as a child or grandchild). During the period of the trust's existence, the income that is distributed to the institution is not taxable to the donor.

# References and Resources

PUBLICATIONS AND ARTICLES

Arnott, Robert, and Frank J. Fabozzi, eds. *Asset Allocation: A Handbook of Portfolio Policies, Strategies, and Tactics.* Chicago, Ill.: Probus Publishing Co., 1988.

Cambridge Associates. *1991 NACUBO Endowment Study.* Washington, D.C.: National Association of College and University Business Officers, 1992.

Cary, William L., and Craig B. Bright. *The Law and the Lore of Endowment Funds.* New York: The Ford Foundation, 1969.

Ellis, Charles D., and James R. Vertin, eds. *Classics: An Investor's Anthology.* Homewood, Ill.: Dow-Jones Irwin, 1989.

Fabozzi, Frank J. *Fixed Income Portfolio Strategies.* Chicago, Ill.: Probus Publishing Co., 1988.

Financial Analysts Federation. *Performance Presentation Standards.* Charlottesville, Va.: Committee for Performance Presentation Standards, 1990.

Fogler, H. Russell, and Darwin M. Bayston. *Improving the Investment Decision Process: Quantitative Assistance for the Practitioner and for the Firm.* Charlottesville, Va.: Institute of Chartered Financial Analysts, 1984.

Investment Counsel Association of America. *The Standards of Measurement and Use for Investment Performance Data.* New York: ICAA, 1988.

Kittell, Cathryn E., ed. *The Challenges of Investing for Endowment Funds.* Charlottesville, Va.: Institute of Chartered Financial Analysts, 1987.

Levine, Sumner N., ed. *The Financial Analyst's Handbook.* 2nd ed.

Homewood, Ill.: Dow-Jones Irwin, 1988.

Rosenberg, Claude N. *Investing with the Best*. New York: John Wiley & Sons, 1986.

Sharpe, William F., and Gordon J. Alexander. *Investments*. 4th ed. Englewood Cliffs, N.J.: Prentice-Hall, 1989.

Wagner, Wayne H., ed. *The Complete Guide to Securities Transactions*. New York: John Wiley & Sons, 1989.

Williams, Arthur, III. *Managing Your Investment Manager*. 2nd ed. Homewood, Ill.: Dow-Jones Irwin, 1986.

PERIODICALS
*Financial Analysts Journal*

*Forbes*

*Institutional Investor*

*Journal of Portfolio Management*

*Money Management Letter*

*Pensions and Investments*

# CHAPTER 11

# Cash Management

by
Dominick F. Carbone
Sarah Lawrence University

Cash Management Group
The Common Fund

Oliver Engert
CoreStates Financial Corporation

Donald R. Price
Stanford University

Abbott Wainwright

# Sponsors

## THE COMMON FUND
363 Reef Road
P.O. Box 940
Fairfield, CT 06430
203-255-7000

*The Common Fund provides comprehensive investment management programs for endowment and operating funds for its member colleges, universities, and independent schools.*

## CORESTATES FINANCIAL CORPORATION
Philadelphia National Bank, FC 1-7-9-20
Broad and Chestnut Streets
Philadelphia, PA 19101
215-973-5638

*CoreStates develops, delivers, and manages cash management services designed specifically for academic institutions.*

# Contents

## 11: Cash Management

C ash management is the discipline of effectively managing cash from the moment a claim for cash is established until an application for disbursement is satisfied. The ultimate objective of cash management is to maximize investment income and to minimize expenses associated with cash flows in the most cost-effective manner possible. Cash management can be defined as having the right amount of money in the right place at the right time. This definition can be translated into the following formula:

Beginning Cash + Collections - Disbursements =
Investable Balances

An effective cash management program ensures that funds in transit move safely and economically and, at the same time, are managed to maximize their ability to earn interest. This activity is accomplished within the constraints of liquidity needs, short- and long-term financing requirements, and a college or university's investment and spending policies. The benefits of a good cash management program can significantly exceed the costs of maintaining the program.

In their quest for the maximum return on cash investments and the reduction of costs, cash managers must look for new, more efficient means of handling funds as money moves from the payor to the college or university, to the investment vehicle, and out of the investment vehicle for disbursement. Before any cash management system can be effective, however, the appropriate institutional environment must exist.

## Institutional Environment

An effective program of cash management relies largely on institutional commitment. Anyone involved with the receipt or disbursement of a college or university's money must understand its value, expressed either as a lost opportunity cost or in terms of the time value of money. Even funds invested overnight can produce revenues. Some institutions pay bills before they are due. Similarly, institutional departments may use an incoming check as an accounting document and delay its deposit to the bank until the accounting and posting are completed. The responsibility of the cash manager is to create an awareness of the critical relationship of time (the time value of money) and cash value (the cash-flow time-line) throughout the institution. It is important that operations that receive cash on a daily basis, such as auxiliary enterprises and the development office, make prompt deposits.

*The cash-flow time-line.* The cash-flow time-line begins when funds become due and ends when they are available for investment or other uses; the time-line begins again in reverse when funds are disbursed from an investment vehicle and ultimately presented for payment. Although that sounds simple, it can be complicated because many people in a college or university control the time-line, including the admissions officer, the provost, the financial or business officer, the controller, and the bursar. These individuals can play an important role in delaying or speeding the collection and disbursement process.

*Staffing.* Appropriate staffing for cash management varies with institutional size and the complexity and thoroughness of the cash management program. Regardless of the college or university's size, the use of a single person to act as cash manager, even on a part-time basis, can be effective. At some institutions, one officer has full responsibility for all details of the cash management program. At others, the cash manager acts as a coordinator and works closely with the treasurer and controller on receipts and disbursements, banking relationships, and short-term investments. Frequently, the responsibility for investing funds is separate from managing the cash flow, although these functions should be coordinated. The level of staffing committed to cash management should ultimately be based on the economic return gained by additional investment income or reduced borrowing costs.

*The cash manager.* The cash manager should pay attention, on a daily basis, to bank balances, receipts, and disbursements. Daily attention provides assurance that cash is being managed correctly, that there is sufficient liquidity to meet requirements, and that surplus funds are being invested. In addition, daily information should be obtained on unexpected incoming funds and disbursements. Meticulous oversight provides knowledge of incoming account receipts and authorized account changes. The level of collected funds in the bank accounts, not the deposited cash balance on the institution's records, should receive the cash manager's attention.

## Other Environmental Factors

Many factors significantly affect the environment of cash management.

BANKS

Banks provide many useful and necessary services to their depositors, but many regulations have been imposed that limit the services that they can provide. Furthermore, regulations vary from state to state. The banking environment has several characteristics that affect cash management.

- State and federal restrictions have led to a banking system that is large and complex; there are 12,000 commercial banking institutions in the U.S. (18,000, including credit unions and savings and loans entities). The sheer number of banks, in addition to other market factors, has resulted in a competitive banking environment that requires a sophisticated understanding of the products and services available.

- Of the many services that banks provide, the most basic is the storing of cash value. However, banks are not permitted to pay interest on deposits in commercial accounts. Consequently, a cash manager must have the goal of reducing idle cash in checking accounts and transferring excess funds into interest-bearing instruments. In response to this need, the financial community provides various sources of short- and intermediate-term investments, and banks offer ways to accelerate cash receipts and decelerate cash disbursements.

- Cost, speed, and security considerations have made electronic collection and disbursement systems a significant area.

Most colleges and universities use local banks for their financial needs and compensate them for services rendered by leaving idle balances. In an effort to enhance community relations, many institutions have accounts with several banks. Consequently, significant sums of interest-free money may lie idle in various commercial accounts. One goal of effective cash management is to reduce the number of separate bank accounts the institution maintains. Idle balances should be consolidated into a "concentration account" from which excess balances can be moved daily into short- and intermediate-term investment vehicles to earn income. Some argue that the maintenance of excess balances is in the college or university's favor, because it eliminates the cost of bank service fees. However, in most cases the fees are offset by the income that can be earned by having idle balances invested in income-producing investments. Most institutions use a combination of fees and compensating balances, with larger institutions leaning toward fees and smaller ones toward balances; very few pay only fees.

Cash managers must consider the creditworthiness of the banks with which they do business. Funds in excess of the Federal Deposit Insurance Corporation (FDIC) insured limit of $100,000 should be thought of as unsecured loans; if the bank failed, these funds would be lost. Several companies evaluate the creditworthiness of banks; these companies should be consulted by cash managers.

## CHECK CLEARING

To appreciate the complexities and issues of cash management, managers must understand the check-clearing process. An example illustrates this procedure: A university on the East Coast pays an invoice for books it purchased from a West Coast supplier. The university writes a check on its local Bank A disbursement account and mails it to the vendor on the West Coast. Several days later the vendor receives the check and deposits it at its local Bank B, which encodes the dollar amount and delivers the check to the San Francisco Federal Reserve Bank (SFFRB) for collection. SFFRB recognizes that this check is drawn on the Philadelphia Federal Reserve Bank (PFRB) and routes the check via an airplane back to the PFRB. The PFRB receives the item, recognizes that it belongs to Bank A and delivers it there (a presentment). Upon receipt, Bank A debits the university's account and passes value (availability) to the PFRB with further credit to the SFFRB. The SFFRB in turn passes the value to Bank B, which credits the vendor's account with available funds. This total process can take six or seven days. Usually two to four days of this time are involved in the check's transit through the U.S. postal system and other transportation vehicles, plus any delay associated with the on-campus internal mail delivery system. Figure 11-1 is an outline of the check-clearing process.

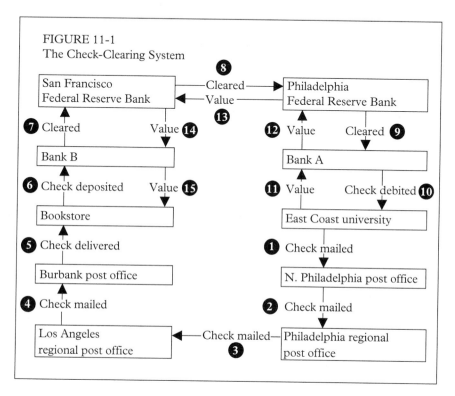

FIGURE 11-1
The Check-Clearing System

Check processing is managed by special computers known as high-speed readers and sorters, which automatically read computer numbers printed on the bottom of each check, called the magnetic ink character recognition (MICR) line. Data on this line contain all the relevant information needed to return the check to the payor's Federal Reserve district bank and bank account. Key routing information is also printed in the upper portion of the check. Because checks pass through these readers and sorters at high speeds, the MICR line is sometimes damaged or destroyed. In this case, MICR lines can be reconstructed from the information located in the upper portion of the check.

In cases where large volumes of checks travel between two banks, one bank usually batches all of its checks written on the other bank's account and directly transports these to that other bank, bypassing the Federal Reserve System. These "direct sends" improve collection times and reduce check-clearing costs.

## FUNDS AVAILABILITY

An availability schedule is a predetermined timetable that indicates when a check drawn on another bank will be recognized as collected and funds will be made available to the depositor. Availability is often calculated on a check-by-check basis, though banks have several options in assigning availability to their customers' accounts. Checks drawn on distant banks clear more slowly than checks drawn on local banks because of the physical distance the checks must travel. The cash manager should request a copy of the availability schedule from the college or university's bank and compare it with the schedules of other banks, paying close attention to the collection time of frequently received checks. If the college or university bank's schedule is inferior to others, the bank should be asked whether this is the best schedule it will offer. Funds availability schedules may sometimes be improved through negotiations.

Although some banks have numerous availability schedules, others have only one schedule or no schedule at all. In some cases, the bank makes funds available on a factored basis: for example, 85 percent next-day availability. In this case, if a college deposits $100 on Monday, $85 would be available on Tuesday and $15 would be available on Wednesday.

## FLOAT COST

Collection float is the loss of interest on funds between the time when money is due and the payor mails a check or transfers funds and the time when this money is available for use by the college or university. There are several components of this float: "mail float" is the time a check spends in the mail system, in both the U.S. Postal Service system and the college or university's mail room; "processing float" is the time it takes the payee to deposit a check in the bank; "availability float" is the time it takes the bank to provide funds for a check.

Disbursement float is the mirror image of the collection process, in which the payor tries to hold on to available funds for as long as possible.

When the collection process is accelerated or the disbursement process is decelerated, the potential gains are measured in funds availability. The faster funds move along the incoming cash-flow time-line, the sooner the money can be invested and start earning income. The more slowly funds move along the outgoing cash-flow time-line, the longer the money can be invested and continue to earn income.

For example, assume that, in a $200 million operating budget, $50 million is received on a noncyclical basis; these funds include the tuition receipts of monthly installment plans, bookstore sales, and other daily remittances. Because there are approximately 250 business days per year, one can assume that $200,000 is received on the average day ($50 million divided by 250). If the availability of these funds can be accelerated by even one day (meaning the institution has use of them one day sooner) by depositing them earlier or accelerating the processing of remittances, the institution would realize a $200,000 increase in available or investable funds. At an 8.5 percent annual interest rate, $17,000 per year would be gained in interest income ($200,000 multiplied by 8.5 percent).

Payment receipts that are sent directly to the college or university should be segregated from the regular mail by means of a separate post office box at a central post office, where mail is not delayed by having to be forwarded to a local branch office. Other techniques are available to move funds faster (see "Collections" section below). The cash manager should review each cash-handling technique along the time-line to attempt to reduce borrowing costs, banking costs, and in-house clerical time.

## INTEREST RATES

Interest rates and the interest rate curve affect the cost of banking services as well as the investment horizon for short-term funds. If compensating balances are used to pay for banking services, the balance needed to recompense services varies inversely with general market rates (see "Bank Relations," below). The lower the interest conditions in the marketplace, the greater the level of compensating balances the college or university must maintain to cover service needs. The opposite is also true: as interest rates escalate, the required amount of compensating balances is reduced because of the increased investment return by the bank, which is considered as payment for bank services.

Furthermore, because the potential benefit for accelerated movement of funds is significant during times of high interest rates, more resources can be put into this effort. During very low interest rate periods, the reduced level of benefits in funds movement tends to decrease the resources (costs) that can be put into this effort.

In scheduling short-term investments to meet liquidity needs and at the same time maximize investment income, the cash manager should consider the level and direction of interest rates; these change over time. The interest rate curve provides important information necessary to determine the length of time in which short-term funds should be committed.

## Bank Relations

A cash management program is not possible without a satisfactory relationship between the college or university and its bank(s). In developing good banking relations, the cash manager must first realize that a bank provides a number of services that customers cannot provide for themselves. The cash manager also must realize that these services involve a cost to the bank and require the bank to earn a reasonable profit.

In a good banking relationship, both the bank and the college or university should pay attention to the total package of services provided, rather than to individual service costs. Costs should be negotiated with the bank, but other factors are also important: the quality of service provided, the promptness of attention given to problems, the willingness of the bank to introduce new cash management techniques and services to the institution, and other subjective qualities. As a customer, the institution should tell the bank how well it is performing its services by giving it a periodic "report card" on the quality of its services, its effectiveness in improving the cash management system, and the speed of its problem resolution.

As mentioned above, there are two ways in which banks are usually compensated for their services: either the customer pays a fee for each service or the customer maintains a balance of funds sufficient in size to meet the bank's cost of services. The compensating balance allows the bank to earn compensation through investment or lending of idle balances that remain in the institution's accounts. Banks prefer that customers maintain compensating balances for two reasons: compensating balances are an inexpensive source of money to fund loans, and they ensure liquidity for the bank's balance sheet.

Fees are becoming more widely used for certain specialized banking services, such as stop-payment orders and computer services. However, compensating balances remain the most widely accepted method for paying banks for services. The cash manager should recognize the bank's need for compensating balances and understand what constitutes a required compensating balance. On the other hand, maintaining balances at a level higher than is necessary to properly compensate the bank for the level of service received is wasteful. Good banking relations, consistent with the efficient management of a college or university's cash, call for a businesslike approach to determining the proper level of compensating balances in bank accounts.

Cash managers should consider preparing requests for information (RFI) or requests for proposals (RFP) for existing or new bank services. These requests enable the cash manager to learn about services that a bank is willing and able to provide. At its simplest, an RFP is a letter that requests detailed information from banks on the services they provide and their cost. An RFP should be specific as to:

- The due date of the response

- The suggested format of the response

- The person who may be contacted for any questions

- The college or university's current banking arrangements

- The college or university's most important banking needs

- Additional banking services that the college or university is interested in

- When the bank can expect a decision on its proposal

## Collections

A collection system should have four objectives:

- To collect receivables in a cost-effective manner

- To convert collections into available funds as rapidly as possible

- To identify surplus cash on a daily basis and move it into income-generating investments

- To update receivables data quickly and accurately

An examination of the collection process should begin with identifying the sources of cash flows into the institution and the typical collection methods used by the college or university. Payments are usually received in one of three ways:

- Over the counter at various departments, such as the bursar's office, the bookstore, and the cafeteria (These funds are deposited at the college or university's local bank.)

- By mail to the college or university or directly to the institution's bank (lockbox)

- Electronically to the college or university's bank as initiated by either the institution or the payor

Payments may be in the form of cash, checks, electronic means such as wires, automated clearing house transfers, and charge cards. Tuition and fees represent the bulk of inflows for smaller institutions, with endowment, gifts, and bequests playing a lesser role. For larger institutions, the opposite is true, with endowment, gifts, and corporate and government research grants making up a larger portion of inflows, and tuition and fees representing a smaller portion.

## PAPER MECHANISMS

The simplest example of a paper collection mechanism is the bursar's office receiving a check for tuition payment, whereupon a staff member updates the student's records and endorses and deposits the check at the local branch of the institution's bank.

Pre-encoding checks is a somewhat more sophisticated technique whereby the institution endorses and encodes a check for the proper dollar amount prior to making a deposit. Encoding of checks by the institution reduces bank charges and may speed availability, but the labor and equipment costs and the delays in check deposits due to the encoding process cannot be ignored. A cost-benefit analysis should be prepared to determine the specific net cost benefit to the institution.

A streamlined operation can ensure that no more than six hours elapse between receipt of payment and deposit in the bank. There are significant opportunities to speed the cash-flow time-line; one way to do this is by using a lockbox.

***Lockboxes.*** A lockbox reduces mail float because remittances are mailed directly to central postal processing centers, bypassing the smaller, less efficient local post office and the institution's mail room. Special zip codes are used, further speeding delivery to the bank. Typically, an institution receives mail once or, at most, twice a day, while the bank may receive lockbox mail 24 hours a day, seven days a week, with up to 24 pickups each day. Many banks receive the majority of the day's mail by 5:00 a.m. Check processing and collection time is lessened with the use of lockboxes because of highly sophisticated systems and round-the-clock operation.

There are two types of lockboxes: wholesale and retail. Wholesale lockboxes are for institutions with moderate item volume and large dollar remittances; retail lockboxes are for those with small dollar remittances and large item volume, and whose payments are accompanied by machine-readable invoices. The purpose of a wholesale lockbox is to accelerate the availability of checks in the amount of $1,000 or more, while the purpose of a retail lockbox is to help manage a high volume of activity and automatically update receivables information. Typically, bank service charges are higher for wholesale lockboxes than for retail lockboxes because the remittance processing for wholesale lockboxes is less automated and requires faster processing to meet availability deadlines.

A lockbox can contribute significantly to several of the objectives of a collection system. For example, a student sends a tuition payment with the tuition invoice to the institution's lockbox. Depending on the bank's lockbox service and the institution's volume of receipts, the bank clears the box several times daily, taking the receipts directly to its processing center, processing the checks, and placing them immediately into the collection system. Photocopies of the checks are attached to remittance information (such as invoices and correspondence) and dispatched by the bank via courier to the institution. Sophisticated banks incorporate up-to-the-minute reporting on funds credited to an institution's account and their associated availability. This facilitates the investment of available funds.

If the bank captures invoice information from tuition bills (such as name of the student, social security number, semester being paid, and amount being paid), data may be transmitted electronically via personal computer (PC), tape, or data transmission to the institution's mainframe. Typically, this value-added option accelerates the posting of information for matriculation purposes and reduces the amount of internal processing at the institution for posting receivables.

A lockbox can optimize the availability of funds by accelerating the check clearance schedules and meeting availability deadlines set by the Federal Reserve Bank. In contrast, a typical 3:00 p.m. over-the-counter deposit at the local bank is not processed for availability purposes until later that evening, after the availability deadlines have passed. Additionally, in-house clerical expenses for processing remittances and preparing deposits are eliminated by a lockbox, and accounts receivable processing expenses can be reduced through simplified manual posting or eliminated through automatic update via electronic transmission of receivables information. The audit controls of a lockbox system are typically much more elaborate than those found in a bursar's office. The time required to deposit funds into the institution's bank account may be reduced by two to three days by shortening mail-processing, remittance-processing, and clearance time. In summary, a lockbox can reduce mail float, minimize remittance-processing float, and improve check-clearing or availability float.

CHOOSING A PROVIDER. Several issues must be addressed when selecting a lockbox service provider. First, not all banks have the same intercity mail times—the time it takes an envelope to arrive in one city when mailed from another varies by post office/lockbox location. Independent cash management consulting firms gather and maintain such data. Most major banks will make these data available on request.

Second, the bank's availability schedule is very important. The lockbox bank should provide an aggressive schedule of availability when compared to competing banks. The efficiency of the bank's clearance of funds is a significant added value.

Third, the bank's quality of processing, level of customer service, information delivery capabilities, and overall technical facilities should be considered. The quality of processing can be measured by a ratio of errors, such as the number of errors per 10,000 items processed. The quality of customer service can be determined from past experience or references.

Fourth, price should be a consideration, particularly with a retail lockbox. The average value of checks processed should be sufficiently high so that improved availability and reduced handling costs offset the cost of the lockbox. Using a lockbox for low-value items such as student loan payments is often not cost-effective. If an institution uses low-cost student labor and a system that deposits over-the-counter checks the same day they are received, it can nullify the availability advantages and the alleged labor savings of lockboxes. Some institutions use lockboxes primarily to save on in-house processing costs.

There are two components to a lockbox price: explicit bank charges, such as fixed monthly maintenance and variable per-item processing charges, and implicit bank charges, known as availability. The following example demonstrates these components.

An average semester tuition remittance is $5,000, and 15,000 students will use the lockbox service.

| BANK A | | BANK B |
|---|---|---|
| | Aggregate fixed | |
| $50.00 | monthly charges | $50.00 |
| | Aggregate variable | |
| $ 0.30 | per-item charges★ | $ 0.65 |

★Includes item processing, photocopying, and daily courier.

On the surface, Bank A appears to offer a more cost-effective system. Preliminary calculations show that $10,500 can be saved each year by awarding the business to Bank A. (15,000 students multiplied by 2 semesters equals 30,000 remittances; $0.65 [Bank B's price] minus $0.30 [Bank A's price] equals $0.35 savings when utilizing Bank A. 30,000 multiplied by $0.35 equals $10,500-per-year savings.) However, closer inspection indicates that Bank A accelerates collections by approximately two days while Bank B accelerates collections by three days. In other words, Bank B obtains available funds one day sooner than Bank A. Taking this information into consideration, the following savings can be found by using Bank B.

| | |
|---|---|
| $5,000 | Average remittance value |
| ÷ 250 | Business days per year |
| $ 20 | The value of accelerating a single check's availability by one business day |
| x 8.5 percent | Annual interest rate |
| $ 1.70 | Additional interest income earned on a per-check basis due to the one day of accelerated funds availability |
| x30,000 | Remittances |
| $51,000 | Total interest gain |
| -10,500 | Less incremental cost of the more sophisticated system |
| | |
| $40,500 | Net total benefit of choosing Bank B |

Bank B can accelerate collections faster than Bank A because it uses a primary post office rather than a secondary one, it picks up the mail around the clock rather than during business hours only, and it is a major clearing bank that uses direct sends to move checks directly to distant banks instead of clearing them through the Federal Reserve System, as does Bank A.

ELECTRONIC MECHANISMS

The two primary types of electronic transactions are wire transfers (FedWire) and automated clearing house (ACH) transfers. Under each category are numerous subtypes.

A FedWire transfer is the electronic movement of funds on a real-time basis from the payor bank to the payee bank via transfers between Federal Reserve Bank accounts. A FedWire transfer can be initiated when the cash manager informs the college or university's local bank to make a transfer. The bank checks the institution's account balance; if sufficient funds are available, the bank debits the institution's account and credits the bank's general account at the local Federal Reserve Bank. The local bank also provides the local Federal Reserve Bank with instructions to debit the local bank's account and credit some other Federal Reserve Bank account to finally credit the intended payee's account. This transaction can be done through either the Federal Reserve Bank or, if the bank handles both debit and credit parties, an intrabank transfer. Once a wire transfer has been executed, it cannot be stopped.

ACH transfers use a network of computerized processing centers, often operated by the 12 Federal Reserve Banks, which transfer funds between ACH member institutions and settle the debit and credit in a one- to two-day period. Prearranged instructions are provided by either the payor or payee. ACH transfers differ from FedWire transfers in that they take longer and do not provide for immediately available funds, but they are significantly less expensive (for example, a FedWire transfer can cost as much as $20, while an ACH transfer may cost only 15 cents). In addition, ACH transfers may be returned (like a check) whereas FedWire transfers are final.

ACH transfers are typically used for recurring payments that have a known due date, such as payroll checks, interest payments, and rent payments. An ACH item takes one or two days to clear, but if the due date is known, such as the 15th of the month, the ACH transfer of funds can be initiated on the 13th so that the transaction settles, or value passes, on the prescribed due date. Under the ACH umbrella are numerous types of payments, as detailed in Figure 11-2.

The differences between types of payment shown in Figure 11-2 relate to the initiator of the payment, the receiver of the payment, and the sophistication of the payment itself, that is, how much invoice or other data are carried along with the transfer of money. For example, a direct payroll deposit, which comes under PPD, the most common ACH transfer type, contains basic information such as the individual's name and bank account number. These data accompany the transfer of funds so that the individual's bank can easily identify the recipient. A CTX, on the other hand, is one of the most sophisticated ACH formats and can be processed by only a handful of banks. It is usually initiated by large corporations and received by trading partners or other large corporations. This type of payment can accommodate up to 4,500 invoices, associated discounts and allowances, and other relevant billing information. Furthermore, a CTX is constructed in such a manner that a bank can transmit this information directly into the recipient's mainframe for automatic receivables updating.

***Preauthorized debit.*** Preauthorized debit is a collection method

FIGURE 11-2
ACH Transactions

| Type | Initiator | Receiver |
|------|-----------|----------|
| Preauthorized Payments and Disbursements (PPD) | Corporation/institution | Employee/customer |
| Customer-Initiated Entry (CIE) | Individual | Corporation/institution |
| Cash, Concentration, and Disbursements (CCD) | Corporation/institution | Corporation/institution |
| Vendor Express (CCD+) | Government/corporation | Corporation/institution |
| Corporate Trade Payment (CTP) | Corporation/institution | Corporation/institution |
| Corporate Trade Exchange (CTX) | Corporation/institution | Corporation/institution |
| Tax Payment (TXP) | Corporation/institution | Government |

used for regularly recurring equal-amount payments within the ACH network. The PPD format is usually used for preauthorized debits. The payor approves the transfer of funds from the payor's bank to the payee's bank on predetermined dates. This collection system can be used for monthly tuition payments, room and board fees, student health plan insurance payments, association dues, computer equipment lease payments, and pledge gifts.

***Vendor Express.*** All institutions that receive U.S. government payments of any kind are now being drawn into Vendor Express because the government intends to make all grant and contract disbursements to institutions in the form of ACH transfers rather than checks. Almost all banks are now able to receive certain ACH transfers. An institution must work with its bank to determine if the bank and the institution can process Vendor Express and obtain timely notice of ACH incoming credits. Institutions may need to establish a terminal-based information reporting system to capture the remittance information that accompanies Vendor Express (CCD+) payments. Some companies also use the CCD+ format to pay vendors electronically.

*Point-of-sale transfers (POS) and other methods.* POS is an electronic funds transfer mechanism operated through a computer terminal at cashier checkout counters in bookstores and similar campus outlets, as well as in the bursar's office.

Credit card and, at institutions that use debit cards, debit card transactions are automatically transferred to the institution's bank, the payor's account is debited, and the institution's account is credited. There is no need to handle the paperwork involved in a deposit, and the funds are available immediately, thus saving labor costs and speeding the collection process.

Institutions should be aware of the costs associated with accepting large dollar payments with credit cards. For purchases of lesser value, such as bookstore sales, accepting credit cards may help increase overall sales. However, there may be a discount of 2.0 to 2.5 percent associated with accepting such payments. (The actual level of discount depends on the volume of transactions.) For example, if a student charges $5,000 tuition per semester on a credit card, the 2.5 percent processing discount (or $125 fee) would result in the institution's retaining only $4,875. At some institutions, more than 20 percent of the students charge tuition on credit cards. If a college has 15,000 students and average semester tuition receipts of $5,000 per student, and 20 percent charge their tuition, with charge card discounts at 2.5 percent, the institution would forgo $750,000 in revenues each year.

Many colleges and universities do not accept charge card payment of tuition and fees. Others may charge their own fee to offset the bank's discount fees. Others find that charge cards are worth the cost because the institution collects the money up front, rather than having to accept payment on an installment plan. This may be a practical way to collect fees from certain student groups, such as evening students, graduate students, or continuing education students.

A paper-based charge system costs considerably more than a terminal-based credit card system does. The discount cost of credit card sales in either case is based primarily on the average dollar size of the transaction and not on the transaction volume. Savings can be obtained by using a terminal-based system because such a system is less costly for banks to manage.

***International collections.*** As institutions are faced with a shrinking pool of domestic applicants, they have turned to international markets to augment enrollment levels. However, this practice can create significant problems regarding collecting funds from foreign banks. For example, a prospective French student may send a tuition check drawn on her local bank account in the amount of 3,000 French francs. When the check is finally received it must be sent back to France for collection and then converted to a U.S. dollar equivalent. There are numerous risks and costs associated with this procedure.

- The process can take 8 to 12 weeks (lost investment opportunity cost).

- The U.S. dollar equivalent is not known until the item is actually collected (exchange rate fluctuation risk).

- The processing fee for such a remittance may cost the institution $50 (bank transaction cost).

- By the time the item is presented against the account in France, funds may no longer be available or the account may be closed (payment risk).

- In addition to the above, in less developed countries, the payment may not be convertible into U.S. dollars when it is presented, because of a foreign currency exchange freeze (foreign exchange conversion risk).

These risks, costs, and time delays are experienced while the student has already enrolled and started classes. International electronic wire transfers such as SWIFT messages, CHIPS settlements, and Tested Telex messages, which are processed in a manner similar to the FedWire, help mitigate these problems. These payments can be made from most large banks in any country.

The benefits of using electronic wire transfers for international transactions are that

- funds are transferred and received within 72 hours, thereby accelerating availability;

- payments can be made in U.S. dollars, thereby eliminating exchange rate fluctuation risk;

- the processing fee for international electronic items is only a fraction of the cost of fees for international paper items; and

- stop payments and insufficient fund hassles (payment risk) are eliminated.

The benefits also include the elimination of mail float, reduced processing float, and fewer collection problems. Furthermore, electronic items cannot be "lost in the mail." Electronic transfer offers a reduction in bank processing fees, the potential to update receivables information automatically with the data that accompany the transfer of funds, and the reduction of manual reconciliation.

***Concentration of funds.*** In a concentration account system, widely distributed funds are gathered into one location and used to fund disbursement requirements. Excess funds can be swept into an investment vehicle to begin earning income rather than sitting idle in a number of different banks and accounts. The process begins when funds in the form of currency and checks are collected at multiple locations and deposited in multiple accounts in field banks. The funds from these relatively small-balance accounts are then transferred to one cash-concentration account.

The mechanisms for concentrating funds are checks, depository transfer checks (DTC), wire transfers, and zero balance accounts (ZBA). A DTC is a check drawn on an outlying field bank and made payable to the institution's concentration account. Few paper deposits are processed; most deposits are "electronic" DTCs that use the ACH mechanism to concentrate funds from field accounts. "Paper" is used only when the field bank is not a member of the ACH network. Receipt of DTC funds is based on the normal one- to-three-day clearing process. Either the field bank instructs the concentration bank to debit the field account and credit the concentration account, or the bank submits an electronic or paper DTC into its concentration account when it receives notice of the field bank deposit.

A DTC in electronic format is otherwise considered an ACH debit. The electronic funds are usually available the following day. This method is generally used to concentrate recurring or small-dollar payments. Large-dollar or time-critical items are usually concentrated via FedWire to receive same-day availability.

A ZBA is a deposit and/or disbursement account that provides control of balance levels of multiple accounts in the same financial institution. Collection activities of individual schools, divisions, or locations are maintained at the local level, while aggregate cash investments and movement of funds remain closely controlled at the institutional treasury level. When a concentration account (parent) and subsidiary zero balance (child) depository accounts are established, balances in the subaccounts are maintained at zero. Daily transactions are posted at the end of each day. When the field depository account is a ZBA, the deposit is automatically transferred to a concentration account. This is possible only when the field account and the concentration account are in the same bank.

ACH transfers are increasingly being used for the concentration of funds. The main office uses a terminal-based system to initiate a debit ACH against the field bank account when the field office notifies the main office of the amount of the day's deposit. The money is transferred one day after the ACH is initiated.

The benefits of concentration accounts are that

- they reduce nonproductive balances at field banks;
- they require less clerical effort and subsequent cost in utilizing these balances;
- they improve monitoring of cash inflow activity at outlying locations; and
- they allow larger amounts of money to be available at one or a few locations (pooling of funds) to more efficiently cover disbursement requirements.

A concentration account can be invaluable for institutions with geographically dispersed deposit locations, such as multiple campuses, separate operating units, state university systems, and bicoastal lockbox networks. When developing a concentration system, the cash manager should examine the number of locations where cash or receivables are handled, the average dollar size of transactions, the availability of funds at the original deposit banks, and the administration needed to oversee the system. For example, a special education school that is located in 28 communities throughout the U.S. accepts remittances at each campus. These funds are concentrated periodically at the main location. Concentration could be accomplished by drawing checks at each campus and mailing them to the concentration account, but this takes too long. The funds could be sent daily from each institution by FedWire transfer, but this is costly. The best solution is for the central office to use a DTC. In such a case, the branch office should inform the main office of the amount of the daily deposit.

## OTHER COLLECTION CONSIDERATIONS

In spite of the technology that enables collections to be made quickly, high technology is of little value if individuals at sending and receiving organizations are not efficient. Adequate training of employees directly associated with the movement of an institution's funds is critical to the success of the cash management operation. While some of this training can be accomplished with on-the-job instruction, many professional associations offer training courses.

The cash manager should consider procedures that encourage the early collection of payments to the college or university. For example, tuition payments are a principal source of cash receipts for most institutions. To improve cash flow, the cash manager should consider advancing the due date for payment of student receivables and/or increasing deposits required from incoming students. Preaddressed return envelopes can ensure that payments are made to a precise institutional address and not delayed in the institution. Bar codes on return envelopes also help speed them through the mail system.

Many institutions offer a deferred payment plan for a fixed fee that allows the student to pay the term's bill over several months. The fixed fee may be replaced by an interest charge. Such an interest rate or charge would compensate for large payments that are postponed and the length of time that payment is postponed. If the volume warrants and if fees are not paid on a timely basis, the institution might also assess an interest or finance charge on receivables or change the due dates for tuition and/or fee payments. Any institution considering these measures must carefully evaluate the effect of the measures on students, the extra time necessary to record multiple payments, the assessment of interest on late payments, and the public relations consequences.

Whenever a cash manager finds that checks have been held for some time, he or she should communicate with the department concerned to discover the reason. At the least, such contact is a reminder of the time value of money and should lead to improved performance. The cash manager should work with department heads who are likely to receive large checks to arrange the quick routing of these major receipts to the institution's bank.

The cash manager may have to arrange to have government funds processed on letters of credit. With such arrangements, the bank can act as the agent for the institution. This is particularly important when a college or university is using a bank in a different city from that in which the institution is located. Such a bank can be designated as the recipient of funds on the letter of credit, saving several days in mail time. Prompt processing of letters of credit eliminates the need to advance the institution's own funds to cover federal expenditures pending receipt.

Purchasing departments are increasingly converting purchasing documents from paper to electronics. They are establishing partnerships and exchanging data with major suppliers in standardized formats known as electronic data interchange (EDI). The most immediate benefit of EDI is in the form of reduced inventories due to the speed of reordering, but cost savings can be realized along the entire procurement/disbursement cycle. The cash manager should be the coordinator for his or her institution's involvement in EDI.

## Disbursements

The two major types of disbursements in colleges and universities are payroll and vendor payments. As with collections, there are two mechanisms for disbursements: paper and electronic. The primary objective of the disbursement portion of a cash management program is to reduce costs. This involves:

- Timing cash disbursements to maximize discount benefits and avoid early payment

- Minimizing the cost of issuing and processing disbursements

- Knowing when large-dollar disbursements are actually going to clear, to minimize the cost of overdrafts and to retain management control of the disbursement function

• Maintaining a satisfactory audit trail of payments

Four disbursement issues warrant close management: the lost opportunity cost of excess funds that remain idle in a disbursement account; the penalty and interest costs of accidental overdrafts resulting from disbursements that exceed account balances; the transfer cost of moving funds into a disbursement account; and the opportunity cost of lost trade discounts. The cash manager should be familiar with the following terms of disbursement.

• The "issuance date" is the day on which a check is written and mailed.

• The "payment date" is usually considered the postmark date on the envelope.

• The "funding date" is the day on which funds are deposited to cover the disbursement.

• The "presentment date" is the day on which the disbursement, i.e., check, is presented to the institution's bank for payment.

• "Two percent/10 net 30" is one of many terms of discounts offered on payments. This one offers a 2 percent discount if paid in 10 days; otherwise the full amount is due in 30 days.

## FUNDING DISBURSEMENTS

There are usually three ways of funding disbursements: impressed accounts, zero balance accounts, and controlled disbursements. These differ in the timing and method of funding.

***Impressed accounts.*** The basic disbursement account is an impressed account, which requires immediate funding for all issued disbursement items. Usually the issuance and funding are simultaneous. A check is issued and mailed, and the recipient presents it for payment. The check is returned to the originating bank and then returned as paid to the payor. This process may take up to a week. If the account is funded at the time of issuance, sufficient funds are in the account to cover the presentment whenever it occurs. This type of account can also be "stagger funded," meaning that a series of funding actions are taken in anticipation that checks that were issued will clear on different days. Payroll accounts are a good example of the use of stagger funding: 20 percent may be funded on pay day; 60 percent on the day after; and 20 percent two days after.

*Zero balance accounts.* Alternatively, an automatic ZBA transfer can be used to fund the disbursement account. This has the advantage of determining the precise date on which the funds will be deposited in the account. FedWire and ACH transfers can also be used to move funds into a disbursement account.

With ZBAs, separate bank accounts for each of several different institutional entities or disbursement needs can exist in a single bank without leaving any balance. Thus, forecasts are not required for each subaccount, but a forecast for the total funds required in the master account is made. Each evening the required funding for disbursement checks that have cleared that day in the subaccounts is covered or "zeroed out" by funds flowing from the master account.

*Controlled disbursements.* Controlled disbursements provide daily notification of the exact dollar amount of disbursements that will be posted against an account that day. For example, at 9 a.m. the bank advises the institution that $50,000 is to be posted that day against the account. Thus, $50,000 is transferred, usually by ZBA or FedWire transfers, to cover the requirement. Therefore, no excess balances remain in the account. With an impressed account, where there can be multiple daily presentments against the account, the bank cannot provide notification in sufficient time for exact funding needs. In a controlled disbursement account, there are one or two presentments daily (early in the morning). The amount of the residual balance is known early each day so that excess funds can be put to work earning income. If the master account has insufficient funds to cover the checks presented in the controlled disbursement account, a short-term investment can be liquidated and funds transferred to cover the requirement. A line of credit may also be accessed to avoid the penalizing costs of overdrafts. An additional advantage of the controlled disbursement account is that the time and frustration of disbursement forecasting are avoided. Forecasting can almost be eliminated with a controlled disbursement account.

Many banks maintain controlled disbursement accounts for their customers in affiliated banks. With these banks, the controlled disbursement bank accounts are handled like ZBAs and the money is sent from the customer's bank to the affiliated bank automatically. This avoids the cost and labor of sending wires. Another option is the maintenance of a controlled disbursement account in a bank that is affiliated with a money market fund, where a similar automatic funding opportunity may be available.

Generally, all institutions with annual disbursements in excess of $10 million can make effective use of a controlled disbursement account, as well as those that make daily investment and borrowing decisions. This system delays the funding of an account until the check is presented for payment and thus reduces excess balances in the account, optimizes investment opportunities by obtaining disbursement information early in the day, reduces overdraft charges due to inaccurate cash forecasting, and may extend the disbursement float.

The cash manager should evaluate banking costs, notification time, and service quality. Notification time is important, because the earlier the bank notifies the customer, the sooner the customer knows the funding portion for early-in-the-day investing opportunities. Controlled disbursement accounts generally have higher fees than impressed accounts, because of the technology used.

***Account reconciliation.*** Many banks provide information for managing and reconciling high-volume accounts efficiently and accurately. In a simple version (partial reconciliation), the bank provides, in check-number sequence, the date and the amount of all checks paid. This information may be reported in paper format or electronically. Electronic reporting enables automatic reconciliation of checking accounts by the institution.

Full reconciliation is the reporting of canceled and stopped checks, as well as paid items or paid and outstanding items of regular and controlled disbursement accounts, in various formats. The college or university provides the bank with a list of issued-check information (i.e., the check numbers issued, the date each check was issued, and the dollar amount of each check). The bank merges this information with its data regarding the date paid and amount paid for each check and delivers a fully reconciled statement of the account at the end of each month.

Banks may offer flexible statement cut-off dates to meet monthly, quarterly, and fiscal-year reporting needs. With an account reconciliation system, a college or university can issue on-line stop payments from its own PC and thus reduce stop-payment costs. There is immediate confirmation of the stop payment and a new check can be issued at once. The most important benefit in establishing an account reconciliation system is the significant reduction in clerical costs.

**Check truncation.** Some banks offer check-safekeeping options (check truncation), whereby the bank provides a report with copies of paid checks, eliminating the need to store canceled paper checks. Mail, delivery, and some clerical costs are eliminated, and bank fees are reduced because the bank does not have to sort checks manually.

## ELECTRONIC MECHANISMS

Electronic mechanisms for disbursements are used to automate disbursement processing and reduce clerical costs.

**Preauthorized credits.** Preauthorized credits are a disbursement vehicle for recurring payments to employees, vendors, and others via the ACH system, including payroll, travel and expense reimbursements, annuity and pension payments, and intrainstitutional transfers. Typical users are systems with a high volume of recurring payments to a stable payee base, such as employees and pensioners. The most common application is direct deposit of payroll through PPD.

The college or university generates a tape or transmission of payroll transactions that contains both the payor's and payee's accounts. The tape or transmission is received by the payroll bank, which transmits the data through the ACH system for distribution to the various payee banks. The institution's account is debited and a credit is made to the payee's account on the payroll date. Savings are achieved in the payroll department because of fewer lost checks, elimination of check-handling costs, and reduction of the cost for printing and storing checks. Bank fees are appreciably less for ACH credits than for check clearing. The substantial costs associated with placing stops on checks are eliminated, and the bank account reconciliation operation is simplified. Benefits for the institution are in the reduction of costs required in preparing and issuing paper payments, elimination of the risk of lost and stolen checks, increased predictability of cash flow, and reduced check-handling and clearance costs. Benefits for the payee are convenience and the security of deposits.

**Cash, concentration, and disbursement (CCD).** CCD is the transmission of batched electronic payments between a college or university and institutional or corporate receivers. This format is usually used for the payment of pension and health premiums, loans, and investment management fees. Payments may be initiated from PC software packages or mainframe ACH systems. CCD has grown in popularity in recent years because of its flexible nature and ease of use.

**Personal computers.** PCs are increasingly being used for transaction initiation, performing the following functions.

- ACH transactions—debits and credits

- On-line stop payments

- Domestic wire transfers—repetitive and nonrepetitive

- International wire transfers

- International foreign exchange drafts

Generally, significant savings in bank service charges can be realized by initiating these transactions on a PC, as compared to manual or telephone initiation. Furthermore, they can be initiated at the cash manager's convenience.

## EVALUATING A DISBURSEMENT SYSTEM

The cash manager must consider issues such as centralized versus decentralized disbursement and trade-offs between lengthening the disbursement float and maintaining good vendor relations when evaluating a disbursement system. Cash management systems work most effectively in a centralized operation. However, a decentralized operation can be made more efficient if all accounts are centralized in one bank, with ZBAs available to each decentralized unit (either geographically or organizationally). If a disbursement system is inefficient and payments are delayed, vendors will become dissatisfied and may institute tighter credit standards for the institution by requiring cash on delivery (COD), payment before delivery (PBD), or interest payment for delayed payments.

## OTHER DISBURSEMENT CONSIDERATIONS

As with collections, technology is of little value in disbursements if the human factor is not efficient and if procedures that reduce cash outlay are not in place. For example, institutions should take advantage of invoices that offer discounted terms. Even in times of high interest rates, normal trade discounts are substantially higher than any interest rate that could be earned on the investment of a similar amount of funds. (A commonly accepted figure for the cost of lost discounts is in excess of 36 percent per year.) Unless there are specific agreements to the contrary, any bills that do not provide a discount should be treated as being payable within 30 days. While it is economical to batch bills to a single vendor so they can be paid in a single check, the cash manager should be sure that the accounts payable office is sensitive to the due dates of various invoices, so that an early date on one does not trigger the payment of all.

Care should be taken to prevent the institution from becoming so concerned with deferment that it neglects the advantages of special disbursement methods instituted for cost reduction. Specifically, the use of "check with order" or "purchase order draft," a system that leads to substantial reduction in workload in the purchasing department, should not be discarded because of its negative effect on cash flow. Because it is normal practice to limit the dollar value of such orders, the net effect on cash flow may not be material, but it should be analyzed.

Many higher education institutions conduct business overseas. Typically, institutions initiate necessary payments via an international wire transfer mechanism, which can become expensive, especially if a total payment is less than $10,000. Alternatively, foreign drafts may be issued in indigenous currency on a foreign correspondent's bank account. Several banks offer this service via a PC-based software program that simplifies the international payment process and greatly reduces bank processing fees. Institutions that issue five or more drafts per month should consider using such a system.

## Information Reporting Services

### ACCOUNT ANALYSIS STATEMENTS

Account analysis statements list the average daily ledger and average daily collected balances, generally on a monthly basis. An account analysis statement allows the cash manager to track funding positions during the month and to know how cash is working. An account analysis statement can be provided through either paper reports or electronic transmissions. This statement represents an invoice, because it recaps the individual services being provided by the bank and details the amount and fee for each transaction. In other words, the account analysis statement also functions as the banking bill. Like all bills, it must be reviewed for invoicing errors before payment. This type of reporting is important because it allows the cash manager to track banking activity and balance position over the course of the year, resulting in better analysis and forecasting on a month-to-month basis. It also allows the cash manager to monitor the bank's service fees.

## PC REPORTING

PC reporting can provide the cash manager with up-to-date information to make accurate funding and investment decisions. Banks have the capability of providing balance reporting and transaction information on a previous-day basis and current-day basis for both debits and credits. PC reporting allows the cash manager to manage the components of the cash management equation in a timely fashion. It provides the beginning balance, information on incoming credits on a current-day basis, and notification of disbursement needs. Many colleges and universities receive account balance information by a telephone call from the local bank or a direct PC link to their bank account. The PC link will become more popular as the cost of computer hardware continues to decline.

## DATA TRANSMISSION

Data transmission of collections and disbursements reduces clerical expenses by eliminating manual posting of receivables and payables information. Data are provided electronically in a format that automatically integrates the ledger system with a PC or mainframe.

# Management of Working Capital

In the strictest definition, working capital equals current assets minus current liabilities; working capital is the resources available to keep operations running through the short term (less than one year). If an institution depends on resources outside of its working capital cycle to stay afloat, its survival is doubtful in the long term. Cash, inventories, accounts receivable, and any asset that is realizable within the next 12 months constitute working capital. Liabilities include accounts payable, accrued expenses (primarily payroll), and current debt obligations.

Many institutions have two peaks in receiving revenue during the year, even though expenses are at a consistent level. These peaks occur when tuition payments are being received at the start of each term. The financial or business officer and the cash manager are responsible for managing this variability in cash and cash equivalent availability.

Smaller institutions with limited resources may manage this variability by actively monitoring balances, investing when the cash level is above a predetermined minimum, and securing a line of credit with a financial institution to maintain the minimum when the cash level falls below this level. The cash manager must choose among bank products (earnings credit, certificates of deposit, savings accounts, sweep vehicles) and nonbank products (money market funds, mutual funds, short-term investment funds). These investments are limited because the institution must relegate itself to short-term returns, which may be low and volatile.

Larger institutions add another dimension to the working capital dilemma. Operating revenues may rise to such a high level in peak times that the college or university severely limits itself by not utilizing investments with longer maturities, thereby giving a higher return. Typically, the annual operating budget incorporates a minimum return on the investable balances. By relying solely on short-term investments, the college or university jeopardizes a large part of its revenue base. Prudent fiscal management dictates that the cash manager look to more predictable returns through longer maturities.

When reviewing a cash management plan, the business manager must

- project cash-flow expectations during the year;
- identify both short- and intermediate-term investment levels;
- monitor cash and receivables balances to determine what can be invested and where;
- maximize cash flow by effectively collecting and disbursing funds; and

- protect the institution's operating assets by investing in secure investment vehicles that have the necessary liquidity for the particular cash management plan.

The cash manager must determine the level of investment in longer-term (less liquid) vehicles, thereby determining what will be invested on a day-to-day basis. It may be advantageous to choose an intermediate-term investment level that is higher than what is available in operating cash. By locking up a high level of working capital in these investments, the college or university would need a credit line for the brief periods when daily cash investments fall short of cash needs. However, the higher investment yield from intermediate-term investments more than compensates the institution for the borrowing expenses during short cash-poor cycles. Although borrowing expenses may be greater than the investment yield when funds are borrowed, the advantages of larger investments in longer maturities can offset this expense. The mix of cash, short-term investments, and intermediate-term investments determines the predictability of investment income in the current fund and overall performance.

Until recently, a number of colleges and universities enjoyed a working capital line that had little or no associated costs. If the credit line was used at all, it was for brief periods in the summer months. There was no associated charge for the line other than the interest rate on seasonal borrowing. However, since changes in the requirements of the Federal Reserve System, a bank must now allocate capital to available lines whether they are used or not. To cover the resulting costs, banks must find some form of compensation. Typical structures include an annual fee for availability, an unused fee, and compensating balances. The cost of maintaining a credit line should be considered when a cash manager is deciding upon an investment strategy.

Another element in managing working capital involves accrual accounts, primarily accounts receivable on the asset side and accounts payable on the liability side. An important aspect of accrual accounts is management of the turnover ratios that indicate how quickly these accounts are being paid by the college or university. Accounts receivable are included in working capital because they represent funds that have been realized or committed. The effectiveness of turning receivables into cash in the shortest amount of time has a definite effect on investment balances. Accounts payable need similar management. An institution that distributes funds to vendors too quickly depletes its investable balance. Management of these accounts includes separating the discounted invoices for payment within 30 days and then scheduling the remainder within the stated terms, not sooner. Again, by properly managing accrual accounts the college or university can maximize investment income. As positive operating surpluses become harder to maintain, the total performance of the cash management plan will increase in importance, whether it is monitored or not.

## Cash-Flow Projections

Planning and controlling cash flow are important tasks of the cash manager because cash flow affects the college or university's ability to pay obligations, including salaries and wages; to acquire assets; and to meet unexpected needs. In order to meet liquidity requirements, managers need information about historic cash flows for a given period. An adequate working capital position does not by itself imply an adequate cash position, because working capital may consist of accounts receivable, inventories, and other noncash items. Nor does an adequate cash position imply an acceptable working capital position, as large current liabilities may require more cash than is available.

An analysis of cash flow shows whether the pattern of cash flow from operations will enable an institution to meet its payment schedules properly or whether the institution must arrange for short-term credit. A cash-flow statement provides the necessary information to plan effectively for meeting short- and intermediate-range cash needs. The cash-flow statement summarizes cash receipts and disbursements by major categories or items and can point out a net change in cash in a given period. In a computer-based system, it is easy to enter data on receipts and disbursements and to program the computer to prepare a cash-flow statement. If such a system is not in operation, the necessary information can be obtained in an analysis similar to that needed to prepare a statement of changes in financial position (see Figure 11-3).

The forecasting of cash is critical in developing investment plans. Cash forecasting can be either a simple manual procedure or a sophisticated computer operation. Cash-flow analysis is historical in nature, and projections should be based on estimates or pro forma statements.

FIGURE 11-3
Sample Cash-Flow Projections Spreadsheet Report

| Report period | 11/25 actual | 11/26 actual | 11/27 actual | 11/28 actual | 11/29 actual | 12/1 estimate | 12/2 estimate | 12/3 estimate | 12/4 estimate | 12/5 estimate |
|---|---|---|---|---|---|---|---|---|---|---|
| Projected cash receipts | | | | | | | | | | |
| Wire transfers | | | | | | | | | | |
| Lockbox receipts | | | | | | | | | | |
| Local branch deposits | | | | | | | | | | |
| Short-term loan proceeds | | | | | | | | | | |
| Investment maturities/income | | | | | | | | | | |
| Total projected cash receipts | | | | | | | | | | |
| | | | | | | | | | | |
| Projected cash disbursements | | | | | | | | | | |
| Wire transfers | | | | | | | | | | |
| Payroll | | | | | | | | | | |
| Vendor | | | | | | | | | | |
| Tax payments | | | | | | | | | | |
| Loan repayments | | | | | | | | | | |
| Total projected cash disbursements | | | | | | | | | | |
| Net projected cash flow | | | | | | | | | | |
| Beginning cash | | | | | | | | | | |
| Total cash | | | | | | | | | | |
| Desired cash level | | | | | | | | | | |
| Surplus/[borrowings] | | | | | | | | | | |

Projection of cash flow is an important part of cash budgeting and integral to the total budgeting process. Estimates of future cash requirements should take into consideration special operating requirements and any expansion plans.

When the demands for cash during a given period are expected to exceed available cash, the shortfall must be met by such measures as the conversion of short-term securities or short-term credit obtained from a bank. A bank line of credit is often used to meet these short-term or seasonal cash requirements. During periods when cash inflow is expected to exceed cash outflow, the cash management plan should provide for reduction of the short-term debt or an increase in temporary investments or both. The greater the fluctuations of cash flow, the greater the need will be for careful planning of cash needs and cash investments.

## Accounts Receivable

Student receivables reflect a college or university's registration policy. For institutions that are highly selective or can sustain a level of desired enrollments, the decision to permit a student to enter is generally clear: the student should pay the entire amount due or registration is not permitted. However, colleges or universities that for enrollment reasons must be or prefer to be less rigid about student payments prior to registration can and do incur a significant level of student receivables. Charges from the bookstore or from fees or fines while the student is enrolled are minor compared to tuition, room, and board.

The bursar or other person responsible for accounts receivable generally balances several conflicting issues when dealing with a student who owes the institution money. This individual must balance the success of collecting past-due funds against the loss of potential alumni goodwill and support. Potential legal ramifications can occur with claims and counterclaims of contractual dispute. The bursar must attempt to separate potentially slow payers (they pay what is due, but it takes time and a lot of patience) from those who promise to pay and do not. The latter, in most cases, should be denied continued enrollment at the institution.

These issues are similar whether a student is currently enrolled, is a graduate, or has dropped out of the institution. The difference is in the leverage that is available to the collector. Continued enrollment or reenrollment for the next semester is the leverage that can be used on an active student. A plea for the needs of the "alma mater" and the threat of withholding a transcript are the leverage for a graduate. In all cases, after all reasonable methods have been exhausted, the remaining threats are referral to a collection agency (and an impact on the individual's credit rating) and legal action to recover the amounts past due.

## Internal Controls

Many large colleges and universities have a specific organization that is responsible for monitoring the flow of funds in and out of bank accounts and handling cash and securities. But for the vast majority of institutions, issues of safety and the authorized use of funds rest in the treasurer's office. Generally, the institution's external auditor samples control procedures involving cash and comments on any weak areas of cash handling during the annual audit. (See Chapter 15, Auditing.)

Areas that should receive attention by the cash manager are in the collections function, the disbursement function (both vendor and payroll), and the posting of student accounts. The simplest control is hands-on management—overseeing daily work activity, randomly inspecting work, reviewing, and asking questions. Another control is dual check-signing responsibility, which requires the treasurer and a second designated official to sign checks issued in excess of a certain amount. Lastly, particularly at small institutions, dual responsibility should exist for all areas that involve cash. No one who is involved in dealing with cash or disbursements or who is substituting for someone who does have that authority should be permitted to perform an entire function alone.

## Current Issues

College and university cash managers must understand some issues that are emerging in the 1990s.

*The changing regulatory climate.* Legislative and regulatory trends, at both the state and the federal level, threaten a degree of uncertainty for cash management. As more savings and loans fail and commercial banking drives FDIC rates higher, the need to reduce compensating balances also increases. Pending regulations on overdrafts could affect the timing of wire disbursements. Regulations concerning same-day presentment could affect the viability of controlled disbursement accounts. Regulations concerning the finality of automated clearing house transfers should make cash managers review these transfers promptly to reject any unauthorized debits.

*Electronic exchange of information and value.* The stage is set for the continued development and application of electronic data exchange technology. Though the U.S. is far from being a "checkless" society, the need for greater transaction speed and security of funds, along with the globalization of markets, will work to foster greater use of electronic banking media. This dimension may shift a significant portion of the cash-flow time-line to real time in the exchange of funds in collections and disbursements. Bank charges for manual and paper-handling services will continue to increase relative to fees for electronic services.

*A smaller and highly concentrated financial services market.* As larger banks absorb smaller, less competitive providers of banking services, and as large banks themselves merge with each other, the cash manager must become more sophisticated and knowledgeable. Deregulation will continue to shape a changing financial services marketplace. The regulatory atmosphere in which financial providers now exist is being transformed at a rapid pace. Cash managers must keep up with these changes to meet their institutions' cash management goals and objectives.

*An international marketplace for financial services.* Increased globalization of the higher education marketplace will require a broader and somewhat different knowledge of cash management principles to face the complexities of foreign exchange and international banking.

# References and Resources

Altman, Edward I., ed. *Handbook of Corporate Finance.* New York: John Wiley & Sons, 1986.

Beehler, Paul J. *Contemporary Cash Management: Principles, Practices, and Perspectives.* 2nd ed. New York: John Wiley & Sons, 1983.

Bort, Richard. *The Corporate Cash Management Handbook.* Boston, Mass.: Warren, Gorham and Lamont, 1989.

Davis, Henry A. *Cash Management and the Payments System: Ground Rules, Costs, and Risks.* Morristown, N.J.: Financial Executives Research Foundation, 1986.

DiPaolo, Vincent, ed. *The Handbook of Cash Flow and Treasury Management.* Chicago, Ill.: Probus Publishing, 1988.

Driscoll, Mary C. *Cash Management: Corporate Strategies for Profit.* New York: John Wiley & Sons, 1983.

Gallinger, George W., and P. Basil Healey. *Liquidity Analysis and Management.* Reading, Mass.: Addison-Wesley Publishing Company, 1987.

Haag, Leonard H. *Cash Management and Short-Term Investments for Colleges and Universities.* Washington, D.C.: NACUBO, 1977.

Hill, Ned C., and William L. Sartoris. *Short-Term Financial Management.* New York: Macmillan, 1988.

Kallberg, Jarl G., Kenneth L. Parkinson, and Joyce R. Oachs. *Essentials of Cash Management.* 3d ed. Newtown, Conn.: National Corporate Cash Management Association, 1989.

Kallberg, Jarl G., and Kenneth Parkinson. *Current Asset Management: Cash, Credit, and Inventory.* New York: John Wiley & Sons, 1984.

Van der Wiede, James, and Steven F. Maier. *Managing Corporate Liquidity: An Introduction to Working Capital Management.* New York: John Wiley & Sons, 1985.

# CHAPTER 12

# Debt Financing and Management

by
Eva Klein
Eva Klein & Associates

# Sponsors

## COLLEGE CONSTRUCTION LOAN INSURANCE ASSOCIATION

2445 M Street, NW, Suite 450
Washington, DC 20037
202-835-0090

*The College Construction Loan Insurance Association (Connie Lee) is a triple-A rated, congressionally authorized bond insurer for higher education facilities financing.*

## JOHN NUVEEN & CO. INCORPORATED

333 West Wacker Drive
Chicago, IL 60606
312-917-7930

*John Nuveen & Co. Incorporated is the oldest and largest investment banking firm devoted exclusively to the underwriting, syndicating, trading, and packaging of municipal bonds.*

## MBIA, INC.

113 King Street
Armonk, NY 10504
914-765-3430

*MBIA, Inc., is a major provider of bond insurance for colleges and universities.*

## MANUFACTURERS HANOVER TRUST CO.
Post Office Box 1763
Hicksville, NY 11802
800-MHT-7722

*Manufacturers Hanover Trust offers guaranteed student loans, alternative loan programs, budget programs, and loan consolidation services.*


## SPRINGSTED INCORPORATED
85 East Seventh Place, Suite 100
Saint Paul, MN 55101-2143
612-223-3000

*Springsted Incorporated provides debt-related financial advisory services to colleges and universities nationwide.*

# Contents

## 12: Debt Financing and Management

C olleges and universities may increasingly need to seek the opportunities that debt financing affords for capital facilities development as an alternative to internal financing or capital gifts and grants. Higher education has neglected existing physical plant for the past two decades, resulting in a cumulative deferred maintenance of $40 to $60 billion by some estimates. At the same time, new facilities needs arising from intensified competition for qualified faculty, increasing costs for advanced research, and changes in undergraduate enrollment patterns must be accommodated. Periodic changes in federal tax policy, for example on deductions allowed for charitable gifts, together with periodic recessions, can constrain both individual and corporate giving to higher education. In addition, colleges and universities are likely to compete more directly than ever with elementary and secondary education, healthcare, social services, and the arts for public and philanthropic dollars.

These factors make capital formation and the choice between internal and external methods of financing even more important and more complex than they have been in the past. In the 1990s, colleges and universities must accomplish more with fewer resources and must find the most cost-effective ways of funding personnel, plant, and operating costs. In this environment, all institutions should consider how debt, in combination with internal resources and aggressive fundraising programs, can play a part in the acquisition or maintenance of needed physical facilities.

This chapter provides an overview of debt financing and debt management. It defines basic debt-finance terms, explains typical financing vehicles, describes common standards and measures of creditworthiness, outlines the bond issuance and rating processes, and discusses debt policy, capacity, and related debt management issues. The current legal, tax, and regulatory environment, which is subject to continuous change, is treated only generally. For detailed understanding of such issues, which are integral to the structuring and implementation of a borrowing, institutional administrators should seek the advice of a professional financial advisor or bond attorney.

## Debt Securities

In the United States, the nonfinancial business sector and the government sector are net borrowers of funds in the economy while consumers and, to a lesser extent, financial institutions are net lenders of funds; that is, while all types of entities may engage in both borrowing and lending, typically consumers (through savings) and banks provide more funds to the economy than they borrow, while businesses and governments borrow more than they lend.

The economic purpose of borrowing is to change the timing of an individual or an organization's expenditures vis-à-vis the timing of its income or revenues: a borrower uses someone else's funds for a needed purpose today, rather than deferring the expenditure until the income is available in the future. For making the funds available, the lender is entitled to a return in the form of interest payments. For a college or university, the question of the timing of expenditures for capital facilities in relation to the timing of future tuition revenues (borrowing versus "pay-as-you-go" financing) has special implications: because students avail themselves of capital facilities for only a few years, a college or university that pays for facilities from its current income does not distribute the cost of those facilities to the many generations of students that will use them. In contrast, a 20- or 30-year bond issue distributes costs into future years, presumably over the useful life of the facility.

By issuing corporate debt securities, a business entity can raise needed capital without diluting ownership or equity interest in its assets and earnings capability; debt actually increases return on equity. Typically, most corporations have capital formation plans that call for a mix of equity and debt financing. The mix is often highly sophisticated and closely managed. Modern financial management principles suggest that colleges and universities, like business corporations, should have capital formation and management plans in which debt is an element. For colleges and universities, debt is an alternative not to ownership equity but to internal funding from gifts, reserves, or current revenues; in the tax-exempt municipal market, debt often is the most cost-effective alternative.

The domestic U.S. (and increasingly global) markets for the buying and selling of capital in various forms are called capital markets. In addition to currencies and commodities, there are three basic forms of securities that make up the capital markets: the stock market (equity securities); the bond market (debt securities); and the money market (wholesale market for high-quality, short-term debt securities). Colleges and universities issue debt primarily, though not exclusively, in the tax-exempt municipal bond market, which differs distinctly from the taxable or corporate bond market and from the government bond market (U.S. Treasury securities) in issuance volume, liquidity, types of investors, and yield behavior.

## BONDS

A "bond" is a promise to repay a specified sum ("principal") plus compensation ("interest") to a lender for use of the money. Payments of principal and interest are made on specified dates. The terms "interest," "rate," or "coupon" denote the compensation to bondholders during the life of the bond. Interest is expressed commonly as an annual percentage rate, although actual payments may be paid semiannually, quarterly, monthly, weekly, or daily. The "maturity" of a bond is the date when the principal amount becomes due and payable. A "serial bond" has a series of maturities, with partial amounts of principal coming due annually or semiannually over a period of several years. The "par value" of a bond is the principal amount that is due at maturity. A bond that is traded at a price below its par value is a "discount bond"; a bond that is traded at a price above its par value is a "premium bond."

Historically, bonds came in one of two forms, bearer bonds and registered bonds. "Bearer bonds" are negotiable by anyone who holds them. Bearer bond certificates include interest coupons that the bondholder clips at payment dates and presents for payment at a bank; payment is made by the paying agent of the borrower to whomever holds and submits the coupons. "Registered bonds" also are issued as bond certificates but are registered with respect to ownership; consequently, they provide greater security against theft as well as the option of automatic payments made to the bondholder. By law, all bonds issued since 1983 are required to be issued in registered form; therefore, only colleges and universities with outstanding bonds issued before 1983 have investors holding old bearer bonds. With widespread automation in the capital markets, increasing numbers of bond issues are being issued as "book-entry bonds"; these are registered bonds whose ownership is recorded in an automated central system by a depository such as Depository Trust Company. Physical bond certificates are not issued in book-entry issuances.

## BOND YIELDS

The "yield" on a bond is the rate of return, expressed as a percentage, that the investor will earn on the investment. Although "nominal yield" may be used to indicate the stated interest rate or the coupon, the return to an investor is described typically in terms of different calculations of bond yields. "Current yield," which describes current income on a bond earned from interest payments, is calculated as follows:

$$\frac{\text{Coupon interest payment}}{\text{Price of bond}} = \text{Current yield}$$

As the equation indicates, the price and the current yield of a bond are inversely related; when the price goes up, the yield goes down and vice versa.

Investors typically analyze bonds in terms of their "yield to maturity" or their "yield to call." Yield to maturity is the annual rate of return, compounded semiannually, earned from all payments of principal and interest, assuming that the bond is held to maturity. Unlike current yield, yield to maturity takes into account the time value of money. There are four variables involved: the bond price, the coupon rate, maturity in years, and yield to maturity. When the first three are known, yield to maturity can be derived; conversely, when the last three are known, the price of the bond can be derived. The calculations formerly involved the use of bond value tables and interpolation, but now bond calculators compute results instantly. The calculation implicitly assumes that interim interest payments are reinvested at the same rate. Because the assumption of reinvestment at the same interest rate does not always apply, yield to maturity actually varies with the average annual return on reinvested interest.

A formula used to compute yield to maturity that reflects average annual return on investment is:

1. Average annual return on investment = annual interest + or - prorated discount or prorated premium

2. Average investment cost = $\dfrac{\text{purchase price} + \text{maturity cost}}{2}$

3. Yield to maturity = $\dfrac{1}{2}\left(\dfrac{\text{average annual return on investment}}{\text{average investment cost}}\right)$

The other yield calculation of interest to bond investors is the "yield to call." Municipal securities typically are issued with "call" provisions, which give the issuer the right to redeem (or prepay) the bonds after a specified period of time has passed and at an established call price, expressed as a premium over par value. Yield to call is the rate of return to the investor if the bonds are called by the issuer on the call date. When dealers sell bonds to investors, they generally also must quote the yield to call, if it is lower than the security's yield to maturity.

INTEREST RATE BEHAVIOR

Interest rates in the economy generally are driven by business cycles, the inflation expectations of borrowers and lenders, and the money supply.

**The business cycle.** As the economy grows, demand for borrowing by corporations and municipal borrowers typically increases and interest rates tend to rise. When the business cycle turns down, demand for borrowing tends to decline, as do rates.

**Inflation expectations.** Interest rates are composed of two components, one of which is a factor for the time value of money, which represents the cost to the lender associated with the unavailability of the funds for the duration of the loan. This is referred to as the "real rate of interest" and represents the cost of the use of money, assuming there is never inflation in prices. The other component of interest rates is a factor for inflation, reflecting the change in purchasing power the lender expects to experience when the money is repaid. When inflationary expectations change, interest rates change also. For example, when lenders expect inflation to increase, they require higher rates of interest; however, borrowers are willing to pay higher rates when they expect prices to rise, because they expect to repay the obligation with inflated dollars. Consequently, inflation expectations of lenders and borrowers combine to affect interest rates, and inflation projections are a major factor in interest rate forecasts.

***The Federal Reserve Board and the money supply.*** One of the major central banking functions of the Federal Reserve Board (the Federal Reserve or the Fed) and its 12 regional Federal Reserve Banks is to control the supply of money in the economy, thereby influencing both inflationary expectations and the level of interest rates. The Federal Reserve sets the interest rate (the "discount rate") at which banks may borrow money from it and establishes reserve requirements for banks that, in turn, drive their cost of funds. Most important, however, are the policy actions of the Federal Reserve's Open Market Committee, by which the Fed buys or sells government securities to increase or to reduce the money supply available in the banking system.

Interest rates, then, are determined largely by the supply and demand for funds in the economy or the availability of and demand for credit. The interest rate is the price that will cause supply and demand for money to come into balance. The Flow of Funds Reports published by the Federal Reserve trace the flow of funds in the economy. Using data from these reports, analysts can ascertain the relative historical and current activity of various categories of borrowers and lenders, as well as project future demand for credit and the potential supply of funds that will be available to meet that demand.

## THE TERM STRUCTURE OF INTEREST RATES AND THE YIELD CURVE

In choosing among different securities, investors must consider risk, liquidity, and return. In addition to credit or "default risk" (the risk that the borrower may be unable to make timely principal and interest payments on the security), investors also face price risk. "Price risk" is the risk that the price of the bonds will fall because of an increase in the general level of interest rates. The longer an investor waits for his or her repayment, the greater the risk of fluctuations in interest rates, because there is more time for variations in interest rates to occur. Therefore, securities with longer maturities typically carry higher rates of interest to compensate for this increased risk. This term structure of interest rates is portrayed commonly as a graph called the "yield curve," with maturities plotted on the x-axis and yields plotted on the y-axis.

In a normal rate environment, the yield curve is upward sloping, or positively sloped, reflecting higher yields for longer maturities. When market conditions cause short-term rates to exceed long-term rates, the yield curve is inverted; when short- and long-term rates are close to equivalent, the curve is flat; when intermediate-term rates are higher than short- or long-term rates, the curve is humpbacked.

Like the yield curve for other classes of debt securities, the yield curve for municipal or tax-exempt securities normally is positively sloped, but its shape does vary. Understanding yield-curve behavior is important to both occasional issuers of bonds and to managers of sustained debt issuance programs, because it is a factor in the decisions about when to borrow and how to structure the maturities of a bond issue.

## Municipal Securities and the Tax Exemption

Municipal bonds or securities—debt obligations of state or local governments—have been issued since the early part of the nineteenth century. The market changed dramatically in 1913, when the Sixteenth Amendment to the Constitution established the federal income tax. Income earned on municipal securities was exempted from income taxation; as a result, yields on these securities fell dramatically and the municipal securities market became distinctly separate from the corporate bond market. The municipal market has expanded continuously throughout this century, especially since World War II.

Municipal securities today include many classes of debt obligations issued by states or political subdivisions of states, which may be local governments, agencies of state governments, or special statutory authorities created by state governments for the purpose of debt issuance. Municipal securities differ from corporate debt securities in that the interest income on these obligations is exempt from gross income for federal income tax purposes. The basis for the federal tax exemption arises from the constitutional doctrine of reciprocal immunity, under which the federal government and state governments cannot interfere in each other's affairs, including by means of taxation. In U.S. tax law, this is interpreted to mean that the federal government cannot tax as income the interest paid on the debt of nonfederal governmental entities. To do so, it is argued, would impair the ability of the states to finance operations. Section 103 of the Internal Revenue Code provides the statutory exemption from federal taxation of interest earned on municipal securities; this section of the Code is amended from time to time to change the manner and degree to which the exemption is granted.

Furthermore, most states exempt from taxation the interest they pay state resident investors on their own securities issues and on municipal bonds issued by obligors within their borders, although most do tax interest earnings on securities issued by other states. A few states exempt from taxation the interest on all municipal bonds. A triple tax-exempt security is one that is exempt from federal, state, and city income taxes; for example, a New York City bond purchased by a New York City resident would be exempt from federal, New York State, and New York City income taxes.

This tax-exemption privilege is the principal advantage that public borrowers have over corporate borrowers. An investor who is not required to pay federal and other income taxes on interest earned is willing to accept a lower rate of interest on the investment than would be required for an equivalent taxable investment. This difference is called the "taxable yield equivalent" of municipal securities. It is computed as follows:

$$\frac{\text{Tax-exempt yield}}{100 \text{ percent - marginal tax bracket}} = \text{Taxable yield equivalent}$$

For example, an investor who earns $200,000 and is in a hypothetical 45 percent marginal tax bracket and who buys a tax-exempt municipal bond with a 7 percent yield earns a taxable yield equivalent of nearly 13 percent. Using these hypothetical numbers, a college or university borrower would pay 7 percent, whereas a corporate borrower of equivalent creditworthiness would pay 13 percent. The higher the investor's tax bracket and taxable yield equivalent, the greater the value of the tax exemption and the lower the interest rates that tax-exempt borrowers must pay to induce that investor to buy the bonds. It is for this reason that changes in federal income tax rates affect interest rates in the municipal tax-exempt bond market.

## TAX-EXEMPT AND TAXABLE YIELD CURVES

Municipal market borrowers need to be aware of the relationship between tax-exempt and taxable interest rates. The relationship changes as a result of a variety of factors. The relationship, or ratio, will become increasingly important for college and university borrowers to understand as, in the future, they will need to consider borrowings in both the tax-exempt and taxable markets as part of their financing programs. (Reasons for taxable borrowing are discussed below.)

In the long run, municipal market rates generally move in tandem with rates in the corporate and government bond market. In the short run, however, municipal market rates move independently of other fixed-income rates and are subject to their own technical or indigenous factors. Most of these factors are aspects of supply and demand.

***Overall supply and demand of municipals.*** Price and yield can be affected by simple fluctuations in the amount of issuances flowing into the market at a given time in relation to demand. For example, in December 1985, numerous higher education issuers brought securities to market at the same time to avoid the impact of tax law changes that were to go into effect in 1986. Bond yields rose to offset this temporary surge in supply. If timing is not urgent, financial advisors normally attempt to bring a higher education issue to market when supply for higher education bonds and/or for municipals is low, relative to normal demand levels.

***Credit quality preferences.*** The municipal market can be subject to different demand for issues of varying credit quality, depending on whether investors, as a whole, are more or less risk-averse at a given time. An extremely risk-averse market can drive down the prices and drive up the yields for even the highest-rated securities. Thus, the yield curves for securities of different credit rating classes can have different shapes.

***Tax law changes.*** The municipal market is susceptible to changes in tax law that modify eligibility for issuance in ways that affect supply; that raise or lower individual or corporate tax rates; or that modify provisions for tax deductions or other aspects of the incentive to invest in tax-exempt securities. Tax legislation in the 1980s provided several major examples of how tax law can affect demand and investor behavior that, in turn, cause interest rates to rise or fall.

For example, commercial banks largely withdrew from investing in certain types of tax-exempt securities (other than "bank-qualified" issues) after a tax law change removed a deduction that had been allowed for 80 percent of interest costs paid by a bank on funds used to purchase or hold tax-exempt securities. Banks buy municipal debt when the yields offered on these securities exceed the cost of capital to purchase them. Elimination of the deduction increased the cost to buy and hold municipals beyond a level at which the investment could be attractive to most banks. Consequently, bank demand or "appetite" for buying tax-exempt securities diminished radically.

As a second example, the introduction of the alternative minimum tax (AMT) affected yield and demand for certain types of tax-exempt securities. Because certain classes of municipal securities are now subject to taxation under the AMT, the yields on these securities must be higher than yields on non-AMT bonds.

As alluded to above, a profound change occurs when there is a major increase or decrease in the maximum individual or corporate tax rates, because the yield relationship between taxable and tax-exempt investments is directly affected. The Tax Reform Act of 1986 reduced individual and corporate income tax rates. In 1991, the highest individual tax rate was 31 percent and the top corporate rate was 34 percent. Recalculation of the taxable yield equivalent, using the hypothetical investor discussed above as an example, would yield very different results. If the investor who was in a 45 percent marginal tax bracket and who is now in a 31 percent tax bracket buys the same tax-exempt municipal bond yielding 7 percent, he or she now would have a taxable yield equivalent of almost 10 percent. Now the 7 percent tax-exempt investment is compared with a taxable investment of only 10 percent rather than 13 percent. To the extent that desirable taxable investment alternatives are available at 10 percent or more, yields on tax-exempt investments will have to rise to induce investors to buy them. From the perspective of the higher education borrower, a tax rate reduction can mean a rise in the tax-exempt interest rates a college or university will have to pay.

## Colleges and Universities as Issuers of Municipal Securities

Because the municipal tax exemption is restricted to public issuers and public purposes, the legal status or type of entity that issues the bonds is fundamentally important in determining whether the borrower is eligible to issue tax-exempt debt. The legal status or type of entity also determines the application of regulatory restrictions on uses or eligible projects, debt limits, treatment of arbitrage (earnings on unspent bond proceeds), financing of costs of issuance, and other related matters. Unfortunately, there are fundamental differences in bond issuance powers and limitations on those powers between public and independent higher education institutions. (See "Federal Tax Law Restrictions on Tax-Exempt Financing," below.)

As agencies of state governments, public higher education institutions are subdivisions of state government and, as such, can be public issuers of tax-exempt debt. Therefore, where state laws permit, a public university may issue bonds directly in the name of the institution. In many states, public colleges and universities are not accorded direct bond issuance powers by the state. In these jurisdictions, the states themselves typically issue debt for higher education capital projects.

In contrast, independent nonprofit colleges and universities are issuers of qualified 501(c)(3) bonds, a special category of municipal securities issued by or in behalf of nongovernmental, tax-exempt 501(c)(3) entities to meet various public purposes. (See also Chapter 9, Taxation.)

## HIGHER EDUCATION FACILITIES AUTHORITIES

To make tax-exempt issuance of securities available to nonpublic entities that develop facilities with public purposes, various state, county, and local special agencies or authorities are created by statute to serve as the legal municipal issuer of such debt. These financings sometimes are referred to as "conduit financings."

Numerous state and local authorities have been created specifically to issue debt for higher education or for higher education and healthcare borrowers. They share the common function of serving as the legal entity for bond issuance, but the range and scope of their activities vary considerably. In some states, higher education facilities authorities have extensive policies on credit strength requirements, as well as large staffs to provide substantial assistance in, if not total direction of, the selection of financial intermediaries, capital finance planning, and the conduct of financings. In other states, authorities have smaller staffs and their roles may be limited to establishing policies and procedures and to reviewing and approving specific financing requests from higher education borrowers.

State-level higher education facilities authorities include:

- California Educational Facilities Authority
- Colorado Postsecondary Educational Facilities Authority
- Connecticut Health and Educational Facilities Authority
- Illinois Educational Facilities Authority
- Indiana Educational Facilities Authority
- Maine Health & Higher Education Facilities Authority
- Maryland Health & Higher Education Facilities Authority
- Massachusetts Health & Education Facilities Authority
- Michigan Higher Education Facilities Authority
- Minnesota Higher Education Facilities Authority
- Missouri Health & Education Facilities Authority
- Nebraska Educational Facilities Authority
- New Hampshire Higher Education & Health Facilities Authority
- New Jersey Educational Facilities Authority
- Dormitory Authority of the State of New York
- Pennsylvania Higher Education Facilities Authority
- Rhode Island Health & Education Building Corporation
- South Dakota Health & Education Facilities Authority
- Vermont Education & Health Buildings Finance Agency
- Virginia College Building Authority
- Washington Higher Education Facilities Authority
- Wisconsin Health & Education Facilities Authority[1]

A few states, including Massachusetts and New York, have two or more state-level agencies or authorities that have legal powers to issue debt for higher education institutions. In addition, city or county authorities also have been created to issue debt on behalf of one or more colleges or universities within their jurisdictions. Typically, these local authorities are found in states where the municipal legal structure includes charter cities. States in which there are multiple city or county issuance authorities include Texas, New Mexico, and Pennsylvania.

Independent colleges and universities located in jurisdictions that include more than one legal entity through which they can issue debt should explore their options; the programs, requirements, flexibility, and levels of assistance provided may vary considerably between issuing authorities.

## HIGHER EDUCATION BOND ISSUANCE

Compared with other industry groups, colleges and universities historically have used debt financing conservatively. Independent higher education institutions have tended to rely heavily on fund-raising for major capital construction. Public institutions have relied heavily on state appropriations, although the state may rely, in turn, on its general obligation debt to fund capital projects. Some colleges and universities have charters, endowment bequests, or policies that preclude incurring debt; others have never needed to borrow externally, having been able to generate enough capital from internal resources and gifts. Until the 1980s, the issuance of publicly sold bonds and the use of complex debt financing structures as part of a broader capital development program were undertaken by only the larger, better-endowed, or more financially sophisticated institutions; smaller institutions relied more typically on tax-exempt loans directly from local banking institutions. During the 1980s, numerous changes in federal tax laws, bank lending programs, and institutional management capacity, combined with continuing fiscal pressures, led increasing numbers of colleges and universities to enter the public tax-exempt debt market. Figure 12-1 shows that the volume of higher education bond issuance increased markedly in the 1980s, indicating this broader participation of higher education institutions in the public debt markets.

Between 1980 and 1990, higher education borrowings grew at an average annual rate of 25 percent per year (an inflation-adjusted annual

FIGURE 12-1

Summary of Long-Term Higher Education Bond Issuance, Including Private Placements

FY 1980 through FY 1990

| Year | No. of Issues | $ Par Amounts (millions) |
|------|---------------|--------------------------|
| 1980 | 32  | 812.2   |
| 1981 | 45  | 847.9   |
| 1982 | 70  | 1,649.4 |
| 1983 | 96  | 2,276.0 |
| 1984 | 145 | 3,266.0 |
| 1985 | 305 | 9,821.8 |
| 1986 | 236 | 6,676.6 |
| 1987 | 225 | 3,790.4 |
| 1988 | 296 | 5,805.6 |
| 1989 | 307 | 6,021.5 |
| 1990 | 270 | 7,927.7 |

Source: Securities Data Company, May 8, 1991.

rate of 20 percent). The record peak of $9.8 billion in 1985 was due to the rush to issue bonds as higher education issuers and their bankers anticipated the major restrictions that the Tax Reform Act of 1986 would bring. In general, higher education borrowing activity in the early 1990s is significantly greater than it was a decade ago. In 1990, higher education bond issuance reached almost $8 billion, representing a significant increase of 31.7 percent over 1989. This increase may signal a new cycle of expanding demand for financing. Because of major needs for new construction and deferred maintenance problems on campuses, it is likely that higher education issuance volume will continue to grow through the 1990s.

Even with this markedly increased volume, higher education financings represent only 6 percent of the total municipal tax-exempt market. Constraints of credit strength, lack of name recognition, lack of financial sophistication, and the small size of some borrowing needs have kept many colleges and universities out of the tax-exempt debt market or confined their borrowings to participation in large pooled financings. Still others have not needed to borrow. It is estimated that only 10 percent of the nation's 3,000 higher education institutions have issued rated public tax-exempt debt, although certainly many others, if not most, have borrowed from banks and internal funds. In addition, it is reasonable to assume that a significant additional number of institutions have issued unrated debt or participated in tax-exempt pooled financings.

The Tax Reform Act of 1986 restricted the potential future total of higher education financings in the tax-exempt market by limiting to $150 million the amount of tax-exempt debt outstanding allowed to independent nonprofit colleges and universities. Many of the largest and most creditworthy independent institutions are not able to increase their tax-exempt market activity. On the other hand, as needs continue unabated, as the industry gains financial sophistication, and as investment bankers devise new issuance techniques, more institutions may be expected to venture into tax-exempt financing to finance new facilities and to fund long-overdue deferred maintenance.

Because higher education has been a relatively minor player in the tax-exempt bond market, investors have not always understood higher education issues as well as other types of tax-exempt bonds. On the other hand, higher education is regarded as having a good track record in creditworthiness; defaults on higher education debt are generally believed to be infrequent, although statistics are not available. Major institutional investors today know how to evaluate these securities, but achieving successful issuance and cost-effective interest rates still can depend on the skill of the institution and its bankers in presenting the institution's case—telling its story—to potential investors.

There are two public debt markets in which colleges and universities can be borrowers. The most traditional and typical is the tax-exempt municipal market. More recently, as a result of restrictions on independent institutions' ability to issue tax-exempt debt, a number of institutions have begun to enter the taxable bond market.

## Overview of Municipal Debt

The categories of municipal debt are based on fundamental differences in underlying security structure. Colleges and universities are issuers of bonds in only some of these categories, but they may be indirect beneficiaries of the proceeds of others.

## GENERAL OBLIGATION BONDS

In the tax-exempt municipal market, general obligation bonds are long-term obligations that are backed by the full faith and credit of the issuer, a state or local government. The credit structure of these bonds is based on the taxing authority of the issuer, without limitation. General obligation bonds are the original form of municipal debt.

Colleges and universities, like hospitals and other nongovernmental entities, have no taxation powers; by definition they cannot be issuers of general obligation bonds in the true sense. (This is not to be confused with the fact that a college or university bond issue can be secured by a "general obligation pledge" of the institution's revenues.)

In many states, the state itself issues general obligation bonds, the proceeds of which are designated to fund construction of facilities for the state's higher education system. Florida, Illinois, and California finance higher education facilities through state general obligation debt. General obligation bonds also are used to finance construction of facilities for K-12 school systems.

## REVENUE BONDS

Revenue bonds are a relatively newer form of municipal financing than general obligation bonds. Once constituting a small fraction of the total municipal market, revenue bonds today dominate the market: 68 percent of total par issuance in 1990 was revenue bonds.

Revenue bonds are not secured by the general revenues and taxing powers of the issuer; rather, they are issued to support specific projects, the revenues of which are pledged to repay the indebtedness to bondholders. Based on the concept of user fees, revenue bonds have allowed municipal issuers to expand their indebtedness without creating greater burdens on general tax revenues. In the 1950s, highways and utilities were the major purposes for which fees were charged and revenue bonds were issued. Today, revenue bonds are issued commonly for colleges and universities, hospitals, housing, public power projects, small industrial development projects, pollution-control facilities, and other public purposes.

With the exception of state general obligation bonds issued by a state to finance college or university facilities, higher education bonds generally are classified as revenue bonds. Tuition and fees institutions collect may be thought of as roughly equivalent to other types of user fees. As noted above, college and university revenue bonds may carry general obligation pledges of institutional revenues.

## SPECIAL TAX BONDS

Special tax bonds are like general obligation bonds in that they are not dependent upon specific fee revenues for repayment to bondholders; however, they are supported by a specific dedicated tax or taxes rather than by the full taxing authority and general revenues of the issuer. As an example, Florida's motor vehicle tag tax is pledged by the state to repay bond issues for higher education institutions.

## MORAL OBLIGATION BONDS

A hybrid form of general obligation bonds and revenue bonds is a moral obligation bond. This type of bond is secured by revenues from the facility financed, with the additional moral but not legally binding commitment on the part of a governmental entity to pay bondholders from tax revenues in the event that project revenues fall short.

## DOUBLE-BARRELED BONDS

A double-barreled bond is secured legally by both specific user fee revenues from a facility financed and by the taxing power of the issuing governmental entity.

## PRIVATE ACTIVITY BONDS AND QUALIFIED PRIVATE ACTIVITY BONDS

Revenue bonds are categorized as either governmental use or private activity bonds. Private activity bonds are revenue bonds, the interest income on which is subject to taxation unless they are "qualified" (for the tax exemption) private activity bonds. Under current tax law, the tests that are applied to determine whether or not an issue is qualified significantly limit private-sector involvement in tax-exempt financed projects. Even private activity bonds that are qualified to be tax-exempt are still subject to more limitations than are governmental use bonds. Issued by or through a public entity to support a private activity with public purposes, qualified issues are possible in such undertakings as pollution-control facilities, multifamily and single-family housing, stadiums, and small industrial development projects. These bonds are subject to state volume caps; each state is permitted bond issuances amounting to $50 per capita or $150 million, whichever is lower.

QUALIFIED 501(c)(3) BONDS

Colleges, universities, nonprofit hospitals, and other tax-exempt organizations are issuers of an additional subcategory of qualified private activity bonds called "qualified 501(c)(3)" bonds. The term 501(c)(3) refers to Internal Revenue Code provisions that define entities that are exempt from federal income tax. Qualified 501(c)(3) bonds are exempted from the tests applied to other qualified private activity bonds and are not subject to state volume cap limitations; however, these bonds are more limited in their treatment than are governmental use bonds.

These legal differences have significant implications in higher education. Whereas the bonds of publicly supported higher education institutions are treated as governmental use bonds, the bonds of independent nonprofit colleges and universities are considered qualified 501(c)(3) bonds. This fact has created an unfortunate variance in the abilities of public and independent institutions to raise tax-exempt funds. The differences lead to a higher cost of capital or to reduced access to the markets for the independent nonprofit segment of the industry; the independent nonprofit segment claims that more favorable capital costs give an unfair competitive advantage to public institutions.

# Long-Term Tax-Exempt Debt

The most conventional form of tax-exempt debt is the "long-term, fixed-rate bond," in which the interest rate or rates are fixed for a single or multiple maturities. The "final maturity" is the date when the final principal is due to bondholders. Final maturities as long as 20 or 30 years are common. Most issuances are structured with serial maturities and in par amounts calculated to include the costs of the capital project or projects and the costs of issuance of the bonds, including reserves for debt service, also called "sinking funds," and sometimes also reserves for repair and maintenance of the facilities to be built. Several separate issuances or a series of bond issues may be issued under a single bond resolution and be treated as a system of facilities, or issuances may be under separate bond resolutions.

Investors in fixed-rate bonds have two advantages: a fixed rate of return and the possibility of appreciation. When market interest rates decline, holders of bonds at higher rates of interest benefit because their bonds appreciate in value. Conversely, colleges and universities that issue fixed-rate debt have the advantage of fixed interest and principal payments, permitting the institution to budget for debt service with certainty. The risk to the borrowing institution is that, if interest rates decline significantly, the institution may pay more than current market interest rates; however in most instances, there eventually are opportunities to call or refund (refinance) outstanding issues. (See "Management of Existing Debt," below.)

## CALL PROVISIONS

Long-term, fixed-rate bonds typically have "call provisions," which enable the borrower to repay bondholders ahead of schedule, at fixed call dates and at fixed call premiums over the par value. For example, callable bonds are issued with a series of maturities, the longest of which is 30 years. The bonds are callable by the college or university at 10 years at a premium of 102. If the college or university chooses to exercise the call provision, the bondholders are repaid 102 percent of the amount then outstanding; the original debt is extinguished and usually replaced with new debt at prevailing rates.

## TERM AND SERIAL BONDS

"Term bonds" have a single maturity at which all the principal debt becomes due. Normally, term bonds will have a sinking fund structure, by means of which the borrower sets aside funds, so that the entire principal amount is accumulated for redemption of the bonds at maturity. "Serial bonds" (or a serial bond issue) include bonds scheduled to mature each year or in selected years over a period of many years. Serial bonds permit an overall reduction in interest costs because the bonds with shorter maturities pay lower rates of interest than do those with the longer maturities. Serial bond issues can be structured to provide for level debt service or for level principal payments, while

COLLEGE AND UNIVERSITY BUSINESS ADMINISTRATION

allowing the borrower to amortize or reduce the borrowing slowly over time. Typically, an issuance will be structured with both term and serial bonds, that is, a combination of serial maturities and a single term or balloon maturity.

## LEASE STRUCTURES

"Lease revenue bonds" are those in which a municipality or debt-issuing authority issues bonds and leases the built facilities or equipment to an eligible user under a formal lease or loan agreement. This structure is used commonly in higher education finance, with a state education facilities authority as the issuer and lessor and the college or university as the borrower and lessee of the facilities. The lease payments become the basic security for the bond; therefore, the lessee's credit and source of funds for the lease payments are pertinent to the credit quality and marketability of the bonds.

"Lease certificates of participation" are units of ownership in debt that is repaid from lease payments, often on major equipment financings. The investors receive portions of the lease payments in proportion to the certificates they own.

Lease structures can be especially effective for public colleges and universities that are financing major equipment acquisitions, such as high-technology telecommunications systems, major computer acquisitions, and significant scientific/research instruments. An important feature of many lease financings is that security for the debt is contingent on annual appropriations of funds and not on a general obligation of the issuer.

## ZERO-COUPON BONDS (CAPITAL APPRECIATION BONDS)

Capital appreciation or zero-coupon bonds have a coupon interest rate of 0 percent. When issued, they are sold at a deep discount from the par amount. Upon maturity, the investor receives a return in the form of appreciation to the full par amount of the bonds. In higher education finance, zero-coupon bonds have been used to finance tuition savings plans and are useful also for specific instances in which the borrower can benefit significantly from having no interest payments to make for a certain time.

## DEFERRED INTEREST BONDS

Deferred interest bonds are structured so that the borrower begins to pay interest on a predetermined date prior to maturity and semiannually thereafter. The interest accrues at a fixed rate from the date of issuance until the date at which the bonds convert to current interest bonds.

# Short-Term and Variable-Rate Tax-Exempt Debt

Because of the term structure of interest rates, short-term debt normally carries lower interest rates than long-term debt. Long-term variable-rate debt, which emulates the interest rate and maturity features of short-term debt, provides opportunities for flexibility and reduced financing costs.

## NOTES

Notes are short-term obligations, generally with maturities of one year or less, although there is no entirely accepted standard definition for what constitutes a note. Tax-exempt notes of various kinds, including "tax anticipation notes," "revenue anticipation notes," and "bond anticipation notes," enable a governmental borrower to lower the overall costs of borrowing by including some short-term debt in a financing plan. Alternatively, they permit a borrower to finance a construction project temporarily until long-term financing is in place. Used widely by municipal governments, tax-exempt notes are not used as widely by college and university issuers.

## VARIABLE-RATE DEMAND BONDS

Variable-rate demand bonds (VRDB) blend features of long-term debt (bonds) and short-term debt (notes). The issuance has a long-term nominal maturity, for example, 30 years; however, the securities have a demand or put feature whereby the bondholder may "put" the bonds back to the issuer, that is, require the issuer to repurchase the obligation at par plus accrued interest. VRDBs also bear an interest rate that is reset on a yearly, semiannually, monthly, weekly, or daily basis, based on market conditions. Thus, investors in VRDBs are able to hold long-term investments with the benefit of reduced interest-rate risk. If market interest rates rise, the rate that is paid on VRDBs also will rise. Normally, resetting the interest rate to match the yield required by current market conditions makes it unlikely that investors will exercise the demand option. If a demand is exercised, however, the issuer's remarketing agent remarkets the bonds to new investors. For this service, the issuer of VRDBs pays an ongoing annual fee to the remarketing agent.

Because of potential rate volatility and exercise of demand features, VRDBs generally are structured with a commercial bank's letter of credit or a standby bond purchase agreement, to serve as a liquidity backup facility. If an investor demands repurchase and the bonds cannot be remarketed immediately, the letter of credit is drawn down for payment of the repurchase price plus accrued interest to the initial bondholder. Letters of credit typically are provided by commercial banks, which charge an initial and ongoing annual fee for providing this liquidity backup. When the letter of credit also serves as a credit backup, the bonds normally trade in the market based on the credit rating of the letter-of-credit bank, rather than the issuer's. Some VRDB issues have credit support in the form of bond insurance, with a letter of credit to provide liquidity. (For a full discussion of letters of credit, see "Credit Enhancement Techniques," below.)

The college or university borrower faces interest-rate risk with VRDBs that it does not face with fixed-rate bond obligations. An issuer of VRDBs must have enough financial liquidity and flexibility to be able to cover increased payments if necessary. On the other hand, the lower (essentially short-term) rates at which VRDBs are sold have enabled a number of colleges or universities to lower their cost of borrowing successfully. With legal restrictions on advance refunding (see "Management of Existing Debt," below), variable-rate debt also provides the flexibility of optional calls or redemptions by the issuer on very short notice, for example, 30 days for a monthly VRDB. In contrast, fixed-rate debt normally has a no-call period of five to ten years.

VRDBs normally have a one-time fixed-rate conversion option whereby the issuer can, with certain required notices, convert the VRDB to fixed-rate debt. Upon conversion, the bonds become long-term, fixed-rate obligations.

## TENDER OPTION BONDS

Tender option bonds are similar to variable-rate demand bonds but differ in the length of the tender period and the periodic interest-rate resetting. Initially, a tender option bond is structured with the first tender date set at six months to ten years from the date of issuance. Subsequent tender dates occur periodically thereafter. Between tender dates, the interest rate on the bonds remains fixed. This structure is used primarily for housing bonds.

## MULTIMODAL BONDS

Multimodal bond issues permit the issuer to select and change the mode of interest-rate resetting periodically to take advantage of changing yield curves.

## TAX-EXEMPT COMMERCIAL PAPER

Tax-exempt commercial paper is an unsecured promissory note issued in registered or bearer form with a maturity that does not exceed 270 days. Tax-exempt commercial paper is the municipal market's counterpart to taxable commercial paper, which is short-term unsecured debt typically sold only by corporate entities with very strong credit. Tax-exempt commercial paper often is backed by a line or letter of credit. Common maturities are 30 days and 60 days.

Colleges and universities have not been active issuers of tax-exempt commercial paper, which normally must be issued in large par amounts by issuers with triple-A credit ratings, of which there are few in higher education. Tax-exempt commercial paper has been used effectively, however, as a structure for pooled financings initiated by state authorities on behalf of numerous college borrowers. The Dormitory Authority of the State of New York, for example, used tax-exempt commercial paper programs to create two pooled financings that totaled $140 million.

# Pooled Bond Issues

Numerous states have undertaken, through their higher education facilities authorities, to sell bonds to create a pool of funds from which they make small loans to qualifying colleges and universities. The advantages of a pooled financing are significant to small borrowers.

Pooled financing makes it possible for the small borrower to gain access to funds at tax-exempt rates, which otherwise might not be feasible because the small size of the borrowing would make a standalone issue too costly or because the small size or limited market recognition of the institution's name would make marketing its bonds difficult and expensive. Until 1986, it was legally possible to issue "blind pools," a pooled financing for which the borrowers and their projects were not identified in advance. When the proceeds of the sale of bonds were received, the bond program administrator invested them at taxable returns and the issue earned arbitrage on the invested proceeds until loans were made to qualified borrowers. Since 1986, regulations preclude blind pools and related arbitrage earnings. Pools remain a viable form of financing primarily in states where the education facilities authorities have sufficient resources to survey participants for needs and to organize the complexities of pooled financings.

The California Education Facilities Authority and the Dormitory Authority of the State of New York are among the authorities that have issued pooled debt programs to finance projects at numerous colleges in their states.

# Federal Tax Law Restrictions on Tax-Exempt Financing

Higher education bond issues are subject to federal and state taxation and securities law and regulations, as well as to legal and policy restrictions of the institution itself. A comprehensive discussion of the legal framework for bond issuance is beyond the scope of this chapter; however, a number of general limitations under federal tax law are basic to understanding bond issuance in the current environment.

Since Section 103 of the Internal Revenue Code was enacted in 1968, successive legislation has placed restrictions on the tax-exempt borrowing privilege. Legislated reductions in the applicability of the tax exemption generally are responses to concern that the exemption drains revenues unnecessarily from the federal treasury, even if issuers use tax-exempt debt for appropriate purposes.

## PROHIBITION OF ARBITRAGE

Arbitrage arises from the spread between taxable and tax-exempt interest rates. When the proceeds of a tax-exempt issue are invested, prior to being expended, in taxable securities with yields higher than the interest being paid on the tax-exempt bonds, the issuer earns arbitrage profits. Under the Internal Revenue Code and ensuing regulations, municipal borrowers are precluded from earning arbitrage profits in most circumstances and, where such arbitrage is earned, it usually must be "rebated," that is, paid to the federal government. The preclusion is implemented in two ways. The majority of bond proceeds are yield restricted; where yield restriction does not apply, rebate usually is effective in transmitting arbitrage earnings back to the federal government. There are six-month and two-year rebate exceptions that have specific spending guidelines and timetables, as well as a variety of penalty options in the event that guidelines and timetables are not met. Also, debt service reserve funds are limited to 10 percent of bond proceeds, unless prior bond indentures require larger reserves. When bonds are secured with larger reserves, the investment yield on the reserves is restricted to the yield on the bonds. Because the regulations governing arbitrage are exceedingly complex and change periodically, prospective debt issuers are advised to consult bond counsel for current information.

## REIMBURSEMENT REGULATIONS

Complex regulations govern the ability of an issuer to use the proceeds of a tax-exempt bond issue to reimburse itself for project-related expenditures made prior to the date of issuance of the bonds. Generally, the regulations require that the issuer declare reasonable official intent to reimburse the prior expenditures with bond proceeds. A college or university's governing board or the issuing authority, or both, must adopt resolutions of intent with certain prescribed characteristics. The intent also must be "reasonable" in terms of the college or university's financial resources, and timing of the expenditures is a factor.

## LIMITATION ON ADVANCE REFUNDING

Refunding also is subject to complex regulations. Bond issues sold after January 1986 may be advance-refunded only once. Bonds issued earlier may be advance-refunded twice, with certain exceptions. (Advance refunding is discussed below.)

## USE-OF-PROCEEDS TEST

The proceeds of a bond issue must be used for the exempt purpose of the issuer. In higher education, this means that proceeds of a tax-exempt bond issue must be used for projects that are related to the education purposes of the institution. Ninety percent of proceeds of bonds issued by public higher education institutions and 95 percent of proceeds of bonds of independent colleges and universities must be so used. As an example, this restriction precludes the use of tax-exempt financing for inclusion of privately owned and operated retail space in a student union building.

## INDEPENDENT INSTITUTION VOLUME CAP

Independent colleges and universities are limited to a cap of $150 million in the amount of tax-exempt debt that they may have outstanding. The cap excludes hospital financings. While only a limited number of college and university borrowers have reached this cap, a great number have the potential to reach it. Institutional borrowers that reach the volume cap and that need additional funds for projects must look to the taxable bond market or forgo projects until outstanding tax-exempt debt is repaid and cap availability for tax-exempt borrowing becomes available again.

## LIMITATIONS ON COSTS OF ISSUANCE

Independent colleges and universities may only "capitalize" (include in the par amount of the borrowing) costs of issuance of the bonds up to a limit of 2 percent of tax-exempt bond proceeds. Costs subject to this limitation include most transaction costs (except fees for credit enhancements), encompassing:

- Underwriting spreads (bond discounts)
- Legal fees, including underwriters and issuer's counsel and bond counsel
- Financial advisory fees
- Rating agency fees
- Trustee and paying agent fees
- Accounting services fees

This discussion summarized selected highlights of extremely complex legal and regulatory issues. Colleges and universities contemplating bond issuance must consult with qualified bond attorneys and financial advisors for a detailed understanding of the complex legal and regulatory requirements and restrictions that may be in effect when they seek to enter the tax-exempt debt market.

# Forms of Taxable Debt

Various statutory and regulatory changes have imposed significant restrictions on the ability of colleges and universities to engage in certain types of tax-exempt financings. In recent years, some institutions have ventured into the taxable debt markets. These institutions include large independent universities that reached their $150 million tax-exempt volume caps and institutions that sought to finance projects related to economic development that did not qualify, under current law, for tax-exempt issuance. Other institutions have issued taxable debt with options to exchange all or a portion of such bonds for tax-exempt bonds bearing lower interest rates, if and when access to the tax-exempt market became available to them. In the future, institutions are likely to turn increasingly to the public taxable market and to taxable bank loans for needed funds. These categories of taxable debt differ not only in source of funds but also in debt structure and means of access.

TAXABLE BANK DEBT

*Term loans.* A "term loan" is a loan made by a commercial bank for a defined period or term and bearing a fixed or floating rate of interest. Loan terms may be brief, such as 90 days, or long term, such as ten years. A term loan is often secured by a "mortgage," in which real property (land and/or buildings) is pledged as collateral or security for the loan. Banks perform a credit analysis to decide whether or not to make a loan and to determine what features, including the term, interest rate(s), and payment provisions, to offer.

Although reliable estimates of the annual borrowing or total outstanding volume of term loans made by banks to colleges and universities are not readily available, the volume is undoubtedly large, and most colleges and universities are familiar with this kind of financing. An institution often has one or more significant banking relationships in its community; the degree to which it may be able to obtain competitive or favorable terms on a term loan may be tied to the extent of its relationships with its bank or banks.

With a few exceptions of some major commercial banks that have identified education and other not-for-profit organizations as a special customer segment and have dedicated staff to that segment, most commercial bankers may be unfamiliar with fund accounting principles and with measures of credit strength for colleges. Thus, an institution may have to interpret clearly its financial condition and financial statements to lending officers. Nonetheless, banks continue to be a major source of financing that should not be overlooked, especially for smaller or occasional projects that do not warrant the time and transaction costs involved in public debt offerings.

*Line of credit.* A "line of credit" is an amount of funds made available, usually by a bank, to a borrower; it is sometimes referred to as a "credit facility." When funds actually are needed, the borrower exercises or draws down on the line of credit. Upon exercise, the original facility often is converted to a term loan that may remain unsecured and treated as such thereafter. Lines of credit are used commonly to provide liquidity and can be extremely useful in managing cash flows.

*Letter of credit.* A "letter of credit" is a form of credit facility sold by banks, although it may be provided by other entities. Letters of credit are discussed below as a technique for credit enhancement.

## TAXABLE DEBT IN THE CAPITAL MARKETS

Because taxable municipals are still in their infancy and secondary markets have not been developed, they are not yet as liquid as tax-exempt municipals. The single major advantage to the taxable debt alternative is that it does not bear the restrictions as to issuer, purpose of issuance, and other regulatory limitations to which tax-exempt debt is subject. In some ways, taxable borrowings are much simpler to structure, but they are more difficult to market. Also, the cost of funds, by definition, is higher. More significantly, activity in these markets will require college and university business officers to become familiar with entirely new market conditions and approaches. Finally, taxable debt issuance by colleges and universities may be constrained by the lack of familiarity of investors in these markets with higher education issues. This constraint may be overcome with time and increased issuance activity and with efforts to improve information flows in the market.

***Capital leasing or lease-purchase agreements.*** In a "capital lease," the lessee makes a series of lease payments, at the end of which the lessee owns the asset. Capital leases often are a financing option for major equipment acquisitions and may be offered by banks, leasing companies, or equipment vendors. Capital leases are common, for example, in major computer acquisitions.

***Commercial paper.*** "Commercial paper" is unsecured promissory notes of corporations, issued for short-term financing or working capital purposes. The notes are issued at a discount and redeemed at face value. Normally, commercial paper programs are issued only by strong credits in large par amounts and rolled over each time the issue matures. A commercial paper program can be credit-enhanced by means of an irrevocable bank letter of credit.

Because of program size and credit requirements, taxable commercial paper has not been used frequently in higher education. It has been used to generate the funding for special pooled financing programs. It is likely that taxable commercial paper, because of its relatively low cost and flexibility, will be used more often in higher education, most likely for large pooled financings.

***Medium-term notes.*** "Medium-term notes or bonds" (MTN) are taxable securities with intermediate-length maturities, typically from two to ten years, that, unlike longer-term bonds, are not callable by the issuer. They are a good taxable alternative for higher education borrowers because of the large size of the MTN market and because they can achieve an interest rate lower than that required by long-term bonds while allowing the borrower to avoid the volatility of short-term rates.

***Taxable fixed-rate bonds.*** "Taxable fixed-rate bonds" are similar in structure to their tax-exempt counterparts, with maturities of 10 to 30 years, but are sold as public offerings in the taxable U.S. corporate bond market or as private placements. "Private placement" of long-term fixed-rate bonds is, in certain situations, a useful alternative to public offering and sale. Private placements can have maturities as long as 30 years, but 20 years is a common final maturity. Because of their narrower distribution, private placements generally have higher yields than do public offerings by issuers of comparable credit strength—the college or university borrower pays a higher interest rate. The advantages are that issues as small as $5 million may be economically viable; credit enhancement typically is not used; less well-known names can be placed; and the transaction is surrounded by privacy. These bonds are purchased most frequently by investors such as insurance companies that intend to hold them to maturity.

For institutions without tax-exempt capacity and with reasonable name recognition, publicly sold taxable bonds can be an alternative for permanent fixed-rate financing. They also can be viable for smaller institutions that are, for various reasons, unable to gain access to the tax-exempt market. Although lack of familiarity of market investors with higher education names is a drawback to smaller or lesser-known issuers, bond insurance can be used to enhance the credit of such issues.

***Foreign currency denominated bonds.*** The most significant difference between foreign currency denominated bonds and conventional fixed-rate taxable bond financing is that principal and interest transactions are made in a foreign currency. When interest rates are more favorable outside the U.S., an issuer can consider whether access to a foreign capital market can be used as a means to reduce borrowing costs. The issuer must be aware, however, of the possibility of a gain or loss on payments due to changing currency exchange rates. In higher education, the limited name recognition abroad of many institutions makes it difficult to find investors. Larger well-known public and independent universities, authorities that issue pooled higher education financings, or issuers that obtain credit-enhancment from a well-recognized commercial bank are most likely to avail themselves of international market opportunities for capital.

***Taxable variable-rate bonds.*** "Taxable variable-rate bonds" (VRB) are similar in maturity and rate structure to tax-exempt VRDBs, except that rates are taxable interest rates. The market for taxable VRBs is relatively small and illiquid, but they may have applications for specific circumstances in higher education. For example, a few such financings have been accomplished in connection with university-related research parks.

## Security Structures, Creditworthiness, and Credit Enhancement

Higher education bond issues are by definition revenue bonds, except when a state's general obligation debt is issued for a higher education purpose. Security structures for higher education debt therefore involve variations on revenue pledges of the institution, that is, pledges of general credit (general revenues) or pledges of specific revenue streams. In addition, the credit structure of a borrowing can be enhanced, through use of a "credit enhancement product," which substitutes the credit strength of the credit enhancement provider for the credit of the issuer or the issuance.

## FORMS OF SECURITY

*Physical collateral.* Physical assets pledged by a borrower to a lender constitute "physical collateral." If the borrower defaults on debt service payments, the collateral may be taken by the lender or investor, who is free to dispose of the property in any way. Normally, the lender sells the collateral to repay the loan. Facilities acquired or constructed with the proceeds of bond funds commonly are pledged as physical collateral to secure the bondholders. Commercial bank term loans often are structured as mortgages, in which the real property or buildings are collateral for the lending bank.

In the case of corporate debt, physical collateral can be meaningful as security. If a corporation defaults on its bonds, bondholders often can liquidate the property and recover some or all their funds. In the case of college and university financings, physical collateral, other than undeveloped land in locations with development potential, is typically far less meaningful as security to bondholders. It is usually unlikely that bondholders would be able to convert an academic building, dormitory, student center, or athletic facility located in the core of a university campus to another profitable use. In the case of lease financings of major computer systems or other high-technology equipment, physical collateral can be more meaningful, as the assets are suitable to disposition, if necessary.

Bond issues cannot be secured purely by the physical property acquired or built with the proceeds. Bond security structures are based on pledges of income streams and/or other liquid assets.

*Collateralization with endowment and other assets.* A borrower can collateralize a loan with assets other than physical assets. Securities and invested funds are common forms of collateral. In the past, colleges and universities commonly collateralized bond issues with funds functioning as endowment. There was no cost associated with doing so, as the collateralized funds could continue to earn returns. Tax law now requires that the yield earned on invested funds held as collateral for bond issues be restricted to the rate of interest paid on the bond issue, although there are some technical steps that can be taken to make partial collateralization useful. This requirement has changed the implications for collateralization, making it virtually unusable as a form of security.

*Pledge of general institutional credit.* Higher education bonds classified as revenue bonds (those other than state general obligation bonds, issued for higher education) can be secured by a pledge of general institutional resources and, consequently, represent general obligations of the institution. A pledge of the institution's general credit means that all revenues and resources of the institution that legally are not restricted as to use or purpose can be tapped to meet payments to bondholders in the event of imminent or actual default. This form of pledge is sometimes called a "legally available funds pledge." The meaning of such a pledge and its value in terms of the quality of the credit of the borrower depend on the degree of flexibility the institution has in reallocating resources, if necessary, to pay debt service. Policy issues, terms of endowments, state requirements, diversity of revenues, size of funds functioning as endowment, and other factors determine the strength of a pledge of general institutional credit.

*Pledge of tuition and fees.* Another common form of security pledge is a pledge of tuition and fee revenues. This kind of security can be either a limited or unlimited pledge. This structure logically provides less security to the bondholder than does a general obligation pledge, because funds other than tuition and fees cannot be tapped to pay bondholders. When tuition and fees form the security structure, the credit analysis focuses closely on the strength of student demand, the history of enrollments, and the levels of tuition and fees.

*Pledge of a specific revenue source.* Alternatively, an institution can issue project revenue bonds, the repayment of which is backed only by the specific revenues of the project being financed. In higher education financings, security pledges for auxiliary facilities involve pledges of all or portions of the revenue streams from the auxiliary project or projects being constructed, or, collectively, the revenues from the system of auxiliary facilities. Auxiliary financings include student or faculty housing, food services, campus retail stores, parking, stadiums, research facilities, and other financings for which user fees are charged. Bond indentures include pledges of a given portion of the revenues for repayment of the indebtedness of those facilities. In many publicly supported colleges and universities, a state or governing board policy establishes a required ratio of debt coverage. In other cases, institutional financing policy, rating agencies, or the market itself drives the amount that can be borrowed against a specific stream of revenues. An example is a policy requirement that net project revenues, after costs of operations, must equal 1.5 times debt service, where debt service is defined as the highest annual amount that must be paid during the life of the bond issue.

## CREDIT RATINGS

The method by which capital market investors are able to make relatively simple judgments about the credit quality of alternative debt securities is the application of credit ratings to these securities. Without a standard process of ratings, which enables relative comparisons and establishes classes or categories of credits, each investor would have to analyze, in exhaustive detail, the underlying business operations, financial strength, and security structure of each bond investment under consideration.

A "rating" is a measure of the likelihood of timely and complete repayment of principal and interest on debt. Commercial bank lenders and other financial institutions perform internal credit analyses and assign ratings for their own credit decision purposes. The public debt markets are served by independent rating agencies that develop credit standards, formulate and apply credit analysis techniques, and establish and maintain ratings on issuers and issues.

Normally, a bond or note issue is rated prior to its sale, although some issues are sold as unrated. Based on the judgment of the financial advisor or underwriter, one or two ratings may be sought for the issue. After a rated bond issue is sold, the rating agency or agencies review the credit on a continuous basis and may amend the rating, based on changes in the issuer's financial condition. The rating assigned, both initially and upon amendment, directly affects the marketability and the yields on the bonds.

The three primary independent rating agencies are Standard &

Poor's Corporation (S&P), Moody's Investors Service, Inc., and Fitch Investor Services, Inc. S&P has rated 425 college and university issues and Moody's has rated 340. (A number of bond issues and institutions have been rated by both.) Fitch, recently reestablished, also has begun to rate college and university issues.

***Long-term debt ratings.*** Long-term credit ratings fall into two categories: investment grade and noninvestment grade. Long-term investment grade ratings assigned by S&P, Moody's, and Fitch are as shown in Figure 12-2.

---

FIGURE 12-2
Investment Grade Long-Term Bond Ratings Assigned by S&P, Fitch Investor Services, Inc., and Moody's Investors Service, Inc.

| Capacity to Pay | S&P/Fitch | Moody's |
|---|---|---|
| Strongest/Highest Grade | AAA | Aaa |
| Very Strong/High Grade | AA+ | Aa1 |
| Very Strong/High Grade | AA | Aa |
| Very Strong/High Grade | AA- | — |
| Strong/Upper Medium Grade | A+ | A1 |
| Strong/Upper Medium Grade | A | A |
| Strong/Upper Medium Grade | A- | — |
| Adequate/Medium Grade | BBB+ | Baa1 |
| Adequate/Medium Grade | BBB | Baa |
| Adequate/Medium Grade | BBB- | — |

---

***Short-term debt ratings.*** Ratings of short-term obligations assigned by Moody's are designated as Moody's Investment Grade (MIG) and range from MIG1 through MIG4. Short-term ratings emphasize the liquidity of the borrower and short-term cyclical elements, rather than long-term credit risk. The ratings that Moody's assigns to issues with a demand feature are designated as VMIG1 through VMIG4. When Moody's rates VRDBs, it may assign both a standard long-term rating for scheduled payments and a VMIG rating for the demand feature. VMIG ratings also may be assigned to commercial paper programs that have no demand features. All MIG and VMIG ratings indicate investment grade securities.

S&P's categories for short-term ratings are:

- SP-1: Very strong or strong capacity to pay principal and interest. Issues possessing overwhelming safety characteristics are given a plus (+) designation

- SP-2: Satisfactory capacity to pay principal and interest

- SP-3: Speculative capacity to pay principal and interest

Credit ratings are assigned to issues, not to issuers of bonds. They evaluate the institution's capacity to repay a specific bond obligation given the security structure of that issue. Nonetheless, the process of analyzing the creditworthiness of the bond issue includes a comprehensive analysis of the issuer's overall credit characteristics and resources.

## CREDITWORTHINESS AND CREDIT ANALYSIS

Credit analysis in corporate finance relies heavily on the use of financial and operating ratios, norms for those ratios, and qualitative factors. Similarly, the financial condition of colleges and universities can be measured by standard ratios that include:

- Balance sheet ratios

- Operating ratios

- Demand ratios

- Contribution ratios

- Creditworthiness ratios

Credit analysis for higher education debt issuance relies heavily on methodologies that establish criteria for various ratios.[2]

The following illustrative discussion of creditworthiness is based on factors used by S&P in assigning its ratings to higher education bonds. Most of the analyses of creditworthiness performed by issuing authorities, other rating agencies, and credit enhancement providers are variations on this general framework.

Figure 12-3 summarizes critical characteristics that S&P considers. The analysis extends to the state that supports a public institution.

---

FIGURE 12-3
S&P Critical Ratings Considerations for Higher Education Bonds

**Public Colleges/
Universities**

**Independent Colleges/
Universities**

State Characteristics:
    State General Obligation Rating
    State Support for Higher Education
    State Support for Specific Institution

University Characteristics:
    Legal
    Demand
    Financial
    Debt

University Characteristics:
    Legal
    Demand
    Financial
    Debt

Source: S&P Higher Education Creditworthiness Seminar,
    April 18, 1989.

---

Even though a rating is applied to the specific debt obligation, the credit analysis covers the entire institutional entity. The analysis takes into account the total revenues and total debt of an entire system or all projects. S&P indicates that an institution's debt service payments should not exceed 10 percent of total educational and general revenues and considers a 5 percent surplus in the unrestricted current fund balance a positive factor. When evaluating the strength of a legally available funds pledge, S&P considers all unrestricted fund balances, which ideally should be twice the amount of debt; in auxiliary revenue pledges, the key factor can be the "essentiality" of the auxiliary facility, that is, how essential the facility is to the institution.

In rating variable-rate debt, S&P analyzes three hypothetical debt service scenarios to test the institution's vulnerability to rate changes:

- Expected level of debt service

- Maximum level of debt service (for example, interest rate of 15 percent)

- Put scenario, assuming a high rate of interest, plus any demand or put options that may be exercised within the first year

In addition, rating analysts determine whether the institution's investments are well-matched to the put mode of the debt, to ensure that the borrower will have the liquidity to repay bondholders if the demand or put feature is exercised. For example, a bond issue with a 30-day demand feature should be matched by investments with 30-day maturities, held by the institution.

**Demand.** Credit analysts consider student demand to be perhaps the most critical factor in creditworthiness; they analyze demand for a college or university in light of national and regional demographic and college enrollment trends. S&P's factors for analysis of public and independent college and university demand vary, as summarized in Figure 12-4.

The demand analysis also takes into account market competition, in terms of:

- Competitor schools

- Effects of tuition levels on applications

- College or university marketing and external relations

- Volatility and other extraneous factors

**Financial performance.** Factors in the analysis of financial condition include revenues, expenditures, unrestricted fund balances, operating margins, and endowment. Critical factors in revenue strength are diversity and flexibility. S&P examines revenue categories by the parameters shown in Figure 12-5.

The principal factor in analyzing expenditures is the mix of fixed versus variable costs. Expenditure categories reviewed include:

- Instructional services

- Student services

- Plant maintenance and operations

- Mandatory transfers

FIGURE 12-4
S&P Student Demand Analysis Factors for Public and Independent Colleges
and Universities

| Public Colleges/ Universities | Independent Colleges/ Universities |
|---|---|
| Application trends | Application trends |
| State acceptance mandates | Acceptance rates |
| Hierarchy of schools | Matriculation rates |
| Selectivity and quality | Student quality |
| Geographic diversity | Geographic diversity |
| Match of legislative priorities for programs with student application trends | PT, FT, and graduate students |

Source: S&P Higher Education Creditworthiness Seminar,
April 18, 1989.

Because fixed costs are of great concern, factors such as the percentage of tenured faculty, the portion of student services costs that are fixed, and other items of budget inflexibility are reviewed closely.

In analyzing endowment, key factors considered are the total value of endowment, which may differ significantly for public and independent institutions; historical trends in endowment growth; and the ratio of funds functioning as endowment to total endowment. In analyzing unrestricted funds, analysts consider:

• Unrestricted current funds balance

• Unrestricted plant funds balance

• Funds functioning as endowment

• Institution-designated unrestricted funds

• Institution-restricted funds for debt service (reserves)

***Debt structure and capacity.*** In evaluating debt structure, analysts examine the security pledge intended for the bond issue being rated and legal requirements such as the additional bonds test (de-

FIGURE 12-5
S&P College and University Revenue Factors in Credit Analysis

| Categories of Revenues | Parameter(s) Evaluated |
|---|---|
| State appropriations | Percentage of total and trends |
| Tuition | Percentage of total and elasticity |
| Gifts and grants | Composition of and dependence on |
| Endowment and investment income | Spending policy |
| Auxiliary operations | Nature, extent, essentiality |

Source: S&P Higher Education Creditworthiness Seminar,
April 18, 1989.

scribed below) or reserve requirements. In assessing debt capacity, analysts evaluate overall debt as a percentage of total operating budget and as compared to endowment and unrestricted funds. Further, they consider the debt financing philosophy and plans of the college or university, including such factors as matching of long-term debt with long-term assets and the mix of short- and long-term debt and fixed and variable-rate debt in the capital financing plan.

*Typical higher education ratings.* Very few college and university bonds have "natural" triple-A ratings, although many higher education bonds achieve the triple-A rating with credit enhancement. In 1991, S&P assigned a triple-A rating to six universities. An equally small number of colleges are rated triple-B, at the other end of the investment grade spectrum. Most higher education ratings fall in the single-A range, with a distribution of ratings over the spectrum. Ratings for public universities are tied closely to the credit ratings of their states; these institutions typically have ratings that are one to three rating grades below the state's rating, with the exception of a few flagship research universities that may have ratings equivalent or nearly equivalent to that of their state.

## CREDIT ENHANCEMENT TECHNIQUES

Because bond investors are compensated for greater credit risk by higher interest rates, the credit quality of an issue is the significant factor in the cost of borrowing. A major innovation in the municipal market has been the creation of techniques and products sold by banks and financial guarantee insurance companies that are aimed at enhancing a bond issue's credit standing. In effect, a credit enhancement provider commits to paying bondholders if a borrower cannot make principal and interest payments, thereby assuming the credit risk that the bondholder normally would bear. The bond issue thus assumes the credit standing of the credit enhancement provider rather than that of the borrower. A borrower whose credit rating on an issue would be in the A range without a credit enhancement could pay lower interest rates based on the triple-A credit rating of the credit enhancement provider. For such a borrower, the critical issue is whether the cost of the credit enhancement will lower interest costs sufficiently to result in net savings on the financing. For borrowers at the margins of being able to issue investment grade securities based on their own credit, credit enhancement may be the critical factor that makes a bond issue marketable. For such borrowers, the cost-benefit analysis is clear: without the credit enhancement, the borrower would not gain access to tax-exempt funds.

The credit enhancement provider is compensated for assuming risk by means of fees or premiums. In credit-enhanced issues, rating agencies typically assign a rating based on the credit enhancement provider's rating. The credit enhancement provider, rather than the rating agencies, performs the exhaustive credit analysis of the borrower.

In addition to collateralization, which can help strengthen a bond issue, the following three credit enhancement techniques are used:

***Guarantees.*** A third party may provide a guarantee of the payment obligation of a borrower. The guarantor is usually a corporation or other entity related to the borrower. In higher education, a college or university could guarantee the debt of one of its 501(c)(3) related foundations or corporations or a religious organization could guarantee the debt of a related college. A guarantee may be collateralized with cash, securities, or other assets capable of being liquidated if the borrower and the guarantor fail to honor the payment obligations.

***Letters of credit.*** Letters of credit (LOC) are issued by commercial banks and other financial institutions to provide for the payment of debt if the borrower fails to make payments. The borrower is then obligated to repay the letter-of-credit provider, in which case the borrower's obligation to the LOC provider may be converted to a term loan. "Standby LOCs" provide for payment in full at the time of default and are usually used to provide liquidity protection for variable interest rate issues. Under a "direct pay letter of credit," the bond trustee draws on the letter of credit without first looking to the institution for payment.

The term for an LOC may be three to ten years, with the most common term being five years. An "evergreen LOC" is one in which the term is extended automatically each year unless the provider gives formal notice that it will not extend the term.

The borrower pays an initial or up-front fee and an ongoing annual fee, which is subject to change, for maintenance of the LOC commitment. LOC fees also vary considerably with the credit quality of the issuer and with overall market conditions. LOCs for higher education bonds are provided by U.S. and foreign commercial banks, including Japanese and European banks. The extent to which commercial banks are active LOC providers depends on their own credit ratings.

LOCs are limited in term and subject to both renewal and cost risks; therefore, they are most appropriate for VRDBs. An LOC's value in a variable-rate financing is rarely disputable because, except in rare instances, VRDBs are not marketable without the LOC support.

***Bond insurance.*** Bond insurance is an insurance policy provided by a state-regulated financial guarantee insurance company. The policy is issued at the time of bond closing and guarantees timely payment of principal and interest to bondholders over the life of the bond issue. An insurance premium is determined by multiplying the premium rate by the total debt service payable. The premium rate charged is determined by the insurer, based on its evaluation of the credit quality characteristics of the insured institution. Bond insurance premiums are usually payable in full at the time of issuance. In certain instances, however, premiums are paid annually on the basis of the outstanding principal amount of the bonds.

Bond insurance is typically the credit enhancement of choice for long-term, fixed-rate bonds because the insurance is for the entire term of the bonds and is irrevocable and the entire cost of insurance is known at the time of issuance. Bond insurance is provided by a small number of financial guarantee companies that are structured and capitalized specifically for financial guarantee products for the municipal securities market. The value of bond insurance is indisputable for a borrowing college or university that is creditworthy but at the margins of being able to sell debt successfully in its own name; insurance may make an otherwise unmarketable bond issue marketable. For institutions with stronger credit, bond insurance may be effective in lowering the overall costs of borrowing. The usefulness of bond insurance in raising a college's credit rating from single-A to double-A or triple-A must be analyzed by the financial advisor or underwriter, who can determine whether the cost of the bond insurance premium would be more than offset by the expected savings in interest costs that will be achieved by the triple-A rating.

***Credit-enhanced higher education volume.*** Figure 12-6 shows the growth in LOC-backed and insured higher education volume over several years.

The relative volumes of LOC-backed and insured higher education bonds tend to follow changes in market interest rates. In years when long-term rates are attractive and borrowers tend to favor long-term fixed-rate issuances, bond insurance volume may rise. When short-term rates are more favorable, LOC-backed volume may rise as VRDB issuance rises. Overall, approximately one-quarter of total long-term higher education debt issuance, including private placements, is credit-enhanced.

# Accessing the Market

OVERVIEW OF THE FINANCIAL INTERMEDIATION PROCESS

In commercial bank lending, the borrower and lender negotiate directly, without an intermediary. In capital markets, a financial intermediary's services are required. The professionals who specialize in structuring and selling the bonds of municipal entities are public finance or municipal finance bankers. These professionals, along with bond attorneys, work with issuers to structure bond issues and with investors to sell bonds. They typically are in separate but related departments of investment banking firms, in commercial bank securities affiliates, or in firms that specialize in financial advisory services to the municipal market.

There are two basic forms of bond sale: private placement and public offering. Each has different structures and requirements.

FIGURE 12-6
LOC-Backed and Insured Higher Education Long-Term
Bond Issues
1981 through 1990

| Year | LOC volume (millions) | LOC-backed as percentage of total HE bonds | Insured volume (millions) | Insured as percentage of total HE bonds | Combined credit-enhanced as percentage of total HE bonds |
|------|------|------|------|------|------|
| 1981 | 95.2 | 11.2 | 22.3 | 2.6 | 13.8 |
| 1982 | 55.4 | 3.4 | 238.6 | 14.5 | 17.9 |
| 1983 | 83.2 | 3.7 | 361.2 | 15.9 | 19.6 |
| 1984 | 377.4 | 11.6 | 881.1 | 27.0 | 38.6 |
| 1985 | 1,744.0 | 17.8 | 2,218.4 | 22.6 | 40.4 |
| 1986 | 173.8 | 2.6 | 735.4 | 11.0 | 13.6 |
| 1987 | 198.6 | 5.2 | 767.6 | 20.2 | 25.4 |
| 1988 | 274.1 | 4.7 | 1,131.9 | 19.5 | 24.2 |
| 1989 | 297.3 | 4.9 | 1,283.4 | 21.3 | 26.2 |
| 1990 | 116.6 | 1.5 | 1,769.3 | 22.3 | 23.8 |
| Ten-Year Total | 3,415.6 | .0 | 9,409.2 | 19.2 | 26.2 |

Source: Securities Data Company.

***Private placement.*** In a private placement, the banker identifies
a limited number of investors interested in buying the entire issue of
securities to be offered. This method usually is preferred for small issues
that would be uneconomical to offer for public sale or for issues with
credit weaknesses that may not gain public market acceptance. Private
placements are simpler than public bond sales and the costs of issuance
are lower; however, the interest rate paid may be somewhat higher.

***Public bond sale.*** The public offering or sale is used more often
than private placements, especially for large bond issues offered for sale
by creditworthy borrowers. Public offerings come in two forms. A
"negotiated sale" is one in which the investment banking firm or bank
securities affiliate engaged by the issuer structures the financing and
undertakes to sell the bonds. In a "competitive" sale, an investment
banking firm, independent financial advisory firm, or bank securities
affiliate may serve as financial advisor for structuring the bond offering.

On a certain date, the financial advisor solicits competitive bids from other underwriting firms that bid to purchase and resell the bonds. The financial advisor assists the issuer in selecting the bid that represents the lowest-cost financing based on net interest cost or true interest cost (see "Determining the Actual Cost of Interest," below). A negotiated or competitive sale of bonds can be accomplished by a single intermediary institution, bidding and acting alone, or by a "syndicate," a group of intermediaries that divide the bonds among themselves based on their knowledge of customer interest in buying the securities. The process called "underwriting" indicates that the financial intermediary firm guarantees that the issuer's bonds will be purchased; if the underwriter cannot market all the bonds to investors, the firm itself buys the bonds.

## THE PARTICIPANTS

A number of parties are involved in the conduct of a publicly sold tax-exempt bond issue.

*Issuer/issuing authority.* For independent college and university borrowers, debt issues are conduit financings conducted through special issuing authorities. For public institutions, the issuing function is performed by the state, by an issuing authority, or by the institution itself. The role that the issuing authority plays varies from state to state and within some localities. At a minimum, the board of directors of the issuing authority must review the application of a potential borrower and approve the financing. The board must pass a resolution authorizing the issuance of bonds in its name on behalf of the borrowing institution. The board, directly and through its staff, maintains fiduciary responsibilities for ongoing management of the debt. In cases where the issuing authority is a large organization, the board may play a far more significant role.

Some issuing authorities appoint a standing pool or syndicate of underwriting firms and assign them to conduct an institution's financing. Alternatively, an authority may engage in a proposal competition process to appoint a financial advisor and/or underwriter for a college or university. Other authorities are even more active in the structuring and marketing of financings and in the actual construction and ongoing management of the facilities financed. States with large numbers of colleges and universities and consequently high volumes of higher education bond activity, such as New York, California, and Massachusetts, tend to have higher education facilities authorities that perform a broad array of financial functions.

**Underwriter.** An underwriter is an investment banking firm or a syndicate of investment banking firms that markets an issuer's bonds to investors. If a single firm is engaged, it is referred to as the sole manager of the underwriting and sale. If a group or syndicate is involved, there is a lead or senior manager and one or more comanagers of the issue's sale. In a negotiated underwriting, the underwriter's public finance department bankers work with a college or university to plan the financing and to determine when and how it should be brought to market. The underwriter provides guidance on structuring the bond issue, determines whether credit enhancement is needed, and assists the institution in obtaining credit enhancement. The underwriter is responsible for coordinating the preparation of the "Official Statement," which describes the institution and its finances, the project or projects being financed, and the financial structure for security, collateral, and credit enhancements, if any. The municipal securities underwriting and sales department of the underwriter firm works with the public finance department's bankers to structure and ultimately sell the bonds to the final investors.

**Underwriter's counsel.** Underwriter firms are represented in transactions by their own legal counsel, who assist the underwriter in coordinating the preparation of the "Official Statement."

**Financial advisor.** In a competitive-bid bond sale, the team that performs the functions described above up to the point of sale is referred to as the financial advisor. The financial advisor is responsible for all elements of planning and structuring and for the solicitation of competitive bids. The financial advisor assists the issuer in evaluating the comparative costs of bids submitted to select the winning underwriting manager or syndicate. In some cases, bond issuers engaging in a negotiated offering employ a financial advisor as well as an underwriter. In this situation, the financial advisor's role is to review the decisions of the underwriter, especially with respect to prices at which the bonds are marketed. In some cases, a financial advisor is retained on a long-term basis to provide ongoing technical support and advice on debt management programs to a frequent issuer.

**Bond counsel.** Bond counsel are attorneys who, representing the interests of future bondholders, prepare an opinion to indicate that the bonds meet all requirements and tests to be issued validly in accordance with law and that the interest earned on them can be excluded from gross income for federal income tax purposes. Bond counsel also render an opinion with respect to state tax law treatment of interest on the bonds. Bond counsel attorneys are an integral part of the financing team and provide ongoing advice on numerous aspects of the transaction.

*Issuer's counsel.* Attorneys who represent the interests of the issuer (and borrower) in various details of the financing structure are called issuer's counsel. This role may be performed by the institution's general counsel in the case of independent institutions, the state attorney general's office in the case of public institutions, counsel of the issuing education facilities authority, or an outside law firm engaged by the issuer.

*Credit enhancement provider.* If bonds or notes are credit-enhanced, the commercial bank provider of the LOC or the bond insurance company also participates in the development of the financing transaction. The credit enhancement provider plays a significant role in determining the creditworthiness of the borrowing college or university and in structuring the security and pledges involved in the transaction.

*Credit enhancement provider's counsel.* Attorneys typically represent the interests of the credit enhancement provider.

*Trustee.* The bond trustee, normally a financial institution with trust powers, represents the bondholders in a fiduciary capacity to enforce the terms of a trust agreement or indenture. The trustee bank is paid a fee by the issuer.

*Paying agent.* Normally a bank or trust company, the paying agent is responsible for payments of principal and interest to bondholders on behalf of an issuer. The issuer makes periodic payments to the paying agent, which then disburses payments to bondholders. The entity that serves as paying agent also may provide other services to the issuer in connection with registration and record keeping for the bonds. In some cases, an issuer's treasurer may serve as paying agent.

*Remarketing agent.* In the case of VRDBs, a remarketing agent remarkets bonds when necessary because of demand options exercised by bondholders. The underwriter who manages the initial offering of bonds is usually engaged to serve as remarketing agent and is paid an annual fee for this service.

## THE RATING PROCESS

The rating process is an extensive, intensive, and formal version of the credit analysis process that should be performed by a potential issuer, with the assistance of its bankers, whenever an institution contemplates a bond issuance. If a credit enhancement is sought, the provider of the enhancement also conducts a full credit analysis prior to the formal rating process. In some instances, a rating agency may be asked to provide an opinion early on about whether an issuer should attempt a public bond sale.

The mechanics of the formal rating process begin with the issuer's application to one or more rating agencies, well in advance of the anticipated date of sale of the bond issue. The issuer decides which and how many ratings to seek, based upon the advice of its financial advisor or underwriter.

The issuer then submits detailed information about itself and the proposed issue. A "Preliminary Official Statement" is prepared and submitted to the rating agency with several years of operating statistics, audited financial statements, planning documents, legal documents relating to the security, and other specific information requested by the rating agency. For higher education issues, this information typically covers all aspects of the institution's history, management, organization, students, faculty, programs, and finances.

When the rating agency receives the required information, the issue is assigned to an analyst, who evaluates credit strength of the proposed issue using the institution's data; statistics from the rating agency's database; and medians or other normative measures that the agency has developed from its experience with similar issues and issuers.

During this phase, the principal officers of the issuing college or university, its financial advisors, and the rating agency analysts meet. The meeting affords an opportunity for the institution to present information that is difficult to convey in written form. Sometimes the meeting is in the form of a site visit to the campus. A site visit is required or recommended if the institution never has issued debt before or if it has not issued debt in some time. Decisions about meetings or site visits are made by the rating agency; alternatively, the issuer can request a site visit. An issuer should follow the advice of its underwriter or financial advisor in matters of managing the rating process. Bankers also work with the college or university to prepare and rehearse for rating agency presentations and/or site visits.

Upon completion of meetings or site visits, the credit analysis is completed and a rating recommendation is formulated. The analyst's recommendation is reviewed internally at the rating agency by the rating committee. When the rating is assigned, it is released first to the issuer, who may appeal and present additional information, and then to the public. A credit report then is distributed.

The process followed by Moody's Investors Service is summarized in Figure 12-7.

## BOND DISCLOSURES

Issuers of debt are expected to disclose all material facts about themselves and the proposed borrowing that may be pertinent to the analysis of the credit quality of the investment. Such information is provided in the "Preliminary Official Statement" and in the final "Official Statement." Investors rely on this information in making their decisions. Responsibility for disclosure lies with the issuer.

In recent years, the subject of disclosure adequacy has been debated widely. The Securities and Exchange Commission (SEC) has indicated its expectation that financial advisors and underwriters should bear responsibility for the completeness and accuracy of disclosures made by an issuer. They are required to exercise "due diligence" in seeking and making available all possibly pertinent information, including any that may represent present or future adverse conditions. The bond industry has attempted to establish new standards for disclosure. An example of industry-suggested disclosure guidelines for colleges and universities is provided at the end of this chapter.[3]

## BOND DOCUMENTS

The following basic documents are part of a public tax-exempt bond sale.

***Bond resolution.*** The first technical and legal document in a bond transaction is the bond resolution, which must be adopted formally by the municipal issuer. For a public institution, the bond resolution is adopted by the institution's governing board. For an independent institution, the bond resolution is adopted by the board of directors of the state or local authority that will issue the debt on behalf of the college or university. The bond resolution sets forth the terms and purpose of

---

FIGURE 12-7
Mechanics of the Rating Process

  1     Application
  2     Municipal calendar entry
  3     Assignment of issue to analyst
  4     Receipt of documentation
  5     Preliminary research
  6     Meeting and/or on-site visit (optional)
  7     Completion of analysis
  8     Analyst's rating recommendation
  9     Sign-off procedure with area manager
10     Presentation to municipal department rating committee
11     Committee decision
12     Rating assignment
13     Rating released to issuer
14     Rating released to public
15     Distribution of municipal credit report
16     Annual request to issuer for data

Source: Moody's Investors Service, *Moody's on Municipals: An Introduction to Issuing Debt*, New York, 1987, 42.

---

the bonds and the financial responsibilities of the parties involved.

*"Preliminary Official Statement."* The "Preliminary Official Statement," coordinated by the financial advisor/underwriter, is intended to disclose all information pertinent to marketing bonds to investors. It describes the issuing institution, its programs, its management, and its long-range plans, and it includes historical data. The statement describes the facilities to be financed or other purposes of the financing and the proposed terms of the financing. All significant risks are described. Financial statements and the results of a feasibility study, if performed, are included. This document is the primary vehicle for disclosure of all material information to potential investors. (See Note 3.)

*Trust agreement or indenture.* At the bond closing, the issuer and the bond trustee execute the trust agreement or indenture, a contract between the issuer and the trustee for the benefit of the bondholders. The indenture sets forth the rights and responsibilities of the issuer and the trustee. In the case of independent institutions, the higher education facilities authority is the issuer that executes the trust agreement with the trustee bank.

***Note or loan agreement.*** The note or loan agreement sets forth the terms of the loan and is executed by the borrower and the issuer. In higher education, it is an agreement between the borrowing institution and the higher education facilities authority that is issuing the debt on the institution's behalf.

***Mortgage or lien agreements.*** If the borrowing is secured by physical collateral (an interest in real property), a mortgage is executed and recorded in the local county clerk's offices. If a collateral interest in personal property is pledged, such as computers or other equipment, a security lien agreement granting such interest to the bondholders is executed and recorded.

***Credit enhancement agreements.*** Bond issues that are credit-enhanced have additional documentation of the terms and conditions of the LOC or bond insurance. In the case of LOCs, the reimbursement agreement is executed between the borrower and the LOC bank. In the case of bond insurance, the insurance agreement is executed.

***Legal opinions.*** Each party to the transaction is represented by counsel. The most important opinion document required is bond counsel's opinion that the bonds are validly issued and that the interest on the bonds meets all requirements to be excluded from gross income for federal income tax purposes. All counsel involved in the transaction issue written opinions to indicate that the actions taken in the transaction are duly authorized.

***"Official Statement."*** The final version of the "Official Statement" is prepared after the bonds are sold. The final "Official Statement" contains the actual interest rate(s) at which the bonds were sold.

***Assignment of CUSIP numbers.*** The Committee on Uniform Security Identification Procedures (CUSIP), under the auspices of the American Bankers Association, developed a uniform system for numbering and identifying municipal, U.S. government, and corporate securities. A CUSIP number is assigned to each bond in the offering and is its identification throughout its life.

***Transcript.*** All official legal documents pertaining to the bond transaction are bound and preserved as the transcript of the bond issue. The transcript is compiled by bond counsel.

## TRANSACTION COSTS

A publicly sold bond transaction entails a variety of costs in addition to interest, principally for the various professional services required to bring an issue to market, for credit enhancements, and, in the case of variable-rate debt, to maintain the ongoing remarketing function. The basic costs for a publicly sold bond issue include:

- Underwriter's spread
- Bond counsel's fee
- Underwriter's counsel's fee
- Issuer's counsel's fee
- Rating agency fee
- Trustee's fee
- Paying agent's fee
- Issuing authority's fee
- Printing expense

Issues that are insured or supported by an LOC have additional costs:

- Bond insurance premium or initial and annual letter-of-credit fee
- Bond insurer's or LOC bank's counsel fees

Variable-rate bond costs include annual fees for the remarketing agent.

*Underwriter's spread.* The largest single transaction cost, the underwriter's "spread" compensates the underwriter for buying the issuer's bonds and taking the risk of reselling them to investors. The components of the spread are:

- Management fee (for structuring and managing the financing)
- Underwriting fee (for assuming the risk of reselling the bonds)
- Takedown (commission to municipal sales personnel for selling bonds)

- Expenses (for out-of-pocket costs)

In private placements, the placement fee includes components for management, selling, and expenses. There is no underwriting fee in private placements, because the intermediary assumes no risk for resale of the bonds.

Transaction costs attendant to a bond issue may be "capitalized" (included in the par amount of the bond issue) and thus do not represent cash requirements for the borrower. For nongovernmental issuers, including independent colleges and universities, capitalized transaction costs are limited to 2 percent of the par amount of the bonds; however, the costs of credit enhancement are excluded from the 2 percent limitation.

## DETERMINING THE ACTUAL COST OF INTEREST

For a bond issue with a single maturity, the "actual cost of interest" is the coupon interest rate if the bonds are sold at par value. Because most bond issues are structured with serial maturities, the actual cost of interest is complicated to calculate. The actual cost of the interest that the issuer of new bonds will pay is calculated differently from the rate of return to the bond investor and must be understood in order to determine, in a competitive bond sale, which bidding underwriter syndicate is offering the bid that results in the lowest interest cost to the borrowing institution. Calculations of net interest cost (NIC) and true interest cost (TIC) are used to present this figure for comparative purposes. It is important to note that the underwriter's spread, described above, is incorporated into NIC and TIC calculations.

***Net interest cost.*** NIC is a simplified formula that is an industry standard. It states the total amount of interest that must be paid over the life of a serial bond issue, without regard to the time value of money. To determine the NIC, the sum total of interest payments for the entire bond offering is divided by the product of the amount of bonds outstanding multiplied by the number of years they are outstanding. The formula is:

$$NIC = \frac{\text{Total Interest Payments} + \text{Discount (or - Premium)}}{\text{Bond Year Dollars}}$$

"Bond years" are the number of bonds outstanding, in $1,000 denominations, multiplied by the number of years they are outstanding. "Bond year dollars" are this amount multiplied by $1,000 for each bond.

*True interest cost.* Critics of the NIC method argue that it is misleading to ignore the present-value element of the calculation, which results in a distortion of the result of bid comparisons. TIC takes the timing, as well as the total amount, of interest payment, into account. TIC is the rate at which all cash flows must be discounted so that the sum of their present values equals the proceeds of the bond issue. The TIC is computed by trial and error, rather than by an algebraic formula. Because this is done easily with computers, issuers of debt now can request that bids be expressed with TIC as a basis.

# Management of Existing Debt

REFUNDING AND DEFEASANCE

A "refunding" is the issuance of new bonds to replace an outstanding bond issue. Refunding is used to:

- Reduce the borrower's interest costs if the market is such that new bonds can be issued at interest rates lower than that of the currently outstanding bonds

- Remove a restrictive or burdensome covenant imposed by the terms of the existing bond indenture

- Reorganize existing debt

"Defeasance" is the termination of the rights and interests of the bondholders and extinguishment of their lien on the pledged revenues of the borrower in connection with a refunding. When final payment on bonds is made or when provision is made for all future payments, bonds are said to be defeased.

Because of the transaction costs involved in a refunding, when reducing interest costs is the objective, interest rates need to drop considerably to make the cost of refunding worth the benefits. A rule of thumb used by some underwriters and financial advisors is that the present value of the savings, net of transaction costs, over the life of the refunding bonds, should be at least 3 percent.

Colleges and universities must sometimes agree to bond covenants that hamper their management flexibility. An example is a tuition or fee covenant, under which certain levels of fees must be maintained. If and when an institution is in a position to refund its bonds without the restrictive covenant, a refunding may be advantageous.

## CURRENT REFUNDING

"Current refunding" is the issuance of new bonds to replace an existing bond issue when the existing issue is callable for redemption at the time of the issuance of the new bonds or will be callable within 90 days of the date of issuance of the new bonds. Because the college or university has the right to call the bonds, an approaching call date is an opportune time to do a current refunding, if it will prove cost-effective. The proceeds of the new bond issue, called the "refunding bonds," are used to repay the old bonds, called the "refunded bonds." The college or university is left with the refunding bond issue outstanding and, presumably, with more favorable debt-service payments.

## ADVANCE REFUNDING

Bond investors are protected from early repayment of bonds by the no-call period. An institution that wishes to refinance its bonds prior to a call date must do so by means of an advance refunding. "Advance refunding" entails depositing with the trustee the proceeds of the refunding bonds in a yield-restricted escrow fund, the principal and interest of which are calculated to be sufficient to pay the principal and interest maturing on the refunded bonds until maturity or until the first optional call date. Bonds that are refunded so that the escrowed funds are sufficient to pay all debt service until maturity are called "escrowed to maturity." Bonds that are refunded so that the refunding bond proceeds are escrowed until the first call date are called "prerefunded bonds." The entire issue is often called for redemption at the call date.

Special U.S. government securities are used for the escrow accounts in advance refundings. These State and Local Government Series securities (SLUGS) are sold by the U.S. Treasury through individual subscriptions to states and municipalities. The maturity structures and interest rates on SLUGS are tailored to conform to the yield and arbitrage restrictions imposed under Section 103 of the Internal Revenue Code. There are two basic types of advance refunding.

*Gross refunding/defeasance.* In a full cash or gross refunding, the size of the refunding bond issue is sufficient to repay the principal and interest on the refunded bonds. A gross refunding includes a series of special obligation bonds. The proceeds are invested and the interest earnings used to pay the principal and interest on the special obligation bonds. A larger amount of principal outstanding may result but the annual debt service may be reduced, because the special obligation bonds are secured by the earnings on the refunding bonds.

*Net cash refunding/defeasance.* In a net cash refunding, the size of the refunding bond issue is a principal amount that, with the interest that will be earned on the funds, is sufficient to repay the principal and interest on the refunded bonds. Proceeds of the refunding bonds are invested in SLUGS and used to redeem or retire the refunded bonds. A variety of specific advance funding techniques are used to accomplish various debt management objectives.

*High-to-low refunding.* The most common refunding structure used by colleges and universities is the high-to-low refunding, in which debt at a higher interest rate is replaced by debt at a lower interest rate. Savings are achieved by the lower debt-service payments on the refunding bonds. This structure is associated with advance refundings when the market affords opportunities for achieving lower interest rates and the escrow is structured for redemption of the refunded bonds at the first optional call date.

*Low-to-high refunding.* Low-to-high refunding is used when a college or university wishes to eliminate unfavorable legal provisions or covenants in the original bond issue even though interest rates may be higher. Such a refunding replaces debt at a lower interest rate with debt at a higher interest rate. The escrow fund is planned to be invested to the final maturity of the refunded bonds rather than to the call date. Earnings on the escrowed funds are restricted to the yield of the refunding bonds, but the yield on the refunding bonds is higher than the yield on the refunded bonds. Consequently, the amount of money required in escrow is smaller and the principal amount of the refunding bonds is smaller than the principal amount of the refunded bonds. Thus, the debt-service payments normally are identical to those the college or university had before.

***Crossover refunding.*** In a crossover refunding, the escrow fund established with the proceeds of the refunding bonds is used to pay debt service on the refunding bonds until the first call date of the bonds. At that time, the use of the escrowed funds crosses over and is used to repay the refunded bonds.

***Window refunding.*** A window refunding is used to combine refunding of an existing bond issue with a new money issue for new projects. The refunding bonds are structured so that only interest is paid in certain, usually early, years. New issue money then fits into "window" years; the effect is relatively level, manageable debt service.

***Partial refunding/defeasance.*** The economic benefits of refunding tend to be greater for bonds with the longest maturities and highest interest rates. Shorter serial maturities, noncallable maturities, or low-interest-rate portions of issues may not be good candidates for refunding. In a partial refunding, only selected maturities, generally those offering maximum opportunities for savings, are refunded.

***Limitations on advance refundings.*** Bonds issued after the effective date of the Tax Reform Act of 1986 may be advance-refunded only once. Bonds issued earlier may be advance-refunded twice if the institution has never advance-refunded the bonds. Thus, to take advantage of significant refunding opportunities, careful planning on the part of the higher education institution and its advisors is required.

## ADDITIONAL BONDS TEST AND PARITY DEBT

Once a college or university has bonds outstanding, issuance of additional debt requires additional analysis of the capacity of the revenues available to be pledged for new obligations. Investors in long-term securities require protection from material changes in the financial capacity of the borrower to repay its obligation. Bondholders are concerned, therefore, about bond issuances subsequent to that of the bonds they hold, especially if a later issue will have claims to the same pledged revenues as those on which they expect to rely. For the protection of bondholders, a legal test, codified in the bond resolution, determines the ability of an issuer to sell additional bonds backed by the same pledged revenues. This "additional bonds test" is expressed as a ratio of historic revenues to expected future levels of debt service.

"Parity bonds" are two or more bond issues in which each bond issue has the same level of priority of claim against pledged revenues. The initial issue is called the "prior issue" and subsequent issues are called "additional parity bonds." The bond indenture of the prior issue normally establishes the requirements to be met before additional parity bonds can be issued.

## HEDGING TECHNIQUES

"Hedging" is a debt management technique aimed at reducing the borrower's risk and, where possible, achieving economies. Hedging has long been used in corporate finance and is being used increasingly by municipal securities issuers in debt management programs. There are two basic strategies for hedging: investment hedging techniques and derivative hedging products.

***Hedging with investments.*** A college or university issuer can use investment techniques to take advantage of the lower rates that variable-rate debt normally affords and, at the same time, create a hedge internally to protect against interest-rate risk. Investment hedging is a matter of matching assets and liabilities to achieve a positive correlation between total asset returns and debt-service costs. The institution uses operating funds, funds functioning as endowment, or other unrestricted funds to make investments so that the interest rate sensitivity on the invested assets mirrors the potential rate volatility of the debt.

***Hedging with derivative products.*** In addition to hedging by investment strategies, borrowers can purchase derivative products that provide a hedge against debt risk. Two such derivative products are interest rate "caps" and "swaps."

A cap is an interest-rate insurance vehicle in which the seller of the cap, usually a bank or other financial intermediary, agrees to pay the buyer the difference between an agreed-upon index of variable interest rates and a negotiated interest-rate ceiling or cap. For example, a cap is purchased at 7.10 percent; the interest rate in the index, normally selected so that it will closely track the cap-buyer's bonds, rises to 7.25 percent. The college now must pay 7.25 percent on its VRDBs; however, the seller of the cap pays the college the difference of .15 percent (15 basis points). Thus, with the cap, the college or university borrower is assured that its interest cost will not exceed 7.10 percent.

An interest-rate swap is an agreement between two parties to exchange interest payments, generally for a period of one to ten years.

It is typically, but not always, an exchange of a fixed-rate and a variable-rate cash flow, based on the debt management needs and interest-rate expectations of the two parties. Swaps emerged as a corporate finance tool in the late 1970s. By 1989, worldwide interest-rate swap volume had reached $1.4 trillion, indicating the popularity of the technique. It is estimated that municipal interest-rate swaps outstanding exceed $10 billion.[4]

A swap allows a college or university to convert temporarily the interest rate paid on floating-rate debt to fixed rate, or vice versa, without permanently converting the debt by refunding the existing bonds. Thus, interest-rate management can be achieved without the complexities, costs, and limitations attendant to refunding. For the variable-rate swap, payments are keyed to an index. In the municipal market, an index of short-term, tax-exempt securities such as the Kenny Index, the Banker's Trust Tax-Exempt Note Rate, or the taxable London Inter-Bank Offering Rate is used.

Hedging is an extremely complex and technical area. For additional details on caps and swaps, as well as information about numerous other derivative hedging products, institutions should consult their financial advisors.

# Debt Capacity, Policies, and Planning

## DEBT CAPACITY AND POLICY

The concept of "debt capacity," the level of debt an institution can bear prudently, is elusive and depends on a variety of legal, policy, and financial management factors. Conservative financial policies on the part of state governments and private governing boards have tended to prevail in higher education; borrowing is not always considered an appropriate financial strategy because it reduces financial flexibility for institutions that may experience fluctuations in demand for their services or unexpected increases in costs. A college or university's prescribed debt limits can be set statutorily by state governments, by a governing board, or by management. In these cases, the debt limits are, de facto, the institution's debt capacity. Otherwise, the market itself, often as represented by the decisions of the rating agencies, effectively dictates debt capacity.

Although the debt capacity of any institution is a function of numerous specific factors, such as the strength of state support, student demand, and unrestricted assets, many colleges and universities may have some degree of unused debt capacity; some may have significant potential to add debt to their balance sheets without loss of financial stability.

*No debt.* Some independent colleges and universities have charter or endowment provisions that preclude them legally from engaging in borrowings. Other institutions, while not legally prohibited from borrowing, have historical policies of avoiding debt to which they have been able to adhere without difficulty. Institutions with no debt avoid the fiscal and legal constraints that debt obligations entail; however, they also have a more limited range of choices for capital development and may be forced to defer needed projects.

*Statutory debt limits.* A number of public institutions have debt limits prescribed by statute or other legal bases; these institutions usually also have restrictions on what kinds of projects they may use their debt capacity to finance. Such debt limits may be expressed as an upper limit for the ratio of debt service to unrestricted current fund expenditures and mandatory transfers. Alternatively, for auxiliary systems, debt limits may be expressed as the relationship between system net revenues and debt service.

*Debt policy.* A number of public and independent institutions that are active issuers of tax-exempt debt have developed nonstatutory internal debt policies that govern the level of debt liability they intend to incur. Normally, such policies are developed with professional assistance and approved in formal resolutions by the governing board of the institution. Elements of the debt limit policy may be developed separately for revenue-generating auxiliary facilities and for non-revenue-generating academic facilities. Some colleges and universities have specific policies for other aspects of debt management. For example, an institution might decide to use debt only for auxiliaries that generate revenue or only for major renovations and maintenance, reserving new construction for donor or internal funds.

*Rating agency preferences.* S&P generally uses the "10 percent rule" (debt service payments should not exceed 10 percent of total educational and general revenues) to determine when debt load has reached a limit at which it may consider downgrade of the rating. A rating downgrade is a serious event with negative consequences for the institution's costs of borrowing; this ratio is one way of expressing an average or approximate debt capacity limit for most institutions.

## CAPITAL PLANNING AND BUDGETING

The performance of long-range capital planning and budgeting is a difficult but necessary art in colleges and universities. An institution that has a strong, ongoing strategic planning process tied directly to its operating and capital budgeting processes is in the strongest position to evaluate debt opportunities and build them successfully into a broad capital development plan.

With a multiyear framework of strategic needs and priorities, a capital budget that incorporates estimates of building and renovation costs should be developed. As time passes, the capital budget must be updated to reflect projects that are completed, changing priorities, and cost differences. (For more information on capital budgeting, see Chapter 6, Budgeting.)

A capital development plan also addresses alternatives for financing that may include:

- Appropriations

- Internal/operating funds ("pay as you go")

- Internal borrowings from unrestricted reserves or funds functioning as endowment

- Focused fund-raising or capital campaigns

- Bank debt

- Tax-exempt debt in public markets

- Taxable debt in public markets

- Private-sector development, via ground lease or joint ventures with a real estate developer

Analyses must be made as to which financing methods are feasible for or best suit each planned project. To some extent, these decisions are self-evident, based on statutory debt authority of state-supported institutions, some of which have authority to borrow only for revenue-producing auxiliaries. Even without legal restrictions, it is evident that revenue-generating projects are better candidates for debt financing. In other cases, potential donors are only interested in certain types of facilities. Many capital financing plans are embedded in capital campaign plans. Inevitably, some projects are neither attractive to donors nor fundable from operating funds and may lend themselves only to debt financing.

## EXTERNAL VERSUS INTERNAL BORROWING

Colleges and universities frequently face the decision of whether to fund a project internally with borrowings from reserves or funds functioning as endowment or whether to incur bank or bond debt. Institutions often prefer to engage in internal borrowing because it is simpler, normally requiring only management's decision and the approval of the institution's governing board, and does not entail restrictive commitments to external parties. It is not, however, the most cost-effective alternative if a tax-exempt financing is viable. A simple rule of thumb to consider is that an institution should not use internal funds for capital acquisitions or development that are appropriate for debt issuance if the average rate of return on invested funds exceeds the expected "all-in cost" (interest plus transaction costs) of bond debt. If an institution uses invested funds earning higher interest rates than the institution would pay on debt, then the difference in lost interest earnings may be considered an "opportunity cost." For example, if an institution can achieve an all-in cost of funds of 7.5 percent and is able to earn an average of 8.1 percent on taxable investments, it would be more expensive to borrow internally from invested funds than to borrow externally and the opportunity cost of borrowing internally is 0.6 percent multiplied by the amount borrowed.

## BANK DEBT VERSUS PUBLIC DEBT MARKETS

Another major consideration is whether a project is of the type and size to warrant the effort and expense of a publicly offered bond issue. In many cases, colleges and universities should explore bank debt alternatives, particularly with local banks where they maintain account relationships. Although the interest rates may be higher, conventional term loans or mortgage loans may have the advantage of timeliness, simplicity, and minimal transaction costs. In many instances, a private placement of bonds may be a good alternative to either a bank mortgage or a public bond sale. A private placement widens opportunities for potential lenders without all the complications of a public bond sale.

## BORROWING VERSUS DOING WITHOUT

A college or university may have a project suitable for bond financing, sufficiently strong credit, and available debt capacity but may prefer, for reasons of fiscal policy, lack of familiarity with bond financing, or internal institutional politics, not to borrow. One alternative is to forgo the needed facility or renovations. In such cases, an analysis of the comparative costs of borrowing with the potential hidden costs of not doing the project can be useful. Quantifying hidden costs is more difficult than comparing internal and external borrowing alternatives, but it is not entirely impossible. In many cases, institutional managers already know that inadequate facilities are precluding them from attracting or retaining resources—research funding, new faculty, or more students—but may find the addition of a debt-service burden difficult to defend to various internal constituents, especially faculty.

For example, an institution with severe maintenance problems in its student housing facilities may have reason to believe that it is losing potential freshmen and/or suffering enrollment attrition in part because of the negative impression that plant deterioration makes on students and their parents. The institution could conduct a survey of current students and parents and departed students and their parents, to determine the extent to which poor residential facilities are or were a factor in their dissatisfaction. Admitted students who chose not to attend also might be surveyed. The resulting data can lead to an estimate of the hidden costs of not performing major renovations to student residences. Perhaps the cost of lost tuition and fees over time would far exceed the annual debt-service cost of financing the renovations. Similar analyses may be made of the impact of inadequate research facilities on research grant volume or on faculty and graduate student recruitment.

It is likely that this kind of analysis will become more common because of the huge amounts of major maintenance that colleges and universities have deferred. Donors generally are not very interested in naming gifts for new roofs and underground utility lines, and there are limits to the amount of funds that unrestricted annual giving can contribute to facilities maintenance. There is also the matter of intergenerational equity—the question of whether current operating funds, including student tuition, should be used to fund long-term improvements. A well-planned and well-managed debt program can be a primary resource for resolving many of the plant renewal problems facing higher education.

## IMPACT OF DEBT PROGRAMS ON INSTITUTIONAL MANAGEMENT

Taking on a debt program has both positive and negative implications that should be well-understood by governing boards and senior management. A well-conceived debt management program broadens options, affording opportunities for facilities acquisition and development that may not be available by other financing methods. It also provides budgetary discipline, because when a college or university funds major maintenance with debt, it no longer can yield to the annual temptation to reallocate maintenance budget lines to other budget categories; the debt service that enabled upgrade of the physical plant is a fixed cost. Debt-financed maintenance and renewal projects also can be accomplished immediately, while their cost is distributed over their useful life.

On the other hand, taking on debt has potential negative impacts that need to be evaluated, including:

- Impact on operating budget

- Restrictions imposed by bond indenture covenants

- Increased management requirements and workload

Institutions contemplating debt financing also should be aware of accounting rules for treatment of debt.[5]

***Impact on operating budget.*** Many colleges and universities must weigh carefully both the real impact of adding debt service to their fixed cost of operations and the political impact on internal constituencies of doing so. While it may be positive that debt service imposes the discipline of funding plant-related needs and spreads the cost over the useful life of facilities, it may be a negative in that it diminishes operating budget flexibility. For many institutions, there is the additional problem of achieving an appropriate balance between funding debt service for facilities and funding faculty salary increases, student financial assistance, and other major budget priorities. The realities of conflicting priorities and campus perceptions about those priorities, especially among faculty, must be considered. If debt issuance seems appropriate, steps should be taken to educate internal constituencies to the advantages prior to undertaking the financing.

**Covenants.** A "bond covenant" is a legally enforceable commitment made by the issuer to perform or not to perform some act. Covenants typically are stated in the bond resolution or bond indenture. Common covenants include such commitments as:

- Maintaining use charges for the financed facility so that they provide sufficient pledged revenues, called a "rate covenant"

- Completing, maintaining, and operating the project financed

- Maintaining liability and other insurance coverage on the facility financed

- Issuing parity bonds only if the "additional bonds test" is met

- Taking no action that would violate Internal Revenue Code restrictions on invested proceeds earnings, causing the bonds to become arbitrage bonds

- Segregating and accounting for funds

- Not selling or encumbering the facility or project financed

Colleges and universities contemplating debt issuance must consider how such covenants would affect institutional management. Removal of a covenant that at one time may have been acceptable or unavoidable but that has become onerous or avoidable for the institution may be an occasion for an advance refunding, if the refunding bonds can be issued without a similar covenant.

**Staff and management requirements.** In addition to the financial and legal restrictions imposed by bond indebtedness, colleges or universities that contemplate a single bond offering or a sustained debt management program must be prepared to allocate the human resources and time required for this financial activity. Additional staff may be required, contributing marginally to the cost of debt.

The process of planning and executing a publicly sold bond issue is time consuming and labor intensive. The most direct effect is on the institution's chief financial or business officer and/or treasurer and their staff. The institution's president, other officers, and board members also are involved to a lesser extent. This intensive process may last a few or many months. No matter how small the institution's financial staff is, at least one person must be familiar enough with debt financing to be able to work effectively with underwriters, financial advisors, bond attorneys, issuing authorities, and others, including internal constituents.

Sustained debt management programs, including those with mixes of fixed and variable-rate debt, require continual monitoring to ensure that:

- Timely and accurate payments are made

- All records and relationships with the trustee, paying agent, and remarketing agent are maintained

- Changes and expected changes in variable rates are monitored

- Investments matched with liabilities are maintained

- Opportunities for refunding or use of hedging products are integrated into debt management

- Arbitrage rebate calculations are performed

## Summary

As higher education institutions meet new strategic and financial challenges, colleges and universities that have not yet done so are likely to seek to include debt in their capital development programs. Debt financing and management are extremely complex undertakings, requiring both internal expertise and reliance on the assistance of skilled professionals external to the institution. Professionals who are experienced in higher education finance can provide the nuances, details, and time-sensitive advice that all colleges and universities need when undertaking debt financing.

# Notes

1. National Association of Higher Education Facilities Authorities.

2. Two resources for information about generic techniques for financial ratio analysis for higher education institutions are *Ratio Analysis in Higher Education* (New York: KPMG Peat Marwick, 1987), and Nathan Dickmeyer and K. Scott Hughes, *Financial Self-Assessment* (Washington, D.C.: NACUBO, 1987). *Ratio Analysis in Higher Education* provides the following key ratios and describes in detail their derivation and their implications.

Summary of Financial Ratios

| | |
|---|---|
| Balance Sheet Ratios | Expendable fund balances:plant debt |
| | Plant equity:plant debt |
| | Expendable fund balances:total expenditures and mandatory transfers |
| | Nonexpendable fund balances:total expenditures and mandatory transfers |
| Operating Ratios | Net total revenues:total revenues |
| | Net educational and general revenues:total educational and general revenues |
| | Net auxiliary enterprise revenues:total auxiliary enterprise revenues |
| Contribution Ratios | Tuition and fees:total educational and general expenditures and mandatory transfers |
| | Federal government revenues:total educational and general expenditures and mandatory transfers |
| | State government revenues:total educational and general expenditures and mandatory transfers |
| | Local government revenues:total educational and general expenditures and mandatory transfers |
| | Private gifts, grants, contracts:total educational and general expenditures and mandatory transfers |
| | Endowment income:total educational and general expenditures and mandatory transfers |
| Demand Ratios | Instruction:total educational and general revenues |
| | Research:total educational and general revenues |
| | Public service:total educational and general revenues |
| | Academic support:total educational and general revenues |
| | Student services:total educational and general revenues |
| | Institutional support:total educational and general revenues |
| | Operation and maintenance of plant:total educational |

<table>
<tr><td></td><td>and general revenues</td></tr>
</table>

and general revenues

Scholarships and fellowships:total educational and general revenues

Creditworthiness Ratios    Available assets:general liabilities

Debt service:unrestricted current fund revenues

Matriculants (freshmen and transfer students): completed applications (freshmen and transfer students)

Opening fall (full-time equivalent) enrollment—this year: opening fall (full-time equivalent) enrollment—base year

3. The Government Finance Officers Association (GFOA) and the National Federation of Municipal Analysts (NFMA) have addressed the issue of new standards for disclosure. NFMA published a handbook of suggested guidelines for disclosure on a sector-by-sector basis (*Disclosure Handbook for Municipal Securities,* 1990), which suggests that the following information be disclosed by college and university bond issuers in the "Official Statement."

Description of Issuer/Obligor
- A.    The Institution
  - 1.    History
  - 2.    Location and affiliations
  - 3.    Principal administrators and board members
    - a.    Brief professional background
    - b.    Manner of selection
    - c.    Name, address and telephone numbers for chief financial contact person, financial advisor and other consultants
    - d.    Term of office

- B.    Administration and Management
  - 1.    Structure of organization
    - a.    Relationship to state funding policies
    - b.    External governmental relationships
  - 2.    Faculty
    - a.    Full- and part-time: five-year trend
    - b.    Number and percentage tenured: five-year trend
    - c.    Number and percentage with advanced degrees
  - 3.    Labor relations
    - a.    History
    - b.    Percent of unionization
  - 4.    Retirement plan status

C.   Description of Institution
1.   Programs offered
2.   Tuition and fees, including policies
3.   Financial aid programs and policies
4.   Enrollment profile
   a.   Head count and full-time equivalent (FTE): five-year trend (historic and pro forma)
   b.   Acceptance rate: five-year trend
   c.   Matriculation and attrition rate: five-year trend
   d.   Average SAT and/or ACT entrance exam scores: five-year trend
   e.   Discussion of any marketing efforts undertaken by institution
   f.   Geographic distribution of student population
   g.   List of competing schools
5.   Plant and facilities
   a.   Insurance coverage
   b.   Dormitory and facilities utilization
   c.   Liabilities and/or litigation

Terms of Debt
A.   Nature of Security
1.   Pledged revenue(s)
2.   Rate covenant
3.   Provisions for issuance of parity debt and test
4.   Reserve fund requirements and funding provisions
5.   Redemption provisions (for all possible circumstances)
6.   Legal features
   a.   Discussion of any pending proceedings that could affect entity's ability to perform its obligations (or could trigger an extraordinary call), including opinion as to possible outcome
   b.   Taxation
   c.   Validation or voluntary procedure which could have been used to validate
   d.   Litigation
   e.   Events of defaults and remedies
   f.   Foreclosure proceedings and other issuer covenants
7.   Specifics regarding crossover refunding transaction, if applicable
8.   Specifics regarding escrow arrangements, trustees and refunding timetable, if applicable

B. Debt
    1. Amount, security and lien status
        a. Outstanding indebtedness, including leases and all contractual obligations
        b. Projected and planned indebtedness
    2. Service
        a. Debt service schedule—cumulatively and by individual issue
        b. Debt service reserve requirement and balance for each issue
        c. Debt service coverage by issue and projected

Capital Improvements
    A. Bond Proceeds/The Project
        1. Sources and uses of funds, including capitalized interest
        2. Construction costs and timetable details
        3. Contractual arrangements with builders

    B. Capital Program and Additional Financing Plans

Financial Data
    A. Financial Reports, Including Breakdown by Major Individual Campuses in State Systems
        1. Annual audits—two years
        2. Auxiliary enterprises operating statements
        3. Current fiscal year's budget

    B. Operations
        1. Revenues by source:five-year trend
        2. State appropriations:five-year trend
        3. Expenditures by function:five-year trend
        4. Interfund transfers
        5. Administration's summary of operations and projections
        6. Endowment and similar funds—status
            a. Management and spending policies; status
            b. Portfolio policy for investments, including restrictions
            c. Percentage of endowment fund that is quasi-endowment
            d. Cost and market value
            e. Fund-raising experience, including alumni giving
            f. Details of major fund drives planned or in process
            g. Foundation involvement—detailed information

    C.    Financial Statistics
1. Tuition and fees, historic and projected—five years
2. Endowment funds per student (market value/FTE): five-year trend

Secondary Market Disclosure
    A.    Financial Information
1. Annual audits should be made available in a timely fashion and should include breakdowns by major individual campuses in state university systems
    a.    State appropriations and grants
    b.    Auxiliary enterprise statements
2. Endowment fund update relevant to that provided at the time of debt issuance
    a.    Market value
    b.    Fund-raising
3. Debt information update
    a.    Debt service and reserve requirements and fund balances
    b.    Debt service coverage, as required by indenture, for each issue
    c.    Future capital plans and financings

    B.    Supplemental Information
1. Enrollment and faculty (FTE) levels, student acceptance and attrition rates
2. Changes in key personnel or investor contact
3. Other changed information that would have been a significant aspect of disclosure at the time of sale

    C.    Notification of delinquent monthly payments of bond fund, unscheduled draws on letters or lines of credit and technical violations of the bond indenture

4. Laura Levenstein, "Interest Rate Swaps Expand Debt Management Alternatives," in *Topics in Structured Finances*, Vol. 2, no.4, Moody's Investors Service, Inc. (September/October): 1990.

5. See *Financial Accounting and Reporting Manual for Higher Education* (Washington, D.C.: NACUBO, 1990), and Robert Forrester and Coopers & Lybrand, *Handbook on Debt Management* (Washington, D.C.: NACUBO, 1988).

# References and Resources

PUBLICATIONS AND ARTICLES

Daley, Joseph C., Charles E. Carey, and George A. King. *A Guide to Municipal Official Statements.* 2nd ed. Englewood Cliffs, NJ: Prentice-Hall, 1990.

Dickmeyer, Nathan, and K. Scott Hughes. *Financial Self-Assessment: A Workbook for Colleges.* Washington, D.C.: NACUBO, 1980.

Forrester, Robert T. *A Handbook on Debt Management for Colleges and Universities.* NACUBO Capital Management Series. Washington, D.C.: NACUBO, 1988.

Hennigan, Patrick J. *Capital Financing for Higher Education: Market Perspectives and Framework for Analysis.* New York: J. P. Morgan Securities, 1988.

Kaiser, Harvey H. *Crumbling Academe: Solving the Capital Renewal and Replacement Dilemma.* Washington, D.C.: Association of Governing Boards of Universities and Colleges, 1984.

King, George A. "Rethinking Higher Education Capital Finance." *Capital Ideas* 3, nos. 2 & 3 (October 1988).

KPMG Peat Marwick. *Ratio Analysis in Higher Education.* 2nd ed. New York: KPMG Peat Marwick, 1987.

Levenstein, Laura. "Interest Rate Swaps Expand Debt Management Alternatives." *Topics in Structured Finance* 2, no. 4 (September/October 1990).

Moak, Lennox L. *Municipal Bonds: Planning, Sale, and Administration.* Chicago, Ill.: Municipal Finance Officers Association, 1982.

Moody's Investors Service. *Moody's on Municipals: An Introduction to Issuing Debt.* New York: Moody's Investors Service, 1987.

National Association of College and University Business Officers. *Capital Formation Alternatives in Higher Education.* NACUBO Capital Management Series. Washington, D.C.: NACUBO, 1988.

National Federation of Municipal Analysts. *Disclosure Handbook for Municipal Securities*. Pittsburgh, Pa.: National Federation of Municipal Analysts, 1990.

Public Securities Association. *Fundamentals of Municipal Bonds*. Rev. ed. New York: Public Securities Association, 1990-91.

Standard & Poor's Corporation. *CreditReview: Bond Insurance*. A supplement to *CreditWeek* (November 26, 1990).

Standard & Poor's Corporation. *CreditReview: Private Universities*. A supplement to *CreditWeek* (September 24, 1990).

Standard & Poor's Corporation. *CreditReview: Public Universities*. A supplement to *CreditWeek* (April 23, 1990).

Standard & Poor's Corporation. *Higher Education CreditReview*. A supplement to *CreditWeek* (April 17, 1989).

PERIODICALS

*The Blue List* (A daily list of bond prices used by dealers who trade bonds in the secondary market; the source of information for prices at which an institution's outstanding bonds are trading at any time.)

*The Bond Buyer* (A daily news publication that provides full coverage of forthcoming negotiated and competitive bond offerings, just sold bond offerings, interest rate trends, market analysis, regulatory news, and other news relating to the municipal bond market. It publishes various indices of general obligation and revenue bonds.)

*The Bond Buyer's Directory of Municipal Bond Dealers—"The Red Book"* (A semiannual directory of financial intermediation service providers, including municipal bond dealers, municipal bond credit enhancers, government officials, associations, municipal finance consultants, and municipal bond attorneys.)

*CreditWeek* (Published by S&P; comments on fixed-income topics, news affecting the bond industry, and specific industry/entity credit analyses.)

*Moody's Bond Record* (A monthly listing of all Moody's current debt ratings.)

*Moody's Bond Survey* (A weekly publication that covers factors and issues that affect the values of bonds.)

*Moody's Municipal & Government Manual* (An annual information manual on 20,000 municipalities and more than 1,000 federal, state, local, and regulatory agencies.)

## INDICES

*20-Bond G.O. Index* (*The Bond Buyer*'s index of 20 general obligation bonds with 20-year maturities. While the individual ratings of the 20 bonds vary from triple-A to lower investment grades, the overall index has a rating roughly equivalent to single-A. This index is of some interest to higher education issuers as an overall market indicator, but it is an index of general obligation issues, which are not issued by colleges and universities.)

*11-Bond G.O. Index* (A subset of the 20-Bond Index that includes those of higher credit quality, approximately equal to a double-A.)

*25-Bond Revenue Index* (An index of 25 revenue bonds, the type issued by colleges and universities, with maturities of 30 years, and with ratings that range from double-A to single-A. This index, which is the most pertinent for higher education issuers to follow, occasionally includes a higher education issue.)

*Kenny Indices* (Kenny S&P Information Services provides information about the market environment for variable-rate debt and compiles indices for subscribers and clients on a customized basis. After each repricing, Kenny conveys new index values to remarketing agents, trustees, and issuers.)

RATING AGENCIES

Fitch Investor Services, Inc.
1 State Street Plaza
New York, NY 10004
212-908-0500

Fitch Investor Services, Inc., sold its rating system to S&P but retained rights to use it. Recently recapitalized, Fitch began rating colleges and universities in 1989.

Moody's Investors Service, Inc.
99 Church Street
New York, NY 10007
212-553-0470

Moody's publishes *Moody's Bond Record; Moody's Municipal & Government Manual; Moody's Bond Survey;* and other specialized publications.

Standard & Poor's Corporation (S&P)
25 Broadway
New York, NY 10004
212-208-8000

S&P publishes *CreditWeek* and holds occasional one-day seminars on higher education creditworthiness aimed at college and university financial and business officers and investment bankers.

MUNICIPAL BOND INDUSTRY ORGANIZATIONS

Government Finance Officers Association of the United States and Canada (GFOA)
180 N. Michigan Avenue, Suite 800
Chicago, IL 60601
312-977-9700

GFOA is a professional association of state and local government finance officers that holds conferences and sponsors activities on topics relating to public finance.

National Federation of Municipal Analysts (NFMA)
P.O. Box 14893
Pittsburgh, PA 15234
412-341-4898
NFMA represents analysts who make credit recommendations for both issuers and buyers of municipal securities.

Public Securities Association (PSA)
40 Broad Street
New York, NY 10004
212-809-7000
PSA is the national trade organization of dealers and dealer banks that underwrite, trade, and sell state and local government securities and U.S. government and federal agency securities.

## MUNICIPAL BOND INDUSTRY REGULATION
Municipal Securities Rulemaking Board (MSRB)
1818 N Street, NW, Suite 800
Washington, DC 20036-2491
202-223-9347
The Municipal Securities Rulemaking Board was established by Congress as part of the Securities Acts Amendments of 1975 to develop rules governing securities firms and banks involved in underwriting, trading, and selling municipal securities. The board, which is composed of members of the municipal securities industry and the public, is a self-regulatory body that sets standards based on the expertise of industry members.

## HIGHER EDUCATION ASSOCIATIONS
National Association of College and University Business Officers (NACUBO)
One Dupont Circle, Suite 500
Washington, DC 20036
202-861-2500
NACUBO publishes material on debt financing and management, sponsors seminars on debt financing, and contains the financial management center, which can provide information on debt financing and management.

National Association of Higher Education Facilities Authorities (NAHEFA)

NAHEFA is a professional membership organization of the managers of these authorities. It does not maintain a permanent office address; contact member authorities for program information.

## DATA SERVICE COMPANIES

Investment Dealer Digest Information Services (IDD)
    2 World Trade Center, 18th Floor
    New York, NY 10048
    212-432-0045

IDD gathers information about municipal bond issues from public sources and maintains an extensive database.

Securities Data Company (SDC)
    1180 Raymond Boulevard
    Newark, NJ 07102
    201-622-3100

SDC is the municipal new issues source for *The Bond Buyer*. It also is a provider of new issue information to the financial services community, including municipal underwriters, financial advisors, and bond counsel firms. SDC maintains and can retrieve data for higher education and teaching hospitals.

## BOND INSURERS

AMBAC Indemnity Corporation
    1 State Street Plaza, 17th Floor
    New York, NY 10004
    800-221-1854

AMBAC is active as an insurer of higher education and related healthcare bond issues.

Capital Guaranty Insurance Company
Steuart Tower, 22nd Floor, 1 Market Plaza
San Francisco, CA 94105-1413
415-995-8000
Capital Guaranty Insurance Company has insured higher education bond issues.

College Construction Loan Insurance Association (Connie Lee Insurance Company)
2445 M Street, NW
Washington, DC 20036
202-835-0090
Connie Lee was created by Congress as a private, for-profit corporation whose mission is to provide financial guarantees on the debt of colleges, universities, teaching hospitals, and other educational institutions. When it commences activity as a primary insurer, Connie Lee will provide bond insurance and related guarantee products on debt obligations only for the higher education and teaching hospital sectors of the municipal market. Its congressional mandate will require it to insure some higher education credits that otherwise would not gain market access.

Financial Guarantee Insurance Company (FGIC)
175 Water Street
New York, NY 10038
800-352-0001
FGIC is somewhat less active in higher education bond issues than other companies but does consider some financings.

Financial Security Assurance, Inc. (FSA)
350 Park Avenue
New York, NY 10022
212-826-0100
FSA entered the municipal market in 1990 and has started to insure higher education bond issues.

Municipal Bond Investors Assurance Corporation (MBIA)
113 King Street
Armonk, NY 10504
914-273-4545
MBIA is the largest municipal bond company and is an active insurer of higher education and related healthcare bond issues.

OTHER RESOURCES
Student Loan Marketing Association (Sallie Mae)
1050 Thomas Jefferson Street, NW
Washington, DC 20007-3871
202-298-3003
Sallie Mae, a private, for-profit corporation whose primary purpose is to serve as a secondary market for student loans, also offers an array of programs for higher education facilities financing. Sallie Mae's financing programs include both taxable and tax-exempt debt, fixed or variable rates, and lines of credit. Sallie Mae also offers a special program that permits small borrowings on a tax-exempt basis.

University Support Services, Inc.
1776 Massachusetts Avenue, NW
Washington, DC 20036
202-331-9350
University Support Services, Inc., is a private, nonprofit corporation whose purpose is to provide programs for financing to higher education. The initial and largest program offered is the ConSern Loans for Education Program, which provides supplemental student loans at favorable rates, based on a taxable commercial paper program.

CHAPTER 13

# Retirement Program Administration

by
Hans H. Jenny
VISTA, Limited

# Sponsors

## MUTUAL OF AMERICA

666 Fifth Avenue
New York, NY 10103
212-399-1551

*Mutual of America is a not-for-profit life insurance company that specializes in providing pension and tax-deferred annuity plans to higher education institutions.*

## TIAA-CREF

730 Third Avenue
New York, NY 10017
800-842-2733

*TIAA-CREF, a nonprofit national pension system, offers retirement and tax-deferred annuity plans and life, disability, and long-term care insurance designed for higher education.*

# Contents

## 13: Retirement Program Administration

Change is ever present in management endeavors, and retirement program administration is no exception. Fundamental, if not revolutionary, changes have taken place in higher education retirement programs. Much of the impetus for change came from new laws and governmental regulations; some changes were introduced by companies in the business of providing retirement products and services, and some have occurred as a result of innovations originating in higher education or among employers throughout the U.S. economy. Although the Age Discrimination in Employment Act of 1967 (ADEA) and the Employee Retirement Income Security Act of 1974 (ERISA) are examples of landmark legislation, the laws and regulations that followed in rapid order during the 1980s established significant new benchmarks for retirement program administration both within and outside of higher education.

In higher education, managerial responsibility for retirement program administration is not assigned according to a uniform pattern. There are enormous differences among institutions in the assignment of authority to make decisions regarding retirement programs and, more important, to affect financial outcomes.

This chapter concentrates on common characteristics of collegiate retirement program administration and some of the significant current issues in this field. It provides a brief overview of the major provisions of law and some of the key questions college and university administrators must answer when they establish and administer a pension plan. This chapter first defines the nature and scope of retirement program administration and then describes the major types of pension plans that are its primary focus. Retirement program administration is a complex undertaking that involves many details. This chapter is an attempt to provide a general overview of issues in retirement program administration and to highlight some new directions institutions need to keep in mind as they review their programs.

## The Nature and Scope of Retirement Planning

For the purposes of this chapter, "retirement program" is defined as the planning and implementing of employee retirement; it encompasses the institutional and individual activities that affect an employee's status (financial and otherwise) as he or she approaches and enters retirement, as well as issues that influence and facilitate employee decisions about retirement.

A comprehensive retirement program includes some or all of the following elements:

- Social security benefits (unless the institution is exempted by law)

- A basic retirement or pension plan

- Any tax-deferred employee savings through supplemental retirement arrangements

- Continued health insurance coverage during retirement

- Continued life insurance coverage during retirement

- Postretirement benefits other than pensions and insurance

- Nonfinancial postretirement benefits

- Phased and/or early retirement arrangements, including descriptions of the circumstances for retirement and the financial arrangements pertaining to it

- Formal or officially sanctioned preretirement (planning) counseling[1]

- Formal or officially sanctioned postretirement counseling and support

Colleges and universities differ in their selection of these benefits and the nature and scope of the benefits selected. Regardless of how small or extensive an institution's retirement program is, the program should focus on the financial well-being of employees in retirement. Another important consideration is the financial impact of the retirement program on the institution.[2]

Employees have two major financial concerns when they think about retirement. They consider their retirement income and how ill health and disability might affect their financial circumstances. Escalating medical costs pose a major dilemma when employees think about retirement, especially in situations in which postretirement health benefits are inadequate or unavailable. With the disappearance of mandated retirement, the lack of postretirement health benefits may prevent many employees from retiring as early as they might if such coverage were available.

There are four major sources of potential retirement income:

- Social security (where such coverage applies)

- The employer-sponsored basic pension plan and any supplemental plans that may exist

- Personal savings and investment income and, in some instances, inheritances

- Postretirement employment

The U.S. Social Security Administration estimates that for the nation as a whole almost 75 percent of retirement income is derived from the first three sources.

In designing their retirement programs, employers are focusing their retirement income attention on the first two of the four potential income sources. The American Association of University Professors (AAUP) and the Association of American Colleges (AAC) describe the retirement planning objectives for colleges and universities: "After-tax income equivalent in purchasing power of approximately two-thirds of the yearly disposable salary (after taxes) during the last few years of long-term employment."[3] Many pension plans that have as their objective some percentage of salary replacement and are not integrated with social security aim at a replacement percentage without reference to social security. Because employees' tax situations differ enormously, it may not be practical to use the AAUP-AAC "after-tax" objective. Instead, colleges and universities appear to have settled on salary replacement percentages--retirement income targets—derived from pretax salary gross amounts.

In addition to financial security, employees look to their employers for a varying array of pre- and postretirement assistance, including preretirement planning, counseling, and certain benefits that extend into retirement. Colleges and universities must decide whether or not they want to extend to retirees the amenities they enjoyed during their working years, such as access to cultural events at no or modest cost, open use of libraries and laboratories, and access to office space and clerical support. In the past, faculty members often were routinely given such benefits as a professional courtesy, but because many institutions face space shortages and rising costs, such postretirement amenities can no longer be taken for granted.

The effect of inflation on retirement income has also become a major consideration of retirement planning. College and university employees are interested in providing protection against the ravages of inflation.

Retirement programs entail significant expenditures for employers. In addition, certain employee benefit liabilities can arise, further increasing institutional costs. Because of these factors, a college or university's financial exposure due to its retirement plan may conflict with employee interests.

## Objectives of Retirement Programs

Retirement programs have three broad objectives:

- To enable long-term employees to retire with a reasonable level of economic security by providing them with a certain amount of retirement income and other retirement benefits and services

- To provide and enhance flexibility in short- and long-range personnel planning

- To attract and retain professional talent

Higher education has long been known for the quality of its employee benefits and retirement programs. Retirement programs represent an important and often strategic element in college and university human resources management and planning. Competitive considerations play a strategic role in attracting and retaining qualified personnel, and colleges and universities have an interest in providing suitable compensation packages and personnel relations environments.

The AAUP-AAC's "Statement of Principles on Academic Retirement and Insurance Plans" espouses a philosophy that links a college or university's mission with the interests of its employees: "The purpose of retirement plans . . . for faculty members and administrators is to help educators and their families maintain their standard of living . . . . The purpose of such plans for institutions is to increase the educational effectiveness of the college or university."[4] Of course, faculty and administrators are not the only employees served by retirement programs; these programs usually apply to all types of full-time employees except students.

Retirement program administration has three major functions:

- Development and articulation of a retirement policy

- Program design, implementation, administration, and maintenance

- Program review, enactment, and improvement

When fully implemented, these functions constitute an integrated set of dynamic arrangements that must comply with existing legal, regulatory, and other requirements. They also must ensure that, over time, the retirement program can be adapted to changing circumstances.

***Developing a retirement policy.*** When developing a retirement policy, the following issues should be addressed.

WHEN CAN OR SHOULD EMPLOYEES RETIRE? Traditionally, retirement policy makers were able to distinguish between "mandatory" and "normal" retirement age. Today both concepts have only limited application.[5] The 1986 amendments to the ADEA eliminated "mandatory" retirement but permitted compulsory retirement at age 70 for tenured employees through December 31, 1993. The National Academy of Sciences performed a study of the potential effect on higher education of eliminating this exception and concluded that keeping it would not be justified. Thus, unless legislation in its support is enacted, "mandatory" retirement in higher education will be a thing of the past by January 1, 1994.

The term "normal retirement age," however, still is in use. To define the income objective of a pension plan, a "pension plan target age" at which an employee will receive an actuarially unreduced payout must be identified. This target age determines the pension plan's potential funding requirements. Retirement before the target age reduces benefits; retirement after the target age increases them. In addition, when they describe their pension benefits, colleges and universities must focus on the level of benefits at one or several such target ages.

ARE THERE POSSIBILITIES FOR PHASED OR EARLY RETIREMENT? Many colleges and universities have introduced formal phased and/or early retirement programs. Some of these are open-ended until revoked; others are instituted for a limited time only and cease to exist unless formally renewed. Generally, such options require certain minimum eligibility qualifications for participation.

WHAT ARE THE SPECIFIC POSTRETIREMENT EMPLOYEE BENEFITS? Postretirement employee benefits include the basic retirement or pension plan; supplemental retirement arrangements; health care plans; life insurance; postretirement professional benefits such as access to laboratories, computers, offices, clerical support, and libraries; and other nonprofessional institution-supplied amenities such as access to sports and cultural events. Minimal retirement benefits normally include the basic pension plan, some kind of health benefit, and, less frequently, some life insurance coverage.

DOES THE INSTITUTION USE AD HOC RETIREMENT ARRANGEMENTS? Colleges and universities normally operate under written retirement policies that address policy areas in detail. In the absence of or in addition to formal arrangements, administrators may make decisions on an ad hoc basis or provide informal counseling, both of which could expose the institution to potential litigation if affected individuals later change their minds or claim discrimination, inappropriate pressure, or that they suffered financial and other damages. In spite of this, however, ad hoc arrangements and "handshake agreements" are frequent because they allow an institution to respond to specific employment and retirement situations.

WHAT, IF ANY, PRE- AND POSTRETIREMENT PLANNING AND/OR COUNSELING ACTIVITIES ARE PROVIDED BY THE INSTITUTION? What are the nature and scope of pre- and postretirement planning and counseling activities? Is their execution assigned to specific administrators? Is there institutional budget support for such activities? Does the institution formally assist retiring employees to develop second careers or earn additional money? There are vast differences in institutions' responses to these questions.

***Program design, implementation, and maintenance.*** Once institutional policy on the retirement program has been established, the program itself must be set up. Retirement program administration, design, implementation, and maintenance are the predominant ongoing burden for college and university retirement program administrators. The following issues must be considered.

DO PENSION PLAN AND OTHER RETIREMENT BENEFITS EMBODY APPROPRIATE INCENTIVES? Retention of key faculty and staff is one factor to consider when designing a retirement plan; another is how to facilitate timely retirement so that there is a mutual advantage to both the employee and the institution. Colleges and universities need to determine if their plan provisions encourage the premature retirement of highly qualified and productive employees. Another issue is whether or not generous plans with large lump-sum death or survivor benefits encourage late retirements.

It may be difficult for administrators to answer such questions before testing specific plans and adapting them over time. From the institution's point of view, additional considerations are:

- Can the institution afford a basic and an incentive-driven phased or early retirement plan? This issue is complex because of the ancillary considerations. For instance, are those who retire early being replaced? If so, at what levels of compensation? Are marginal revenue losses resulting from enrollment reductions equal to or larger than marginal cost savings resulting from retirements, early or otherwise?[6]

- Is the institution in a retrenchment or expansionary mode? Is the demand for professional and other personnel declining or expanding?

- Can the institution afford retirement benefits? This question is asked more often in connection with pre- and postretirement health care costs. When institutions are forced to consider their own financial interests ahead of those of employees, benefit retrenchment or shifting of a larger portion of costs to employees and retirees may become necessary.

DO RETIREMENT BENEFITS ADHERE TO CURRENT LEGAL REQUIREMENTS? Legal and regulatory compliance questions are likely to arise often. Legal complexities introduced by ERISA in 1974 and legislation enacted since then that affects retirement benefits and pension plans mean that institutions must continually avail themselves of the best possible legal advice.

ARE RECORD KEEPING AND PLAN REPORTING ADEQUATE AND TIMELY? The responsibility for accurate records is shared by the principal parties of a pension contract: the employer, the employee, and the plan administrator or carrier. The institution's retirement program administrator should clarify who should keep which records. ERISA and the Internal Revenue Code (IRC) stipulate the records and reports that independent colleges and universities must keep and distribute to participants. In certain retirement plans employees are responsible for once-a-year instructions to the plan administrator concerning contributions via salary reduction. Institutions must keep records of premium remittances, participants' premium allocations, salary reduction agreements, and all Internal Revenue Service (IRS) related information. But with the ever-widening use of telephones to give instructions to the provider, institutions can no longer be held responsible for keeping track of all transactions.

HOW OFTEN AND IN WHAT MANNER ARE EMPLOYEES INFORMED ABOUT THEIR BENEFIT STATUS? For contributory plans, institutions need to ensure that payroll deductions are accurate and that employees understand them. Institutions should explain any changes in the cost of retirement benefits. For certain types of pension plans, information about investment performance, capital accumulations, annuity choices, and changes in the law must be provided to plan participants. Although the IRS and the Department of Labor (DOL) stipulate some reporting requirements, they do not always prescribe the precise format; sometimes they provide choices among different forms. Institutions and plan providers may differ in the extent, frequency, and quality of retirement benefit reporting to employees and plan participants. Institutions need to review both the extent and the effectiveness of the information provided.

HOW ARE EMPLOYEES INFORMED ABOUT THEIR RETIREMENT BENEFITS? Colleges and universities should review enrollment procedures and coverage requirements periodically to ensure that there are no loose ends. If a plan is voluntary, are eligible employees contacted periodically regarding their possible participation? Are written waivers obtained from nonparticipants? How often are these updated? If the plan is mandatory, what are the procedures ensuring that employees are contacted about their enrollment?

DOES THE INSTITUTION TRANSMIT PLAN CONTRIBUTIONS IN A TIMELY MANNER? The DOL requires that premiums be remitted within 90 days of withholding or accrual, although premiums must be paid at the earliest reasonable date. Participants should be able to assume that institutional contributions and withholdings will be transmitted promptly.

DOES THE INSTITUTION ORGANIZE OR ENCOURAGE THE FORMATION OF EMPLOYEE-SPONSORED SUPPORT GROUPS (OTHER THAN COLLECTIVE BARGAINING ENTITIES) DEALING WITH RETIREMENT MATTERS? Many colleges and universities have well-established employee-sponsored pre- and postretirement support groups; some of these function with considerable administrative encouragement and direct support. Academic units devoted to the study of problems associated with aging often spearhead voluntary faculty- or employee-sponsored discussion and action groups. Because some institutions see potential legal pitfalls in direct involvement with these groups, the institutions may distance themselves from activities that could be perceived as providing advice. Some institutions have written policies expressly forbidding members of the administration to offer advice concerning employee choices. Nevertheless, it may be appropriate to review periodically whether or not there is a constructive role in this area for administrative support.

WHO IS IN CHARGE OF RETIREMENT PROGRAM ADMINISTRATION? Many institutions, large ones in particular, have decentralized the process of retirement program decision making and administration. They may delegate "benefits administration" to the human resources department; many institutions may have a "benefits officer"; faculty retirement issues may be under the jurisdiction of key academic administrators. In view of the complex legal aspects of retirement plans, it is essential that institutions establish clear lines of administrative responsibility. ERISA requires private employers to appoint a "plan administrator." If the chief financial or business officer is not permitted to deal with certain retirement administration matters with specific employee groups, these restrictions need to be spelled out and the official charged with the responsibility in question must be clearly identified. The institution must comply with legal requirements regardless of who oversees a particular aspect of retirement program management.

IS THE INSTITUTION COVERED BY ADEQUATE EMPLOYEE BENEFIT LIABILITY (EBL) INSURANCE? ERISA provides penalties for fiduciaries who violate its requirements and makes them personally responsible for imprudence and omissions in the management of assets. A variety of claims can arise from clerical error, inappropriate advice, or infractions such as a breach of fiduciary requirements, inadvertent violations of ERISA rules, dishonesty, fraud, or misappropriation of benefit funds. Institutions must determine whether or not they need special ERISA-related EBL coverage to minimize the risk of financial exposure.

*Periodic program review and management.* The retirement policy and program should be reviewed periodically. The following issues should be considered in a review.

WHAT IS THE SPECIFIC ROLE PLAYED BY THE GOVERNING BOARD? The governing board is ultimately accountable for a college or university's financial condition. In what detail is the governing board acquainted with the retirement program in general and the pension plan in particular? Pension and other retirement benefits represent significant claims against current and future financial resources. The legal requirements raise issues of a governing board's fiduciary responsibilities. The board's duties in relation to changing retirement benefits must be clearly delineated.

ARE THERE PROCEDURES FOR RETIREMENT PROGRAM REVIEW? Changes in laws or regulations compel a review whenever they occur. Other developments, especially competitive ones, may call attention to new opportunities for review. Should institutions establish formal evaluation procedures? Periodic investment performance reviews are important in pension plans where employees' retirement income depends on the investment performance and the financial viability of the investment manager or carrier.

No retirement benefit program can serve all institutions and all employees all the time. Individual, social, and economic circumstances may change significantly over time. Colleges and universities should institute formal procedures that ensure periodic evaluations to determine whether or not existing programs fulfill employee needs and accomplish institutional objectives.

## Retirement Income Planning

College and university retirement income planning for employees is built around social security and the institution's pension plan.

## SOCIAL SECURITY

Except for certain public institutions, participation in the social security program is mandatory for colleges and universities. The Social Security Act of 1935 has been amended frequently, and today the amendments and regulations require thousands of pages of explanation.[7]

**Benefits.** The following retirement-related programs are included under social security:

- Old age or retirement insurance (social security retirement benefits)
- Survivor's insurance
- Medicare for the aged and disabled
- Disability insurance

SOCIAL SECURITY RETIREMENT BENEFITS AND SURVIVOR'S INSURANCE. Social security benefit eligibility depends upon the number of "work credits" or "quarters of coverage" an employee has accumulated at retirement. In 1991, an employee must have earned 40 quarters of work credits to qualify for social security. Older workers closer to retirement age need less than 40 credits. (The specific credits vary; employees and employers should consult the 1983 amendments to the Social Security Act of 1935.) Retirement income benefits can first be claimed at age 62, but there is a permanent 20 percent reduction that rises to 30 percent for those claiming benefits at age 62 by 2022. In 1991, full benefits may be claimed at age 65. Widowers and widows can claim (reduced) benefits as early as age 60. Divorced persons who were married for at least ten years can claim their own benefits at age 62 regardless of their work credit status.

The 1983 amendments to the Social Security Act of 1935 introduced a provision that raises the normal retirement age for receiving social security benefits and increases the reduction for claiming early benefits. The amendments will first apply to persons born in 1938. The normal retirement age will gradually rise from 65 to 67 beginning in 2027.

**Medicare benefits.** Medicare benefits first appeared in 1965, providing health insurance for employees aged 65 and older regardless of whether they work or are retired. Medicare is financed through the

Federal Insurance Contribution Act (FICA) tax and through premiums paid by enrolled persons and by the federal government.

***Disability benefits.*** Disability benefits have been part of social security since 1965. Employees can receive disability benefits before age 65 if they are seriously physically or mentally disabled. "Serious disability" means that one is prevented from performing any kind of work and the condition is expected to last at least 12 months (or has lasted that long) or results in death. To receive disability benefits, an employee must have earned a specific number of work credits, depending upon the age at which disability occurs, or must meet other conditions specified in the regulations.

***Major concerns.*** Social security and Medicare benefits are largely financed by payroll taxes paid equally by the employee and his or her employer. Colleges and universities have two major concerns regarding social security: the costs to the institution for its share of the FICA tax, and whether or not to integrate social security with the pension plan.

INSTITUTIONAL COST OF THE FICA TAX. The size of the FICA tax liability (or expenditure) is a function of the number of employees, the prevailing wage or salary levels, and the size of the tax. In 1991, the employer portion of the FICA tax was 7.65 percent (6.2 percent plus 1.45 percent hospital insurance) for earnings up to $53,400 (indexed) and 1.45 percent (hospital insurance only) for earnings between $53,400 and $125,000 (indexed). Because FICA normally applies to most of an institution's payroll, FICA taxes may frequently exceed the institution's cost for the pension plan.

INTEGRATION WITH SOCIAL SECURITY. Social security benefits must be considered an integral part of retirement planning and funding. As a rule of thumb, social security will replace between 20 and 40 percent of an employee's preretirement income. Social security retirement income offers a larger replacement potential for those with lower earnings and a smaller replacement for those with higher earnings. When a college or university integrates a pension plan with social security, it normally makes a smaller pension plan contribution for the earnings levels to which the FICA tax applies as compared to those levels to which the tax does not apply.

In the aftermath of the Tax Reform Act of 1986, the IRS released regulations on how a plan may incorporate the "permitted disparity" in the social security integration formula. These regulations limit the difference between the contribution percentage rates to the lesser of the base contribution percentage (contribution on the first dollars of salary) or 5.7 percent of salary. The IRS provides a "safe harbor" for plans where the contribution rate increases at a level below the social security wage base (SSWB). This safe harbor further restricts the difference between contributions to an amount less than 5.7 percent. For example, if an institution's employees contribute 4 percent of their salaries to the SSWB, the institution could contribute up to 8 percent (twice the amount of the employees' contribution) to the SSWB.

Defined benefit retirement plans can also reflect the amount of projected social security benefits in their benefit formulas. The IRS regulations are complex and should be reviewed regularly.

Not every college or university integrates its pension plan with social security. There is no uniformity in higher education in this respect except where states mandate a special integration formula for public institutions.

Social security retirement benefits may be augmented by cost-of-living adjustments (COLAs). COLAs are based on the smaller of either the year-to-year difference in the third quarter Consumer Price Index (CPI) or the percentage increase in average U.S. wages. COLAs do not affect directly the cost of social security to institutions.

## THE PENSION PLAN

The basic pension plan and any supplemental retirement arrangements sponsored by an institution represent the centerpiece of college and university retirement programs. In general, there are two fundamentally different types of pension plans: "defined benefit" and "defined contribution" plans. Under a defined benefit plan, retirement income is predetermined by a formula that takes into account years of covered service and prevailing salary levels, normally in the years immediately preceding retirement. Under a defined contribution plan, the emphasis is on the periodic contribution into the fund on behalf of and/or by the employee.

All public employee pension plans are defined benefit plans. Defined benefit plans are also available, though less frequently, in the independent sector of higher education, often in connection with collective bargaining contracts for nonprofessional employees. Defined contribution plans are found throughout the independent higher education sector; in addition, many states make available defined contribution plans to their higher educational institutions, mostly for faculty and administrators.

***Defined benefit plans.*** In defined benefit plans, the future pension is determined in advance by means of a benefit formula. There are three types of formulas:

- Flat-benefit formula: Each year of service may yield a flat dollar or percentage of wage or salary benefit.

- Career-average formula: A percentage of pay is earned each year, adding up to the full benefit at retirement; or, at retirement, all earnings are averaged out and the benefit is a percentage of this career average.

- Final-pay formula: The last year (or years) of employment constitutes the base from which, combined with total years of covered service, a pension payout is computed; it is often adjusted to take into account the age of the retiring employee.

Most public institutions use a final-pay formula, averaging the highest years' wages or salaries, multiplying this average by the number of years of credited service, and multiplying the result by a factor that defines the rate of salary recovery. This factor can range from 1 to 2.5 percent. Some systems use step-rate levels designed to be integrated with social security, where the final benefit is the sum of each step-benefit calculation.

In higher education, salary replacement tends to be based on the "last few years" of full-time employment, which translates into the last years at the highest wage or salary level. The last-few-years norms are three and five years for most public institutions' defined benefit plans. Key factors are the number of years of participation in a plan and the age at which employees retire. In higher education the standard is a 30- to 35-year participation. Plan policy normally assumes full-time participation over an entire career, without interim deductions of accumulating funds through lump-sum distributions unless they are rolled over into other approved plans.

***Defined contribution plans.*** Defined contribution plans are characterized by periodic contributions made by employers and/or employees. The contributions are then invested on a tax-deferred basis; investment earnings accumulate over time to constitute the capital basis for retirement income. There are no predetermined payout formulas or payout benefits. The payout amounts depend on the combined effects of the amount contributed, the performance of the types of investments chosen, the compounding effect of reinvested investment earnings, the length of time of plan participation, any early lump-sum distribution, applicable actuarial mortality assumptions, and the specific payout option(s) chosen by participants.

To achieve a specific salary replacement, institutions must estimate the long-range potential effects of alternatives that combine most of the above elements under specific investment return assumptions. Plan contributions and investment earnings accumulate to individual employee contracts (or accounts).

In higher education, most independent-sector plans are defined contribution plans; most states have "optional retirement (defined contribution) plans" (ORP) as an alternative to their defined benefit plans. Several modern defined benefit plans, including ORPs, offer multiple investment choices and multiple vendors. In some states, ORPs are the only pension plans offered to college and university faculty and administrators; in others, they supplement the state system. Historically, the most widely disseminated defined contribution plans in higher education have been offered by Teachers Insurance and Annuity Association and the College Retirement Equities Fund (TIAA-CREF) under section 403(b) of the IRC (called 403(b) plan contributions).

TARGET BENEFIT PLANS (TBP). A TBP is a defined contribution plan that sets forth a defined benefit payout objective at a target retirement age and/or for specified ages.[8]

At a specified age, the target benefit requires a certain amount of capital, which is a function of the size of past contributions, investment returns, and the length of participation in the plan. Other important elements in determining the target benefit are actuarial assumptions and the types of final payout (e.g., single-life annuity, with or without guarantees for survivors). The target benefit is funded solely from amounts contributed periodically, plus any compounded net total return. The following should be considered in determining a participant's periodic contribution rate:

- The amount contributed will depend on the factor (e.g., a formula benefit of 1 percent, 1.5 percent, or 2.5 percent) by which the salary average and years of service are multiplied.

- Contributions are smaller for younger participants and larger for older participants.

- Contributions normally increase each year for each participant.

- The final accumulation and payout may be smaller or larger than the original target benefit, depending upon cumulative investment results.

TBPs aim for more nearly uniform final (salary recovery) benefits regardless of an entrant's age. Some TBPs express the retirement benefit as a percentage of final pay prior to retirement rather than basing it on length of covered service. Some defined contribution plans accomplish similar results by using contribution schedules that increase with age.

***Section 401(k) matching retirement plans.*** An employer may match on a predetermined basis an employee's contribution to a retirement arrangement. There are several such arrangements in higher education, and they are also popular in for-profit business under section 401(k) of the IRC. However, Congress eliminated tax-deferred 401(k) arrangements for tax-exempt employers in the Tax Reform Act of 1986. If and when 401(k) arrangements become available to nonprofit organizations, colleges and universities may wish to use them in lieu of 403(b) plans. Because of their popularity in the business sector and their relative simplicity, matching retirement plans have considerable appeal to higher education.

***Contributory and noncontributory plans.*** For each type of plan described above, contributions may be made by the employer, by both the employer and the employee, or by the employee alone. The employer has the right to require employees to contribute to a pension plan; the employee's contribution to a plan also may be voluntary. As a result of the Tax Reform Act of 1986, voluntary matching plans are subject to a special nondiscrimination test. This test sets the employer's average matching contribution for highly compensated employees (HCEs) on the basis of the average matching contribution for non-HCEs.

The actual structure of contribution patterns varies greatly. Some institutions offer a basic noncontributory plan as well as a matching (usually voluntary) contributory plan. Examples are a plan with a 10 percent employer-only contribution; a plan that requires all eligible employees to participate as a condition of employment where both the employee and the employer make a 5 percent contribution not subject to the matching test. Other examples are a plan that is not compulsory but has, for those participating, a 5 percent employer match of a 5 percent employee contribution that must pass the matching test (a 5-5 percent split); or a combination of a basic noncontributory plan of 8 percent plus a voluntary matching incentive plan of 3 percent by employer and employee.

In addition to contributing to a retirement plan, employees can contribute to a tax-deferred annuity or a supplemental retirement arrangement on a before-tax basis via salary reduction contributions. Employees can also make voluntary contributions to any plan on an after-tax basis within the total contribution limit imposed by law. In 1991, laws limited 403(b) plan contributions by capping the employee's salary reduction amount and limiting the combined employer-employee contributions both as a percentage and as a dollar amount. For all types of contribution arrangements, both defined benefit and defined contribution plans may integrate their contribution and benefit schedules with social security.

## ADVANTAGES AND DISADVANTAGES OF DIFFERENT TYPES OF PENSION PLANS

Each type of pension plan has certain advantages and disadvantages that must be weighed before a plan is introduced or when an existing plan is being evaluated.

***Defined benefit plans.*** The primary advantage of a defined benefit plan is that the size of the benefit at retirement can be determined with relative ease. A participant need only estimate the size of the wage or salary to which the benefit formula applies, in light of the years of covered service and his or her age at retirement. At public institutions, defined benefit plan managers usually provide tables that illustrate the formula benefits for various ages and service lengths. An advantage of a defined benefit plan for the employee is the virtual absence of investment risk, especially in a fully funded plan. However, there could be a risk if the financial standing of public entities weakens, if investment managers assume excessive risks, and if independent institutions with underfunded plans should default. Under ERISA, benefits of private deferred benefit plans are protected by the Pension Benefit Guaranty Corporation (PBGC).

The two major disadvantages of defined benefit plans concern the participant and the employer. For participants, a major question is the portability of the defined benefit. In public institutions, portability is normally limited to the jurisdiction over which a particular plan extends. In some instances, public pension systems provide credit for prior service with other public institutions. In independent institutions, defined benefit plans tend not to be portable beyond an employer; an exception may be a collective bargaining pension plan agreement covering more than one institution (a multiemployer plan). Another major disadvantage for employees in public institutions is that they exert no direct influence on pension plan policy and benefits, because defined benefit public employee retirement plans are not developed at the institutional level, where employee input might be expected.

For employers, a major uncertainty, if not disadvantage, of defined benefit plans concerns the funding requirements. In public institutions, the funding responsibility for retirement normally lies with the state or a public agency. Individual institutions fund their share of the defined benefit via contributions, which are charged to annual budgets, and withholding from participants' paychecks if the plan is contributory. In the event of deficiencies, institutional budgets could be affected if the state decides to charge deficiencies to user institutions. In the independent sector, institutions with defined benefit plans assume the full funding risk. Depending on investment practice and outcomes, a pension plan may be overfunded, underfunded, or adequately funded. In principle, overfunding is easily corrected but subject to ERISA, which requires caps for overfunding. Underfunding, which violates ERISA requirements, may be more difficult to correct, especially by institutions in financial trouble. The employer also faces relatively high costs of administering a defined benefit plan. For instance, IRS Form 5500 must be completed by an independent certified public accountant, and independent actuarial advice is needed to determine and verify individual benefits.

Another disadvantage of defined benefit plans that are based on the participant's highest earnings is that benefits accrued later in one's employment will have a greater value than those accrued earlier. If consecutive earnings prior to retirement are the highest, both early retirement or transfers to a job outside the system will result in benefits based on the lower retirement exit earnings.

*Defined contribution plans.* A primary advantage of defined contribution plans to the employer is that costs are highly predictable because they are normally limited to the employer's plan contributions. A major advantage for participants is that, once vesting has occurred, the participant "owns" accumulated benefits. Furthermore, he or she may at some point gain access to all or part of the retirement capital proper, depending upon the specific decisions made by the institution about the cashability and rollover of assets upon retirement and IRS constraints.

A disadvantage for participants is that they face investment risk. This risk is implicit in plans where employees make no investment or contribution allocation decisions and cannot predict the eventual investment result. The risk is explicit in plans that allow participant-directed investments, whether or not employees make contributions. The plan administrator still has ERISA-imposed fiduciary responsibilities and liability exposure, but some DOL regulations are designed to "relieve fiduciaries of certain liabilities" such as investment losses incurred by participants making direct choices among a broad range of investments.[9]

As investment choices multiply for higher education institutions with defined contribution plans, participants are exposed to more potential investment risk; this could be viewed as an outright disadvantage or as an enhanced opportunity. In general, defined contribution pension systems embody potentially greater employee involvement, especially when compared to public institution defined benefit systems. For the employer, this heightened employee involvement may imply a need for more information or counseling services.

Another related disadvantage for participants in a defined contribution plan is the uncertainty attached to estimating the future retirement benefit. This is the case especially for younger participants, when economic assumptions must cover many years; it is less of a problem for participants who are close to retirement. But even then, if retirement capital is subject to sharp short-term market fluctuations such as those experienced in October 1987 and October 1990, estimates can prove to be highly inaccurate. Retirement income estimates are available on annual benefit statements and/or through a growing list of software made available by insurance and investment companies or by independent vendors.

TARGET BENEFIT PLANS. TBPs are quite rare in higher education, but they offer a major advantage over the other plans for institutions that hire older personnel who will spend relatively few years with the institution before they retire. For a participant in a TBP, contribution rates may significantly exceed rates for employees in other plans, so as to ensure adequate capital accumulations in retirement. Long-service employees who enter a TBP at an early age will have a much lower contribution rate throughout their careers. As long as target benefits fall within a nondiscriminatory range of benefit objectives for other covered employees, this alternative gives employers added flexibility for attracting highly compensated professionals. A disadvantage for the institution is its higher-than-normal contribution cost. There are no special funding requirements other than those for contributions.

# Pension Plan Review

Higher education is in many ways unique in matters of pension plan administration. Many private businesses with pension plans administer the plans themselves. They have their own investment staff and sometimes their own actuaries. Some companies hire legal and actuarial expertise but manage plan investments internally. Other companies contract with outside experts for all pension plan administration details.

In contrast, colleges and universities have traditionally relied on external pension plan managers. In public institutions, defined benefit plans normally are under the jurisdiction of a public agency that may further assign certain functions—investment management in particular—to third parties. The management of defined contribution plans in both public and independent institutions traditionally has been delegated to external private entities. Independent college and university defined benefit plans are sometimes managed internally, sometimes not. Because the concept of defined contribution pensions in independent higher education recognizes the importance of portability, external management through a single agency predominated from the outset. Today, more than 1,500 higher education institutions provide TIAA-CREF options as their only pension plan or in conjunction with other pension plan providers. Since the introduction of individual retirement accounts, supplemental retirement arrangements, more self-directed investment choices, and the Securities and Exchange Commission's (SEC) agreement with TIAA-CREF, numerous other suppliers have entered the field and now provide pension services to colleges and universities. More choices among competitors and products will become available in the future.

## ASPECTS OF PENSION PLAN EVALUATION

When funds transfer and lump-sum distribution opportunities became available on March 1, 1990, colleges and universities with TIAA-CREF contracts were asked to make specific choices regarding these options. Institutions were asked by TIAA-CREF whether or not they wished to add any or all of the new investment choices that had been introduced in the 1980s (the CREF Money Market, Bond Market, and Social Choice accounts) and whether or not they wanted to adopt transferability and/or lump-sum distribution (cashability) options. The need to make these and other substantive decisions concerning pension plan philosophy and policy created an opportunity for colleges and universities to debate—if they had not already done so—whether or not to add products from pension plan managers other than TIAA-CREF. An opportunity such as this, when an entire industry is asked to review its pension plans, does not present itself very often. Normally, the initiative for a thorough review lies with individual college and universities. In this historic instance, the opportunity for a review of pension plans arose amid widening competition, after the major supplier of higher education defined contribution plan products enlarged its offerings in response to considerable outside pressure and criticism.

When making decisions on which options to provide, institutional administrators should

- review the relative adequacy of the basic plan's contribution level;

- study the historical investment performance of competing providers;

- study the financial health of competing providers;

- review the comparative reporting, back-office, and compliance support capabilities; and

- assess employee and participant needs, preferences, and points of view.

The discussion that follows is limited to defined contribution plans, but most of it also applies to defined benefit plans.

## PENSION PLAN ADEQUACY

When reviewing a pension plan, the initial question asked must be: Is the plan's current contribution rate sufficient to yield, at retirement, the salary replacement originally contemplated? The stated pension plan retirement income is normally expressed as a percentage of preretirement salary replacement made possible by a plan participant's pension, with or without considering social security payments. Usually, the example of a level single-life annuity with or without a 10-year guarantee is used as the target.[10]

Whether or not prevailing contribution rates were initially determined or revised in terms of specific salary replacement targets, they should be so determined at some point to provide an idea of their relative adequacy. A wealth of empirical information is available that enables administrators to obtain data about prevailing salary replacement rates. Institutions should be able to collect pertinent data from retired participants and from plan administrators, who can provide estimates of replacement ratios based on specific case models. Retired employees are a useful source for testing salary replacement propositions.

The most difficult aspect of the evaluation for defined contribution plans lies in assumptions about investment outcomes. Given a specified salary replacement target, which combinations of assumed compound interest (or total return), plus plan contributions reflecting salary increases, will most likely achieve it over the stipulated career years? There may be more than one answer. A single interest rate assumption may be sufficient, but what specific rate should be chosen? At a guaranteed 3 percent investment return upon retirement, as is the case in many fixed-income annuities, targeted salary replacement would imply the need for significantly higher future retirement capital accumulations than are prevalent at existing contribution rates. Prevailing accumulations and 3 percent returns would produce annuities of less than one-half those realized between 1970 and 1991. The interest rate assumption would ideally be derived from a weighted average of assumed long-range returns for each investment choice. But because the contribution allocation among diverse investments cannot be known, this procedure may be too complex and too uncertain. By using plausible sets of average annual return assumptions and factoring these into contribution and length-of-service models, reasonable projections of long-term capital accumulations can be developed; these are the basis on which the salary recovery potential can be estimated. Regardless of how it is done, a reasonable long-range average interest rate or a rate of total return assumption must be made.

The normal mid-range average contribution rates in higher education defined contribution plans lie somewhere between 10 and 15 percent, not counting social security. Figure 13-1 presents examples of replacement ratios excluding social security, clearly demonstrating the difference contribution rates make.

If social security benefits are added, salary recovery on lower incomes would be greater. This is also true in integrated plans. Over the benchmark 30- to 35-year career target, average 10 percent contribu-

---

FIGURE 13-1
Salary Replacement Rates

| Entry Age | Yrs. Svc. | 10 Percent Level Plan Repl. Ratio | 14 Percent Level Plan Repl. Ratio |
|-----------|-----------|-----------------------------------|-----------------------------------|
| 25 | 40 | 60.6 percent | 84.8 percent |
| 30 | 35 | 50.3 | 70.4 |
| 35 | 30 | 41.0 | 57.4 |
| 40 | 25 | 32.5 | 45.4 |

Based on the following assumptions: Salaries increase 6 percent per year; average investment return is 8 percent; and benefit payout is at an 8 percent investment return, taking into account 1983 actuarial data, for a single life annuity, 10 years guaranteed. The annual rate of salary increase also affects the replacement ratio. Rapid escalation of salaries near retirement may reduce the replacement ratio, other things being equal.

Source: *Benefits Alert*, April 8, 1991: 3-4.

---

tion plans may not be adequate if institutions wish to push level benefit salary recovery beyond the guidelines espoused by the AAUP-AAC "Statement of Principles on Academic Retirement and Insurance Plans." On the other hand, the same 10 percent plan invested solely in equities, achieving above-market-average total rates of return (exceeding the 8 percent return of the illustration), will result in much higher recovery. Long-term contributions invested in a balanced equity portfolio have the potential of earning much better than an 8 percent annual total return.[11] A 10 percent contribution rate, combined with monthly dollar-cost averaging when contributions purchase units in an equity portfolio with fluctuating prices, is an excellent retirement capital accumulation vehicle. For defined contribution plan participants who balance their allocations among multiple investment choices or concentrate the total contribution into fixed-income investments, thus reducing both risk and potential total return, contribution rates in excess of 10 percent may be needed to achieve higher salary replacement.

It is essential that administrators not make interest or investment return assumptions on the basis of current events. Salary increases, investment returns, or interest rates do not move forward at constant rates. If, because of inflation, salaries begin to increase rapidly toward the end of one's career, the intended salary recovery may not come about; in contrast, high total returns and interest rates such as those experienced during the 1980s might be interpreted as requiring smaller contribution rates. Neither situation may be sustained in the long run.

## INVESTMENT PERFORMANCE

When colleges and universities transfer their pension plan management responsibilities to third parties, they hire investment management expertise. Many of the same selection and investment performance evaluation principles that guide choices of endowment fund investment managers should apply in the selection of the pension "fund" investment manager(s). (For a full discussion of this subject, see Chapter 10, Endowment Management.) In general, the pension fund's investment manager should have a track record of solid effective performance extending over several market cycles.

Pension plan administrators and third-party carriers must act in the best interests of plan participants and beneficiaries. ERISA stipulates "prudent expert" investment behavior for fiduciaries in the management of pension funds. But with the rapid increase in participant-directed investment decisions, it is not always easy to say who the investment "manager" actually is: Is it the company whose mutual funds one is purchasing or is it the participant who directs his or her monies into specific investments?

Historically, pension plan capital has been invested to preserve principal in anticipation of a fixed annual return. With the realization that inflation reduces the purchasing power of a capital asset as well as of the income that it is expected to produce, CREF's variable annuity concept was introduced, proving that a balanced equity fund can be a superior long-range pension plan vehicle. Competing variable annuity investment products followed, and today plan participants, where colleges and universities make them available, have a surfeit of investment choices.

Colleges and universities take the initiative when defining investment policies of their endowments. In pension fund administration, institutions and participants judge others' investment policies and track records. When TIAA-CREF predominated, an institution chose a plan provider and left the issue of investment performance for participants to ponder. In the new environment of multiple investment choices, external providers, and investment products, institutions have an increased responsibility for evaluating their provider's investment know-how and track record. This responsibility exists not only when selecting providers but also when evaluating how the provider manages the accumulating contributions. DOL regulations absolve institutions of certain liabilities, but institutional responsibility under ERISA has always been to act in the best interests of its employees, who put considerable trust in management's ability to make a sound choice. Employees are seldom in a position to conduct continuing expert oversight and need the institution's support and professional credibility in evaluating investment policies and performance.

Regulations proposed by the DOL in 1991 provide limited fiduciary relief to participant-directed plans. Under ERISA, an employer is not responsible for a retirement plan participant's investment allocation decision if the plan provides at least three diversified funds that enable the participant to effectively alter his or her potential return and investment risk and allow participant elections at least once every three months. The plan administrator must also disclose information on the investment options to participants. However, a plan administrator is liable for loss if the plan's selection of an investment option is imprudent.

An investment manager's performance should never be judged on the basis of short-term quarterly returns only. It is customary, unless grievous errors are committed, to observe investment performance over at least a two- to four-year period, preferably over a full market cycle. An excellent time for judging performance is during a period of protracted decline in market values. Nevertheless, institutions should consider making available to participants periodic, perhaps quarterly, reports of the ongoing performance of each officially authorized investment. The content of such a report can be quite simple and limited to a listing of the various net asset values and total returns. A long-range performance history should be developed that shows performance in one, three, five, ten, and more yearly intervals. It is also important that, in addition, such reports track the performance of compatible broad market indexes for comparable investments. Again, if a college or university already has a professionally sound reporting scheme for its endowment investments, it should be able to adapt the same to its pension fund investment alternatives.

## IS THE PENSION SAFE?

Insurance companies, mutual funds, and other companies that manage pension fund investments receive ratings by such entities as Standard & Poor's and Moody's. They are also audited under various federal and state laws. Does a high rating make the money safe? To a degree, it does. But there remains a need for oversight through an independent governing board, the periodic independent assessment of investment and payout performance, and vigilance on the part of the contracting college or university in cooperation with its plan participants.

Such oversight does not mean significant expense, because much of the information necessary for evaluation is readily available in public records and literature covering the financial markets. Colleges and universities have research and analytical talents on their governing boards, on financial staffs, and among their faculty. On some occasions, it may be useful to hire expert advice, which comes at a relatively small cost when compared to the vast sums of money at stake.

## THE PENSION PLAN PROVIDER

Not every company that manages pension funds is prepared to give institutions and participants the assistance they need. Plan providers' back-office support is important to colleges and universities because they themselves are hard-pressed to keep costs down. Such support increases costs to companies that need to make a profit; the investment return is reduced by whatever costs are charged to the plan. Colleges and universities should expect full service, but they also have an interest in cost containment by their plan administrators. They should deal with providers who have the capability for on-line transmission of transaction data, compliance reporting, and touch-tone telephonic transaction service.

Support from the plan provider in compliance matters is also crucial. New companies may not always have staff who understand and respond to the needs of educational institutions. Providers should train their personnel in the special needs of higher education institutions. Changes in laws and regulations affect all colleges and universities. There are many competing insurance companies and mutual funds that are competent in such matters and have extensive experience dealing with individual policyholders and pension plan participants. For institutions that contemplate expanding their roster of plan managers and investment choices, there is a surfeit of capable competition. But there are also providers with limited expertise and poor investment performance records. The issue is how to choose the best.

## EMPLOYEE PARTICIPATION

Institutions differ in their governance structures, especially in the extent of employee involvement in major areas of managerial policy. At many institutions, faculty and other employees have a considerable voice in the evolution of pension plans and retirement policy. Colleges and universities that have introduced options beyond the traditional TIAA-CREF choices report significant employee participation before making the final decision. Consultation with employees and plan participants is useful, if not essential, when an existing plan is being evaluated and when policies are established that affect the future financial security of employees. Policy matters that can be adapted to participants' needs without additional cost to the institution should be given a high priority.

***The participants' point of view.*** There is no single participant point of view vis-à-vis pension plans. Each employee sees benefits in light of his or her individual circumstances. Nevertheless, there is much common ground. Colleges and universities can provide a pension plan environment that restricts or enhances participants' freedom of choice and the plan's scope of flexibility without any direct effects on institutional costs.

***The participants' decisions.*** The introduction of CREF in 1952, making participants a party to the investment policy- and decision-making process, required that an investment choice between fixed and variable annuities be made—a choice between two entirely different types of investments. For many it proved to be a vexing choice, for others a welcome opportunity. Today, the potential for more investment choices is greater, and employers must decide how many and which specific choices to offer and how many outside managers a plan should use. A key consideration is the degree of risk that should be allowed or introduced.

How institutions enhance plan flexibility depends to a large extent on the quality and knowledge of the employer and the employee leadership. Some employee groups are better informed than others; the same is true for employers. Participants are asked to make decisions on their own behalf akin to those made by governing boards when formulating an asset allocation policy for endowments. Although the sums involved may be larger in the endowment decision, asset allocation decisions are difficult to make regardless of who makes them. It is a decision that employees should not be asked to make entirely alone.

Institutions have a responsibility to assist employees by making them fully aware of potential opportunities and pitfalls and to help employees learn how to make the appropriate decisions. Colleges and universities need to remain sensitive to the special difficulties some participants will face when it comes to allocating contributions among different investment vehicles. A special effort may have to be made to teach them how investment allocation decisions are made.

***The accumulation phase.*** During the accumulation phase, a plan's major objective is the long-term maximization of the accumulation of capital. This fundamental concept must be conveyed to participants, who must be made aware of the trade-offs between long-term investments in fixed-income funds compared to funds with asset and income growth. The accumulation phase, especially for younger participants, is probably not the right moment for stressing an investment policy geared toward the stability of retirement income. It is the right moment to aim for capital appreciation. The new environment of increased flexibility and enhanced investment choices responds positively to participants' needs.

Not every investment vehicle on the market, however, is suitable for pension plan investment, and too many choices may lead to confusion among those who are less expert in allocating their contributions. Institutions and participants must resolve the question of what constitutes the most appropriate mix of acceptable risk. There also is the issue of critical mass: How many employees must participate in an investment option to make it cost-effective? Suppliers differ in how they answer this question. Empirical evidence suggests that 25 percent of eligible employees may add alternative investments when they are first offered and that 50 percent or more may do so subsequently.[12] Widening the field of choice is in the long-term interest of pension plan participants.

**The payout phase.** In the payout phase, the policy issue centers on how to provide individual participants with a reliable annual income stream appropriate to their particular financial circumstances. Again, the investment decision revolves around the question of appropriate asset allocation.

In principle, annuities are a form of "total return" payout, whereby in each payout period a slice of current income and historical capital accumulation is distributed to the participant. Therefore it should not matter if the accumulation grows because of a high interest yield or as a result of superior capital appreciation. Indeed, in annuity funds that are valued at current market prices, the payout does reflect total investment return plus whatever factor is associated with life expectancy. In fixed-income funds that are not market priced, the payout fluctuates with the cost yield of the investment portfolio, adjusted for life expectancy. Fundamentally, all annuities are variable, but some are more so than others. These variances force the participant in a multi-investment pension plan to create an asset allocation policy that stresses the investments' future income streams, a policy that will probably be different for many (but not for all) participants from the one best suited to the accumulation phase. Once again, less well-informed participants may need considerable assistance as they try to make the right allocation decision.

Thus annuities alone may not be the most appropriate payout vehicle for every participant. Some employees may wish to move their capital accumulation when they leave higher education for other employment; others may not be satisfied with the available investment options before or at retirement. Among the more sophisticated participants, the lack of adequate combined payout and investment flexibility during retirement may lead to transfers from one plan provider to another. Even those who prefer annuities may seek more flexible arrangements elsewhere than the ones being offered by the institution's current plan.

THE CONCEPT OF MINIMUM DISTRIBUTION. The Tax Reform Act of 1986 introduced the "minimum distribution" requirement for most tax-deferred arrangements (TDA), including 403(b) plans, and, in so doing, introduced an important new payout option that competes with annuities and lump-sum distributions. Exceptions exist for government and church employees and all others who reached age 70 1/2 by January 1, 1988. Furthermore, minimum distribution must not begin before age 75 for contributions and earnings accumulated before January 1, 1987. In general, for contributions and earnings received on or after January 1, 1987, minimum distributions must begin no later than the April 1 following age 70 1/2. Minimum distributions have the singular advantage of initially preserving much of the tax-deferred retirement capital accumulation. While a minimum distribution requirement or a mandated starting date imposed by law compels a payout even though a plan participant may be able to postpone significant withdrawals indefinitely, the minimum distribution offers an important flexibility some retired employees may wish to explore.

Some pension plan providers believe that retirement income should always lead to an annuity type of payout. The minimum distribution requirement modifies the lifetime annuity concept and introduces an alternate retirement capital distribution system over an expected lifetime, called the minimum distribution option (MDO). The MDO provides a benchmark for discussing the range of available payout options.

LUMP-SUM DISTRIBUTION (LSD) AND ROLLOVERS. Lump-sum distributions from pension plans in the business sector of the economy are frequent and often sizable. In 1988, 8.5 million workers reported receiving in excess of $48 billion in LSDs from previous employers. In higher education, LSDs are a relatively new phenomenon.

Within the pension plan context—that is, the long-term preservation of accumulated (or accumulating) retirement capital—LSDs imply rollover of the distribution within the law to other TDAs. A 403(b) LSD can be rolled over into another vendor's 403(b) plan, or it can be rolled over into an individual retirement account (IRA). If they are not rolled over within 60 days of payout, LSDs are taxable as ordinary income and a 10 percent tax penalty applies for participants less than 59 1/2 years old. If LSDs are rolled over, the capital is preserved and earnings continue to accumulate tax-free. Congress has considered bills advocating compulsory transfers of LSDs to defined contribution plans or IRAs and raising the tax penalty for early IRA withdrawals. Thus, there is evidence that many legislators believe that retirement capital should be kept intact as employees change jobs and transfer funds from one plan to another.

Plan participants need the flexibility inherent in LSDs that are intended to be rolled over into other TDAs, and institutions that are in the process of reviewing their plans need to decide whether or not and on what terms to provide this flexibility.

***Portability, accessibility, and preservation of pension benefits.*** When employees change jobs, the question of what happens to pension benefits arises. A pension benefit is portable when employees can carry the value of accrued benefits from one employer to another. The plan provider or sponsoring employer must make the decision concerning the plan's degree of portability. To make sure that optimum retirement income becomes available, it is essential not merely to carry past accrued benefits from job to job but also to continue contributions and appropriate investment policies until retirement.

The Employee Benefit Research Institute (EBRI) conducted a study on the question of how much larger retirement benefits would be if employees were able (or willing) to keep their accrued retirement benefits intact. EBRI estimates that retirement income would have nearly doubled even under conservative investment assumptions.

In higher education, the extent of portability varies between types of plans. Because the benefit formulas favor the latest (or highest salary) years of employment, defined benefit plans tend to discourage employment mobility once vesting has occurred, especially during the last decade of employment prior to retirement. Potential mobility is greater if a participant does not leave a defined benefit "system." In higher education, portability is greater in defined contribution plans, even though contribution rates may differ as an employee moves around.

Accessibility is another matter. A principal disadvantage of defined benefit plans is that a participant does not have access to the accumulated retirement plan capital. Such access is possible under defined contribution plans, provided the employer has incorporated appropriate provisions into the plan documents. Plan providers that invest in long-term securities may limit access to full lump sums either by providing gradual access to a fund over a certain time period or by reducing the lump-sum payment by "cash surrender charges." These charges usually cease for holdings that exceed a stipulated number of years. For example, while TIAA has changed its policy to grant gradual access over 10 years, access by the participant remains limited. In a report on mandatory retirement, the National Research Council Committee on Mandatory Retirement in Higher Education suggested that "in the context of ensuring an adequate pension income over time, allowing faculty to withdraw pension funds at or before retirement is less desirable."[13] If institutions, as employers, are interested in ensuring that their retirees benefit from sustained retirement income, they may wish to limit accessibility to accumulated capital to prevent employees from losing or squandering their most important asset.

On the other hand, as financial circumstances and participants' needs change, retirees may prefer more payout flexibility (more accessibility to capital) than some plan providers offer. Many 403(b) plan providers are supplementing their accessibility options beyond those currently available from TIAA-CREF.

***Inflation and the retired participant.*** High salary recovery at retirement is one thing, but maintaining payout purchasing power over time is quite another. Most colleges and universities have not devised long-term pension inflation protection. The social security component of retirement income and public employee pension plans offers varying degrees of anti-inflation protection. Occasionally, a state system will make an ad hoc or one-time cost-of-living adjustment. In the same vein, independent colleges and universities have sometimes instituted supplements for retired employees when the gap between their annuities and the exploding price level began to cause hardships. Institutions with defined contribution plans have taken the position that balanced equity funds—funds emphasizing asset and income growth—are an appropriate means to counter inflation during the accumulation and the payout phase. Many pension plan providers offer specific retirement income growth portfolios with proven records of long-term dividend increases.

TIAA's graded benefit payment method may answer in part the concerns raised by inflation and may be a response for those preferring more or less assured increases in payout from year to year. A participant choosing this alternative begins with a low initial annuity, followed annually by predetermined increments. By itself, the graded method cannot be considered "inflation protection," but for participants who can afford the lower initial annuity, it may be a partial alternative to the stock market or to an annually fluctuating payout. Participants seldom complain about large rising payouts; they tend to gripe about the sort of double-digit reductions equity-based variable annuities sometimes experience. Even "level benefit plans" such as TIAA experience long-term payout fluctuation. Payout tends to rise and fall with changes in interest rates. There is little solace in the admonition that one should expect such reverses in variable and fixed annuities.

If equity funds or other investment vehicles do not accomplish the desired income objective, colleges and universities may be confronted with the question of what, if anything, to do about it. The issue is complex, because inflation is at work during both the accumulation and the payout phase. Exactly what is the inflation shortfall? Salary increases during the accumulation phase reflect inflation, though not always completely. Salary increases make contributions rise. Thus, over the long term, equity-based investment pools as well as fixed-income funds can incorporate some if not all of the inflation trend during the accumulation phase. Therefore, the total accumulation at retirement embodies some quantifiable inflation adjustment. Institutions could try to compensate for any difference by providing supplementary contributions at or after retirement, provided these meet the legal maximum contribution limits. They could also choose proven investment managers and vehicles with a high probability of matching or surpassing the rate of inflation, as well as specially chosen investment instruments that provide income growth during retirement.[14]

Investment transfer options, tax-sheltered rollovers, and LSDs are of strategic investment importance to retired participants. If a college or university believes that it should not play an aggressive investment policy role, it can provide transfer flexibility to participants as an alternative. Overall, however, colleges and universities may have to deal with inflation more actively in the future than they have in the past.

The issue of the nature and degree of the college or university's involvement in the pension plan investment policy and guidance is a significant concern in higher education. The focus is on the scope of investment alternatives, as well as on the degree of tolerable or permissible investment risks. How colleges and universities assist employees in making complex contribution allocations as well as transfer, rollover, and lump-sum payout decisions may become a more vexing and prominent concern.

## Comparative Plan Evaluation

A matrix or a checklist can be used to facilitate the evaluation of competing pension plan providers. In such a matrix, the horizontal axis would show the names of the providers being considered, their addresses, their telephone numbers, and the key contact persons for specific pension plan concerns. On the vertical axis, key elements on the basis of which the choices are made would be listed. This method can help determine the basic information needed for participants to make investment choices. In this sense, the institution can inform without providing advice. A checklist might include:

- Each investment option
- The investment policy underlying each option and a description of the composition of funds
- A description of each investment's short- and long-term performance history, in comparison with major indices
- A comparative standing of the investment options and policies
- The most suitable options for accumulation
- A list of transaction costs such as charges for writing checks, management fees, maintenance fees, severance fees

- A description of the specific payout arrangements that can be made: annuity, income only, regular or irregular monthly payments
- If money is transferable to other companies, and minimum amount, maximum amount, and any pertinent charges
- If money is transferable within the company
- If touch-tone telephone switching capability exists
- When payout can start and any penalties that may be assessed
- What happens when the participant leaves the institution for reasons other than retirement
- How contributions are made
- The company's reporting practices (monthly, quarterly) for the participants and the institution
- Specific compliance assistance support, including sources and names of supporting documentation
- Names of other institutions using company's services; references of officers who can be contacted
- Ratings by companies such as Dun and Bradstreet, Moody's, and Standard & Poor's
- The company asset base and other vital financial statistics

Other information that might help for comparative purposes includes:

- Company organization—investment staff, sales staff, administrative staff; if the institution works with specific individuals, if staff will make on-site visits
- Articles and news clippings describing the company's philosophy and performance, including critical analyses, if any, in major journals or newspapers
- Age and service record of individuals in charge of funds; personnel turnover; educational and professional background of key officers of the company

## Pre- and Postretirement Support

Once an institution has a pension plan, it must maintain communication with employees. If participation is voluntary, some institutions feel that they must encourage employees to participate in the plan. If it is not, the institution may have to explain why being part of a pension plan is necessary. As pension plans become more difficult to understand, especially in their legal, investment, and payout complexities, employees increasingly need support in making their decisions.

The primary responsibility for pre- and postretirement planning lies with the employee, but institutions may assist employees in planning for retirement and provide postretirement information and advice. In higher education, the responsibility for employee relations concerning benefits and pension plans tends to be shared between the human resources office and the business office. Academic deans are sometimes responsible for certain types of communications regarding the faculty. Larger institutions may hire "benefits officers"; some institutions have pension plan specialists.

The institution can play a dual role in employees' decisions: it can inform and it can advise. It is important to define clearly both the responsibilities of specific individuals within the administration and the nature of the many different kinds of information and advice they are authorized to provide.

Sometimes information and advice are difficult to separate. For instance, when an administrator informs an employee of the requirements that must be met before participating in a pension plan, the employee is in fact advised to abide by these requirements. But when the employee must make a contribution allocation decision or must choose among payout alternatives, the administrator should limit his or her role to providing relevant background information, leaving the actual choice to the employee. The administrator may inadvertently influence the choice by suggesting a specific contribution or payout alternative.

Many institutions do not want their administrators to give advice that might lead to future litigation. Specific recommendations concerning pension plan contributions and payout alternatives could lead to litigation and financial liability exposure. It is essential that institutions clearly identify the nature of "prohibited" types of advice.

Retirement program planning is ideally a joint employer-employee responsibility. Where employees are unionized or strong employee committees exist, pension plan and retirement planning issues may be a permanent agenda item. In institutions where administrative leadership is taken for granted or expected, the very existence or absence of retirement program activities will define the institution's attitude on the subject.

Institutions are of course free to abstain from or engage in any counseling activity of their choice. By and large, most colleges and universities appear to see their role limited to communicating information and facilitating decisions.

## COMMUNICATION

*Disseminating information about the plan.* The employer is responsible for disseminating information about the pension plan. This may seem obvious, but in practice the information provided by institutions varies with respect to depth, clarity, and sophistication. A partial list of the information institutions provide above and beyond the literature issued by pension plan companies follows.

- The summary plan description, required by law

- Annual (required) or other periodic reports about benefit status

- Periodic comparative investment reports, especially in multiprovider and multiproduct situations (These plans include documentation of the products offered by each supplier, costs of participating, transfer privileges, withdrawal rights, portability, frequency of reports, and other pertinent information.)

- Special supplementary documents, which may explain the employee's rights and responsibilities under existing laws and describe the limits of tax-sheltering, the procedures for salary-reduction decisions, and how to approach payout decisions

- Documents describing the pension plan's historic investment performance and employee participation rates

- Periodic (quarterly) reports of each manager's investment performance if the institution has multiple suppliers (Often, this comparative information includes data on key market indices, the relative performance of other similar funds, and any necessary explanations so that lay readers may understand what is being presented.)

- Documents describing procedures (if any) for instituting changes in the pension plan
- Periodic newsletters describing institutional activities concerning pension plans, retirement benefits, and other personnel matters

Some colleges and universities may limit written communications to a descriptive benefits document report, while others may provide extensive and frequent materials. In all institutions, there probably is much oral communication between employees and specific administrators concerning details of the pension plan. Many institutions are concerned about the time-consuming aspects of individual counseling. Smaller colleges in particular may need to rely on cooperative efforts among similar institutions.[15] Publications and workshops provide administrators with relatively inexpensive expert how-to information.

## LEADERSHIP AND FACILITATION

If colleges and universities have been reluctant (for liability exposure reasons) to engage in direct retirement planning and advising, they are increasingly interested in seeing employees organize their own pre- and postretirement planning and counseling activities. Faculties and other employees who are highly organized may carry out such activities under union and AAUP sponsorship; pension plans and retirement planning concerns are often matters that appear during collective bargaining.

Institutions have encouraged many voluntary arrangements whereby employees gather to study, discuss, and instruct one another concerning retirement matters. Institutions can facilitate the process by providing a place for groups to meet and bringing experts before the groups. Periodic meetings with representatives from the institution's retirement plan administrators should be encouraged. If necessary, the administrator should take the initiative in arranging meetings. Many employee groups enjoy having spouses, other family members, or retired friends as part of such voluntary retirement planning efforts. Employee interests concerning retirement go beyond strictly financial matters. Institutions might consider the following types of program content:

- Personal financial planning, including budgeting and elementary finance principles

- Estate planning and tax liability

- Health planning (nutrition, exercise, medical checkups)

- Postretirement housing (how to finance, where)

- Second career or part-time employment options

- Future lifestyle (work versus leisure time, travel, continuing education, volunteer service)

Recurring themes heard on campuses are "I never get around to doing much about planning for retirement," "Take-home pay is already so small, saving money is impossible," "The literature that is distributed by institutions and plan managers is too complicated to understand," and "There is a long time before retirement, so why hurry?" The litany is endless. However, employees who attend meetings regularly and stay informed profit from the knowledge they gain. Administrators should not discontinue their efforts in the face of adverse publicity or apathy but should redouble their efforts to improve communications.

Employees should begin planning for retirement at a young age, preferably no later than at age 30. In practice, however, active interest in expanded retirement planning begins between five and 10 years prior to the time an employee plans on retiring. Institutions should focus their efforts at employees aged 45-50 but include everyone else. Once an institution decides to facilitate retirement planning and counseling, for instance, through the use of regular workshops for faculty or staff, it should seek the best professional in-house or external help to create the appropriate atmosphere, maximum voluntary attendance, and an ongoing program attuned to participant needs.

## RESPONSIBILITIES OF RETIREMENT PLAN PROVIDERS

Retirement plan providers have certain responsibilities as fiduciaries and as parties to contracts under ERISA and IRC requirements. The quality and scope of service available to institutions vary among providers. Institutions should consider the following.

***The nature of the products that are available.*** Many providers offer similar investment vehicles, the investment performance of which, however, may differ. Providers also differ in the degree of flexibility they provide in fund transfers and payout and the costs of such services. Some providers charge for providing benefit illustrations tailored to a specific contract or for providing alternatives. An important first step in evaluating a plan provider is to see how the specific services offered differ from those of other qualified firms and what they cost. Many insurance companies and mutual funds have changed their product mix for higher education considerably over the years.

*Enrollment support.* The support of the provider during the enrollment of participants and the timeliness and the accuracy of participant and institutional records are important considerations. Among the enrollment-related services are workshops, meetings with key employee groups and administrators, new employee orientation, employee reaction to the quality of information provided, and surveys to assess how well employees are understanding the information provided and the effectiveness of counseling.

*Maintenance services.* Once a plan has been adopted and participants are enrolled, it is important to distinguish among the different maintenance services provided. Record keeping is a first requirement. Institutions expect providers to assist with filing IRS Form 5500 and other required documents, such as the summary annual report. Many providers offer plan administration manuals, but these should be customized for each institution. Institutions with TIAA-CREF plans have become accustomed to extensive service support, and they will expect no less from new providers. Higher education's principal defined contribution plan provider has set a standard against which others can be measured.

*Communication with employers and employees.* Communications cover a wide spectrum of activities, from marketing to performance reporting. Providers differ in the quality and detail of written communications. Many providers offer toll-free telephone service to both administrators and plan participants. Free hot lines for retiring personnel may be available. Providing a name to contact may be an early order of business.

Administrators should not prefer one provider over others simply because it supports the more mundane administrative functions surrounding retirement plans. In the final analysis, the investment performance and the degree of plan flexibility offered are the factors that matter. In the recent past, many college and university administrators charged with the supervision of the retirement plan did not address the investment performance question with sufficient vigor and regularity. In some institutions there is apathy or complacency among participants, who believe that, as long as investment performance follows the major market indicators, there is nothing to worry about. There is both ignorance among participants and an opportunity for leadership by administrators on the subject of transfer and payout flexibility—especially concerning the potential need to create or protect an inheritable estate. Although lack of knowledge can be understood and excused as far as employees are concerned, it is not forgivable in retirement plan administrators.

## Legal Considerations

Legal matters constitute a major aspect of pension plan administration. The most prominent laws affecting pension plans are the Equal Pay Act (1963), Title VII of the Civil Rights Act (1964), ADEA (1967), and ERISA (1974), including all of their subsequent amendments; the IRC also affects pension plans.

The legal environment in the 1990s is dramatically different from that in which most college and university pension plans were first introduced, and the legal and regulatory requirements are considerably more complex. The legal requirements affect retirement plan participants as contributing employees and as retirees collecting their retirement income.

All private pension plans are subject to all of the laws listed above, but ERISA does not affect public pension plans. For defined benefit plans at public institutions, some specific provisions have been enacted to facilitate the transition to compliance with the latest amendments; in other instances, sections of laws are directed to unique public pension plan characteristics.

The significant legal constraints on retirement plan administration fall under the following categories:

* ERISA

* IRC requirements

    * Defined contribution plans

- Tax-deferred annuities

- Profit sharing

• Nondiscrimination requirements

ERISA

In 1962, President John F. Kennedy appointed a Committee on Corporate Pension Funds and Other Retirement and Welfare Programs. In 1965, the committee published a report recommending that private pension plans should continue to play a major role in providing retirement security to American workers. The report suggested numerous changes in how private pension plans should be regulated.

ERISA was Congress's response to the committee's report. Jurisdiction for enforcing the new law was assigned to both the DOL and the Treasury Department, a jurisdictional arrangement that caused numerous problems that were addressed in Reorganization Plan Number 4, in 1979.

### Title I: "Protection of Employee Benefit Rights."

REPORTING AND DISCLOSURE. Title I of ERISA is devoted to the protection of employee benefit rights. It stipulates that employees must be provided with "Summary Plan Descriptions" (SPD) and that participants and beneficiaries must receive benefit statements that are accurate, easily understood by an average person, and written in "plain English." Each participant must have access to financial information about a plan by means of a summary annual report, which can be derived from IRS Form 5500, which is filed annually. Participants are entitled to other documents, including an annual report of accrued and vested benefits. Plan modifications must be reported by filing amendments, and when private defined benefit plans are to be canceled, the Pension Benefit Guaranty Corporation (PBGC) must be notified. Public pension plans are exempt from the requirements of ERISA.

FIDUCIARY REQUIREMENTS. Under ERISA, plan sponsors must act in the sole interest of plan participants and beneficiaries. They must adhere to the "prudent person" or "prudent expert" rule and attempt to minimize large losses. The fiduciary requirements extend to plan administration activities, including selecting the plan administrator(s) and the investment manager(s) and formulating investment policy. The fiduciary standard is enforced by both the IRS and the DOL.

Fiduciaries who violate ERISA standards may become personally liable for losses, and they may have to return personal profits resulting from actions deemed to be in violation of the standards. Violations may result in criminal or civil actions and can lead to revocation of the plan's tax-deferred status. The DOL may sue violators on behalf of participants. The fiduciary standard prohibits conflicts of interest and identifies and defines the prohibited transactions, not all of them germane to non-profit higher education. It also prohibits discriminatory action by plan administrators against persons pursuing their legal rights and employees who are seeking DOL assistance or who may sue in federal court.

Department of Labor regulations relax this fiduciary standard for defined contribution plans with participant-directed investments. While the regulations focus on Section 404(c) plans, tax-sheltered 403(b) plans subject to ERISA allowing participant-directed investments may elect this exemption. The regulations insulate the fiduciary from liability for losses that result from investment control exercised by a participant or a beneficiary. The regulations provide a number of safeguards for fiduciaries and applicable definitions that circumscribe fiduciaries' liability. For participant investment control to exist, independent investment decisions must materially affect return and risk and must be based on at least three diverse investment options, each displaying different and distinct risk and return characteristics. Furthermore, these options must be such that the risk for large losses is minimized. The regulations also stipulate that investment elections must be permitted at least once in any three-month period. Under certain circumstances fewer opportunities for participant investment decisions may be offered, but the minimum "three investment options" rule must be met before a fiduciary's liability can be relaxed. Allowing participant-directed investments is an opportunity and not a requirement.

ASSIGNMENT OF BENEFITS. Title I prohibits benefit assignment but stipulates certain exceptions (e.g., use of benefits as collateral, payments pursuant to qualified domestic relations orders).

***Title II: "Minimum Standards and Qualified Plan Rules."*** ERISA does not require employers to establish pension plans. Once they do, however, the law stipulates certain minimum standards. Institutions may incorporate more liberal rules unless specifically prohibited. Among the many issues, the following are of special interest.

PLAN PARTICIPATION. Eligibility must begin by age 21 and cannot be postponed by more than one year or beyond 1,000 hours of employment. The exceptions to this are special teaching institutions and fully vested plans; for special teaching institutions, eligibility must begin by age 26 after one year of service; for fully vested plans, by age 21 after two years of service.

VESTING REQUIREMENTS. For employee contributions, the right is immediate; for employer contributions, ERISA stipulates two alternative minimum vesting requirements:

- Full vesting after five years (without any vesting prior to the five-year period), also known as "cliff" vesting

- Three-year zero vesting, followed by 20 percent graduated annual vesting for four more years, with full vesting in the eighth year

The Retirement Equity Act sets forth rules concerning vesting effects when an employee stops employment and returns to service at a later time.

BENEFITS. Institutions may provide more liberal benefits than stipulated in ERISA, but they must at least offer:

- A qualified joint and survivor annuity for participants who have been married for at least one year; the benefit is at least one-half of the employee's benefit but the joint and survivor annuity is normally lower than a single life annuity

- A waiver of a joint and survivor annuity, which must be approved with the consent of a spouse or beneficiary, and must be written in front of a plan administrator or notarized

- Most plans must have a preretirement survivor benefit that adheres to specified guidelines for vested participants married a year or more

DEFINED BENEFIT ACCRUAL. ERISA requires one of three possible accrual methods. Accrual does not need to be even or constant over time, but it normally extends over the participant's total plan participation. The law does not mandate specific benefit levels but deals with the rate of accrual. Benefits cannot be reduced or canceled because of age; employees who work beyond normal retirement and participate in a plan will continue to accrue benefits.

FUNDING REQUIREMENTS. Plan assets must be invested separately from other employer assets, for example, in the form of trust agreements, in an insurance company in an allocated or unallocated account, or through individual policies. Combinations of these approaches may be used. ERISA establishes minimum funding requirements for private defined benefit plans, money purchase, and TBPs. Institutions should familiarize themselves with the specific guidelines. The maximum funding cap is 150 percent of termination liability. The description of the limits is complex; managers should refer to the IRC and other applicable regulations for clarification.

CONTRIBUTION LIMITS. Contribution limits differ depending upon the type of plan. For instance, Section 403(b) defined contribution plans compel a smaller tax-sheltered limit than 401(a) plans. At enactment, a general $30,000 cap (eventually indexed) was established on total contributions; covered compensation was also limited at $200,000 (indexed). Salary reductions (403(b)) were limited to $9,500 (indexed in the future) but could be increased for long-term employees if certain conditions are met. There are penalties for excess contributions.

***Title IV: "Plan Termination Insurance."*** Title IV established the Pension Benefit Guaranty Corporation (PBGC) to serve as an insurer of private defined benefit plan payments under certain circumstances. Plans that provide a monthly retirement benefit must pay premiums to the PBGC.

Institutions planning to establish new defined benefit plans should study this title carefully. It contains numerous restrictions and conditions and may entail a contingent employer liability upon plan termination.

## IRC REGULATIONS FOR PENSION FUNDS

IRC regulations limit total plan contributions and the amounts of compensation that can be legally tax-sheltered. Limitations are specific to a particular type of plan. Section 403(b) plans and Section 401(a) plans differ in certain respects; a somewhat larger tax sheltering is permitted when 401(a) plans are combined with 403(b) plans. Institutions need to study the rules that apply to their particular plan and determine whether moving to a different plan jurisdiction (i.e., from

403(b) to 401(a)) might be advantageous in spite of potentially higher administrative costs.

When evaluating IRC regulations, institutions should consider the following questions:

- Are salary reduction contracts meeting the regulations' requirements?

- Have the maximum excludable amounts been audited under the applicable sections of the IRC?

- Are plan contributions within the Tax Reform Act of 1986 limits, or new limits imposed by subsequent legislation?

- Are participating employees fully aware of the tax consequences of early withdrawals and restrictions on hardship withdrawals?

- Does the institution have a published loan policy within the limits of the law?

Because there are other TDAs (e.g., IRAs, rollover IRAs, 401(k) profit-sharing accounts), institutions should be aware of the legal requirements and limitations. This advice is especially pertinent for institutions that permit cashout, which may lead to permitted TDAs. For public institutions, Section 457 plans (nonqualified unfunded deferred compensation arrangements) may be of interest. The Tax Reform Act of 1986 extends such plans to the private nonprofit sector. Several tax provisions are unique to this section. A key limitation is that rollovers to an IRA are prohibited; in addition, there are no tax penalties at withdrawal. Contribution limits on 457 plans are combined with contributions to 403(b). The Tax Reform Act of 1986 also extended Section 457 to cover the deferred compensation plans of private nonprofit employees. There are also legal requirements for integrating plans with social security.

## NONDISCRIMINATION REQUIREMENTS

All pension plans are covered under the nondiscrimination rules. Nondiscrimination provisions will not be enforced for public institutions' pension plans until 1993. The general nondiscrimination standard can be summarized as follows: pension plan contributions or benefits must not favor highly compensated employees (HCE) over other employees. In general, HCEs should not benefit from contribution or benefit rates that exceed those of non-HCEs covered under the plan.

HCEs are defined as:

- Five percent owners of an institution

- Employees who earn more than $75,000 per year

- The top 20 percent of employees who earn more than $50,000 per year

- Institutional officers who earn more than $45,000 per year (indexed since enactment)

The following employees are excluded from nondiscrimination provisions:

- Students in 403(b) plans not subject to the FICA tax

- Part-time employees in 403(b) plans working less than 20 hours per week

- Employees covered by collective bargaining agreements

- Employees with nonresident alien ststus but no U.S. employment (they are employed by a foreign company)

- Employees who fail to meet minimum age or employment requirements, provided the requirements are not waived for any employee

The law and subsequent regulations provide for "safe harbor" and "unsafe harbor" tests, and other testing options. The minimum participation test that determines if enough employees are covered requires plans to cover 50 employees or 40 percent of eligible employees. The minimum coverage tests evaluate the adequacy of non-HCE coverage. A plan must satisfy one of two tests. Under the Ratio-Percentage Test, the percentage of non-HCEs covered by the plan must equal 70 percent of HCEs on the plan. The Average Benefits Test has two parts. The average benefits of non-HCEs must be at least 70 percent of the average HCE benefits, and the classification must be reasonable according to safe/unsafe harbors and the facts. The matching test applies to contributory plans and plans accepting after-tax contributions and ensures that the average contribution percentage for HCEs passes one of three possible numerical tests. Some plans may benefit from restructuring requirements. These tests are intended to ensure that HCEs do not benefit from contribution rates and benefits that exceed those of non-HCEs covered under the same plan. Under these tests, voluntary or noncontributory plans are most vulnerable in institutions where a large percentage of participating employees is highly paid.

The nondiscrimination rules are complex, and institutions must pay special attention to them and to the general nondiscrimination standards of Section 401(a)(4) of the IRC.

## AN APPROPRIATE PLAN

What is an appropriate plan for a college or university under the law? Retirement law focuses generally on all tax-deferred arrangements, from 403(b) plans to individual retirement accounts, with points in between. One of these is the "401(a) plan." Figure 13-2 shows key differences between the 401(a) plan and the 403(b) plan.

In the past, a majority of colleges and universities used 403(b) plans. In the aftermath of the Tax Reform Act of 1986, which imposed nondiscrimination requirements on these plans, more institutions may be interested in qualifying their plans under section 401(a). Although Figure 13-2 does not provide all the relevant detail, it does highlight key differences. The size of total tax-sheltered contributions—especially those made via salary reduction—may be affected if the two plans are combined. The potential for salary reduction is greater for a 401(a) plan when it is combined with a 403(b) plan, as compared to using a 403(b) plan alone. Employers interested in maximizing their employees' total contributions to a retirement plan may wish to study how a 403(b) plan can be supplemented by a 401(a) plan.[16] The ability to average LSDs for federal income tax purposes under 401(a) may be an important consideration for participants. The audits of 401(a) plans are more extensive than those for 403(b) plans and may have higher administrative costs.

FIGURE 13-2
Differences in How the Law Treats 403(b) and 401(a) Plans

| Compliance Items | 403(b) | 401(a) |
|---|---|---|
| ERISA, Form 5500 | No detailed information; no financial audit | Detailed information; financial audit required |
| Vesting | Immediate recommended because of calculation of maximum exclusion allowance | Delayed vesting permitted |
| Minimum distribution | Age 70 1/2 (April 1 following, with grandfathering of pre-1987 accumulation) | Age 70 1/2 (April 1 following) |
| Income averaging (five years) | No | Yes |
| Limits to contributions | One overall limit for employer and employee contributions, including TDAs; separate TDA cap | Separate limit for employer contributions, and employee TDA contributions |
| Nondiscrimination testing | These are all the same in both types of plans | These are all the same in both types of plans |
| Definition of highly compensated employee (HCE) | Statutory and alternative definition of HCE as over $50,000 (indexed) | Statutory only |
| Excludable | 410(b) categories plus non-FICA students and employees working less than 20 hours per week | 410(b) categories |
| Special safe harbor | Notice 89-23 | None |
| Public plans nondiscriminatory after 1993. | Full compliance | Pre-ERISA rules |

# Notes

1. "Formal or officially sanctioned" means that one or more institutional officials and employees have been assigned to these tasks and that employees can expect to receive relevant information, assistance, and/or advice. However, the expression does not define the nature of such counseling.

2. In the words of one institution: "The goal of [the] . . . program is to provide protection, security, opportunity and services to faculty and staff members. The goal of the . . . retirement plan is to provide security for you in the future." (Johns Hopkins University, *Your Retirement Plan* (Baltimore, Md.: Johns Hopkins University, 1990), 1.)

3. American Association of University Professors, "Statement of Principles on Academic Retirement and Insurance Plans," in *Academe* (January/February 1988): 37-38.

4. American Association of University Professors, *Academe*, 37-38.

5. In Illinois, for instance, the Equal Employment Opportunity Commission forbids the use of the term "normal" in connection with retirement plans.

6. A sound economic guideline is that marginal revenues should always equal marginal costs and that the cost substitution effect (one type of cost replaces another) should be neutral or result in smaller total costs. See Hans H. Jenny et al., *Another Challenge: Age 70 Retirement in Higher Education* (New York: TIAA-CREF, 1979), 45-51.

7. For more information on social security benefits, see F. F. Jehle, *The Complete and Easy Guide to Social Security and Medicare: With Sections on Disability and SSI Programs* (Madison, Conn.: Fraser Publishing Company, 1991).

8. Donald S. Grubbs, Jr., *Target Benefit Plans: Pension and Profit-Sharing Plans, Series A, Folio 2* (Philadelphia, Pa.: American Law Institute-American Bar Association, 1980); TIAA-CREF, "Target Benefit Plans," in *Research Dialogues* no. 22 (New York: TIAA-CREF, 1989); U.S. Internal Revenue Service, *IRS Revenue Ruling 76-464*; U.S. Internal Revenue Service, *Reg. SEC. 1.410(a)-4*.

9. The Department of Labor proposed regulations under Section 404(c) of ERISA (*Benefits-Alert*, April 8, 1991: 3-4).

10. Because most participants choose guaranteed payments to a beneficiary for ten or more years, annuity providers and plan illustrations often give ten-year (or more) illustrations of eventual benefits. The American Association of University Professors has recommended a benefit of two-thirds of preretirement salary net of taxes and other mandatory withholdings; some institutions have decided on a "maximum"—for some, this is as much as 100 percent before tax recovery with or without social security.

11. R. G. Ibbotson and R. A. Sinquefield, *Stocks, Bonds, Bills, and Inflation: The Past and the Future* (Charlottesville, Va.: Financial Analysts Research Foundation, 1982), is a classic source on the topic of short- and long-term investment returns.

12. Ibbotson and Sinquefield.

13. P. Brett Hammond, *Ending Mandatory Retirement for Tenured Faculty* (Washington, D.C.: National Academy Press, 1991), 82.

14. TIAA-CREF, "An Increasing Annuity Based on Nominal Interest Rates

and Debt Instruments," *Research Dialogues* (New York: TIAA-CREF, April 1986), describes a response for those who may find the GRA unattractive because of the initial payout reduction. It proposes a "graded benefit" annuity variation and a formula for calculating required contribution levels that begin a payout at retirement similar to the more conventional level benefit method. "At a substantial cost, the original replacement ratio . . . may be regained by users of the graded method . . . by upward adjustments in the contribution rate of a defined contribution plan or of the benefit liability assumptions of a defined benefit plan."

15. In addition to the various professional organizations for college and university managers, there are formal and informal regional networks well-suited to smaller institutions. These networks may meet rarely and conduct much of their business by telephone and fax.

16. By combining a 403(b) with a 401(a) qualified plan, the maximum tax-deferred contribution can often be increased under section 415(e)(5) and IRS regulation 1.415-7(h)(1).

# A Historical Overview: Laws and Other Highlights

Higher education has played a path-breaking role in the history of retirement program development in the United States. The following highlights summarize the essence of an evolution spanning more than a century:

| | |
|---|---|
| 1636 | Plymouth Colony settlers' military retirement program. |
| 1797 | Gallatin Glassworks' profit-sharing plan. |
| 1869 | Mutual Life Assurance Association for New York City Teachers is the first retirement plan for teachers. |
| 1875 | American Express Company's private-employer pension plan. |
| 1892 | Columbia University, New York, establishes first pension plan for independent university teachers. |
| 1893 | Chicago establishes pension plan for public school teachers. |
| 1895 | California creates local teachers' retirement plans. |
| 1896 | New Jersey establishes first state retirement system. |
| 1905 | Andrew Carnegie transfers $10,000,000 to a group of trustees, the revenue to be used to provide pensions for college teachers. The fund is incorporated as The Carnegie Foundation on May 8, 1905. |
| 1906 | The Carnegie Foundation is reincorporated as the Carnegie Foundation for the Advancement of Teaching (CFAT). |
| 1916 | CFAT issues "A Comprehensive Plan of Insurance and Annuities for College Teachers," which proposes a contributory system for college pensions. |
| 1918 | Teachers Insurance and Annuity Association (TIAA) is founded jointly by CFAT and the Carnegie Corporation of New York and operated by CFAT until 1936. TIAA provides a fully vested and portable pension system for non-profit educational institutions. |
| 1935 | U.S. Congress creates the Social Security Act, amended in 1965 to establish Medicare health insurance protection. |
| 1942 | An Internal Revenue Code (IRC) amendment establishes guidelines for the design and operation of pension, profit sharing, and stock bonus plans. |
| 1950 | Social security is extended to most private educational insti- |

tutions on a voluntary basis.

1952   College Retirement Equities Fund (CREF) creates a common stock investment and annuity option for what henceforth is known as the TIAA-CREF retirement system.

1962   Keogh Plans are established by the Self-Employed Individuals Tax Retirement Act of 1962.

1967   Age Discrimination in Employment Act (ADEA).

1974   The Employee Retirement Income Security Act (ERISA) establishes rules concerning vesting and investment practices in private pension plans and creates the Individual Retirement Account (IRA).

1978   Amendments to the Age Discrimination in Employment Act (AADEA) raise the minimum age for mandatory retirement to 70 and require review and amendment of employee benefit plans to meet legal requirements; exempts tenured faculty through June 30, 1994.

1980s   Acceleration of competition between TIAA-CREF and other suppliers of annuity and retirement investment products. Colleges and universities rapidly introduce options other than TIAA-CREF annuity and investment options.

1982   The Tax Equity and Fiscal Responsibility Act (TEFRA) imposes (tax-sheltered or tax-deferred) benefit and contribution limits.

1983   NACUBO forms a committee to study TIAA/CREF.

1984   The Retirement Equity Act of 1984 (REACT). The Deficit Reduction Act (DEFRA) extends freeze of cost-of-living adjustments in social security retirement income through 1988. The Commission on College Retirement is formed to study TIAA/CREF and retirement plan issues.

1985   The Consolidated Budget Reconciliation Act of 1985 (COBRA).

1986   The Tax Reform Act establishes new limits for tax-sheltered or tax-deferred pension plan contributions and extends nondiscrimination requirements to pension plans; ADEA is amended to eliminate mandatory retirement at any age for most workers; exceptions continue for tenured positions in higher education.

1988   CREF introduces Money Market Account; TIAA-CREF

Settlement Agreement with SEC concerning transfer of fund balances.

1989    SEC approves TIAA-CREF Settlement Agreement.

1990    CREF introduces Bond Market and Social Choice Accounts.

1990-91    TIAA/CREF account balances transfer becomes effective (1990 for CREF and 1991 for TIAA over a ten-year period).

This list, while incomplete, conveys how changes in legislation and in the most widely held defined contribution retirement plans (TIAA-CREF) has accelerated. The most significant changes have occurred since ERISA, which created the IRA and opened the door to retirement plans for mutual funds and other investment management entities. The unprecedented pace of change in IRC provisions relating directly and indirectly to pension plans—changes occurring every few years throughout the 1980s—coupled with Internal Revenue Service (IRS) regulations, will continue to have significant repercussions for retirement plan administration.

Sources:

Employee Benefits Research Institute. *Fundamentals of Employee Benefit Programs.* 4th ed. Washington, D.C.: EBRI, 1990.

Mamorsky, Jeffrey D. *Employee Benefits Handbook.* New York: Warren, Gorham & Lamont, 1989.

NULaw Services. *1990 Tax Facts on Life Insurance.* Cincinnati, Ohio: National Underwriter, 1990.

Rosenbloom, Jerry S. *The Handbook of Employee Benefits.* 2nd ed. Homewood, Ill.: Dow-Jones Irwin, 1988.

TIAA-CREF. *Keeping Your Plan in Shape: Nondiscrimination Guidelines for 403(b) Plans.* New York: TIAA-CREF, 1990.

# References and Resources

American Association of University Professors. "Statement of Principles on Academic Retirement and Insurance Plans." *Academe* (January/February 1988): 37-38.

Biggs, John H. "Retirement Objectives in Higher Education." Panel Discussion at National Benefits Conference, Washington, D.C., December 6-7, 1990.

Bodie, Zvi. "Inflation Insurance." *Journal of Risk and Insurance* 57, no. 4 (December 1990).

Commerce Clearing House. *A Fresh Look at Deferring Compensation: The Nonqualified Plan Alternative.* Chicago: Standard Federal Tax Reports, 1988.

Consortium on Financing Higher Education. *Early Retirement Programs For Faculty: A Survey of Thirty-Six Institutions.* Washington, D.C.: Consortium on Financing Higher Education, 1987.

Employee Benefits Research Institute. *Fundamentals of Employee Benefit Programs for Education Employees.* Washington, D.C.: EBRI, 1990.

Ford Foundation Advisory Committee on Endowment Management. *Managing Educational Endowments.* 2nd ed. New York: Ford Foundation, 1972.

Gray, K. *Retirement Plans and Expectations of TIAA-CREF Policyholders.* New York: TIAA-CREF, 1988.

Gray, W. S., III. *Determinants of Investment Portfolio Policy.* Charlottesville, Va.: Institute of Chartered Financial Analysts, 1981.

Hallman, G. Victor, and J. S. Rosenbloom. *Personal Financial Planning.* 4th ed. New York: McGraw-Hill Publishing Co., 1987.

Hartford, G. A., and G. W. White. *New TIAA-CREF Employee Options: New Institutional Responsibilities.* NACUBO Advisory Report 90-2. Washington, D.C.: NACUBO, 1990.

Ibbotson, R. G., and R. A. Sinquefield. *Stocks, Bonds, Bills, and Inflation: The Past and the Future.* Charlottesville, Va.: Financial Analysts Research Foundation, 1982.

Jenny, Hans H. *Early Retirement: A New Issue in Higher Education— The Financial Consequences of Early Retirement.* Wooster, Ohio, and New York: College of Wooster and TIAA-CREF, 1974.

Jenny, Hans H., et al. *Another Challenge: Age 70 Retirement in Higher Education.* New York: TIAA-CREF, 1979.

Kellums, S. E., and J. L. Chronister. *Life after Early Retirement: Faculty Activities and Perceptions.* Baltimore, Md.: Association for the Study of Higher Education, 1987.

Kimball, S. I. *Transferability of Funds Invested with TIAA-CREF.* New York: Commission on College Retirement, 1987.

King, F. P., and T. J. Cook. *Benefit Plans in Higher Education.* New York: Columbia University Press, 1980.

Lozier, G. G., and M. J. Dooris. "Is Higher Education Confronting Faculty Shortages?" Paper presented at the annual meeting of the Association for the Study of Higher Education, November 21-24, 1987.

Maginn, J. L., and D. L. Tuttle. *Managing Investment Portfolios: A Dynamic Process.* New York: Institute of Chartered Financial Analysts with Warren, Gorham & Lamont, 1983.

Mamorsky, Jeffrey D. *Employee Benefits Handbook.* New York: Warren, Gorham & Lamont, 1989.

Markowitz, H. M. "Portfolio Selection." *Journal of Finance* (March 1952). (This article introduced rational portfolio selection theory.)

Massy, W. F. *Endowment: Perspective, Policies, and Management.* Washington, D.C.: Association of Governing Boards of Universities and Colleges, 1990.

McCardle, Frank B. "Proposed DOL Regulations on Participant-Directed Investments." *Benefits Alert* (April 8, 1991): 3-5.

Munoz, J. T., S. F. Harran, and E. R. Maclosky. "Alternative Retirement Investment Opportunity: A How-To Approach." *Business Officer* 21, no. 12 (June 1987): 35.

National Association of College and University Business Officers. *Final Report of the Ad Hoc Committee on TIAA-CREF.* Advisory Report 85-1. Washington, D.C.: NACUBO, 1985.

NULaw Services. *1990 Tax Facts on Life Insurance.* Cincinnati, Ohio: National Underwriter, 1990.

Piacentini, B. J. S., and T. J. Cerino. *Data Book on Employee Benefits.* Washington, D.C.: Employee Benefits Research Institute, 1990.

Roper Organization. *Report of the Pension Issues Study.* New York: Washington Higher Education Secretariat Pension Issues Committee and TIAA-CREF, 1987.

Rosenbloom, Jerry S. *The Handbook of Employee Benefits.* 2nd ed. Homewood, Ill.: Dow-Jones Irwin, 1988.

TIAA-CREF. "An Increasing Annuity Based on Nominal Interest Rates and Debt Instruments." *Research Dialogues* (April 1986).

TIAA-CREF. "Comparing SRA Income Streams: Annuitization versus Minimum Distribution." *Research Dialogues* (February 1991).

TIAA-CREF. *Keeping Your Plan in Shape: Nondiscrimination Guidelines for 403(b) Plans.* New York: TIAA-CREF, 1990.

TIAA-CREF. "Target Benefit Plans." *Research Dialogues* (July 1989).

TIAA-CREF. *TIAA-CREF: The Future Agenda.* Report of the Special Trustee Joint Committee. New York: TIAA-CREF, 1987.

Williamson, J. P., and H. A. D. Sanger. *Investment Manager's Handbook.* Homewood, Ill.: Dow-Jones Irwin, 1980.

CHAPTER 14

# Risk Management and Insurance

by
Arthur G. Broadhurst
United Educators Insurance Risk
Retention Group, Inc.

# Sponsor

# Contents

## 14: Risk Management and Insurance

I n the financial arena, risk is the probability of an occurrence likely to result in financial loss. Because risk is an unavoidable fact of life, no college or university can operate without some exposure to risks that can cause death or injury or severe loss or damage to campus property or the property of others. Loss can be in the form of direct first-party loss to the institution itself (from fire, earthquake, theft, disappearance, or business interruption) or third-party loss resulting in institutional liability (such as negligence, wrongful death, wrongful termination, or collision).

An area of risk that receives a great deal of attention is the public perception of harm (whether justified or not) arising out of institutional operations. This perception not only has the potential to damage an institution's image and reputation but also can lead to financial loss through protracted and difficult litigation. In the litigious society of the United States, even the most seemingly inconsequential act or incident may give rise to a claim or a lawsuit.

Because risk involves uncertainty in regard to possible adverse outcomes and consequences, the potential for serious financial harm to an institution has led many institutions and their financial or business officers to focus on managing the elements of risk and loss as a part of the institution's overall financial management strategy. The risk of damage to persons or property is a financial risk, similar to other business risks such as credit risk, balance sheet risk, and investment risk; thus, the prudent financial manager takes steps to protect the institution from these various exposures to loss. Risk management is a specialized form of financial management; the risk management function should be placed directly and prominently among the responsibilities of the chief financial or business officer. Although the implementation of a risk management program may be delegated to someone else, the responsibility for risk management remains with the chief financial or business officer.

Risk management is the formal process of assessing exposure to risk and financial loss and taking the necessary action to minimize risk. However unfortunate or regrettable a loss may be in human or emotional terms, to a college or university loss invariably means potential financial loss. The function of risk management is to reduce the college or university's exposure to financial loss occasioned by damage to persons and property. Risk management requires reducing both the frequency and severity of incidents that are likely to result in financial loss, as well as the financial impact of such incidents and events as do occur.

Colleges and universities cannot prevent accidents from happening, but they can take steps to reduce their frequency and severity. Likewise, they cannot prevent damage suits or claims from third parties, but they can take steps to lower the chances of a successful adverse judgment or to reduce the amount of damages awarded. Without a risk management program, administrators have no way to assess an institution's potential exposure to risk and therefore have no rational way to protect it against loss. A good risk management program, carefully conceived and effectively implemented, provides reasonable assurance to financial managers and the governing board that the campus community is doing what it can to protect itself and its constituents from harm and financial loss.

Risk management is generally associated with insurance because insurance is the most common and best-known technique used to minimize financial loss, although it is not the only technique available. No college or university can afford to make the mistake of assuming that by purchasing insurance it transfers the responsibility and the risk of catastrophic loss to an insurance company and therefore can ignore its responsibility for risk management. Financial and business officers should remember that the primary interest of an insurance company is to protect itself against serious financial loss. Insurance carriers protect themselves from unacceptable levels of loss, as market conditions permit, by narrowing insurance policy terms and conditions, raising premiums, reducing limits, writing exclusions into policies, and requiring coinsurance by the institution. Financial administrators who neglect any aspect of their risk management responsibilities jeopardize their institutions.

This chapter looks at several aspects of effective risk management. After addressing the importance of institutional policy and commitment, it examines the overall risk management function. Important risk management concepts are elaborated, including the identification of exposure to loss, risk control, and risk financing. The methods of becoming insured are also described: the role of agents and brokers, consultants, and insurers are placed in the context of that bidding process. Types of insurance are then described, followed by a brief discussion of occupational safety and health and the human subjects of risk management.

## Institutional Policy and Commitment

Successful risk management requires that staff in widely differing functional areas of the college or university work together with the common objective of identifying and managing exposures throughout the institution. Unless the president and the governing board realize the importance of risk management and actively support it, a risk management program is not likely to be successful.

Institutional commitment to a risk management philosophy and program should be clearly defined and formalized in a policy statement adopted by the governing board of the college or university. The policy statement should describe the goals and objectives of the risk management program and designate responsibility (and appropriate authority) for the program's implementation. The policy statement may assign the oversight responsibility for risk management to the finance committee of the governing board or to a subcommittee on risk management and insurance.

## The Risk Management Function

In smaller colleges or universities, the chief financial or business officer may serve as risk manager. In larger colleges or universities, the risk management function is likely to be delegated to a risk management specialist or to the director of a fully staffed risk management department.

The risk management function is very complex, because risk is inherent in all institutional operations and departments. The risk manager does not so much manage risk as manage a process that requires all departments of the institution to understand the importance of risk management in their areas and to cooperate in achieving common risk management objectives. The risk manager should have clear and open lines of communications with every department head and should enjoy sufficient independence and authority to make effective decisions relating to identification and evaluation of risk, loss control and prevention, loss financing, and transfer of risk.

The risk management function may include:

- Advising the president and governing board on significant potential sources of risk exposure

- Reporting coverages, premiums, and losses

- Recommending limits and retention levels (the amount of insurance the college or university should carry and the amount of risk the institution can reasonably assume through deductibles and coinsurance), loss-prevention programs and practices, risk-transfer devices, and consulting services

- Preparing underwriting information

Because risk management involves responsibilities in such widely differing functional areas, the staff member assigned the primary responsibility for risk management should be an administrator who works well with both professional and nonprofessional staff, particularly with those areas most important to the risk management and loss-control process: physical plant, athletics, human resources, transportation, security, student affairs, medical services, intellectual property, and technology transfer. The risk manager needs to have a good understanding of the range and nature of institutional operation and style, as well as a fundamental understanding of risk management, loss control, risk-transfer and risk-financing devices, and insurance. Imagination, technical competency, interpersonal skills, and communication skills are important in gaining the support and cooperation of administrative colleagues, faculty, and staff.

The risk manager coordinates many facets of the risk management program and works with insurance brokers and consultants, attorneys and adjusters, safety engineers, inspectors from regulatory agencies, and other external agencies and persons. Usually the risk manager is the link between the institution and its insurers and claimants when an incident occurs or a claim is filed.

# The Risk Management Process

The risk management process involves identifying and evaluating potential exposure to loss, reducing the institution's loss potential to the degree feasible and consistent with achieving its mission, and selecting financial mechanisms for paying for losses that occur. These principles apply to all business organizations, but the program needed to carry them out varies with the size and sophistication of a college or university, its particular circumstances and resources, and the inclinations and capabilities of the personnel responsible for risk management.

## IDENTIFICATION OF EXPOSURE TO RISK

Identification of exposure to risk is the first task in establishing a risk management program. A review of existing financial statements, property records, and other files will indicate physical assets to be preserved, but the risk manager should insist on up-to-date evaluation. Attention should be paid to special equipment, library and art acquisitions, special functions such as conference and facility rentals, licenses and contracts, new building plans, acquisitions, and changes in space utilization. Accounting officers, legal counsel, physical plant directors, and academic administrators should be consulted in the risk identification process. The identification process may be complicated by multiple locations, foreign operations and programs, joint ventures, research and development contracts, technology transfer, and related entities. The identification process is never-ending; the lines of communication must be kept open, and the risk manager should exercise initiative to keep abreast of changes that might affect risk handling.

## RISK CONTROL

Some established techniques have evolved by which risks can be controlled.

***Avoidance of risk.*** A college or university can avoid risk by not accepting it or by not entering into a situation with potential for risk. For example, a university may choose not to accept a research grant for development of new explosives technology to avoid potentially unacceptable physical damage, injury to persons, or political risk exposure. Although such a choice is not always possible or, if it is possible, it may have unacceptable practical or political consequences, risk avoidance is both possible and desirable in some situations.

***Loss prevention or reduction of risk.*** The adage "an ounce of prevention is worth a pound of cure" provides a guide for the control of risk. Risk can be reduced, eliminated, or managed by a well-planned institutional loss-prevention program. For example, a college or university may determine that safety considerations require the razing of an unsafe high-rise dormitory or installing a sprinkler system in the dormitory.

***Retention, assumption, or acceptance of risk.*** The methods of retention, assumption, or acceptance of risk are of particular concern to an institution. Constant vigilance is necessary to avoid unintentional acceptance of risk through unknowing exposure. Some risks must be retained because insurance for a given risk cannot be purchased, because the cost of the insurance is not justified by an apparent risk, or because the insurance simply is not affordable. Examples of risk that may have to be retained, assumed, or accepted are earthquakes, wars, pollution, and accidental glass breakage. The importance and economic value of risk assumed must be considered in relation to the size of the institution's assets and operations and the probability and severity of loss.

***Transfer of risk to others.*** Risk may be contractually transferred to others. For example, a facility lease may require the lessor to assume all property and liability risks on the leased property. This arrangement is referred to as a "hold harmless" agreement. Contracts entered into by the college or university should be approved by legal counsel and reviewed by the risk manager so that indemnity and insurance provisions can be considered. Only properly designated persons should sign contracts or obligate the college or university through a written agreement. Many risks can and should be insured. Such action reduces financial loss to the amount of the premiums (and deductibles and coinsurance). Risk may also be limited by disclaimers and assumption-of-risk agreements such as posting a notice (e.g., in a parking lot) disclaiming any responsibility for accident or injury and warning that third parties engage in the activity at their own risk. Legal counsel should be consulted to ensure that "proper notice" or assumption of risk occurs. Counsel should also be consulted about the limited effectiveness of disclaimers and assumption-of-risk agreements as a means of avoiding liability.

RISK FINANCING

Because risk may become loss with financial consequences, each college or university must determine the most efficient method of financing its loss. Loss may be financed directly from institutional funds as losses occur (risk retention), from commercial insurance, or through self-insurance, loss reserve funds, or external funding arrangements such as a letter of credit. A combination of these approaches is normally used. At its simplest, commercial insurance is used in combination with deductibles (the insurer pays loss exceeding the self-insured retention) or coinsurance (the insurer pays a percentage of the loss, perhaps 90 percent). At more complex levels, the combination may involve an actuarially determined, formal self-insurance layer or "captive" insurance program that is reinsured or protected against catastrophic loss by "excess of loss" commercial insurance. Ultimately, the loss funding decision depends on how much management of its own loss expense an institution is willing and able to bear and how much security the institution is willing to buy through insurance premium payments.

Sometimes insurance is described as a risk-transfer mechanism because it transfers the risk of financing loss away from the institution to an insurance company. Insurance finances risk by spreading the payment, in the form of premiums, for incurred or potential losses over time.

Fundamental issues in selecting the mechanisms for financing loss are frequency of occurrence and probable severity of loss of any given risk. How likely is a risk to result in loss? What is the possible financial impact of the worst case imaginable on the institution? How often can a loss be expected? In other words, one way for colleges and universities to look at the issue of financing risk is to consider the probability of loss from a particular risk. The more predictable, and therefore certain, the frequency and severity of a given loss, the more reasonable it is to finance the risk internally. The less likely a risk is to lead to loss, the more difficult it is to predict the extent of loss that risk might produce, and the more reasonable it is to cushion the institution from sudden and severe financial loss by pooling (or insuring) the risk.

Frequency and severity are relative terms. A small college with limited resources might consider five instances of vandalism in a year "frequent" and a $25,000 uninsured loss severe or even catastrophic. A larger university might deem the same losses and costs infrequent and insignificant. Each institution must determine its own level of tolerance for risk and decide the amount of loss that it can afford to bear from its own resources and the amount it must fund over a long period of time (whether through insurance premiums or payments into a loss reserve fund).

Losses that are predictable in frequency and low in severity, such as pilferage, minor vandalism, disappearance of books from the library, minor storm damage, and vehicle collision damage may be handled as retained losses and funded directly through a portion of the risk management operating budget. Use of insurance with an appropriate deductible allows the institution to assume a level of risk for self-funding routine losses but limits the institution's exposure (either per claim or aggregate-for-all) if losses turn out to be more severe in frequency or extent than assumed by the deductible. Insuring high-frequency, low-severity risks is not only expensive but can adversely affect the institution's insurance program, because underwriters become nervous about frequent claims and losses, regardless of their cumulative value. It is a wiser use of risk management money to manage and fund small losses internally and to use insurance to protect against more serious losses. Each institution needs to determine, in consultation with its advisors, brokers, and insurers, which risks it can reasonably assume and what level of deductible or risk retention is suitable in each instance. This decision should be made in light of the institution's history of losses, its financial resources, and the resources of its risk management department.

Self-insured retentions may be funded from the annual operating budget as losses are incurred or through reserves arising from appropriation or allocation of the institution's fund balance, depending on the capability and needs of the institution. Generally accepted accounting principles do not allow for the establishment of a reserve for self-insurance arising through charges to current-year operating expenditures, since an identifiable loss has not as yet occurred. However, the allocation or appropriation of a portion of the current fund balance as an unrestricted loss reserve is permissible, so long as actual loss is charged as an expense when incurred. The institution may establish a liability account for self-insured losses that are known but not settled at the end of the accounting period.

**Self-insurance.** A formal self-insurance program requires the establishment of reserves for losses, the charge of "premiums" and allocation of losses as the losses are incurred, systematic accounting for losses, and loss-prevention and claims-control services. The institution acts as its own insurer. Traditionally, self-insurance has been considered most useful in financing relatively stable and predictable areas of loss, particularly if the aggregate level of self-insurance exposure is "capped" by excess catastrophic insurance that is purchased commercially. Until recently, the use of self-insurance was limited largely to property and workers' compensation, but many institutions now use some form of self-insurance program for other liability risks.

Advantages of self-insurance as a loss-funding mechanism include:

- Reduced premium costs resulting from the elimination of high-frequency, low-value claims and the related administrative costs

- Greater institutional control of coverages and claims handling (Good claims handling can have a substantial impact on the reduction of claims costs, especially in workers' compensation areas.)

- Retention of premium dollars and investment income and, in the case of workers' compensation and liability, retention of reserves for losses until losses are actually paid

- Elimination of commercial insurance-carrier profits, premium taxes, and agents' or brokers' commissions

Disadvantages of self-insurance may include:

- Loss of expense predictability because of the spread of risk among many other entities

- Administrative time and expense of operating an "insurance company" within the institution (This hidden cost should be considered. Administration of a program takes time, personnel, and resources.)

- Possibly less objective claims handling (where personal bias can affect settlements) than by commercial companies (This service can be contracted for separately.)

- Claims-handling complaints arising against the institution rather than against an insurance carrier

- Possibly less efficient subrogation and collection from other parties at fault

- Possible lack of integrity or adequacy of self-insurance loss reserves, which should be regularly valued by a casualty actuary in any event

If an exposure is not a deductible against primary insurance but is totally self-insured with an "excess of loss" cap provided by commercial insurance, other disadvantages occur, including:

- Possibly less effective inspection and loss-prevention services by the insurance carrier, since it is less exposed to loss

- Less effective efforts to keep administrators and supervisors loss-conscious because the insurance carrier no longer applies external pressure to meet safety standards

These disadvantages can be overcome by proper management of the risk function. Some institutions may assume greater responsibility for loss control when their own funds are directly at risk.

Management techniques integral to the successful administration of a self-insurance program include the following.

WRITTEN COVERAGE DOCUMENT. It is essential that self-insured coverage be defined by insuring agreements, conditions, and exclusions so that coverage is understood by all parties and arbitrariness in claims can be avoided.

ADEQUATE FUNDING. Funds must be available to cover both normal (expected) losses and unexpected (shock) losses to the extent of the agreed-on level of coverage per loss and for aggregate losses for each policy year.

INTEGRITY OF RESERVES. Self-insurance coverage exists only to the extent that loss reserves are adequately funded. Accumulated loss reserves must be held inviolate from use for purposes other than the self-insurance program. Ideally, interest on invested reserves is retained within the reserves, and a self-insurance premium charge formula is developed to ensure the adequacy of the reserves for incurred but not reported losses, as well as specific case reserves, and for the administrative operating expenses of the program. For this reason, a number of institutions have developed "captive" insurance companies.

Self-insurance as a loss-funding mechanism has taken on increased significance in general liability and medical professional liability issues. The primary reason for the expansion of self-insured programs is that adequate commercial coverage is unavailable at reasonable costs.

Self-insurance is not a suitable approach for all institutions. Some institutions are not large enough, have insufficient reserves, or have inadequate loss-management resources to support a self-insurance program. Risk managers may have difficulty persuading an institution's administrators to assume greater financial risk. Each institution should consider limitations on the use of self-insurance for educational and medical facilities because of accountability, cost distribution, and other standards developed by federal agencies and industry regulators such as the Financial Accounting Standards Board and Medicare.

***Captive insurance.*** A formal self-insurance program can be organized as a captive insurance company. There are two types of captive insurance companies: a "single-parent captive" is a wholly owned insurance subsidiary designed solely to insure the parent's exposures; a "group captive" is jointly owned and operated by several institutions. Captives are insurance companies and meet the same legal requirements as any other insurance company organized within the same jurisdiction. Colleges and universities have developed a number of single-parent captives, typically for general liability and medical or hospital exposures. A number of group captives serve the higher education community. Group captives operate like traditional insurance companies and serve their members' insurance needs.

Single-parent captives have more specialized functions, such as direct underwriting of the parent's risks, purchase of stop-loss and aggregate excess-of-loss insurance, and purchase of excess reinsurance. In practice, some college and university captives use a "fronting" approach, in which a conventional insurance company licensed to operate within an institution's jurisdiction issues an insurance policy and provides loss-prevention and claims handling services. The institution pays a premium directly to the fronting insurance company. The insurance company then purchases reinsurance from the captive. The cost of such a program includes a fronting fee based on the original gross premium, the expense of financial guarantees to cover the full exposure of the fronting carrier, and the expense of any other required services not provided by the fronting company.

Colleges and universities typically form a captive to obtain coverage for exposures not insurable in commercial markets; to obtain broader, more flexible, and more permanent coverage than is available commercially; to lower the overall cost of insurance protection and to protect the integrity of self-insurance reserves; to develop stability of coverages and premiums; and to charge the premiums as current expenditures and to grants and contracts.

It is usually easier to obtain excess coverage if a captive insurance company has been formalized, especially if the captive is fronted by an established commercial carrier. Furthermore, although reinsurance markets are not ordinarily accessible to a self-insured institution, they are directly accessible to a captive.

Captive insurance companies, whether single-parent or group, are generally organized and licensed in a jurisdiction that has favorable captive laws that make it easier for a small special-purpose insurance company to operate. Favorite domiciles (locations for organizing and licensing captive insurance companies) are Vermont, Illinois, Colorado, Bermuda, and the Cayman Islands. The most important factors to consider when deciding on a domicile for a captive include ease and speed of formation of the captive; capitalization requirements and tax rates; regulation of premium rates and coverage; reserve and investment requirements; actuarial requirements; and availability of necessary professional services. The formation and operation of a captive require a long-term commitment. Institutions cannot jump in and out of a captive from year to year as premium levels and management interest fluctuate.

*Risk retention group.* The Legislative Risk Retention Act of 1985 permits the formation of risk retention groups. A risk retention group resembles a group captive insurance company but has more flexibility in operating on the national level. United Educators Insurance, created by several higher education associations, is the best-known example of this principle in higher education.

## Becoming Insured

Insurance involves the pooling of financial resources and spreading the cost of risk among a large group of policyholders over time. Each policyholder shares a portion of the losses suffered by others. In this way, the annual cost of loss to each policyholder is more predictable and limited and the risk of a catastrophic financial loss to any one policyholder is eliminated.

Several factors affect insurance premiums. The insurance company incurs costs for operating expenses, commissions to brokers, paid losses and loss adjustment expenses, and costs of future losses from events that have happened but have not yet been reported to the company. The company must also provide a return to its stockholders and increase its capital and surplus. The company earns income on investments of its reserves and other funds. The balance of its income must come from premiums. Although no insurance company escapes the basic economics of this formula, the quality of underwriting, loss experience, efficiency of operation, and investment performance differentiate premium levels among companies. The insurance industry seems to operate in cycles of low to high to low premiums for various types of coverage. These cycles may have a negative impact on the budgets of colleges and universities and are partially responsible for the growth of other risk-financing methods, such as captives, in higher education.

## AGENTS AND BROKERS

Although agents usually work on behalf of the insurers and brokers work on behalf of the insured, it is a distinction without a significant difference, so the terms are used synonymously in this chapter. Most commercial insurance is placed through independent agents and brokers; in fact, some of the largest insurance companies underwrite risks only through an agent or broker. There are advantages in dealing with a full-service commercial agent or broker who can assist in determining appropriate coverages, avoiding coverage gaps and duplicate coverage, negotiating special policy endorsements, gaining access to specialty markets, evaluating and comparing policies, structuring self-insured retentions, accessing loss-control services, and managing and reporting claims.

Agents and brokers traditionally have been compensated through payment of commissions by insurers; the payments vary depending on the line of insurance (typically ranging from 5 to 15 percent). On large accounts, however, brokers may perform services for a specified fee rather than for a commission. In smaller institutions, the percentage of commission is generally a fair means of compensating the broker for his or her knowledge and skill. The risk manager must determine the amount of the commission and whether fair services are received for the money spent. It is important to find out what services an agent or broker offers in order to request and evaluate those that are desired.

Opinion differs on whether an institution should be represented by a single broker or by multiple brokers. Proponents of using a single broker argue that the institution receives better attention with one broker and that a unified account may be serviced better than one that is fragmented. It is also easier to avoid potential coverage gaps with one broker. However, multiple brokers may provide broader market coverage, and competition among brokers benefits the institution.

The institution should select its brokers on the basis of the scope of services they offer, their experience, their familiarity with educational institutions and exposures, and the qualifications of the account executive servicing the account. Proximity of a service office is also desirable. An institution's risk management and insurance program is important to its well-being, and its broker should not be chosen on the basis of friendship, patronage, or political relationships.

## THE CONSULTANT

The use of an independent insurance risk management consultant may be desirable on an occasional or regular basis. The consultant may be called upon to review the adequacy of insurance coverage; to design specifications for coverage to submit to brokers; to help in the broker selection process by assessing strengths and weaknesses of firms developing risk management programs; to conduct special studies such as those involving the preparation and evaluation of proposals; to appraise or hire a risk manager; to conduct feasibility studies for self-insurance or pooling; to identify risks and exposures in particular special risk areas that require special markets; to appraise property and prepare schedules of value for insurance; and to recommend appropriate deductible and retention levels.

Consulting fees are charged on a per-hour or per-assignment basis. In many cases, a maximum fee is quoted, to which will be added any out-of-pocket expenses. A few consulting firms work on a percentage of savings; however, this may not be desirable, because it places the emphasis on cost rather than on coverage, service, and other factors that are more important insurance considerations.

An institution's agent or broker may be a good source for information on independent consultants. The University Risk Management and Insurance Association (URMIA) recommends experienced risk managers as consultants on a per diem basis. Many commercial lines agents and brokers consider themselves consultants, so you should make it clear that you are seeking the objectivity of a disinterested third party.

Although a consultant's fee may appear high, a competent and experienced consultant should be able to recommend a high level of protection and ultimately should save money through good insurance and risk management program design and by avoiding duplicate or unnecessary coverage.

Major insurers have loss engineers and loss-control services that may be called on directly or through a broker. Institutions pay for these loss-engineering and safety services through their premiums and should take advantage of them. Most general liability and property insurers require physical inspection of insured premises; the inspection results in a written engineering report that is submitted to insurance company underwriters as a basis for determining premium levels and exposures. Insurers will generally make this report available to their insureds because it is in their interest to have clients work with them to reduce exposure to loss. Insurers also provide specific recommendations to clients as a result of loss-engineering studies. Some insurers require remedial action as a condition of writing insurance or as a factor in renewal. Loss-engineering services provided by insurers are limited in scope, however, and are related to particular insurance coverages available through a certain company. Recommendations made by insurance company loss-control and safety engineering personnel should be taken seriously and action should be taken to correct noted deficiencies. When it is difficult to obtain insurance, institutions with uncorrected deficiencies may find their policies not renewed or their coverage limited.

## CONSIDERATIONS IN SELECTING AN INSURER

Debate continues among risk managers and brokers about the wisdom of using a formal bidding process for broker selection or for purchase of insurance. Putting insurance out to bid on a periodic basis, particularly in a competitive market, may keep the current broker or agent responsive to institutional needs and cognizant of service, may reduce costs, may improve coverages, and may provide the opportunity for changing the institution's agent or broker. Putting insurance out to bid too frequently can lead to inadequate broker service, can emphasize price at the expense of quality of coverage and service, and may weaken broker-college relations, which can be detrimental to the institution in the long run.

An institution should limit its potential insurers to those that are strong enough, financially and administratively, to service its account at the present time and in the future. The institution's broker or consultant can be helpful in making this determination. The relationship between an institution and its insurers should be for the long term. Assuming that the quality of coverage and service is satisfactory and the pricing is reasonable, a relationship of at least three years may be in the institution's best interest.

It may be worth the effort for institutions to select qualified brokers in advance of the bidding process according to ability and desire to provide needed services and their access to markets. Rather than employing a broad public bidding program, it may be more useful to select a limited number of brokers who can best meet the institution's needs. In this way, the institution can be sure that the agency has the necessary capabilities and services and that responsible insurance and reinsurance markets will be available for its use.

The insurance company's decision to accept a risk and setting the price to charge for accepting it are the primary functions of the underwriter. Although many types of insurance are priced from a standard rate manual, numerous variables (credits and debits) to the manual rate are possible, so the underwriter's assessment of the risk is important. The underwriter receives information about the institution from the agent or broker or, in the case of a direct writing company, from a sales representative.

A college or university needs to communicate its needs to insurers by preparing detailed information about the desired coverages and by providing all the information that the underwriter needs to assess the risk and determine the premium amount. The application for coverage generally takes the form of a "submission packet" that provides all necessary information, so that the underwriter can properly evaluate the exposure. Because underwriters have the flexibility to debit or credit a manual rate, it is important that the institution present itself in the best light possible, while providing such full and complete information that the underwriter has no doubt about the institution's exposure or management capability.

Applications for new coverage or for renewal of existing coverage should be submitted at least 60 days in advance of policy expiration. Insurers require adequate time for reviewing each application and supporting documentation and for making underwriting decisions about pricing and coverage. Furthermore, the institution needs time to negotiate prices and terms of coverage and to seek alternative coverages as necessary. The submission packet should include:

- The insurer's application (or a generic application if acceptable to the insurer)

- A description of the college or university—its size and scope of programs; locations of its various operations other than the main campus, including foreign operations and locations; and special risks and exposures (nuclear, underwater, aircraft, research and development, etc.)

- Subsidiaries and related entities to be included in coverage (foundations, bookstores, hotels, joint ventures, auxiliary operations)

- Risk management and safety programs and procedures that might warrant premium credits

- A loss history for the prior five years for the line of coverage being sought

- The amount of coverage desired, including any alternatives the insurance company may propose, and desired retention/deductible levels

- Financial statements (generally required for particular liability coverages, including errors and omissions)

- The date on which quotations are needed and the name and address of the person to whom they should be sent (usually the broker)

A complete submission packet saves delays caused by the need of the underwriters for additional information and provides a good impression of the institution.

## SPECIAL PROBLEMS OF PUBLIC COLLEGES AND UNIVERSITIES

Public colleges and universities face issues different from those of independent institutions in regard to their liability for their actions or the actions of their employees, as well as the appropriateness of purchasing liability insurance to finance loss. Traditionally, states were immune to lawsuits by citizens (as a "sovereign immunity"), but this doctrine has eroded over time as a result of legislative action and judicial decisions relating to issues of public policy and fairness. In some states, courts have imposed limits on the circumstances in which governmental immunity can be used as a defense. Other states have established procedures for claimants under a tort claims act, which usually limits both the circumstances in which a recovery can be made against a state agency and the amount of recovery. Furthermore, whether public colleges and universities are state agencies for purposes of immunity or tort claims acts differs from state to state. In some states, the purchase of liability insurance waives protection from immunity or may limit recovery to the limit of insurance that is available.

Because many of the operations of state colleges and universities are different from the operations of other state agencies and are similar to the operations of independent colleges and universities, they share many of the same risk characteristics and exposures. Traditional governmental functions impose greater liability on state institutions, requiring their financial and business officers to sort out, with the advice of legal counsel, a variety of complex liability issues.

State officials (sometimes all state employees) who are acting within the scope of their duties may have protection for liability by "public officials liability" insurance or by state defense and/or indemnity. Are some or all employees of a college or university employees of the state and entitled to indemnification? In some states the decision as to whether a public official is acting within the scope of his or her duties and whether the official will be indemnified or defended is discretionary. Faculty and other employees of state institutions are concerned about whether they will be protected under certain circumstances.

Equally troubling, there are circumstances in which an "agent" of the institution may not be an employee qualified as a "public official" under state law.

Because state colleges and universities have activities, operations, and programs outside their state boundaries, including athletic trips, foreign travel, and research programs, they are subject to claims from injured parties beyond their borders, whether in another state or another country.

Public colleges and universities may engage in joint projects with other colleges and universities, both public and independent, outside of their state through partnerships or other forms of joint venture, including jointly held corporations. Most public colleges and universities have several "related entities," not exactly subsidiaries but usually independent 501 (c)(3) corporations that serve specific purposes, such as foundations, athletic associations, alumni associations, etc. These independent corporations, although related to the purposes of the college or university, are private corporations designed to keep their funds under the control of the institution rather than the state. Often their status as private corporations means that their activities (and employees) cannot be protected by the state.

Numerous legal actions may be brought against state institutions and employees in federal courts, including civil rights violations, discrimination (in employment and otherwise), antitrust suits (for a range of activities involving everything from athletics to computer sales), and copyright and trademark actions. Additionally, state colleges and universities engage in a wide range of activities, including entrepreneurial and similarly commercial activities, publishing and broadcasting, consulting, land development, and a variety of commercial ventures that can create liability exposures that some states may not be willing to indemnify.

For these and a variety of other reasons an increasing number of state institutions purchase liability insurance.

## PUBLIC BIDDING

State colleges and universities may be required to use a public bidding process. Public bidding is designed to eliminate corruption, politics, and favoritism in the purchasing process and to promote the acquisition of the best coverage at the lowest available cost. As permissible by law, selection should be based on the bid that best matches cost to coverage and service and on the credentials of the bidder. Selection should not be based solely on price. The objectives of public bidding can be frustrated by several factors.

*A bid may be deceptively low.* Many colleges and universities package numerous coverages under a single bid. Because the final premium cost of some types of insurance is based on audits that will be conducted during the term or after its expiration, the bid price may reflect a low "deposit premium." The uninitiated or the careless reviewer of quotations may accept a bid because it is attractively low, yet when the final audit is made, the net cost could actually be higher than it would have been with other companies that prepared more accurate initial quotations. In other words, a quotation may be unrealistically low because it represents merely a deposit against future audits and final premiums.

*Public bidding does not necessarily produce the lowest available cost.* Contract changes (endorsements) during the policy term may require negotiations with the carrier. If there has not been a continuous relationship with the company over time, these negotiations can be difficult and costly.

Some markets may be closed. In a public bidding situation, some large, full-service commercial agencies may not be willing to expend the time and effort necessary to obtain quotations for quality coverage when they perceive that the institution is only seeking a low price. Some markets may be closed to these institutions because another broker has "blocked" that market by submitting to it first. Insurance companies will provide a premium quote only to the first broker who submits an application, unless a subsequent broker provides a "broker of record" letter. Some brokers submit applications to a number of companies to prevent a competitor from obtaining a quote from any of them.

*Periodic bidding may affect the quality of the bidding process.* Public bidding at each renewal period has an upsetting effect on the market. Each carrier is well aware that it may win this year but lose the next, over a relatively insignificant difference in price. This leads to a reluctance in carriers over time to be aggressive in preparing quotations. Some may submit only token bids. Furthermore, changing carriers frequently creates problems for the risk manager, who may have difficulty in establishing a satisfactory relationship with a single carrier or agency willing to work with the institution. It also complicates the administration of an insurance program, as constantly changing policy terms and conditions increase record-keeping responsibilities.

# Types of Insurance

PROPERTY INSURANCE

In general, insurance policies should be considered in terms of the types of risks they cover. Other than life and health coverages, the two major categories of insurance are property insurance and casualty insurance (including workers' compensation).

Most institutions are insured for fire, lightning, and the replacement value of buildings and contents. This represents the cost to repair, rebuild, or replace a damaged facility with new materials of like kind and quality. Extended coverages usually include damage caused by wind, hail, some explosions, smoke, riot, civil commotion, and vandalism. Other coverages, such as for earthquakes, pollution, or floods, may be included for an additional premium.

In the event of loss or damage to property that is not repaired, rebuilt, or replaced, recovery is usually limited to the extent of actual cash value, or replacement cost less depreciation, rather than replacement cost value.

Fire and extended coverage policies may be inadequate when other property perils are considered, such as earthquake, flood, water damage, or collapse. A "difference-in-condition" or "all risks" policy usually can be negotiated to cover these and other perils.

***Building and content valuations.*** Valuation of institutional property is difficult, especially on a building-by-building basis. Complicating factors include frequent shifting of contents from building to building, acquisitions, new construction, remodeling, leased property, and demolitions. Traditionally, financial reports reflect asset values at book or acquisition cost and may be depreciated. These financial reports are important for identifying assets but otherwise have little significance to the risk manager. The risk manager may wish to order a complete appraisal as a basis for a statement of property values, which is updated each year by increased value factors. It is essential that the risk manager be notified promptly of any acquisitions, dispositions, and demolitions and of any remodeling or alterations that would affect property values substantially. Where possible, existing records should be coordinated and serious consideration given to maintaining automated records of insurable values. Institutions with frequent or continuing construction projects may wish to include builders' risk coverage in basic property policies; an automatic acquisition clause would be valuable in covering new properties. Institutions can use construction cost indices and historical cost records to calculate the current replacement value that should be used.

Coinsurance clauses are designed to prevent an insured from underinsuring its property. If an institutional building is worth $20 million but is insured for only $15 million (75 percent of its value), the insurance company will pay only 75 percent of each insured loss under the principle that the institution chose to self-insure 25 percent of the loss.

An agreed amount clause, wherein the insured and the insurance company agree in advance on the value of the property, is essential for eliminating any penalty that might be assessed if a policy has a coinsurance clause that requires full value coverage. Museum and fine arts policies generally use an agreed amount clause.

Additional components of the property insurance package may be transit insurance, covering merchandise and purchases while in commercial movement, and other types of floater (or movable property) coverage on institutional assets, either in movement or on premises. College or university property located off campus should also be covered; this could include art objects on loan, property in storage, or gift properties. Gift properties should be evaluated carefully from the standpoint of potential risks, as they may have obvious hazards (gravel pit) or unknown hazards (underground storage tanks or chemical waste). Special property insurance is available on data processing systems that can apply to both hardware and software.

**Deductibles.** The deductible amount of an insured loss is that portion borne by the insured before the insured is entitled to any recovery from the insurer. The deductible may apply to each loss, an annual amount of losses, or a combination of both. The purpose of the deductible is to eliminate relatively small and frequent losses from insurance coverage. The financial or business officer should carefully appraise the institution's ability to fund such losses through deductibles.

As large a deductible as feasible should be retained, based on history of loss, present efforts at loss prevention, and market requirements. Premium savings must be weighed against the cost of uninsured losses.

## ELECTRONIC DATA PROCESSING (EDP)

Traditional forms of property insurance are not sufficient to cover the special risks associated with computers. An EDP policy goes beyond the normal property coverage and provides coverage for occurrences such as electrical disturbances, temperature extremes, water damage, and mechanical failure. Perhaps more important, the EDP policy provides funds for reconstruction of media and/or to defray the extra expense that may be required to restore operation at an alternative site while the insured facility or equipment is under repair.

## BOILERS, PRESSURE VESSELS, AND MACHINERY

Colleges and universities use a wide variety of vessels and machines that can accidentally burst or break. Although such accidents are rare, they have great loss potential and are therefore excluded from most property insurance policies. Boiler and machinery insurance, a specialty contract, was developed to overcome this deficiency. (To avoid confusion and ensure smooth settlement of losses, boiler and machinery coverage should be coordinated with the insurer used for property coverage.)

The purpose of boiler and machinery insurance is to prevent loss and to pay for damages after a loss. Thus, inspection service is as important as the insurer's indemnity function (approximately one-third or more of the premium goes toward loss prevention). The value of inspection services is enhanced by the statutory inspection requirements of most states.

Boiler and machinery insurance generally covers the insured's property, damage to the property of others, and defense and legal services. Additional protection against indirect losses may be purchased for the loss of use or occupancy, spoilage, and power outages.

Boiler and machinery coverage is technical. To ensure adequate handling of such coverage, the risk manager should seek expert advice from an underwriter who specializes in boiler engineering and machinery or an outside consultant. A generally accepted practice is to delete the coverages for liability(covered elsewhere), as well as for property already protected under a property policy.

The concept of "maximum loss potential" is an important guide in deciding what policy limit to purchase. Due in large part to good inspection services, boilers are subject to low loss frequency. When occasional loss does occur, however, it is likely to be serious. A good strategy is to accept the limited exposure of a high deductible and insure for high limits to prevent exposure beyond the insurance coverage. As a result, it is preferable that boiler and machinery contracts include a high limit of coverage. The machinery coverage may include such items as electrical equipment and distribution systems, utility systems, air tanks, air-conditioning systems, motors, and furnaces.

## CASUALTY (LIABILITY) INSURANCE

The chief purpose of casualty insurance is to protect the institution from loss as a result of liability imposed by law for injury to persons or to the property of others (for example, slips and falls, auto accidents, and libel). Legal liability normally results from negligent acts or omissions. A comprehensive general liability policy, with appropriate endorsements as necessary to extend coverage, offers the broadest protection, although other liability policies cover specific types of liability (auto, employers, nonowned aircraft, fiduciary, and errors and omissions). Professional liability coverage should be provided in one or more policies, as necessary, to cover doctors, nurses, and other medical personnel; faculty engaged in clinical programs; students involved in clinical experience; and any other faculty and professional staff who provide advice and counsel as part of their duties. Additionally, if a medical or dental school or other specialty has a clinical practice plan from which a portion of the income earned by the clinical practice is returned to the institution, the institution should extend its coverage to the entire program.

## ERRORS AND OMISSIONS POLICIES

Errors and omissions liability coverage is the least understood liability insurance protection available to colleges and universities. As a result, many institutions either fail to make effective use of these policies as a financial management tool or purchase policies that do not provide adequate protection.

Errors and omissions policies are designed to protect against financial loss as a result of "wrongful acts" for which the college and university or its agents and employees may be held liable. These policies generally cover the cost of investigating a claim or defending a suit, damages awarded by a court, and the amount of settlement paid to a claimant (and the legal costs related to that settlement).

These policies are called by a variety of names: directors and officers insurance (D&O), trustee liability, school board liability, and educators' legal liability. While errors and omissions policies are modeled after commercial D&O policies, they have evolved to cover a broad range of institutional exposures and include elements of professional liability policies.

Current errors and omissions policies vary in coverage but, unlike traditional D&O policies, most include some or all employees, volunteers, and the educational corporate entity as insureds. Errors and omissions policies generally provide coverage for claims by employees, including breach of contract, denial of tenure, and wrongful termination claims, which are the most frequent types of errors and omissions claims made against institutions, as well as discrimination, failure to educate, antitrust, and other miscellaneous claims.

The issue of who has the right and duty to defend claims under a policy is a matter of importance. Under some insurance policies, the insurer defends against a claim and may defend or settle the claim with or without the consent of the insured. Under other policies, the duty to defend lies with the insured, and the insurer reimburses or pays directly the reasonable legal expenses, damage awards, or settlements of covered claims.

Insurers generally do not assume responsibility for any expenses incurred before notice of a claim has been filed with them. Institutions should notify their insurer as soon as a claim is made or when they first become aware of an incident that may give rise to a subsequent claim, regardless of whether the insurance company or the institution has the duty to defend. Reporting an incident may establish the right to coverage under the policy in the event that a claim is made.

A claim does not always have to be a suit in order to be covered by an errors and omissions policy. Under some policies, a claim is established whenever anyone gives notice (usually in writing) that he or she intends to hold the institution or its governing board, employees, or agents liable for an alleged wrongful act. For example, the notice could be a letter to the president or a board member from an employee or his or her attorney alleging that he or she was dismissed unfairly and is now seeking compensation for the alleged injury or lost wages.

The fundamental issue in a claim is not the form of the claim but its merit. To be covered by an errors and omissions policy, a claim must allege a wrongful act for which the institution reasonably could be held liable.

To make effective use of errors and omissions policies, college and university officials should know who and what is covered and how the defense of claims will be handled. Those covered should include members of the governing board, employees, student teachers, volunteers, the institutional corporation, and its subsidiaries and related entities (such as alumni organizations, athletic associations, booster clubs, and foundations), whether or not separately incorporated.

At a minimum, an errors and omissions policy should cover the following types of claims commonly made against colleges and universities:

- Wrongful termination

- Discrimination

- Denial of tenure and other employment-related claims

- Copyright infringement

- Antitrust

- Defamation, libel, slander

- Invasion of privacy

- False arrest or detention

- Wrongful entry or eviction

- Sexual harassment or abuse

- Punitive damages

A useful measure of any insurance policy is the comprehensiveness of the coverage it provides. Some policies provide minimal coverage, while others offer considerably broader and therefore more useful and more expensive coverage. A difference of a few thousand dollars in premium may appear to be significant unless compared with the legal costs of defending an uninsured claim, which can easily reach $100,000 before considering damages to the claimant. A policy that does not cover the institution's actual liability or other losses and legal expenses is not a good use of institutional funds.

## EXCESS/UMBRELLA LIABILITY

The excess/umbrella liability policy is an important policy. In its broadest form, it provides coverage for losses that exceed the limits of the primary comprehensive general liability policy and other underlying primary liability policies. High limits provide protection against catastrophic liability. Excess policies may or may not cover exclusions or exhausted aggregate limits of underlying primary policies. Limits purchased by colleges and universities may range from $5 million to $100 million, but the most common limits range from $10 million to $25 million. An excess or umbrella liability policy should "pay on behalf of" the institution, rather than "indemnify" it, to prevent a situation in which the institution must first pay a large claim and then seek reimbursement by the carrier. It is important that the anniversary date of the umbrella policy coincide with the anniversary dates of underlying coverages.

***Workers' compensation.*** Workers' compensation laws require employers to indemnify employees against certain types of losses resulting from work-connected injuries. Most states provide workers' compensation as the sole remedy for work-related injuries. Some employers consider this a medical benefit, but most authorities agree that it more closely resembles liability insurance.

The actual cost of workers' compensation to colleges and universities varies with the benefit level and claims procedures of each state. In some jurisdictions, such as California, New York, Texas, and New Jersey, the financial drain of workers' compensation liability on colleges and universities can be substantial. Many larger institutions now partially self-insure this risk. Even in those cases where self-insurance programs are maintained, it is wise to reinsure liability for catastrophic losses.

When an institution chooses to insure its entire liability, several forms are available. For smaller institutions, rates are charged as a percentage of payroll. The base rate premium is set by the experience of similar employers in the state. Larger institutions may qualify for experience-rated policies that compare the institution's experience over a three-year period with similar employers and provide a credit or debit factor to the base rates. Larger institutions that do not self-insure may find it advantageous to insure under a "retrospective rating" plan in which an insurance company charges the institution a fee for administering the workers' compensation program, with the premium determined by the actual claim payout, modified by certain additional charges for expenses and taxes.

It is important that possible endorsements to the compensation policy be evaluated. Examples are voluntary compensation endorsement, "all states" coverage for employees subject to a jurisdiction outside the state of primary work, foreign coverage for employees who may be abroad, coverage under the Jones Act, the longshoremen and harborworkers' compensation program, or federal maritime jurisdiction.

***Defense Base Act.*** The Defense Base Act, as amended, places special requirements and obligations on contractors. Institutions performing research or other services for the Department of Defense should review this act carefully.

## OCCURRENCE OR CLAIMS MADE

Until recently, general liability coverages were written on an "occurrence" basis—no matter when a claim arose, the policy in effect at the time of the occurrence provided coverage. The effect of this provision is best illustrated by reference to the asbestos industry. By the time asbestos was judged to be a hazardous material, it had been produced for decades. Judgments made in the 1980s in favor of claimants were paid by insurers under policies that were in effect, for example, in the 1940s, because that was the time (or among the times) of the "occurrence." Furthermore, because incidents of exposure to asbestos "occurred" in successive policy years, the insurer's liability to pay damages was determined by the courts to be the maximum annual policy limits multiplied by the number of years in which damage "occurred."

The insurance industry felt that it was blind sided by huge claims against general liability policies that were outdated. In response, the industry developed a "claims made" general liability policy, which provides coverage only if a claim is made (or the possibility of a claim becomes known) during a policy period. The claims-made policy (previously utilized primarily for D&O and professional liability coverage) has a profound effect on the insured's protection. In the asbestos example, it means that the only coverage available to the insured would be the policy limits in effect for the single year in which the claim first is made.

The claims-made policy has not come into common use for general liability policies. Nevertheless, risk managers and business officers need to be prepared for pitfalls such as the following in the event that a claims-made policy becomes part of the institution's risk management programs.

***Nonstandard terms.*** The language and coverage of claims-made policies are not standard, and various forms of claims-made policies are in circulation. The risk manager should examine several sources and try to negotiate the removal of restrictive language.

***Retroactive or "nose" period.*** This is a negotiable date prior to the policy inception subsequent to which a wrongful act will be covered by the policy if a claim is made during the policy period. Ideally, the retroactive period should be unlimited or at least coincide with the expiration date of the last occurrence policy. Otherwise, the institution will have gaps in coverage.

***Extended reporting or "tail" period.*** Tail coverage extends the time beyond the expiration date in which an event that occurred during the policy period may be discovered and reported. The length of the tail and the additional premium are negotiable and should be negotiated when the policy is being acquired (not after the policy expires or is replaced).

Claims-made policies for general liability are a new and different insurance contract, and the risk manager must exercise great care to ensure that the institution has the protection that it believes it has. The claims-made policy was created to limit the exposure of the insurers and, to the extent that it does, it increases the exposure of the insureds.

## DEFENSE COSTS

Traditionally, general liability insurers are obligated to pay the costs of defending the insureds, in addition to paying the policy limits. For example, in a case involving a $1 million policy, an insurer may spend $250,000 to defend an insured in a suit that results in a $1 million settlement. Because the settlement does not exceed the policy limit and the defense costs are covered in addition to the policy limit, the insurer incurs the entire cost of $1.25 million. Some insurance policies, especially claims-made, reject the tradition and provide that defense costs are included in the policy's limits. Colleges and universities should be aware of this possibility and increase their policy limits to offset its effect.

## PER OCCURRENCE VERSUS ANNUAL AGGREGATE

In the past, policy limits were applied on a "per occurrence" basis, so that the full policy limits applied to each occurrence in a single policy year. Many policies are now being written on an "annual aggregate" basis, wherein the policy limit is the total amount the insurance company will pay during the policy year regardless of the number of occurrences. Risk managers typically negotiate an aggregate that is a multiple of the limit per occurrence, such as a $1 million limit with a $3 million annual aggregate. For an additional premium, excess policies can generally be endorsed to "drop down" to cover an exhausted underlying aggregate limit.

## CRIME INSURANCE

Two basic types of policies, "blanket crime" and "comprehensive 3-D" (dishonesty, disappearance, and destruction), are available to cover employees to prevent financial loss due to their activities.

The blanket crime policy is a package contract that, within a single overall limit, provides five major crime coverages: fidelity, on-premises, off-premises, money orders and counterfeit paper currency, and depositor's forgery.

The comprehensive 3-D policy does not provide a single amount of insurance to cover loss from any insured hazard or any combination of hazards. Instead, it has 18 insuring clauses (including the five major crime coverages above) with a separate limit of insurance and a separate premium for each. The insured may select any one or all. These policies should be tailored to the needs of the institution. This requires careful attention by financial officers, auditors, and the agent or broker to assess individual institutional needs.

## UNEMPLOYMENT COMPENSATION

When an employee is dismissed without being at fault for the dismissal, he or she is entitled under law to unemployment compensation benefits. Students usually are not covered, and faculty contracts should be written so that faculty members with contracts for teaching in a subsequent fall term are not eligible to claim unemployment compensation benefits during the summer months.

Management of this risk dictates prudent human resources management practices, especially in larger institutions, which may lay off employees in one department while hiring in another. Close coordination and rethinking of the economics of summer layoff practices are necessary. Careful documentation of discharge for cause is fundamental in controlling this risk, because not all "for cause" dismissals disqualify a discharged employee from unemployment benefits. Institutions generally have an option to fund unemployment compensation benefits either by reimbursement to the state for actual benefits paid to former employees or by payment of a payroll tax. Thoughtful but prompt attention must be paid to each claim for unemployment compensation when notice is received from the state employment office.

For institutions with low employee termination rates, significant cost savings may result from self-insurance through reimbursement to the state for actual benefits paid. Some institutions have determined through feasibility studies or by using consultants that self-insurance is a less expensive method of funding this risk.

## STUDENT ACCIDENT AND HEALTH INSURANCE

Almost every institution has a program to provide student accident and health insurance, either mandatory or optional. In a few instances, student groups administer and purchase this coverage; in others the institution directly purchases the coverage on behalf of its students. Many innovations are being made to the insurance coverage available in this complex, competitive market. Since coverage may be subject to various state and federal discrimination regulations, institutions should see that plans offered to students do not violate them.

## OTHER INSURANCE

There are other types of insurance that colleges and universities may wish to consider for special risks.

***Business interruption.*** Business interruption insurance covers both lost income and continuation of salaries in the event that buildings, contents, boilers, or machinery are damaged or destroyed, thereby curtailing part or all of the institution's activities.

***Extra expense.*** Institutions can buy coverage for extra expenses incurred (above normal operating expenses) to continue operations in the event that property or equipment is damaged or destroyed. Examples of these expenses include overtime payments, temporary rental of facilities, and auxiliary equipment.

***Builder's risk.*** Builder's risk insurance covers buildings during construction. Such coverage should be arranged to include the insurable interest of the owner, contractor, and subcontractors.

***Valuable papers and records.*** Institutions can buy coverage of the cost to restore the damage to, or replace the loss of, papers and records. In colleges and universities, this coverage is primarily used for library books and periodicals. A general property policy usually covers the cost of blank paper and transcribing but not the cost of reconstructing the information in institutional records. A microfilm program (with copies stored in a separate building or vault) could offer better protection than insurance for office records.

***Accounts receivable insurance.*** Institutions can buy coverage of damage to or loss of accounts receivable that results in the inability to collect on receivables in the event that records cannot be reconstructed.

***Miscellaneous bonds.*** Examples of miscellaneous bonds are notary bonds, performance and payment bonds provided by contractors for construction projects, tax-free alcohol users' bonds, and post office operators' bonds.

***Nuclear risks.*** Radioactive contamination insurance, available for covering the cost of decontaminating buildings and controls systems, as well as nuclear "pool" coverages for both property damage and liability exposures, are available for institutions that own or operate nuclear reactors or that use special nuclear materials, as defined by federal agencies.

***Travel accident.*** Travel accident insurance should be provided for faculty and staff while they are traveling on business for the institution.

*Athletic insurance.* Accidental death, dismemberment, disability, and medical insurance should be provided for athletes, cheerleaders, and band members. Packages are offered that include rehabilitation and loss of future income to injured athletes. Such insurance should include protection for travel, play, and practice.

*Foreign liability.* Comprehensive general liability is available to provide legal defense and coverage for the institution and its employees for actions brought in connection with study programs and other activities in a foreign country. Coverage should be extended to include automobile liability and workers' compensation. In some instances, the foreign country may not recognize a U.S. insurance company and a reciprocal policy may need to be issued.

## Occupational Safety and Health

The Occupational Safety and Health Act of 1970 gave a new legal dimension to risk reduction. The act gives the force of law to practices and conditions of employment that are widely recognized as desirable, if expensive. Because the Occupational Safety and Health Administration (OSHA) can levy fines and penalties for violations of the act, the act promotes institutional recognition of OSHA regulations and attention to the means of funding and implementing them. Thus the law acts as a stimulus for making major capital expenditures that might otherwise have been deferred. The alert risk manager should use the act's requirements as an opportunity to reduce risk.

All independent institutions are subject to the act. Many state-supported or related institutions are exempt until their state has enacted a law acceptable to the federal government as a substitute for the act. When enacted, state regulations affect public institutions and are enforced by state inspectors. In addition, many institutions must comply with regulations of the National Institutes of Health, the Food and Drug Administration, the Environmental Protection Agency, and the Nuclear Regulatory Commission.

## Human Subjects

The use of human subjects in research is not unique to colleges and universities, but higher education undoubtedly claims the largest share of research using human subjects. The manner in which an institution treats its human subjects is a concern of risk management. Moreover, the Department of Health and Human Services (HHS) requires a system of peer review for research involving human subjects in order to protect individuals' rights.

Many institutions have now formalized an institutional review board (IRB) with jurisdiction extended beyond HHS-funded research to all use of human subjects in any research activity of the institution. The composition, function, and authority of these IRBs has gradually been refined.

Particularly in the area of medical research, there may be ill effects of scientific research on the human subject. HHS has suggested that human subjects be reimbursed for medical care and disability as a result of their volunteer efforts as subjects. In January 1979, HHS regulations become effective that require that informed consent forms stipulate the benefits, if any, provided in the event of injury arising out of research. Risk managers need to stay informed about the most recent regulations affecting treatment of human subjects.

It is desirable that the risk manager serve on the IRB to become familiar with research involving human subjects. Ideally, the risk manager should also help develop policies that will avoid or modify the risk in this area. Excellent opportunities for risk transfer exist when research is sponsored by organizations that may be required to indemnify the institution against potential claims. This may become apparent only through the risk manager's services on or communication with the IRB. Until such time as it is required by law, an institution may wish to make provision for compensating human subjects for medical expenses incurred as a result of research activities to help reduce the likelihood of a resulting claim.

## Summary

For humanitarian, social, legal, and financial reasons, an institution must make every reasonable effort to protect the health and safety of the campus community and the public from any hazards incidental to its operations. Colleges and universities must protect their financial resources and assets against possible serious losses, thus assisting to accomplish the goals of providing instruction, research, and public service. To meet these objectives in a cost-effective manner, a professional risk management program should be an essential component of every institution's financial management and strategy.

The key elements of risk management are to identify risk to which the institution is exposed, estimate the probability of loss of various risk exposures, determine the optimum method of managing risk, determine the most effective method of financing loss, and implement a plan to carry out and monitor the risk management program.

Some level of self-insurance (risk retention) is appropriate for every institution and is a highly efficient way to finance risk (whether through increasing deductibles or more sophisticated funded programs). Nevertheless, commercial insurance will continue to play a vital role in protecting an institution's resources, and care must be given to the selection of both the insurance intermediary (broker) and the insurer on which the institution ultimately relies. Coverage should be acquired on the broadest possible basis after the assumption of the maximum risk that the institution can safely manage. Resources are available to assist the institution in the development of a risk management program appropriate to its size, resources, and interests.

# References and Resources

PUBLICATIONS AND ARTICLES

Broadhurst, Arthur G. *Risk Management for Schools.* Boston, Mass.: National Association of Independent Schools, 1983.

Head, George L. *The Risk Management Process.* New York: Risk and Insurance Management Society, Inc., 1978.

Madsen, Claudina, and John H. Walker. *Risk Management and Insurance: A Handbook of Fundamentals.* Washington, D.C.: NACUBO, 1983.

*State Liability Laws for Charitable Organizations and Volunteers.* Washington, D.C.: Non-Profits' Risk Management and Insurance Institute, 1990.

Stone, Byron, and Carol North. *Risk Management and Insurance for Non-Profit Managers.* Chicago, Ill.: First Non-Profit Risk Pooling Trust, 1988.

PERIODICALS

*The Delphian: The Journal of Risk Management for Higher Education*

*From the Gym to the Jury*

ORGANIZATIONS

National Association of College and University Business Officers (NACUBO)
>One Dupont Circle, Suite 500
>Washington, DC 20036-1178
>202-861-2500

United Risk Management Insurance Association (URMIA)
>One Dupont Circle, Suite 505
>Washington, DC 20036-1178
>202-861-2538

Further information on insurance companies can be obtained by consulting the publications of A.M. Best Company, Inc., Oldwick, N.J., which provides "ratings" of commercial insurance companies by size and financial strength.

# CHAPTER 15

# Auditing

by
Warren H. Spruill
University of Alabama System

# Sponsor

## KPMG PEAT MARWICK
345 Park Avenue
New York, NY 10154
212-758-9700

*KPMG Peat Marwick focuses on maximizing the value of external and internal auditing for its clients.*

# Contents

## 15: Auditing

Colleges and universities usually are controlled by a governing board (exceptions are military academies and some proprietary and parochial institutions). The board delegates authority to the president, who in turn delegates specific authority for various functions to his or her subordinates. As the delegation becomes more extensive, the organizational structure becomes more complex. In this environment desired results may fail to develop because of circumstantial changes, problems in communication, and willful deviations. Those delegating authority must, therefore, insist on a sound system of internal control.

Every institution must establish periodic assessments of the system of internal control. Auditors evaluate the adequacy of the internal control system and determine if all management levels are in compliance with the system. Colleges and universities experience a variety of audits. Some of these are performed by auditors hired or contracted by the institution. Others are performed on the behalf of third parties, usually state and federal government agencies. This complex network of audits serves a variety of decisionmakers, both inside and outside the organization, who need reliable and relevant information. The institution itself needs audits to check its operations to ensure that programs conform to the expectations of senior management and the governing board. Taxing authorities want to make certain that all taxes have been paid. Lending bodies want to know how financially sound the institution is before agreeing to make large loans.

Audit services are provided by three types of auditors: independent, internal, and governmental. Independent auditors, usually certified public accountants (CPAs), are engaged by an institution to express an opinion on its financial statements. These audits are performed under auditing standards developed by the American Institute of Certified Public Accountants (AICPA). In some public colleges and universities, a state auditor issues an opinion on the annual financial statements. The opinion on the financial statement provides a basis for third parties to know that statements are presented fairly, consistently, and in conformity with generally accepted accounting standards. Independent colleges and universities, as well as some public institutions, engage auditors to perform audits of federal awards. Federal award audits done under the Office of Management and Budget (OMB) Circulars A-128 and A-133 are discussed in this chapter; audit requirements for federal student financial aid are discussed in Chapter 22, Student Financial Aid, and are not covered in this chapter.

Internal auditors are employees of the institution. Internal auditing has a significant role in the management of most institutions, and it has become increasingly varied both in scope and objective. Internal auditing helps to ensure that financial resources are being properly managed and accounted for and that the institution is complying with applicable policies, standards, regulations, and laws. Internal auditing is an independent appraisal function that examines and evaluates an organization's activities as a service to that organization. Internal auditing results in analyses, appraisals, recommendations, counsel, and information concerning the activities reviewed.

Governmental auditors are concerned about compliance with laws, regulations, and the terms of agreements. They are concerned also about the proper accountability of public funds entrusted to the college or university. In addition to federal auditors, public institutions are subject to audit by state auditing agencies.

The Internal Revenue Service (IRS) is concerned about proper filing of returns and payment of taxes on unrelated trade or business income, and it also wants to know if an organization operates within the constraints of its exempt status. IRS auditors check to see that all employment taxes are being properly withheld and paid to the U.S. Treasury, which involves an evaluation of the classification of people paid as employees and people paid as independent contractors. (For a full discussion of this subject, see Chapter 9, Taxation.)

Sales tax audits determine if all payments due have been made. If a college or university claims an exemption of fuel tax for off-road consumption, that claim will be audited. Generally, any financial transaction that has the potential to be taxed is subject to audit. Colleges and universities should maintain adequate records to demonstrate their method of computation and payment of all taxes.

Auditing has experienced a growing role in the management of most institutions over the past 50 years. Auditing assists all levels of management to assure internal and external constituencies that financial resources are being properly managed and accounted for and that the institution is complying with institutional policies, accounting standards, regulations, and laws.

Some auditors spend considerable effort on evaluating internal control. Recent changes in federal auditing requirements have placed greater emphasis on internal control than in the past. Federal requirements have combined external audits and federal audits to the extent that they now can be considered at the same time.

This chapter gives an overview of institutional responsibilities regarding audits; turns to internal audits and long-range planning; discusses the administration of internal audits; and covers external audits. Finally, the chapter notes some trends that will affect audits at colleges and universities throughout the 1990s.

# Institutional Responsibilities

INTERNAL CONTROL

A college or university's system of internal control should ascertain that

- the college or university clearly communicates its established policies, plans, and procedures and the entire organization is in compliance with them, as well as with federal, state, and local regulations and laws;

- institutional assets are accounted for and safeguarded from losses of all kinds;

- information used for decision making is reliable;

- all assigned responsibilities are carried out competently; and

- institutional, federal, and state financial reporting requirements are met.

The Committee of Sponsoring Organizations of the Treadway Commission (COSO) issued an exposure draft of a document outlining a common definition of internal control in 1991. The following points represent fundamental concepts of internal control. COSO believes there are nine components that, taken as a whole, constitute a system of internal control. These are:

*Integrity, ethical values, and competence.* Integrity and ethical values must be practiced at all levels of the organization, and staff performing internal audits must be competent.

*Control environment.* The institutional environment must be conducive to effective control, and a control consciousness must exist on the part of staff.

*Objectives.* Objectives and related implementation strategies and plans must be established for the institution as a whole and for significant activities.

*Risk assessment.* Risks related to achievement of the objectives must be identified and analyzed.

*Information systems.* Information requirements must be identified and systems put in place to provide the needed information.

*Control procedures.* Control procedures must be in place to ensure adherence to policy and to address risks related to the achievement of objectives.

*Communication.* Relevant messages and information must be communicated throughout the institution—downward, sideward, and upward.

*Managing change.* Change that affects the institution's ability to achieve its objectives must be identified and responded to in a timely manner.

*Monitoring.* The functioning of internal control must be monitored, and policies and procedures must be modified as needed.[1]

In each phase of the audit process, attention should be directed to the existence and effective functioning of internal controls—the methods and procedures adopted by an institution to safeguard its assets, to ensure the accuracy and reliability of its accounting data, to promote operational efficiency, to protect its personnel, and to help ensure adherence to institutional policies, accounting standards, regulations, and laws. Management is responsible for establishing and maintaining a system of internal control based on sound principles. Management's obligation to administer financial affairs justifies the careful design, installation, and support of internal control procedures.

Characteristics of a satisfactory internal control system in an institution of any size include:

- Organizational structures that separate functional responsibilities and create a deterrent to fraud

- Periodic monitoring to ensure adherence to prescribed policies

- Authorization, approval, and record-keeping procedures that give accounting control over assets, liabilities, and changes in fund balances

- Employees who are capable of executing prescribed responsibilities

- Clerical practices that ensure compliance with approved authorization and record-keeping procedures

As an institution grows, management problems become more complex, computerized processes become more sophisticated, delegation of authority and responsibility increases, and an effective, responsive system of internal control becomes increasingly important. Responsibility, authority, and operating policies and procedures should be clearly defined and documented through the appropriate records and forms, as well as through a logical flow of record-keeping and approval procedures.

## AUDIT COMMITTEES

The governing board of an institution should appoint an audit committee. Any matters considered essential to ensure the fiscal integrity of the institution may be considered within the committee's purview. Audit committees usually perform the following functions:

- To select, or approve selection of, the accounting firm that audits the annual financial statements

- To meet with members of the accounting firm to discuss the scope of the forthcoming annual audit

- To meet with the accounting firm to review the results of the audit, management letter comments, and other matters of interest to the committee

- To oversee the internal audit function and review or approve the annual internal audit plan

- To receive periodic status reports from the chief internal auditor on internal audit activities, including accomplishments of the annual plan, major deviations, and significant audit findings

Many institutions do not have separate audit committees. Often the governing board at public institutions is too small; even on large boards, the finance committee may act as the audit committee. While a separate audit committee is preferable, under certain circumstances the finance committee can function as the audit committee.

In addition to the above functions, audit committees have several responsibilities:

- To understand the nature and complexity of institutional operations

- To grasp any technical problems the enterprise might encounter in applying generally accepted accounting principles (GAAP)

- To comprehend accounting principles applicable to the institution

- To review the procedures followed by external and internal auditors

- To identify difficulties or problems in complying with regulatory agency requirements

- To report to the full board on the adequacy of internal control over financial and administrative transactions

- To ensure that matters of noncompliance with institutional policies, GAAP, regulations, and laws are resolved[2]

*Audit planning.* Internal auditing provides a comprehensive review of systems and activities of the institution, including management information systems. Effective planning produces a number of benefits.

- It facilitates the effective allocation of resources to the audit function.

- It produces the psychological benefit of encouraging the parties involved to plan ahead and anticipate potential problems or opportunities.

- It enhances communication and cooperation between the auditor and management, because they work together to coordinate efforts toward the goals of the audit.

- It enables the audit committee to assess the effectiveness of audits by comparing the preaudit plan with the actual results.[3]

# Internal Audits

Internal audits evolved because institutional managers needed an independent evaluation of information relating to significant aspects of institutional operations that was more detailed and more frequent than external auditors normally could provide. The expansion and complexity of these operations made it increasingly difficult to monitor the effectiveness with which policies were being followed, objectives were being met, and control systems were functioning. Not only has management's need for information grown, but accountability for the appropriate and efficient use of institutional resources has become a matter of great concern to students, legislative bodies, government agencies, the general public, and all levels of institutional management.

Internal auditing should operate under policies established by the governing board. The institution should have an audit charter, which provides a statement of purpose, authority, and responsibility for internal audits consistent with the Institute of Internal Auditors (IIA) *Standards for the Professional Practice of Internal Auditing*. This statement should define the purpose of internal audits, specify their scope and lines of communication and reporting, and declare that auditors have no authority over or responsibility for the activities they audit. Such independence permits internal auditors to perform their work freely and objectively. The institution's internal auditing policy also should be set forth in the auditors' charter, which should be signed by the president.

Internal auditing is no longer limited to the practice of ensuring appropriate financial activity and policy compliance. Internal auditors now also evaluate the effectiveness of system procedures and activities in operational audits. Thus, the full scope of internal auditing encompasses an examination of financial transactions, including an evaluation of the adequacy of internal controls; an evaluation of compliance with and adequacy of applicable policies and other requirements both internal and external; and a review of the effectiveness of the use of institutional resources. However, not every audit embraces all these objectives. A particular audit may be selective in scope to meet a specific management need. The scope of internal audits varies among institutions because of differences in the nature of their operations, organizational structure, management style and competence, employee capabilities, and concepts of operating control.

The efficiency of any organization is affected by the quality of its management control, which begins with good planning and appropriately delegated authority and continues through performance and reporting the results of that performance. An effective management control system encourages adherence to policies and procedures. It includes carefully designed standards of performance by which a particular activity functions and by which the activity is measured and evaluated. As a result of this measurement and evaluation, operations may be adjusted to conform to prescribed or desired standards.

INTERNAL AUDITORS

Internal auditors must have access to all college or university records that are relevant to the activity under review. Such access, which enables the internal auditor to conduct an effective examination, should be authorized in the college or university's internal auditing policy. The internal auditor should be sufficiently removed from political pressures to ensure that conclusions may be reported without fear of censure. The internal auditor must remain independent from the administrators responsible for the operations under review. In many cases, the chief auditor reports directly to the institution's president or audit committee. In colleges or universities where the auditor reports to the chief financial or business officer, at a minimum, the auditor should have direct access to the audit committee. In any event, the auditor should meet privately with the audit committee at least annually.

***Scope of the internal auditor's responsibility.*** The audit charter sets forth the auditor's responsibility and, as such, it grants the auditor access to people, records, and property. The charter does not spell out what areas should be audited.

The internal auditor should be concerned with every phase of institutional activity. The internal auditor's responsibilities should include:

- Examining financial transactions for accuracy and compliance with institutional policies

- Evaluating financial and operational procedures for adequate internal controls

- Testing the timeliness, reliability, and usefulness of institutional records and reports

- Evaluating the cost-effectiveness of operations and activities

- Monitoring the development, implementation, and major revision of methods, systems, and procedures, including those pertinent to computer applications

- Evaluating and monitoring the computer center's system of internal control to ensure adequate security and controls related to hardware, software, data, and operating personnel and to ensure retrieval of necessary data for audit purposes

- Evaluating control over end-user computing

- Determining the level of compliance with required internal policies and procedures, state and federal laws, and government regulations

- Evaluating program performance

- Coordinating work with external auditors

- Reviewing the contractual and project management control for projects

In addition to reviewing compliance with policies, plans, and procedures, the internal auditor should review their appropriateness in light of current conditions.

*Affiliations with institutional constituencies.* Many institutions have foundations or other entities for which they are fiscally responsible. Although these may be separate legal entities, foundation activities often are intertwined with those of the institution. Foundation personnel may be custodians of institution-owned property and participate in or influence institutional decisions. In addition, some independent colleges and universities have wholly owned subsidiaries. These may be units held as investments or organizations that provide essential support to the institution, such as a hotel. If they are under the control of the institution, the audit committee should decide if they should be included in the audit plan.

Colleges and universities contract for a wide variety of services. These include such activities as construction, food services, janitorial services, and pest control. Competitively bid, fixed-price contracts for commodities are of little audit interest; however, an effective internal auditor needs access to contractor data when the quantity, quality, or price of goods and services is at issue.

***Coordination with external auditors.*** The internal auditor must interact with the external auditor to identify and evaluate the activities being performed. Through such action

- the internal auditor can rely on the scope and frequency of the external and/or federal audit work and reduce the scope of his or her work accordingly; and

- the external auditor may rely on the internal auditor's work, thereby reducing the cost or involvement of outside agents in the institution's activities.

Because the federal government requires external audits for several different purposes, internal auditors should remain acutely aware of federal audit requirements. All audits performed on behalf of the government must conform to federal audit standards.

Once the internal auditor has established relationships with the various constituents and with external auditors, he or she is ready to begin the long-range planning necessary for a comprehensive review or work program.

## SELECTION OF AREAS TO BE AUDITED

An integral part of the internal audit function is the development of a precise audit plan. With the proliferation of desktop computers and the increasing acceptance of risk analysis, many improvements in planning are possible. The relative risk of various activities is the most critical factor in selecting internal audit projects.

In the audit selection process, the internal auditor must take into consideration the three basic responsibilities of management: planning, organizing, and directing organizational activities in order to achieve institutional goals and objectives. The internal auditor views these management objectives in the context of certain control objectives:

- The reliability and integrity of information
- Compliance with institutional policies, accounting standards, laws, and regulations
- The safeguarding of assets
- The economical and efficient use of resources
- The accomplishment of established goals and objectives[4]

In determining what to audit, when to audit it, and for what purpose, the auditor must compare the relative benefits expected from the audit to the estimated costs of conducting the audit. The benefits may include improved control over various parts of the operations, less losses, and the location of trouble spots. There is also the benefit of psychological deterrence: when employees know all activities are subject to review, they may follow policies and procedures more rigorously.

When developing an audit plan, the auditor must

- determine the scope of responsibilities of the auditing function, including any limitations imposed by management or the governing board;
- develop a comprehensive list of all areas subject to review;
- devise a system to assess the risk associated with each area;
- rank areas in order of the magnitude of risk to the institution;
- communicate this risk assessment to the institution's key decisionmakers; and
- select the top-ranked areas as the nucleus of the annual audit plan.

An annual schedule of activities and departments to be audited should be prepared, and a long-range plan of four or five years should be considered when developing the schedule. Files can easily be kept up-to-date on a computer.

In the planning stage, the auditor can only estimate risk. Usually this estimate is imprecise because of the limited amount of available information regarding a project. As more information is made available, the risk assessment should be revised. Even with limited information and the subjective nature of risk assessment, initial risk assessments are useful for two reasons: they give management a framework in which to consider overall risk and, in some instances, they can make management aware of risks it had not considered.

Developing a sound internal audit plan is only half of the job. The plan must be flexible. It must be subject to change as the institution adjusts to changes. The departure of key people, changes in laws or regulations, and other factors can affect the auditor's plan. An effective audit department is sensitive to these changes in the environment. Risk ratings on projects will change continually. Regulations change, as do attitudes about the degree of enforcement of existing rules.

***Inventory of potential audit areas.*** Before an audit can be performed, the scope of the audit must be a manageable size. This makes it easier for the auditor to make staff assignments, to issue reports to the appropriate levels of management, and to provide conclusions on a timely basis. Before risk can be assessed, all potential areas of concern must be identified. Many sources within an institution are helpful in identifying audit areas, including:

- Organizational charts and directories
- Policy and procedure manuals
- Charts of accounts
- Listings of research grants and contracts
- Listings of previous audit reports
- Listings of affiliation agreements
- Construction and capital plans
- Budgets
- Flow charts and internal control documentation
- Lists of audit clauses in contracts

The auditor should ask senior management and external auditors to identify other areas that should be included in the long-range internal audit plan.

An auditor at a university with a teaching hospital has an additional set of concerns when inventorying the universe: effectively identifying the audit areas in a unit that differs, in many ways, from other parts of the university. The Association of Health Care Internal Auditors (AHCIA) has developed a database of audit concerns and related issues.[5]

***Risk assessment.*** After conducting the inventory, the auditor will have a list of potential areas to audit. The next step in the auditing process is to consider the relative level of risk in each area.

There is no one set of risk components that can be used in risk assessment. Areas of consideration may include the following:

- Newness, changed conditions, or sensitivity of the organization, program, activity, or function

- The function's dollar magnitude and duration

- The extent of federal participation, either in terms of resources or regulatory authority

- Management needs, as developed in consultation with the responsible program officials

- The adequacy of the financial management system and controls

- Timeliness, reliability, and coverage of reports prepared by others, such as state and local governments and independent public accountants

- Results of other evaluations, for example, inspections and program reviews

- Mandatory legislative or other provisions

- Availability of audit resources

- The date and results of the last audit

- Financial exposure of the institution's resources

- Potential loss and risk of the institution's resources and public reputation (A potential loss should be viewed in the same manner as a loss that has actually occurred. Failure to apply for matching gifts is one example of a potential loss.)

- Requests by management for special investigations and other audit services

- Major changes in operations, programs, systems, and controls

- Opportunities to achieve operating benefits

- Changes to and capabilities of the audit staff

RISK EVALUATION SCORES. Once projects have been evaluated, a risk evaluation model should be used to determine a risk evaluation score for each project. This score is used to determine the priority of a project in relation to all other projects under consideration. The higher the risk evaluation score, the greater the need for an audit. Projects should be sorted by risk evaluation score in descending order. The result is a prioritized list of audit segments.

Much drudgery can be eliminated from the process of risk evaluation with the use of a personal computer. Several organizations have developed software packages that compute risk evaluation scores. Many internal audit departments also have designed models to run on personal computers.

***Changing priorities.*** Internal auditors generally are not subject to many external pressures about the timing of a project, but some important exceptions should be noted. One exception is the acquisition of major new software systems. Whether purchased or developed internally, these new software systems must be reviewed during their development or prior to their implementation. Deletion and correction of inadequate or incomplete controls while a system is still in the design phase will save time in the long run. It is very expensive to correct control deficiencies after systems have been installed. The auditor, therefore, must be available to review the controls in new systems as they are planned, designed, or developed.[6]

Other events can determine the need for an audit. For example, suspected fraud or embezzlement can upset priorities. Sudden or excessive departures of key personnel should cause the auditor to reevaluate his or her priorities. Certain major acquisitions fall into a priority category similar to new computer systems. The auditor frequently receives special management requests.

Low-PRIORITY AREAS. Projects with very low risk present a special problem for the auditor. Philosophies differ, and the handling of this problem is subjective. Some suggestions follow.

- Do not allocate resources to low-rated projects.

- Budget a small percentage of each annual budget to low-rated projects.

- Schedule periodic surveys in these areas to verify the low-risk score.

- Use these projects as a training ground for new staff members and student interns.

- Review these projects on an extended audit cycle, perhaps every five to ten years.

Some universities have used student interns in their internal audit departments. This serves the dual purpose of providing a valuable learning experience to the student while helping the internal audit department diminish its backlog of smaller jobs.

Every segment of an organization needs some audit coverage. The longer any segment goes without an audit, the more problems are likely to occur. Audit departments that are understaffed should be cautious about diverting resources to evaluate low-priority areas when, as a consequence, areas with large risk scores go unattended.

***Matching audit resources with priorities.*** Once priorities have been determined, the auditor must begin to match priorities with resources. A good rule of thumb when determining audit resources is that 210 staff days of work equal one full-time auditor. This will vary by institution according to such considerations as vacation policies, number of holidays, and time spent in training.

***Determining staffing levels.*** The chief auditor should list in priority order the staff workload and any work that could be done with additional audit resources. These lists provide an excellent basis for a dialogue with the key institutional decisionmakers. The result might be authorization to hire more auditors or the establishment of time cycles, in which the audits would be scheduled over two to five years. Regardless of the outcome, these lists give the audit committee and top management a basis for understanding the trade-off between audit staff size and audit risk. In institutions with limited audit staff, contractors may be hired to perform all or some of an audit. Public accounting and consulting firms are sources of such consultants.

## TYPES OF INTERNAL AUDITS

***Financial audits.*** Financial audits determine whether the financial statements or other reports provide timely, accurate, relevant, reliable, and complete information upon which to make decisions. Financial audits concentrate on accounting controls, which can be divided into three principal areas:

- Control of assets

- Systems of authorization and approval

- Separation of accounting duties from those concerned with operations or custody of assets

In financial audits, the primary concerns are the determination of the reliability and accuracy of financial data, including supporting records, and the evaluation of internal financial controls.

***Operational audits.*** An operational audit evaluates activities, identifies inefficient and ineffective practices, and recommends measures for corrective action. These audits provide an objective examination of operational controls, systems, and procedures. A financial audit can be extended into an operational audit simply by changing the direction of the audit. For example, an auditor who finds an excessive number of computational errors made by clerical staff might ask what caused these errors. That inquiry might lead to a review of personnel practices: Are the right people being hired for the job? Are they properly supervised? Do they have the right equipment? Are they properly trained?

Any department within an institution that has measurable goals and objectives is a candidate for an operational audit, provided that the internal audit department has staff who are competent to perform the engagement. An operational audit ensures that maximum benefit is received for the resources expended. Administrative activities are measured and evaluated against standards set by management. Such performance standards may be communicated by various means, including long-range plans, budgets, job assignment sheets, or production schedules. When performing an operational audit of a highly technical or complex activity, the auditor may require the assistance of a consultant or subject matter specialist familiar with the activity being audited.

**Compliance audits.** Compliance audits are concerned with adherence to applicable policy, laws, regulations, and other administrative requirements. Internal auditors must spend an increasing amount of time on such audits because of the severe consequences of noncompliance with certain regulations. These consequences can be monetary refunds, loss of future funds, or damage to the institution's reputation. In many cases, compliance audits may help prevent adverse findings in an external audit.

**Investigative audits.** Fraud and other financial irregularities are committed by managers, employees, students, and others who have access to an institution's information and resources. The internal audit department is often called upon to do special investigations when such incidents occur or when there is suspicion of such an occurrence.

The IIA's *Standards for the Professional Practice of Internal Auditing* set out the internal auditor's responsibilities in the area of fraud:

- When an internal auditor discovers a significant weakness in internal control, he or she should perform tests to determine if an irregularity occurred because of the weakness.

- When unusual circumstances or transactions occur, the auditor should adopt a skeptical attitude with regard to answers to questions.

- The auditor should be alert in thinking how a fraud might take place.

The internal auditor has two categories of service to offer the institution in dealing with white-collar crime. First, the auditor should recommend means to deter or prevent it; second, he or she should develop methods of detecting it.

DEVELOPING THE AUDIT PROGRAM

A formal, written program for each internal audit project should be developed with the advice and approval of the auditor's immediate superior. This program should establish the general scope of audit coverage.

***Research and preparation for the audit project.*** To perform an audit, the auditor needs information, accumulated through research and a survey of the area or activity to be audited, to develop a profile of the activity to be audited. Thoroughness in conducting preaudit research and the preliminary survey may eliminate time-consuming audit tests. For example, a comparison and analysis of several years' worth of operating results for a unit may yield sufficient information to eliminate similar questions or tests generally required later in the process. Research can help the auditor understand the operations of the audited unit and render more informed recommendations. Research findings often direct the auditor's approach in performing the preliminary survey and hence in defining the scope of an audit.

***Preliminary survey.*** The purpose of a preliminary survey is to obtain or update information on the way an activity is intended to function and the way control procedures are intended to work. Through interaction with the unit being audited, the survey answers the basic questions of who, what, where, when, why, and how. If the survey is not well-planned and thorough, important steps might be skipped in the audit. Although preliminary surveys may vary in style among institutions, certain information, including the following items, should be sought.

- Objectives of the activity, which are generally available in policy statements, management directives, and documents chartering the institution

- Organization of the activity, which should include not only an organizational chart for the activity but also a chart describing the position of the activity in the total institutional structure

- Financial information, which must be identified to determine what is available and where it is located

- Operating instructions, with copies obtained for use in the audit verification and evaluation phase. A detailed study of operating instructions should *not* be made during the preliminary survey

- Operating method, which should be analyzed to identify the flow of data within the institution and resulting records

- Areas of management concern (described by the head of the unit under audit), which should be recorded.

Deficiencies mentioned in prior audit reports should be reviewed with the head of the audited unit, and a determination should be made of what controls have been implemented to correct the deficiencies.

## VERIFICATION AND EVALUATION

The audit program should list tests and procedures required for each step of the process to ensure verification and evaluation of the program. Each audit is unique; thus, it is not possible to develop a standard audit program. If an operational audit is conducted, tests should identify causes for exceptions to policies and objectives, as well as the exceptions themselves.

Audits require a broad range of techniques for testing activities, such as interviewing, observing, and financial analysis. Care must be taken to ensure that all work performed is relevant to the purpose of the audit. Among the techniques that an auditor may use in the audit process are interviewing, creating flow charts, and statistical sampling.

***Interviewing.*** The auditor should strive to develop a comfortable relationship with the head of the unit being audited by interviewing this person. One of the most effective methods for conducting such an interview is the use of a questionnaire that the head of the unit completes in the presence of the auditor, who records the answers. Such a questionnaire ensures consistency of coverage, provides a basis for conversation, and provides documentation.

To be useful, a questionnaire must be prepared in sufficient detail to ensure that major operating areas are not overlooked. A majority of the questions should be worded to avoid "yes" or "no" answers. While some responses may duplicate information developed in other phases of the audit, this duplication is useful in that it provides a basis for comparison.

***Creating flow charts.*** Flow charts spell out the duties of each person involved in a function. They can serve:

- to describe the procedures used in an activity and the interaction of various systems and their influence on other activities;

- to evaluate weaknesses in control;

- to reveal the need for certain steps or tests required in the audit program that otherwise would not have been determined without exhaustive testing and interviewing; and

- to reduce the amount of narrative required to understand the system.

Flow charts can provide a means for analyzing complex operations. Flow charts need not be elaborate, formal, or extensive but merely adequate for the task at hand.

***Statistical sampling.*** Statistical sampling is used in auditing to determine the size of samples, to select the items to be sampled, and to evaluate the results of the sample. When a small set of items is used to make judgments about the population from which they were selected, some risk is taken. The amount of risk taken can be measured by using the laws of probability.[7]

Statistical sampling can greatly expand audit coverage and effectiveness and reduce time spent on the audit. It can enable the auditor to estimate accurately some characteristics of a population by examining a part of that population. This serves to supplement the auditor's judgment and to enhance the documentation of audit procedures.

***Financial analysis and analytical review.*** Financial analysis and analytical review represent forms of inquiry. These tools are used heavily by external auditors when auditing an institution's financial statements and also are useful in the internal audit process. Financial analysis and analytical review are used to highlight discrepancies or unusual relationships. Deviations by themselves do not indicate a problem—they point out areas or transactions where the auditor needs to do further investigation. These areas include:

- Areas of potential savings, for example, excessive freight charges

- Accounting areas, by comparing balances in one report with those in an earlier one

- Major fluctuations, for example, significant increases in payments to consultants, or in banking fees

Techniques include comparing data and analyzing ratios, trends, and regression. These techniques are useful in spotting areas of fraud or embezzlement. For example, in an audit of a campus motor pool operation, an auditor discovered that an excessive number of batteries had been purchased. In determining whether these purchases were reasonable, the auditor divided the number of batteries bought into the number of miles driven by all of the vehicles in the pool. This indicated that, on the average, each vehicle received a new battery every 10,000 miles. With this indication, the auditor used other investigative techniques and found that batteries were purchased for personal vehicles and other unauthorized purposes. The analytical procedures were not used to prove fraud but to point out an unusual condition requiring further investigation.

The audit findings—the results of the audit tests and procedures—are the basis for the auditor's conclusions as to the effectiveness of the audited operations. The audit findings should be evaluated and ranked according to their relevance and materiality.

## COMMUNICATIONS DURING AN AUDIT

An audit project should begin with an opening conference with the head of the unit to be audited. This interview provides the opportunity to establish the purpose and scope of the audit and to explain the methods and objectives of the audit process; it also helps allay any concerns the unit head may have.

During the course of the audit a continuous dialogue should be maintained between the auditor and the head and staff of the audited unit. Some auditors refer to this as a participative or cooperative audit. Communicating with and involving the audited unit's staff ensures that the staff stay informed of the progress on the audit. It also provides a forum for exchanging views on findings as they are developed. Often this approach leads to a resolution of problems before the audit is completed; it also tends to dispel any adversarial attitudes that may be associated with the auditing function.

## THE AUDIT REPORT

After the audit is completed, the findings must be reported, in written form, to management. Customarily a draft of the report is discussed at an "exit conference" with the head of the audited unit. This conference provides an opportunity to clarify points in the report before its formal issuance. The head of the audited unit may include in the report any pertinent remarks he or she has.

The formal audit report should indicate any significant deviations from institutional directives, as well as the consequences of the deviations. It should include a description of the causes of the deviations. The report should conclude with the auditor's recommendations for corrections and necessary changes in operations to prevent similar deviations in the future. Observations, opinions, and recommendations of lesser importance, not included in the formal report but worthy of note, may be reported by memoranda or other means. Confidential or sensitive findings may be transmitted to senior institutional management in a separate letter.

Audits should indicate the type of corrective action that will prevent recurrence of variations from the desired state. When control modifications are suggested, they should be designed to accommodate future operations. The head of the audited unit should have the opportunity to respond in writing to the audit findings prior to issuance of the audit report.

***Follow-up.*** After an appropriate time interval, usually six months, a follow-up review of audit recommendations should be conducted to determine that appropriate corrective actions have been taken by the audited unit. The auditor does not have authority to require implementation of a recommendation; this is a management decision. If the auditor believes, however, that the decision is not in the best interests of the institution, he or she should have sufficient independence and a line of communication for presenting the case to a higher authority for resolution.

## COMPUTER TECHNOLOGY AND THE INTERNAL AUDITOR

***Electronic data processing.*** With the widespread use of electronic data processing (EDP), special problems in control and security of data demand the attention of management and the internal auditor. The objectives and essential characteristics of accounting control do not change by using data processing. However, organizational procedures used in EDP may differ from those used in manual data processing.

EDP controls fall into two categories: general controls and application controls. General controls deal with overall control issues such as implementation, operations, data and physical security, and systems software. Applications controls relate to the methods used to ensure completeness, accuracy, and consistency in an individual application. General controls refer to the overall administration of the management information system area; they indicate how well the unit is run. Application controls apply to specific programs, such as the payroll program. For example, a combination lock on computer room doors to bar unauthorized access is a general control. A device that rejects any payroll transaction that does not have an authenticated social security number is an application control. An EDP control system must be concerned with evaluating the system's definition, related input, and operating procedures to ensure adequate checks on processing and reporting functions. Effective programming, adequate documentation of programs and systems, separation of responsibilities, security of equipment, programs, data and communications, and periodic audits provide the means for achieving internal control in a computerized system that may include one or more mainframe computers, minicomputers, and personal computers.

***Audits of new systems.*** Data-processing systems are developed by internal staff or purchased externally. Some development efforts result in large, complex, integrated systems; others in smaller, distributed ones. Management and internal auditors are concerned with the reliability, integrity, and control of these systems. Each type of system requires different expertise for both data processors and auditors. Regardless of how the proposed system is acquired, the scope of the audit should assess the controls that will be in the system and determine their adequacy in safeguarding institutional assets.

For systems developed internally, the auditor needs to review the systems development life cycle to determine whether the development was documented properly at each particular step and all appropriate development steps were included.

For purchased systems, the auditor should assess the processes for selecting and evaluating both the vendor and the product. These procedures ensure that appropriate steps were taken in evaluating the software, not necessarily that the best purchasing decision was made. Purchased systems can be installed with no changes or with extensive modifications. Any type of system must be reviewed to ascertain its accountability and reliability.

*New technology.* Methods of controlling advanced on-line and distributed systems can differ from those for batch systems; however, the underlying objectives for security and control remain the same. For example, users and transactions require authorization, data and equipment need safeguarding, and applications and systems must be auditable. Operationally, processing results should be accurate and timely, and resources should be used efficiently and effectively.

Organizations have addressed the challenges of distributed systems, advanced networking, communications systems, and powerful workstations by establishing and relying on technical audit personnel and training generalists on the audit staff. Smaller institutions should engage consultants to do these reviews. A good source of experts is a CPA firm.

*Audit tools.* New technology includes easy-to-use audit tools. Computer-assisted audit techniques (CAATS) are available both in mainframes and personal computers. With CAATS, an auditor can extract information, compare files, verify counts and values, and perform other functions such as analytical calculations. Many vendors offer statistical and analytical tools for auditing computer files and records. Other tools useful in auditing include query and ad hoc report-writing systems, spreadsheet packages, graphics systems, word processors, database systems, and application development tools.

*Specialized computer subjects.* Certain areas require a high level of audit expertise. Audits of operating systems or distributed systems in an open systems environment require specialists. In large institutions, the internal audit department should assess the adequacy of internal control in these complex areas. In some institutions, consultants may be hired to do these reviews.

## STAFF QUALIFICATIONS AND TRAINING

Historically, great emphasis has been placed on accounting training as a qualification for an internal auditor. As organizations have become more complex, however, the nature and purpose of the internal audit function have expanded. The audit staff should have a variety of skills and education in areas such as statistics, engineering, operations research, financial and business management, data processing, and systems analysis. Not all of these qualities will be found in any one person, but as many of them as possible should be represented within the staff. As an audit group diversifies, it should keep its primary mission in focus. Any audit department must keep a healthy balance between analysis of internal control on the one hand and internal consulting on the other. Where financial and compliance audits are the top priorities for internal audit departments, accountants should compose most, if not all, of the department staff.

Both the United States General Accounting Office (GAO) and IIA have adopted minimum continuing education standards for internal auditors. In addition, internal auditors holding professional certifications such as certified internal auditor (CIA), certified information system auditor (CISA), certified management accountant (CMA), or certified public accountant (CPA) have continuing education requirements that must be met to maintain certification.

Staff training is a responsibility of management. Since the auditing department may be called on to evaluate a wide range of activities, members of the audit staff should be trained to a high level of proficiency in the use of audit tools and techniques, such as the use of EDP equipment and sampling techniques. On-the-job training, departmental staff training sessions, formal courses, seminars, and training sessions can be used to meet continuing education requirements. Many professional organizations, such as the Association of College and University Auditors, offer courses for internal auditors.

EVALUATING THE INTERNAL AUDIT FUNCTION

College or university management should conduct a periodic independent review of the audit department—in essence, an operational audit of the department. In 1986, the IIA issued a standard on quality assurance that requires an external review by a qualified party at least once every three years. Independent evaluations, referred to as "peer reviews," are offered by the IIA's Quality Assurance Review Service, CPA firms, consultants, and the Association of College and University Auditors (ACUA). For colleges and universities that want an evaluation of their internal audit department, ACUA refers internal auditors from other institutions who have been trained in and agree to adhere to the standards prescribed by ACUA. IIA's *Quality Assurance Review Manual for Internal Auditing* is also an excellent guide for conducting such reviews.

# External Audits

External audits are performed by the following parties:

- Independent CPAs and state auditors
- Federal agency auditors
- State and local government agencies
- The Internal Revenue Service
- The General Accounting Office

In the past, an institution's external auditor and the federal audit agencies played separate roles in the auditing process; certain aspects of those roles have been combined over the years. The move toward a single audit concept culminated with the issuance of OMB Circular A-133, "Audits of Institutions of Higher Education and Other Nonprofit Institutions," in 1990. Institutions now must engage an external auditor to perform a combined audit that serves the needs of both the institution and the federal government.

## OMB CIRCULARS A-128 AND A-133

The Office of Management and Budget (OMB) is a federal administrative agency that develops regulations for other agencies to promote consistency within the government by coordinating and establishing standard procedures for common functions among agencies. Before OMB's predecessor, the Bureau of the Budget, was established, each federal agency was free to initiate its own administrative requirements.

OMB's regulations standardize areas such as reporting, thresholds, cash requests, and accounting. OMB does not issue regulations directly to colleges and universities; it issues regulations to other federal agencies. These other federal agencies require colleges and universities to comply with the regulations as terms of grants and contract agreements.

Circular A-133 is an outgrowth of Circular A-128, "Audits of State and Local Governments"; however, most of the A-128 audits were done by state auditors. Audits under OMB Circular A-133 are a recent phenomenon. In fact, the first audits under this circular were completed before the regulations were finalized, and, because it is so new, many of the terms and concepts in Circular A-133 are unclear. It will be some time before institutions and their auditors will gain a full understanding of this circular.

There are two sets of guidelines for external audits. A public institution that is declared an integral part of a state or local government follows OMB Circular A-128. Independent institutions and public institutions that are not considered a part of a state or local government follow OMB Circular A-133. Entities audited as a part of a state, in accordance with Circular A-128, are *not* covered by Circular A-133.

Circulars A-128 and A-133 are similar, but there are a few noteworthy differences. Circular A-133 has a biennial reporting option, i.e., audits cannot be performed less frequently than every two years; Circular A-128 has an annual reporting requirement, unless the state legislature opted for biennial audits when the circular was first issued. Under Circular A-128, the threshold that defines major programs is $300,000; Circular A-133 has a threshold of $100,000, and research and development and student financial aid, if they exceed this threshold, are defined as major programs. Circular A-128 defines major programs by numbers described in OMB's *Catalog of Federal Domestic Assistance.*[8]

Another important difference in the two circulars is in the reporting of immaterial findings. When OMB developed Circular A-128, it had to meet the requirements of both the Single Audit Act and the Government Accounting Standards. When OMB developed Circular A-133, there was no statute similar to the Single Audit Act, so the Government Accounting Standards provided the only criteria. Circular A-128, therefore, requires all findings, regardless of materiality, to be included in the report. The determination of materiality is left to the professional judgment of the auditor. Circular A-133 permits immaterial findings to be reported in a separate memorandum.

***Coordinated audits.*** Both circulars permit coordination among the federal audit agency, the institution's independent auditor, and its internal auditor. To date, the Defense Contract Audit Agency, which has resident auditors on some campuses, is actively pursuing this approach.

## PROCUREMENT OF AUDIT SERVICES

When procuring audit services, institutions must follow the procurement standards set forth in Circular A-110, "Grants and Agreements with Institutions of Higher Education, Hospitals, and Other Nonprofit Organizations." This requirement is also applicable to Circular A-133. Audit agencies wanted to give colleges and universities latitude beyond having to hire the lowest bidder. The federal audit agencies weigh competence of the auditor more heavily than the price to be paid. For example, under Circular A-128 guidelines, 75 percent of the weight is assigned to audit competence and 25 percent to cost of the audit.

The OMB circulars require that small audit firms and audit firms owned and controlled by socially and economically disadvantaged individuals should be given the maximum opportunity to participate in contracts awarded to fulfill the requirements of these circulars. This may involve a different contracting process for an institution that customarily engages a major CPA firm to conduct its audits. The circulars suggest hiring a consortium of small firms or subcontracting a portion of the audit.

## REPORTS REQUIRED OF THE INDEPENDENT AUDITOR

Even if reporting is biennial, external audits must be performed each year. Each audit must include the following reports, which are distributed to those "requiring or arranging for the audit [and] each federal department or agency that provided federal assistance funds to the recipients."[9]

***An opinion on the institution's basic financial statements.*** The audit procedures must be applied to the basic financial statements, and a supplemental schedule of federal awards must be prepared. Through an oversight, the requirements for preparing this new supplemental schedule do not specify the level of detail that the federal agencies will need. Circulars A-128 and A-133 require reporting of expenditures by major programs only.

***A report on the independent auditor's understanding of the internal control structure and the assessment of control risk.*** This report contains the scope of the work accomplished in the effort to assess the institution's control structure. It also describes the significant controls that ensure compliance with laws and regulations that have a material impact on the financial statements or the management of federal awards.

***The auditor's report on compliance.*** The auditor's report on compliance includes an opinion as to whether or not the major programs were administered in compliance with applicable laws and regulations. This report provides two statements of assurance: a positive one on the items tested for compliance, and a negative one on all others. The report presents material findings that disclose the number of transactions and the dollar value of the universe from which transactions were selected, the sample, and the exceptions. The report gives the dollar amount of costs questioned and recommendations for corrective action. The federal audit agencies have indicated they do not intend to extrapolate from this report; however, if the recommendations are severe, this report may provide the basis for additional audits by the federal agencies.

The three reports may be bound together or presented as separate documents. Any fraud or other illegal act discovered by the auditor is to be reported in accordance with the Government Auditing Standards. The auditor must review the status of conditions noted for correction in the findings and recommendations of prior audit reports and report on uncorrected conditions.

The institution must respond to any findings and recommendations contained in the reports. This response, which is submitted to the federal agencies with the audit report, should describe corrective action taken or planned or a justification for not taking action. Reports must be submitted by the earlier of 13 months after the end of the period being audited or 30 days after completion of the audit. One copy of the audit report must be submitted to a central clearinghouse designated by the OMB. Institutions are required to keep copies of audit reports, including audit reports from subrecipients, for three years from their issuance. Written notification is required of any extension of the retention period.

REFERENCES FOR A-128 AND A-133 AUDITS

The following primary sources are helpful in determining how to comply with a Circular A-128 or Circular A-133 audit.

• Circulars A-128 and A-133, including the related OMB "compliance supplements," which set forth the compliance requirements to be tested

- OMB Circular A-21, "Cost Principles for Educational Institutions," which contains the cost principles against which transactions must be compared

- OMB Circular A-110, "Grants and Agreements with Institutions of Higher Education, Hospitals, and Other Nonprofit Organizations," which contains the administrative standards

- AICPA's *Audits of Colleges and Universities*

- OMB Circular A-88, "Indirect Cost Rates, Audit, and Audit Follow-Up at Educational Institutions," which lists institution's "cognizant agency"—an institution's primary contact with the federal government regarding federal audit matters (In 1991, OMB was redrafting Circular A-21 to include all of the provisions previously contained in Circular A-88.)

## INSTITUTIONS EXEMPT FROM OMB CIRCULARS A-128 AND A-133

Even if an institution happens to be exempt from the OMB requirements, the governing board of an institution should require an annual audit by an independent auditor, who seeks to determine if financial statements issued by the institution are fair representations of its financial position in accordance with generally accepted procedures that have been applied in a manner consistent with similar previous statements. Accordingly, the examination includes tests and other auditing procedures considered necessary for the purpose.

Upon completion of the examination, the independent auditor addresses a formal report to the institution, generally to the governing board. This report usually consists of a statement describing the nature of the examination and an expression of the auditor's opinion. The report often is accompanied by a management letter containing observations made in the course of the audit. Professional standards also require that the auditor inform the board about disagreements with management, major adjustments, and other matters.

Independent auditors are also engaged for specialized audits or technical services. They can assist the business office with expert advice and an independent view of accounting procedures, fiscal systems, and management problems.

Arrangements made with the independent auditor should be in

writing, and the institution should specify the objectives of such arrangements. The auditor will determine the nature and extent of the review required to render an informed opinion and suggest management actions. Effective coordination between the external and internal auditors may reduce the overall audit burden at an institution.

OTHER FEDERAL AGENCY AUDITORS

***U.S. General Accounting Office (GAO).*** The GAO, an arm of the legislative branch and under the direction of the Comptroller General, is charged with ascertaining that both federal agencies and recipients of federal funds are expending funds appropriated by Congress in accordance with congressional intent and in an effective and efficient manner.

***U.S. Internal Revenue Service (IRS).*** Audits by the IRS are performed to determine whether the institution continues to qualify for tax-exempt status under Section 501(c)(3) of the Internal Revenue Code and whether taxes have been paid on unrelated business taxable income. In addition, the IRS may audit an institution to determine if it is properly classifying employees and independent contractors, withholding payroll taxes, and administering employee benefits plans.

The IRS conducts several audits each year at institutions of higher education. In addition, the IRS has on occasion selected certain institutions for the Taxpayers Compliance Monitoring Program. These audits are performed in considerable depth.

***Other groups.*** Institutions are subject to examination by other groups representing taxing authorities, federal and state regulatory agencies, county and municipal agencies, providers of insurance coverage, and private foundations.

# Small Institutions

Small institutions present a unique audit environment. Typically they do not have internal audit staffs; in those that do, the internal auditor usually performs a variety of other tasks that have little to do with internal auditing.

In one sense, small institutions have less need for internal audit. With fewer employees and simpler business systems, smaller institutions are easier to control than large, complex institutions. The chief financial or business officer, who usually has an intimate knowledge of the people, the systems, and the procedures at a small institution, can spot deviations quickly. However, certain matters do need to be evaluated in a small campus environment, including the following.

## RISK ASSESSMENT

The financial or business officer should perform an annual risk assessment of the areas where peer institutions have experienced problems. Departments in which personnel turnover has been higher than normal should be examined and the cause should be ascertained. The financial or business officer should ask the institution's insurance agent for advice about cash-handling activities and other ways to protect assets; it is in the insurance company's best interest to lower claims.

## ORGANIZATION

The financial or business officer should review the institution's organizational structure. Could any duties be reassigned in such a manner as to promote better control? Changes often promote efficiency. If the financial or business officer lacks skill in this area, he or she may wish to consult with the institution's external auditor.

## RECORDS

The financial or business officer should ensure that record-keeping procedures are sound. Complete, relevant records kept for the duration of any statute of limitations requirements are essential to protect the institution.

## BUDGETS

The budget planning, budget authorization, and accounting systems, manual and computer driven, should be linked together. There should be adequate feedback to prevent or detect unacceptable deviations from the budget.

## STAFFING

If an institution lacks staff resources, it may turn to its external auditor for assistance. Certain operational matters may be referred to the external auditor's consulting division.

# Recent Trends and Developments

### INTERCOLLEGIATE ATHLETICS

National Collegiate Athletic Association (NCAA) member institutions have been concerned with financial abuses and lack of integrity in collegiate athletics. In a 1985 survey of 791 institutions conducted by the National Association of College and University Business Officers, 96 percent of the chief executive officers polled believed that the chief executive officer should have ultimate control over the athletic budget. Of these, 99 percent were concerned about problems of integrity and 80 percent were concerned about demands to generate income in NCAA Division I sports.

In response to concerns about the integrity of intercollegiate athletics, the NCAA approved rules requiring independent audits and presidential control of athletic budgets. The audits must be conducted by an independent external auditor.

Many institutions have gone beyond the NCAA requirements for financial audits and have commissioned internal audits to verify the eligibility of student-athletes to participate in intercollegiate athletics. For example, the internal auditors of state colleges and universities in the Tennessee Board of Regents system are required to use an audit program that includes 22 specific analyses, including transcript verification, student financial aid, and academic status and progress. This type of audit verifies the satisfaction of six criteria:

- A student-athlete is admitted in accordance with regularly published entrance requirements

- A student-athlete meets published eligibility or satisfactory progress requirements

- A student-athlete is eligible to receive athletically related financial aid

- A student-athlete's aid does not exceed limitations imposed by the NCAA

- Financial aid awards by sport are in compliance with NCAA recommendations

- Corrections of deficiencies and methods to improve systems in the athletic department are recommended.[10]

The Knight Foundation has been interested in the reform of intercollegiate athletics. Toward that end, it published *Keeping Faith with the Student Athlete.* The report advocates comprehensive, annual policy audits of athletic programs. The recommended audits should examine admission records, academic progress, graduation rates, and the athletic department's management and budget.

## CONSTRUCTION AUDITING

A few internal audit departments have been performing construction audits for decades. Recently many more departments have become involved. The huge sums expended on construction projects, the need to make evaluations while construction is under way, and the potential for serious financial losses when controls are inadequate or fail make this a productive audit area.

## IMPLEMENTING RECOMMENDATIONS

Internal auditors in small departments, or at small institutions, are under pressure to correct the problems they find. Recently, auditors at some large institutions have advocated that all internal auditors play this role, arguing that internal auditors have a full understanding of the problem and a clear vision of the corrective action necessary. While this may be true, implementing one's own recommendations seriously impairs an auditor's objectivity. If auditors are involved in such a process, great care must be taken that the same auditor does not go back later to audit work created by his or her own hand.

## FRAUD AND WHITE-COLLAR CRIME

"Fraud" is an instance or act of trickery. At one time, fraud was thought of as a crime committed by those who had access to cash or cash equivalents. Today, the potential for fraud is prevalent throughout a college or university. Unauthorized changing of grades, kickbacks from vendors, payments for goods and services not delivered (at least, not delivered to the campus), personal business expenses charged to institutional accounts, the manipulation of financial and operating data, and many other potential opportunities for fraud face every college or university.

Institutions should seek legal assistance when an act of fraud is suspected. Some common terms related to fraud follow.

- Defalcation: The misappropriation of money in one's keeping.

- Irregularity in relation to financial statements: The intentional distortion or alteration of records or documents by omission, misrepresentation, manipulation, or falsification; the recording of transactions without substance; the intentional misapplication of accounting principles; or misappropriation for the benefit of management or employees.

- Management fraud: When top management intentionally deceives creditors or independent auditors. Such misrepresentations may hide the theft of assets or exaggerate the institution's financial strength.

- Computer fraud: Any defalcation or embezzlement assisted by tampering with computer programs, data files, operations, equipment, or media.[11]

Auditors should understand the nature of fraud, what encourages it, and the techniques used to deter it. They must advocate the type of control environment that prevents fraud and must know the proper procedures to use during a fraud investigation. Trend and proportional analyses are two techniques to use when determining the existence of fraud.[12]

Because little is known about the nature of fraud, the Institute of Internal Auditors Research Foundation commissioned a study of frauds that occurred in the U.S. and Canada. The foundation concluded that:

- Twenty-nine percent of the frauds involved collusion; 71 percent did not.

- The failure to enforce existing internal controls allowed fraud to be perpetrated.

- Management's overriding of controls was an infrequent cause of fraud.

- Only 18 percent of the frauds were detected by internal auditors; 33 percent were detected as a result of anonymous tips.

A major purpose of the study was to determine which factors motivate employees to commit frauds. The foundation felt that, by identifying motivations, companies could reduce fraud by monitoring the associated employee pressures. Major motivations included a desire to live beyond one's means, a feeling that salary was not commensurate with responsibility, and a strong urge to "beat the system."[13]

The IIA *Standards for the Professional Practice of Internal Auditing* cover the auditor's responsibility for detecting fraud. According to these standards:

- When an auditor discovers a significant internal control weakness, he or she should perform tests to determine if an irregularity has occurred because of the weakness.

- The auditor should maintain a skeptical attitude about answers to questions about special or unusual transactions and should seek evidence to support or refute the response.

- The auditor should be alert in thinking about how a fraud could occur.

- Auditors must look for control weaknesses that expose assets to unnecessary risks and must have the independence to make necessary investigations.[14]

## EMERGING TECHNOLOGIES

In 1991, the IIA released the results of a major research study entitled *Systems Auditability and Control (SAC)*. The study found that all indicators point toward continued changes in technology throughout the 1990s. Hardware will continue to increase in performance capabilities while declining in price. Application and database software developments will challenge traditional ways of computing. Large management information systems (MIS) will give way to end-user computing. The SAC study predicts that, within three to five years, significant change will occur in the following technologies: developmental methodology; storage, processing, communications, database, and interface technologies; and knowledge-based systems. These areas are likely to experience decentralization and changes in standards, communications, operating environments, database management, workstations, and security.

These new technologies compel management and auditors to assess the additional risk associated with their introduction. Risk assessment and the installation of controls are decisions made by management on the collective advice of users, internal auditors, and technical specialists. The risk categories associated with the new technology are similar to the traditional concerns of auditors of management information systems:

- Data accuracy and integrity

- Security, including authorization to use systems and physical protection of hardware and software

- Recovery, backup, and error handling

- Compliance with standards and with internal procedures to ensure compatibility

- Management of the technology risk within the organization

***Developmental methodology.*** Auditors will continue to be concerned about new systems development. The introduction of computer-assisted systems engineering (CASE) and object-oriented software will enhance systems development. In addition to the traditional concerns about systems development, there is heightened concern about the consistent and proper use of these tools. "Change management" and "version control" will become more critical concepts of internal control.

***Storage technology.*** Optical storage technology provides more storage capability, longer storage life, and more error-correction capability and storage mechanisms. Data will become more subject to theft as the size of the storage medium shrinks; other risks concern the compatibility of hardware and software as well as technological obsolescence.

***Communications technology.*** Fast-packet switching and Integrated Services Digital Network (ISDN) are two communications technologies that transmit images, voice, data, and video at higher speeds. No new risks have been identified with these technologies; however, heightened scrutiny will be necessary as access and services are expanded.

**Database technologies.** Distributed database management systems and object-oriented database systems enable data to be shared across several locations with improved availability. These technologies also permit nontraditional documents, like maps, to be stored and managed. Traditional risks include the lack of coordination of database integrity during network or systems failure; lack of change synchronization between locations; and lack of data security at remote sites. New risks are associated with excessive expectations and the tasks of adjusting to the newness of technology.

**Interface technology.** Emerging technologies such as image processing and computer vision promise improved usage of document storage, processing, problem solving, and the automation of tasks. Concomitant risks of fraud, business interruption, and error should be anticipated. Controls to ensure the integrity and security of data—both image vision and real—are vital. These controls should be reviewed by the auditor.

**Knowledge-based systems.** These expert systems use knowledge and inference procedures to solve difficult problems. This software intensively relies on the establishment and maintenance of the logic used for rule making. The risks lie in improper rule logic, inadequate rule maintenance, inadequate rule integrity, and the inability to test all circumstances and conditions.

The auditor must keep a constant vigil because of these expected changes. The number of advances and their greater acceptance suggest a challenging control environment. Audit staffs need training resources in every area. In some of the rapidly changing areas, outside technical assistance should be used.

# Notes

1. Committee of Sponsoring Organizations of the Treadway Commission, *Internal Control: Integrated Framework*—Exposure Draft (New York: COSO, March 12, 1991), 56.

2. James D. Willson and Steven J. Root, *Internal Auditing Manual* (Boston, Mass.: Warren, Gorham & Lamont, 1984).

3. Louis Braiotta, Jr., *The Auditor Director's Guide* (New York: John Wiley &

Sons, 1981).

4. General Standard 300 from *Standards of Professional Practice of Internal Accounting* (Altamonte Springs, Fla.: Institute of Internal Auditors, 1978).

5. For more information, contact Ray Hebert, Audit Library Director, P.O. Box 310, Harrisburg, PA 17108.

6. S. Rao Vallabhaneni, *Information Systems Audit Process* (Carol Stream, Ill.: EDP Auditors Foundations, 1988).

7. Herbert Arkin, *Sampling Methods for the Auditor* (New York: McGraw-Hill Publishing Company, 1982).

8. The *Catalog of Federal Domestic Assistance* is published annually by OMB and is available from the U.S. General Services Administration, Washington, DC 20405.

9. OMB Circular A-133.

10. R. S. Nicks, "Auditing Athletics," *AGB Reports* 27, no. 1 (January/February 1985): 20-23; R. O. Riggs and C. R. Hedden, "Auditing the Records of Student Athletes," *Business Officer* 18, no. 2 (June 1985): 36-38.

11. Comptroller General of the United States, *Government Auditing Standards* (Washington, D.C.: U.S. Government Printing Office, 1988).

12. Lawrence Sawyer, *The Practice of Modern Internal Auditing* (Altamonte Springs, Fla.: The Institute of Internal Auditors, 1981).

13. W. Steve Albrecht, Keith R. Howe, and Marshall B. Rommey, *Deterring Fraud: The Internal Auditor's Perspective* (Altamonte Springs, Fla.: The Institute of Internal Auditors Research Foundation, 1984), xiv.

14. James D. Willson and Steven J. Root, *Internal Auditing Manual* (Boston, Mass.: Warren, Gorham & Lamont, 1984).

# References and Resources

PUBLICATIONS AND ARTICLES

Albrecht, W. Steve, Keith R. Howe, and Marshall B. Rommey. *Deterring Fraud: The Internal Auditor's Perspective.* Altamonte Springs, Fla.: The Institute of Internal Auditors Research Foundation, 1984.

Arkin, Herbert. *Sampling Methods for the Auditor.* New York: McGraw-Hill Book Company, 1982.

Braiotta, Jr., Louis. *The Auditor Director's Guide.* New York: John Wiley & Sons, 1981.

Brink, Victor A. "Forward from Fifty." *Internal Auditor* vol. 48, no. 3 (June 1991).

Committee of Sponsoring Organizations of the Treadway Commission. *Internal Control: Integrated Framework—Exposure Draft.* New York: COSO, March 12, 1991.

Comptroller General of the United States, *Government Auditing Standards.* Washington, D.C.: U.S. Government Printing Office, 1988.

Davis, G. B., D. L. Adams, and C. A. Schaller. *Auditing and EDP.* 2nd ed. New York: American Institute of Certified Public Accountants, 1983.

Institute of Internal Auditors. *The Institute of Internal Auditors' Report on Fraud.* Altamonte Springs, Fla.: IIA, 1987.

Institute of Internal Auditors. *Quality Assurance: Review Manual for Internal Auditing.* 2nd ed. Altamonte Springs, Fla.: IIA, 1990.

Institute of Internal Auditors. *Use of Ratio Analysis by the Internal Auditor.* Altamonte Springs, Fla.: IIA, 1986.

Institute of Internal Auditors Research Foundation. *Standards for the Professional Practice of Internal Auditing.* Altamonte Springs, Fla.: IIA, 1990.

Institute of Internal Auditors Research Foundation. *Systems Auditability and Control.* Altamonte Springs, Fla.: IIA, 1991.

Knight Foundation. *Keeping Faith with the Student Athlete: A New*

*Model for Intercollegiate Athletics.* Charlotte, N.C.: Knight Foundation, 1991.

Nicks, R. S. "Auditing Athletics." *AGB Reports* 27, no. 1 (January/February 1985): 20-23.

Riggs, R. O., and C. R. Hedden. "Auditing the Records of Student Athletes." *Business Officer* 18, no. 12 (June 1985): 36-38.

Sawyer, Lawrence B. *The Practice of Modern Internal Auditing.* Altamonte Springs, Fla.: The Institute of Internal Auditors, 1981.

Willson, James D., and Steven J. Root. *Internal Auditing Manual.* Boston, Mass.: Warren, Gorham & Lamont, 1984.

ORGANIZATIONS
Association of College and University Auditors (ACUA)
    North Carolina State University
    Campus Box 7202
    Raleigh, NC 27695-7202
    919-515-3511

National Association of College and University Business Officers (NACUBO)
    One Dupont Circle, Suite 500
    Washington, DC 20036-1178
    202-861-2500